The Millennium Myth

Praise for *The Millennium Myth*

"The Millennium Myth is a living force active in the soul of humanity, tooling up for yet another expression of its endtime eschatology. In a magisterial act of scholarship and intuition, performed with high competence and lucidity, Grosso, a reader's true friend, has evoked the soul and body of this world-shaking insinuation of vast imminent change and shown us how to embrace the Old Serpent, our supposed nemesis and, rather than chain him up, befriend him and ride his life-affirming energies into the Golden Age."
　　　—Richard Leviton, author of *The Imagination of Pentecost: Rudolf Steiner & Contemporary Spirituality*

"Known by *Magical Blend* readers as a provocative and intensely comprehensive author, Michael Grosso takes us on a tour of the Millennium Myth. The historic perspective of the end of times is revealed in engrossing clarity and is, by the book's end, shown to be a subjective choice we must all make individually and collectively . . . *The Millennium Myth* taps into the totally unpredictable, creative rage of the human heart and imagination. Highly recommended."
　　　—*Magical Blend*

"Michael Grosso's emphasis on the historiography of visionary patterns in the societal imagination is a much needed effort . . . He promises to break new ground."
　　　—Jean Houston, Ph.D., author of *Manual for the Peacemaker: An Iroquois Legend to Heal Self and Society, Public Like a Frog: Entering the Lives of Three Great Americans,* and *Godseed: The Journey of Christ*

"Grosso weaves together a vast collection of writings and thoughts, creates a vivid panorama of beliefs and faiths, and tells us wisely that the Millennium Myth contains a vision of the end of death as we know it."
　　　—*The Book Reader*

The Millennium Myth

Love and Death
at the End of Time

Michael Grosso

QUEST BOOKS
The Theosophical Publishing House

Wheaton, IL U.S.A./Madras, India/London, England

The Theosophical Publishing House
P.O. Box 270
Wheaton, IL 60189–0270

A publication of the Theosophical Publishing House,
a department of the Theosophical Society in America.

*This publication made possible with
the assistance of the Kern Foundation*

Library of Congress Cataloging-in-Publication Data

Grosso, Michael
    The millennium myth : love and death at the end of time /
Michael Grosso.
        p.   cm.
    Includes bibliographical references and index.
    ISBN 0-8356-0711-9 :
    0-8356-0734-8 (Trade Paper)
    1. Eschatology. 2. Eschatology in literature. 3. Future in popular
culture. 4. Sexuality in popular culture—Forecasting. I. Title.
BL501.G76   1994
291.2′3–dc20   94–22720
                                                                CIP

9 8 7 6 5 4 3 2 1 * 95 96 97 98 99
This edition is printed on acid-free paper that meets the
American National Standards Institute Z39.48 Standard

Printed in the United States of America by R.R. Donnelley

For my partner, Louise Northcutt—
with love

Acknowledgments

n my citations I have indicated the many sources I have drawn upon in writing this book. With much appreciation I also want to acknowledge several people who have in one way or another been a help in its production: Rafael Collado, Patti Hamilton, Richard Heinberg, Cliff Landers, Richard Leviton, Louise Northcutt, Ken Ring, Brenda Rosen, John White.

CONTENTS

And so there comes a time—I believe we are in such a time—when civilization has to be renewed by the discovery of new mysteries, by the undemocratic but sovereign power of the imagination, . . . the power that makes all things new.

—Norman O. Brown
Apocalypse

Introduction: Reading the Signs of the Times

For all life longs for the Last Day
And there's no man but cocks his ear
To know when Michael's trumpet cries
That flesh and bone may disappear,
And there be nothing but God left.

WILLIAM BUTLER YEATS
The Hour Before Dawn

This book tells the story of the Millennium Myth, one of the great myths of the world. It tells of the end of time and the rebirth of love, the end of history and the dawn of a golden age. The vision of the Millennium has roots that sink deep and wide in human consciousness; it is a vision that has inspired many great movements and many great souls. At the heart of the Myth is the idea that history—Our Story—is a journey with a goal, a drama with a climax. According to the grand script, the human adventure is heading for a showdown, and humanity is on a collision course with the Eschaton, the end of the world.

The Myth has revealed its message in Western, Eastern, and Native traditions. While some see in the pursuit of the Millennium delusion and social pathology, others find a soulful attempt to come to grips with the meaning of time and history. I have come to see the Myth as both a source of guiding light and a caster of sinister shadows.

Millennialism is a topic that engages many disciplines: politics, history, economics, anthropology, theology. Amid the many possibilities, I focus on the visionary power of the Myth—one man's reconnaissance report. "We are such stuff as dreams are made on," says Shakespeare's Prospero. The makers of the Myth, and those who dance to its tune, are proof of Prospero's point.

About Terminology

Millennium refers to the time after the end of time when the Old Serpent, Satan, will be bound. *Millennium* (Latin for a "thousand years") is a word that belongs to a constellation of images: Armageddon, the Second Coming, the Messiah, the Rapture, the Antichrist, the Day of the Lord, the Woman Clothed with the Sun, the New Heaven and Earth, and many others.

Apocalypse literally means "uncovering." "For there is nothing covered that shall not be revealed; neither hid that shall not be known" (Matt. 10:26). The word has a dark tone; one thinks here of Ragnarok or Götterdämmerung—flamboyant, cosmic violence. I use *millenarian* to stress social movements; *millennial* to denote the whole imaginative sweep of a mentality that luxuriates in extremes. *Chiliastic* is a synonym for millennial, and I occasionally use it because it tickles the ear. I upper case Millennium Myth to denote the entity whose escapades I narrate in this book; for short, Myth, with a capital *M*.

Finally, I spell it *phantasy*, not *fantasy* (both variants are from the Greek *phantazein*). By *phantasy* I mean to stress the power of the psyche; the word goes back to a Sanskrit verb that means "to make visible," "to appear or shine." Thus, the phantasy of the Millennium makes images of alternate worlds visible to the mind's eye. Nothing derogatory is meant, therefore, when I speak of Saint John's apocalyptic *phantasy*, to cite one example. A phantasy may mirror a possible world or help create a new world; I want to underscore this double sense through my spelling.

An Anarchy of Archetypes

One thing is clear: our world is changing rapidly, and the collective imagination is churning with creative turmoil. History is accelerating. The big question is: where are we heading? In the midst of a kind of anarchy of archetypes, some see the faint outline of a "new world order" emerging. With the death of Communism and the slow, lingering illness of Christianity and Western capitalism, people feel the ground beneath them beginning to shake; space is opening up around us, space for new visions, space for new ideas of what is humanly possible.

Never before in history have so many people shared the consciousness that a great cycle of time—a thousand years of human history—is about to end. We are about to enter the seventh millennium—the sabbath of human history. Rising expectations about what this may mean, a sense of impending crisis and impending breakthrough, are heating up the apocalyptic climate.

Rapidly heading toward that beacon year, 2001, the imagination of the End stirs uneasily in us; the mood is intensified by a medley of factors: calendar magic, uncanny signs and wonders, ecological menace, social disorientation, economic instability, and spiritual uncertainty. Large numbers of people are feeling the metaphysical urgency of the times. On December 7, 1993, Norman Lear, the man who gave us Archie Bunker, chided the American Press Club for missing the most important story of our time, the incredible religious fervor welling up everywhere, the hunger for spiritual experience, the growing discontent with the official picture of the true and the real. Lear spoke eloquently of the sprawling spiritual hankerings of millions of Americans, of people he called "unaffiliated gropers."

This book covers part of the missing story. It inquires into the fervor, the mythic source of the groping. Some digging into the national psyche is called for, some insight into our mythical past. It has been said we are a nation deficit in vision; the truth is that American history is steeped in the visionary. One aim of this book is to recall from its near oblivion the visionary roots of America.

Sleeping Sickness of the Soul

We desperately need to recall those roots. The twentieth century has seen more mass destruction of human beings by other human beings and more suicidal behavior toward our home planet than ever before. Everywhere we hear voices questioning the ruling myths, ideals, and images of our culture, and we hear voices crying out for the rediscovery of soul. One such voice belongs to First Lady Hillary Rodham Clinton, who had the *chutzpah* to ask whether "America is suffering from sleeping sickness of the soul."

Frightening evidence of this sleeping sickness may be seen in how government officials handled matters at Ranch Apocalypse in Waco, Texas, where eighty-six Americans, including seventeen children, perished in a flaming compound on April 19, 1993. There was little understanding of the spiritual forces that triggered that tragedy. David Koresh, the leader of the ill-fated cult, was a man enchanted by the Book of Revelation, the most potent expression of the Millennium Myth. To the Branch Davidians, events seemed to be happening according to divine plan; demonic agencies of worldly power were persecuting and threatening to destroy them. Officials had refused to allow family, press, or religious people to talk with the besieged band, thus isolating them and aggravating their fears and suspicions. According to one of the cult's lawyers, Jack Zimmermann, on the morning the tanks charged the compound, "some of the very religious people thought it was the last day of the world."

One might think it ironical that those who perished in Waco were merely extreme believers in the main myth of the Western world, the great hope voiced by the Book of Revelation that a last conflict between good and evil will one day end the pain of life and fix the injustice, banish death by supernatural decree, and liberate the world for God's love. In tune with his doomsday script, the government played to perfection the role Koresh assigned it.

David Koresh was a man trapped by his Bible-spawned beliefs. If he was a madman, his madness runs deep in the culture, for his was the madness of belief in the Savior, in the triumph of good, in the dream of instant passage to heaven. Like countless of his millenarian forerunners, Koresh used sacred scripture to serve his own needs and advance his own ends. And yet, however suspect those needs and ends, Koresh and his followers battened on the same hopes that gladdened the hearts of the first Christians. It is not surprising to hear that Koresh exerted his power "by convincing his flock that sacrifice would assure them of a heavenly reward later as members of the Lord's elite 144,000."[1] (We will keep bumping into this magic number, a figure in the numerology of endtime.)

Since the pilgrims established Plymouth Colony in 1620, the Myth has fanned the American dream. And Koresh took the American dream very seriously. His way of pursuing it was extreme; and yet Koresh was not that odd, since arming oneself for a transcendent battle is as American as Tom Paine or Woodrow Wilson.[2] The Bureau of Drugs,

Tobacco and Firearms, the FBI, and the Attorney General had no sense of the mad logic of Koresh's millennial imagination; in effect, they tried to extinguish a fire by hosing it with gasoline. After the failure to arrest Koresh, which ended in the death of four federal agents and an unknown number of cult members, officials sought to prevent the prisoners from sleeping by blasting them with noise and mocking them with sounds of Tibetan chants, rabbits being slaughtered, dental drills, reveille, and Nancy Sinatra's "These Boots Were Made for Walkin'."

A bad plan. They should have known that sleep deprivation causes hallucinations, a sure way to deepen Koresh's crazy belief that apocalypse was imminent and that he was the Messiah. The official handling of Waco's mystic rebels showed no insight into the psychology of millennialism. Yet that psychology involves forces awakening everywhere today in American society. One might, in fact, see the Waco fiasco as a bizarre spectacle of national self-destruction—a kind of spasm of trying to rid ourselves of our own mythical past. Koresh and his groupies were, in their own way, acting out the myth of the reigning national religion. The impatience of federal agents, compounded by their gun-slinging ignorance, resulted in needless disaster.

David Koresh had predecessors. Joseph Smith, the founder of Mormonism, also alarmed the establishment by his polygamous proclivities and was killed by a mob of self-righteous rednecks. Fresher yet in our memories are the Guyana mass suicides and murders, orchestrated by another sexually eccentric American prophet, Jim Jones. Still another case of false prophetism linked to sexual charisma was that of Charles Manson, also fond of toying with messianic phantasies.

Manson, incredibly, was loved by his followers. He appealed to their weird sense of idealism. Manson heard revelations in the music of the Beatles, especially the song "Revolution 9," which led him to believe that Helter Skelter was at hand. Helter Skelter was his code name for the coming Armageddon of race wars. The divine plan was for black folk to take over white civilization. Blacks would then hail their true messiah, Charlie Manson, who would emerge from his hideaway in Death Valley as the Lord of History. How to start Helter Skelter? Manson decided to do it himself; the grisly murders he engineered were supposed to trigger Armageddon by starting race wars. The whole affair was driven by twisted millenarian phantasies.

An Indestructible Vision

The Millennium Myth, as I show in the following pages, is capable of exerting a wide range of influence on the human mind—an influence that can be darkly twisted or wondrously inspired. "In truth I tell you," said Jesus, "there are some standing here who will not taste death before they see the Son of man coming with his kingdom" (Matt. 16:27–28). Jesus apparently thought the great event was imminent. From the beginning, millennialists have suffered from premature expectations. Christianity itself is but the ongoing fallout of the first failed Millennium, a kind of marking time, a waiting exercise, and is driven by an indestructible longing for the great yet-to-come.

The Millennium Myth attracts the imagination not because of its predictive value, but because it touches on the springs of life itself; it satisfies a deep need for a vision of transformation. No outer disappointment can kill this need. Enthusiasm repeatedly flares up and dies out; in waves that never cease, come stirrings of expectation and fizzings of failure, disappointments and revivals, postponements and reschedulings. So, when prophecy fails, new prophets invariably arise.

Among innumerable possibilities spanning two thousand years, consider a few examples. After the first Christian flare up, a hundred years passed, and the Second Coming never materialized. Around A.D. 156, Montanus the visionary embraced Christianity and at once made two converts, themselves *voyantes* (nowadays called "channels"), Priscilla and Maximilla. Montanus came from Asiatic Phrygia, the center of the ecstatic cult of the goddess Cybele. The two ladies came from noble and wealthy households and were called "madwomen" by orthodox writers of the time. All together they promoted "the new prophecy," which sought to restore the authentic spirit of the early Church.[3] Montanus and his two seeresses proclaimed the imminent descent of the New Jerusalem. The heavenly city was going to float down from the skies and station itself on the soil of Asia Minor in the obscure town of Pepuza. Montanus and his inspired lady friends would make it happen. Said Maximilla, one of the first in a long trail of female millenarians, "I am the word and spirit and power."[4]

The Jewish people had been dreaming of the Day of the Lord since the age of prophecy. Long after the Roman sack of Jerusalem in A.D. 70, Sabbatai Zevi, inspired by the cabala in the seventeenth century, announced that he was the Messiah, and called on believers to create the New Order (*olam tikkun*), literally the "about-turn." People, he declared, should free themselves from the burden of the law, and all holy days should be days of rejoicing. The new Messiah was fond of women, so he elected to lift age-old restrictions against them, a move that miffed the Hebrew patriarchs. Imprisoned in Turkey for treason, Sabbatai opted prudently to save his life by converting to Islam.[5]

The Myth has also flourished in the East, for example, in the Taiping—or "Heavenly Kingdom"—rebellion of 1850. The syncretic prophet Hung Psu kept the Manchu Dynasty at bay for fourteen years, putting on a good show that he was the younger brother of Jesus Christ. Messianic movements such as the Cao Dai (Spirit of God) played a part in the struggle for political independence in modern Vietnam. As early as 1830, the prophet of the Hoa Hao movement, Phat Tay An, foretold the end of the Vietnamese empire that would result from the onslaught of the West.[6] Worship of the Maitreya Buddha "yet to come" inspired antidynastic insurrections in Asia since the fifth century. As recently as 1965, a movement among Burmese peasants began, based on belief in the coming King Maitreya.[7] In 1972, British painter Benjamin Creme was studying the Alice Bailey revelations when he began to "channel" messages that the appearance of Christ-Maitreya was forthcoming. Creme took full-page ads in prominent newspapers like the *New York Times*, announcing that in 1982, "Maitreya the Christ" would appear on world television and communicate with everyone by telepathy. The Myth, as we will see,[8] has an affinity for technology.

Prophecy plays to end-of-the-century angst. In the early spring of 1990, thousands of Elizabeth Clare Prophet's followers gathered in Paradise [sic!] Valley, Montana, preparing to burrow in underground bomb shelters (at a cost of up to ten thousand dollars each). Clare Prophet, leader of the Church Universal and Triumphant, warned that nuclear Armageddon was due on April 23. Fear of death concentrates the millennial mind.

Millions of Americans, exposed to televangelists like Jerry Falwell, Pat Robertson, Pat Boone, Jimmy Swaggert, George Vandeman, and Jim and Tammy Bakker, believe that the Bible is a roadmap of history and that our great planet Earth is shortly to become "late."[9] The idea of such a colossal conflict provides a thrilling myth to live by. Through the lens of the apocalyptic imagination, all the horrors of history assume meaning; life becomes bearable. Thus, one fundamentalist declared during the height of the Cold War:

. . . that Christ will make the first strike [against the demon-
ically inspired Soviet armies]. He will release a new weapon.
And this weapon will have the same effects as those caused by
a neutron bomb. You read in Zechariah 14:12 that 'their flesh
shall consume away while they stand upon their feet and their
eyes shall consume away in their holes, and their tongue shall
consume away in their mouth'.[10]

Early in his career, Ronald Reagan was reading current events as apocalyptic signs of the times. In 1971, he stated to James Mills that Libya's
communist involvement was "a sign that the day of Armageddon isn't
far off." The President added, "For the first time ever, everything is in
place for the Battle of Armageddon and the Second Coming of Christ."

Again in 1976, Reagan discussed the Battle of Armageddon in a
taped interview with George Otis. In 1980, Reagan was still talking
about Armageddon. "We may be the generation that sees Armageddon," he told evangelist Jim Bakker. Jerry Falwell, according to reporter
Robert Scheer, quoted Reagan as saying: "Jerry, I sometimes believe
we're heading very fast for Armageddon right now." These remarkable
words were uttered by a man who had the power to press the button
that would start the nuclear holocaust.

As Ronald Reagan demonized the Soviet Union by calling it the
Evil Empire, George Bush demonized Saddam Hussein by calling him
Hitler. Once America saw Saddam as Hitler, war, in most people's
minds, became the only solution to the Persian Gulf crisis. Joining
the dance, Saddam Hussein was seduced by his own apocalyptic
hyperbole. (Islam has a rich prophetic tradition.) He ranted about
the "mother of all battles" and about George Bush being "Satan in
the White House." Vintage apocalypse talk. Saddam Hussein, hoping
to exploit Arab resentment and frustration, tried to ignite the self-
sacrificial flames of a united jihad against the West. He failed, with
results disastrous for Iraq.

Apocalyptic politics is not unique to bomb-happy Christians or
exploiters of Islamic spiritual longing. Brooklyn-born rabbi Meir
Kahane was assassinated in New York City in November 1990.
Kahane, an orthodox rabbi, believed we are living in the Messianic
Age. Kahane hated Arabs with apocalyptic passion. He thought that
expelling them from Israel would hasten the coming of the Messiah.
About Israeli policy toward the Arabs, Kahane wrote, "Had we acted

without considering the gentile reaction, without fear of what he may say or do, the Messiah would have come right through the open door and brought us redemption." The rabbi explained, "We are not equal to gentiles. We are different. We are higher."[11] Early in 1994, one of Kahane's disciples, Baruch Goldstein, went on a killing spree against Muslims who were praying in the Tomb of the Patriarchs in Hebron.

The Myth casts a big shadow, which we will keep meeting in the following pages. But it would be a mistake to think that that was all the Myth had to recommend itself; for where there is shadow there must be light. The Millennium Myth, as we shall see in many examples, has more humane potentials. Nor does it always appear in religious garb. Since the Renaissance, it has put on a variety of secular masks. In 1989, for instance, Czech playwright turned President, Vaclav Havel, told the American Congress, "Without a global revolution in the sphere of human consciousness, nothing will change for the better." Havel's remark has an American New Age ring to it, and the American New Age movement, as I show later, is rooted in the Millennium Myth.

A Passion for Meaning

The great timeless myths place our lives in perspective. Not about individual but collective salvation, the Millennium Myth speaks to the future of the species and the fate of the Earth. It has a long history of shaping human experience, and for many remains a way to read the signs of the times, a way of putting a hopeful face on the unknown future.

For Bernard McGinn the apocalyptic imagination reveals that history is a "divinely ordained totality."[12] In other words, all the struggles, all the disappointments of history will one day be resolved; in the End, everything will come together. The persistence of the Myth demonstrates how deeply rooted is our need for closure and transcendence. It speaks to the common human passion for meaning, to the wish to reinvent the human story, to the yearning of people to align themselves with something wonderful, something sublime.

Eschatology, the study of the end of the world, nowadays is turning into scientific futurology. The prophet crying in the wilderness gives way to teams of infomaniacs hunched over humming computers. Futurists collect data, forecast global trends, and like old-time prophets, project images of the possible. John Naisbitt's and Patricia Aburdene's bestselling *Megatrends 2000*, a blend of scientific trend analysis and upbeat millennialism, is a case in point.

A pattern of the imagination so widespread and long lasting must, I believe, express a deep human need. One aim of this book is to honor that need. Through that pattern we often fall prey to enchanting images with the uncanny power to jolt, mold, and direct our lives. Jung called such life- and world-shaping thought patterns "archetypes," "psychic dominants," or "primordial ideas." Archetypes exert their most potent magic during times of stress and crisis. Needless to say, ours is a time of high stress and constant crisis. Things are falling apart; the center definitely is not holding. The Dreadful, as Heidegger said, has entered our midst. Since Copernicus, as Nietzsche once said, the planet Earth is rolling from the center toward X. We are a ship at sea, without compass, without map, without captain. After two thousand years of Christianity, we find ourselves in a world turned upside-down by science and technology, a world with huge upheavals in the offing, a world tottering somewhere between doomsday and a new age.

A Quick Take On What Is Coming

The book is divided into two parts. The first is historical and spotlights the influence of the Myth on key turning points in Western history. We begin with the origins of the great vision, going back to Zoroaster and the Babylonian creation epic. Next is a chapter on the medieval prophet Joachim of Fiore, whose achievement was to marry the Millennium Myth to history. Joachim was the first in a long line of prophetic historians, Hegel, Nietzsche, Marx, Comte, and others. In the Renaissance and the Enlightenment, those bright crests in our evolutionary time wave, the mind and soul of the Myth light up in specific historical locales. The Renaissance reveals the all-sided individual and the vast potentials of art and science; the Enlightenment beams into history the modern ideals of equality and pluralism and optimism. In rare cases, the Enlightenment ideal of equality unites with millenarian enthusiasm, as in the American whom George Bernard Shaw once called a "superman"—John Humphrey Noyes, founder of one of the boldest social experiments in American history. Still in the historical mode, chapter 5 views the American Millennium, a place in imaginal time where the near divinity of the "common man" is discovered, a place where each person claims the birthright to compose his or her own "Song of Myself."

The last two chapters of Part One bring us face to face with the nightmare side of the Myth, the fruits of malignant transcendence. The Millennium Myth played a heavy role in the Hitler movement and in Soviet Communism. These social aberrations were monstrous magnifications of Manson's "Family" and Koresh's "Mighty Men." They contained a great deal of twisted idealism mixed with brutal sentimentality. Unfortunately, the forces that helped give birth to these antisocial horrors are still very much with us—poverty, anomie, injustice, and a yearning for messianic, that is, simplistic solutions.

In Part Two, I speculate on how the Myth may be shaping the future of American consciousness. I look at that messy thing called the American New Age through the lens of the Millennium Myth, then proceed to an overview of the many strange and often anomalous phenomena currently being reported in America and elsewhere and find them loaded with millennial overtones. Angels, for example, are Biblical symbols of encroaching endtime, an interesting fact, in light of the epidemic of angel reports we are witnessing today.

I find that the Myth has been working its enchantment on the human love affair with technology. When modern technology converges with the apocalyptic imagination, we get a new phenomenon, which has prompted me to coin a word—*technocalypse*. Technocalypse is changing our biological nature; our lives are becoming increasingly intertwined with machines. We home in on the eschatology of the machine.

Whatever the machine promises to do for us, there remain two themes we need to address: love and death. Love and death thread their way through all the chapters. There is nothing modest about the Millennium Myth; it is determined to abolish death. The Myth—one sees the first glimmers in the epic of Gilgamesh—rebels against death. In the words of Saint John the Divine, "death will be no more," or to take a prophet of different stripe, Timothy Leary has said that "science must snuff death." So we look at prospects for escaping the curse of our mortality and try our hand at sketching a new paradigm of death.

The myth also rewrites the rules of love, sex, and human relations. In a time when savage incivility is rampant, it might pay to rethink the range and quality of our loves, how they humanize and how they bestialize us. As it turns out, the Book of Revelation leads us to the hot core of the Millennium Myth. There we face the dilemma of binding or unbinding the serpent. It is the only way to the miracle promised by the prophets, the miracle of love and sex—emancipated from the devil of fear and oppression.

Let us begin by going back to the origins of the Myth.

Bayerische Staatsbibliothek Munchen, Clm 4452 fol. 201ᵛ

Part I

Historical

Origins of the Great Vision

*For no one is it easier to come into Heaven than the
generous.*

ZOROASTER

The millennial imagination has a history. In the course of time, it absorbs
new motifs and sheds old ones, gathers and loses momentum, becomes
effective in different ways at different times and places. This chapter
looks at the first times and places, the origins of the Millennium Myth.
The main idea of the Myth is that deep and radical regeneration
of human society is possible. The vision of this possibility had a
beginning; let us try to track it down.

The Word Millennium

The classic location of the word *millennium* is Saint John's Book of
Revelation, the last book of the New Testament. Chapter 20 begins:

> Then I saw an angel come down from heaven with the key of
> the Abyss in his hand and an enormous chain. He overpow-
> ered the dragon, that primeval serpent which is the devil and
> Satan, and chained him up for a thousand years. He hurled
> him into the Abyss and shut the entrance and sealed it over
> him, to make sure he would not lead the nations astray again
> until the thousand years had passed.

This is the only place in the New Testament where the desatanized
epoch of a thousand years, the Millennium, is specifically mentioned.

Now, John's vision of a time when the nations are no longer led
astray by an evil principle was the product of a long evolution, and
was itself destined to go through many changes in the centuries to
come. But John's version has been definitive for the Western world.

Very little is known about John, the author of the Book of Revelation. A few scholars identify him with the John of the Fourth Gospel, but the style, spirit, and content of the two books, so different, make this unlikely. The date of composition is also uncertain. The Book of Revelation may have been written any time after the first great persecution of Christians under Nero in A.D. 68 on up until A.D. 95 during the reign of Domitian. The author himself says it was written on the Greek island of Patmos.

Nero had blamed the Christians for a fire that broke out in Rome, thus launching the first persecutions. It was a case of established power looking askance at an alien cult. Tacitus, the Roman historian, had charged the Christians with harboring an uncivil "hatred of the human race," and favored the persecutions. The Book of Revelation proclaims that the persecutions must end, but it goes much further and announces the coming of a supernatural overturning of the existing order. A cosmic cataclysm would generate a new heaven and new earth; all the pain and injustice of the world was going to be wiped away, and even the last enemy, death—the enemy that foiled even the mighty Gilgamesh—would be overcome. As we will see, the idea of overcoming death recurs throughout the history of the Myth.

How did John know all this? The answer is plain from the first sentence of the book: "A revelation of Jesus Christ, which God gave him so he could tell his servants what is now to take place very soon." John was convinced because he received a revelation and beheld a vision of things to come. The Book of Revelation announces unequivocally that "the time is at hand" and ends, high with expectation, with the words, "Amen. Come, Lord Jesus!" This yearning to see the world come to end seems a constant of the human imagination, for "the time" is going to be "at hand" again and again in the centuries to come. The Book of Revelation is the archetypal announcement that the time has come to end time—in other words, to end ordinary history and enter a "new age."

The Heart of the Vision

The time is at hand for a final struggle between the forces of good and evil; cosmic chaos will climax in cosmic regeneration. Conflict, polarity, totality are the essence of the New Testament apocalypse. Nothing is left out. Everything, willy-nilly, is drawn into the battle: man, woman, angel, God, Satan, star, sea, serpent, horse, locust—the whole of creation is sucked into a colossal whirlpool of struggle and transformation.

A voice like a trumpet declares to John, "Write down in a book all that you see and send it to the seven churches of Ephesus, Smyrna, Pergamos, Thyatira, Sardis, Philadelphia, and Laodicea" (Rev. 1:11). The message in each case is a call to Holy War. Each message ends with the refrain, "He that overcomes . . ." He that overcomes will be rewarded and given an occult sign, the keys to the Kingdom, manna from heaven, a white stone with a secret name, and so forth. But he that overcomes will, above all, be given power—tremendous power.

To the people of Thyatira, for example, John wrote, "To anyone who proves victorious, and keeps working for me until the end, I will give the authority over the nations which I myself have been given by my Father to rule them with an iron scepter and shatter them like so many pots" (Rev. 2:26–29). The formula in Greek is *to nikonti doso*, literally "to him overcoming I shall give . . ." It needs to be pointed out about this all-important document of western history that it exudes the language of the will to power. There is scarcely a trace of love, forgiveness, or humility, such as one associates with the Jesus of the Gospels.

John's revelations summon all believers to total war—in the words of Saddam Hussein, to the "the mother of all battles." Here was the message to the Laodiceans: "But since you are neither cold nor hot, I wish you were one or the other, but since you are neither hot nor cold, but only lukewarm, I will spit you out of my mouth" (Rev. 3:16). In John's apocalyptic milieu, there is no room for being "lukewarm," no room for detachment, evenhandedness, skepticism; we are called to take sides, ready ourselves for total commitment and decisive action.

The mother of all battles will be preceded by signs. The logic of the signs is a logic of what Jung referred to as *enantiodromia*—"the passing over into opposites." As we drift toward what seems the worst, we may expect the advent of the best. The nearer to domination by the Evil One, the nearer to the Great Day of the Lord. The Book of Revelation codifies the specifics of what to look for in this terrible but ultimately glorious scenario.

There are two types of signal. One revolves around images of moral and social monstrosity; the other, around images of natural catastrophe. Thus, the Beast and his minions emerge in their sinister and dehumanizing horror. We are confronted with an image of enforced idolatry, the collective worship of material icons of immoral wealth and depraved power. The Antichristian Beast gains power over the masses by demonstrating "miracles" and "great wonders" such as making fire "come down from heaven on the earth in the sight of men" (Rev. 13:13). Anyone refusing to worship the image of the Beast is threatened by death. John's world in bondage to the Beast is a world in bondage to material power.

The ancients saw evil environmentally; thus, the moral decay that arises from the abuse of power infects the environment. John warns that a day will come when the planet, mimicking our inner perversities, will turn into a living nightmare. The sun will blacken and the moon turn to blood. A star will fall from heaven and the bottomless pit will ejaculate smoke and fire-belching monsters. Monsters are big in the apocalyptic landscape, somewhat clunky, Godzillalike symbols of inner disorder.

John makes horror-movie master Roger Corman look like a dandy. In John's endtime script, there will be earthquakes, a war in heaven, angels that pour blood in the sea, vanishing islands and mountains, beasts with many eyes, decapitated heads and claws, thunders and lightnings, plagues and blasphemies, lots of unclean frogs coughed from the dragon's mouth—and finally, a great massing of all the terrible powers of the universe at a little, dusty, dry place called Armageddon.

Given this assortment of evocative but confused images, readers can find what they want in the Book of Revelation. A contemporary environmentalist might see in the image of the bleeding moon a premonition of the wounded ozone girdle. John's vision is full of lakes of fire, images of supernatural combustion, easily seen by dogged end-of-the-world watchers as premonitory of the global warming trend, a yet-to-come nuclear ekpyrosis, or perhaps, more literally, the oil wells that burned for months following the Gulf War in 1991.

Saint John was emphatic in decisively branding the principle of absolute evil: the old dragon, the deluder, and the father of lies. John understood that supreme evil may be loath to advertise itself. That is the whole point about deception and disinformation. Evil that operates on such a high supernatural plane is very clever at hiding itself behind the cloak of good. In John's vision, the sign that endtime is near will be when the Evil One installs himself in the highest places of political power. In his vision, John sees that " . . . the whole world had marvelled and followed the beast" (Rev. 13:3). John was, of course, thinking of his Roman tyrants. The "beast" so muddles the public mind with propaganda that people can no longer distinguish between good and evil.

This disturbing form of unconscious evil is mediated through the talents of false prophets. The idea of false prophets masquerading in high places of power is in some ways appealing; on the other hand, it might, in the suitably disposed, lend itself to paranoia. One might suspect the most powerful, well-kept, and decent-seeming people of being in the secret employ of the Dark One; for, according to apocalyptic logic, the supreme evil knows exactly how to mask itself behind the appearance of supreme good.

John offers us a few diagnostic traits. It will be a mark of these sinister false prophets to perform uncanny healings and other miracles such as "calling down fire from heaven onto the earth while people watched" (Rev. 13:13). Well, by these criteria, just about anybody might be suspect; for example, during the Gulf War, people watched on CNN a fair bit of the American military establishment "calling down fire from heaven onto the earth." Does that make George Bush the Antichrist? Deception is the essence of his Satanic Majesty, deception that enslaves consciousness and leads to the idolatry of things and power—in the Gulf War, oil. It is possible to push this matter of luciferic deception too far, for how can one ever be sure of being on the right side? But let us turn to the positive side of the Millennium Myth.

New Heaven, New Earth

The Book of Revelation would not have enthralled the mind of the West for two thousand years merely by focusing on the underside of the human condition. The wholehearted plunge into the shadowy disorder of evil makes psychological sense only on the assumption of a countervision of redemptive power. Thus we come to the countervailing spirit of optimism, equally important in the apocalyptic legacy. We come, in short, to the Biblical phantasy of the Millennium, perhaps the most powerful source of utopian hope in Western civilization.

The saints and martyrs who did not worship the Beast and the false prophets in power will rise from the dead and reign in heavenly utopia with Christ (Rev. 20:6). John's vision reaches past the Millennium, **19** past the end of this interim paradise to the time when "Satan is loosed out of his prison." This, then, in a chaotic vision heralds the last period of cosmic warfare, where those troublesome characters Gog and Magog are introduced, and where there is a final judgment, and death and hell (in a muddled image) are cast into a lake of fire. This last round of dissension ends for the damned in what John calls the "second death"—in other words, the final state of hopeless alienation from God.

The vision now mounts to its thrilling climax. These are words that sound the depths of human aspiration: "And I saw a new heaven and a new earth; for the first heaven and the first earth were passed away; and there was no more sea" (Rev. 21:1). Here, in my view, is the core positive image of the Millennium Myth. An image of rebirth, revival, and regeneration, it contains the tantalizing suggestion that we may be able to tap into the mystery and creative power of time, that at the end of time as we know it a cosmic breakthrough is possible. It points to a time after the "end" of time.

The reference to the sea is puzzling. Why "no more sea"? The disappearance of the sea is suggestive, possibly the key to understanding the eschatological, or as I might say, the evolutionary dynamics of the Millennium Myth. If we take the sea as a symbol of the unconscious, then the text is saying that the Millennium—the time after the end of time—will come when nothing is unconscious, or as Carl Jung would say, when the unconscious becomes conscious.

This is much the way Jung defined the goal of depth psychology, which he called "individuation." At the end of his book *Aion*, which explores the archetype of the self, Jung wrote, "Just as the central idea of the *lapis Philosophorum* plainly signifies the self, so the *opus* [referring to the unconscious goal of alchemy] with its countless symbols illustrates the process of individuation, the step-by-step development of the self from an unconscious state to a conscious one."[1] Jesus put it like this: "There is nothing covered up that will not be uncovered, nothing hidden that will not be made known" (Matt. 10:26). And Saint Paul said that when the Lord comes, he will "bring to light the hidden things of darkness" (1 Cor. 4:5). This points to the gnostic significance of the Myth.

The gnostic thinks with images. So John says he saw the "New Jerusalem coming down from God out of heaven, prepared as a bride adorned for her husband." One can understand John musing on a "new" Jerusalem; the old earthly Jerusalem had recently been destroyed by the Romans, the memory of which must have been vivid in the prophet's mind.

On the other hand, the *New Jerusalem* also signifies a state of psychic transformation. In particular, one feature of the image should be stressed: *Heaven comes down to earth.* The Millennium Myth is about the liberation of earth—about sacred materialism, not about the abstract heaven of Platonic ideas. In harmony with the idea of sacred materialism, the bride is adorned for her husband; sex and family are divinized, not abolished. The "revelation" pictures hierogamy, a sacred marriage of heaven and earth, of male and female, of inner aspiration wed to outer satisfaction. As we will see in chapters 8 and 12, this has radical implications for sex and marital relations.

Consider another piece of text with gnostic overtones: "And the city had no need of the sun, neither of the moon to shine in it: for the glory of God did lighten it" (Rev. 21:23). No sea, no sun, no moon; the world internalized, "lit up" from within, seen without shadow, without ambiguity, without evil or menace. The only light that shines in this world is the light of God—on a reasonable gnostic interpretation, the "light" of a wholly integrated consciousness.

The gnostic Gospel of Thomas makes the idea of the unconscious becoming conscious pretty explicit. Jesus shows the way to enter the Kingdom:

> When you make the two one, and when you make the inner
> as the outer and the outer as the inner and the above as the
> below, and when you make the male and female into a single
> one.[2]

This is a striking passage. It jumps with images depicting the way to overcome dualistic habits of thought. Consider, for example, the image of male and female made over into a "single one." Thomas's gnostic Jesus is calling for androgyny, transcending sexism, as a step toward recovering paradise on earth. Androgyny is the way toward the wholeness of human love, and, as we shall see,[3] images of androgynous love recur in the futuristics of the Millennium Myth.

Consider another statement from Thomas that reveals a little more about the great vision:

> Disciples said: When will you be revealed to us and when
> will we see Thee? Jesus said: When you take off your clothing

21

without being ashamed, and take your clothes and put them under your feet as the little children and tread on them, then shall you behold the Son of the Living One and you shall not fear.

Before entering the kingdom of heaven, we will have to perform psychic striptease, peel away the lies of our ordinary *personae*, or "personalities."

But the same passage is an inspiration for those fond of acting out their religion on a more literal plane. Nudism has been a recurrent motif, popular among later revolutionary millenarians. Nudism, a form of metaphysics in action, repudiates the Fall; it denies that we have fallen from grace or have really been expelled from Eden. Seen against the backdrop of a gnostic Jesus, nudism becomes an attempt to abolish ugly self-consciousness, the shame and self-loathing that poisons our lives; it becomes a platform for uttering blanket rejections of the curse of repressive civilization and literally points the way back to our paradisal origins. I might mention that William Blake and his wife were fond of cavorting about their home in their Edenesque attire, much to the dismay of some of their visitors.

John sounds another revolutionary alarm when he says, "And I saw no temple therein; for the Lord God almighty and the Lamb are the temple of it." Just as there is no need of the sun, there will be no need of the temple. The temple that counts is no longer made of stones. The real temple of God becomes an inner state; the more installed therein, the more one feels free from external authority. Those who have oppressed us, the people who make and enforce the laws, will lose their hold on us. The temple is the supreme symbol of external authority, but its days are numbered, according to the Myth.

John's Kingdom of God, minus its repressive temple life, would be the end of what Karl Marx called "alienation." Saint John and Karl Marx agree on this millenarian point: God stops being a tool of repression, and will live *with* his people and *in* his people. Temple and church and priesthood, the outward tokens of spirituality, become expendable at the end of history. The outer will become the inner, as the Gospel of Thomas says, and the inner will be free to fully express itself outwardly. This vision of divine egalitarianism will remain alive in our collective mental history for two millennia.

The Moral Tone of John's Revelation

To appreciate the Book of Revelation's impact on history, we need to note its moral tone. It is something very distinctive, and I am afraid, unpleasant, perhaps even revolting. What you find, in the first place, is a prominent lack of compassion; an almost complete absence of any willingness, as we say today, to "look at the other side." Far from making the unconscious fully conscious, this part of the vision is phrased in such a way as to exacerbate the most violently restricted consciousness. Morality in the Book of Revelation is drawn in terms that are absolutely dualistic, rigidly incapable of compromise.

In his last book *Apocalypse*, D. H. Lawrence says that John of Patmos differed sharply from Jesus and Paul. Jesus and Paul loved aristocratically, according to Lawrence; John's soul, by contrast, was not ruled by love but by that dangerous psychic poison diagnosed unsparingly by Nietzsche and known by its French word *ressentiment*.[4] Tacitus, the Roman writer, may have had this resentful side of primitive Christianity in mind when he said of the new cult that it was based on "hatred of the human race." One thing is clear: you cannot fault Saint John for inconsistency; vindictive rage reigns supreme till the last verses of his text:

> This is my solemn protestation to all who hear the prophecies
> of this book; if anyone adds anything to them, God will add
> to him every plague mentioned in the book.

John's revelation must remain intact; no one may tamper with the exact formulation of his words. This suggests an attitude toward words reflected in the practice of Egyptian word magic.[5] Tamper with the spell, and the plagues will befall you. Nothing may be added. John wants to freeze the world, make it static, uniform, hard, translucent, like crystal or precious stones, which play so large a role in his description of the New Jerusalem. Indeed, great attention is paid to the real estate of the New Jerusalem: the gold streets, the jeweled palaces. (In chapter 8, we will look at the symbolism of gems and crystals from a more benign angle.)

John is as opposed to subtraction as he is to addition: "And if anyone cuts anything out of the prophecies of this book, God will cut off his share of the tree of life and of the holy city." One notes the scribal imagination at work; if you edit anything out of the perfect

23

script, *you* are edited out of the book of life. Life is like a book for John of Patmos.

What seems missing, I feel obliged to repeat, is the spirit of Christian love. One looks in vain among the raging words of John's revelation for signs of any concern for sinners; not a trace of regret for the lost soul. And everything is painted with fatalistic conclusiveness. "He that is unjust, let him be unjust still; and he that is filthy, let him be filthy still: and he that is righteous, let him be righteous still; and he that is holy, let him be holy still."

Well, why not leave at least a little room for change? John's pronouncements enshrine a self-righteous indifference to the fate of others. Yet something else is involved besides self-righteous indifference. At work is an active force, a sacred vendetta, a positive will to enjoy inflicting pain. Yet it all takes place under the ironical disguise of that icon of gentle passivity, the Lamb. Thus speaks this martyr to the Lamb: "How long, O Lord, holy and true, shall you not judge and avenge our blood on them that dwell on the earth?" Again, one wonders with D. H. Lawrence what happened to that aristocratic love big enough to forgive and forget.

It is hard to think of a better word than *sadistic* to describe some of the sentiments expressed in Chapter 9 of the Book of Revelation. We are at the part where the Lamb opens the Seventh Seal, which reveals the seven angels and the seven trumpets of doom. When the fifth angel sounds, a star falls from heaven and the bottomless pit yawns. Out of the unholy pit pours a smoke that darkens air and sun. And out of the smoke appear millions of locusts, commanded from on high to hurt "only those men which have not the seal of God in their foreheads." In John's vision, the improperly sealed people are not killed but "tormented five months." It will be "the torment of a scorpion, when he strikes a man."

The next sentence, I admit, causes me some distress; for I cannot help feeling that it is either a prevision of nuclear war or pure psychopathic phantasy: "And in those days," the prophet declares, "shall men seek death, and shall not find it; and shall desire to die, and death shall flee from them." John sees locusts with heads of men and bodies of horses and hair of women and teeth of lions and tails of scorpions that sting like hell. Finally, he gets to the killing part of his vision: a third of humankind is killed, scorched by the fiery breath of unvisualizable monsters. Those who survive the holocaust shall remain unrepentant, and John assures us that new tortures await them.

The moral tone of this book is not inspired by the spirit of love and forgiveness that tradition claims for Christianity. The Christian scholar R. H. Charles, commenting on the author of the Book of Revelation, states, "He looks upon the enemies of the Christian Church with unconcealed hatred. No prayer arises within his work on their behalf, and nothing but unalloyed triumph is displayed over their doom."[6]

If Christian love does not mark the tone of this book, what does? The answer, I believe, is evident: the will to power. In Chapter 1, for example, John refers to Jesus Christ as the one who "made us kings and priests unto God." In return for this we are supposed to give God and his Father "glory and dominion for ever and ever." Glory and dominion? What about that sweet Jesus love that has melted souls for centuries? In place of love, the Book of Revelation exults in sheer triumphalism. "King of kings; Lord of lords" are the words that turn John on, as does the image of ruling over "all the nations with a rod of iron" (Rev. 12:5). The "rod of iron" is prominent in John's Revelation.

Apocalypse in the Gospels

Let us try to trace the origins of the great vision a little further back now in the New Testament. The Gospels contain different, but not necessarily harmonious, prophetic images of last things. Sometimes Jesus speaks as if the Kingdom of God is already present. "The Kingdom of God is within you," he says in an often-quoted passage. He proves it by pointing out that "the blind receive their sight, and the lame walk, the lepers are cleansed, and the deaf hear, and the dead are raised up, and the poor have good tidings preached to them" (Matt. 11:5).

So, in a sense, the Kingdom is present, but there is more to come. Indeed, what is coming is a spiritual revolution. In Mark 1:15: "The time is fulfilled, and the Kingdom of Heaven is at hand; repent ye, and believe in the gospel." Repentance—the Greek word is *metanoia*—refers to the radical change of perspective that follows upon conversion to God-centeredness. In the new outlook, one looks upon the world as something less than permanent.

The Lord's Prayer is perhaps the most famous affirmation of the end of the world. Said daily by untold numbers of Christians, it is a prayer to end the known world and bring about heaven on earth. "Thy kingdom come, thy will be done, on earth, as it is in heaven" (Matt. 6:10). It is, at the same time, the supreme prayer of sacred materialism; for it wishes to extend the power of the sacred on "earth," not send it elsewhere. The Kingdom of Heaven is really on earth, revisited with a new consciousness.

So according to Jesus, as he pointed out with regard to the miracles and good tidings, the Kingdom of God has already begun to ingress on earth. The Gospel then is indeed "Good News." The times are already changing; the poor are waking up to the realization that freedom is possible, and the miracles have begun, the signs and wonders that prove there is a transcendent power to bring about a new heaven and a new earth.

However, if God's Kingdom has begun to dawn on earth, the job is a long way off from completion. Completion calls for the return of Jesus. The Second Coming will be heralded by signs:

> And when you hear of wars and rumors of wars, be not troubled; these things must needs come to pass; but the end is not yet. For nation shall rise against nation, and kingdom against kingdom; there shall be earthquakes in diverse places; there shall be famines; these things are the beginning of travail (Matt. 24:6).

Of course, rare would be the time when these images did not evoke a sympathetic sigh of recognition. Nature behaving anomalously is a sign that the Son of Man is returning. The persecution of the faithful is another sign of the Advent. Jesus is recorded as saying, "But when they persecute you in this city, flee unto the next; for verily I say unto you, Ye shall not have gone through the cities of Israel, till the Son of Man be come" (Matt. 10:23).

What else does this mean but that Jesus expected to return in the lifetime of his disciples. The disciples "shall not have gone through the cities of Israel" before the Son of Man comes. If he does not mean himself by the "Son of Man," who does he have in mind? I call attention to this once more because fundamentalist exegetes like Hal Lindsey seem to ignore passages like the above, when they spin out their phantasies of Armageddon. "Verily, I say unto you, This generation shall not pass away, until all these things be accomplished." "This generation" passed away, but all "these things" were not accomplished.

I know it is possible to torture the text—as we say today, "deconstruct" it—that is, make it mean what you want it to mean. However, I take the text to mean that Jesus thought he was going to come back before a generation passed away, but he did not. One may conclude from this that historical Christianity is the unintended byproduct of a prophecy that failed. On the other hand, it is possible to argue with John Humphrey Noyes that the resurrection in fact constituted the Second Coming and that the reality of endtime has in some sense already begun. Later, we will see how the American visionary Noyes tried to put this belief into practice.

Saint Paul's Rapturous Endtime

Jerry Falwell has stated in public why the thought of nuclear Armageddon never ruffles him; the reason is the "Rapture." Falwell believes that because he is a born-again Christian, Christ will snatch him up out of harm's way in the event of nuclear Armageddon. "I ain't gonna be here," he once said.[7] Where did Jerry Falwell get this strange idea?

The notion of an endtime Rapture is found in the letters of Saint Paul. Paul was a slightly younger contemporary of Jesus. The story of his conversion to the new faith on the road to Damascus is well known. En route to arrest some followers of Jesus, he saw a light and heard a voice: "Saul, Saul, why are you persecuting me?" Paul (the Latin form of his name) recalled later in one of his letters the experience of being raptured out of his body during this extraordinary encounter. "Whether still in the body or outside the body? I do not know," he observed of the experience (2 Cor. 12:3–4).

Paul seems to have had an out-of-body experience, a phenomenon often discussed nowadays.[8] Plausibly, Paul's out-of-body experience was the basis of his phantasy of the mass Rapture supposed to come at the end of the world. The exact words that give Jerry Falwell reason not to fuss over nuclear Armageddon occur in 1 Thess. 4:16:

> For the Lord himself shall descend from heaven with a shout, with the voice of the archangel, and with the trump of God: and the dead in Christ shall rise first. Then we which are alive and remain shall be caught up together with them in the clouds to meet the Lord in the air.

Whatever the source of this vision, it has the power to cast a spell on the imagination of some people, as one may see in the strange case of Jerry Falwell.

The spell is currently still potent. I have in my hands a curious document. In what looks like a bus or train schedule, produced by the Mission For The Coming Days, one reads that "Jesus is coming in the air" on October 28, 1992. On the cover is an artist's conception of a modern city, the streets strewn with disabled vehicles and Christ descending from the clouds on a beam of light. Beneath this illustration is a "Timetable of Rapture (Oct. 28, 1992)." The times are given for the Rapture in New York, Moscow, Tokyo and about eight other major cities. Inside one reads that on the above date "true believers in Christ will mysteriously disappear from the earth."

This will be followed by the Great Tribulation (1993–1999), a period in which Antichrist will take over the world and visit terrors and abominations on sinners and unbelievers. In a move that links the apocalyptic imagination to the environmental crisis, our ozone problem is said to signify the "prelude to the Tribulation." According to the Timetable, the exact date of the Rapture is known through an outpouring of Joel's prophetic spirit on more than one thousand faithful Christians. No further particulars are given.

Daniel's Doomsday Timetable

The Book of Daniel is a favorite of mystics and millenarians, a horoscope for the apocalypse. During the Middle Ages, Jewish writers used it to compute the time of the coming Messiah. Christians used it along with the Book of Revelation for their doomsday timetables.

The Book of Daniel enriched the millennial imagination with the symbolism of the four beasts. The four beasts refer to the four world empires, the "evil empires," that must perish before the conquest of the "fifth monarchy," the reign of God and his saints.

According to itself, the Book of Daniel was written during the Babylonian exile under the reign of Nebuchadnezzar (605–562 B.C.); but some scholars say it was composed at the time of the Jewish persecution under Antiochus Epiphanes (about 165 B.C.). In that case, the four empires were the Babylonian, the Median, the Persian, and the Greek. When Rome became the chief power of the Mediterranean world, and thus the new focus of evil, Daniel's scheme was revised, and the Medes were dropped from the picture.

In the late Middle Ages, the empires were France, England, Spain, and Italy. During the Civil War in England, radical Puritans known as "Fifth Monarchy Men" fought under Cromwell, and the "Fifth Monarchy Men" became the new "Elect."

The Book of Daniel adds to the apocalyptic vocabulary such phrases as the "Ancient of Days" and the "Son of Man" in Chapter 7, the latter mysterious phrase appearing in the Gospels and used by Jesus to refer to himself. Daniel's "Son of Man" comes on "the clouds of heaven" and is the ruler of all nations, peoples, and languages. Like John, Daniel wants to freeze reality, deny the Heraclitean flux, and make the kingdom of the saints "an everlasting kingdom, and all dominions shall serve and obey him" (Dan. 7:27). As with John's Revelation, so with Daniel, prophecy here seems redolent of the will to power.

Daniel's, like John's, will to power is boundless in its ambition, aspiring to achieve dominion over nature itself. The ultimate dominion over nature is dominion over death. Belief in the resurrection of the dead was not prominent in the Old Testament. In Ezek. 37, for example, resurrection was a symbol of national rebirth. However, for the first time a clear statement about individual resurrection occurs in Daniel: "Many of those that sleep in the dust of the earth shall awake, some to everlasting life, and some to shame and everlasting contempt" (Dan. 12:2). The notion that we may awaken from the "dust of the earth" is a breakthrough in the imagination of the possible. The prophecy of bodily resurrection became a major motif of apocalyptic thought and is very much a part of contemporary futuristic speculation.[9]

Other Prophetic Sources of the Vision

Daniel is perhaps the most important Hebrew prophet for the history of the apocalyptic. But there were others; here are a few examples:

In the Hellenistic book 1 Enoch, the idea of the Millennium appears for the first time. Before John, this book foretold that the old heaven and earth would be destroyed, and a new heaven created. "And the first heaven shall depart and pass away, and a new heaven shall appear" (1 Enoch xci.) This is more radical than the older view of an eternal **29**

Messianic kingdom on earth. A more disruptive transformation is imaged in 1 Enoch. The idea of disruption is crucial. At the heart of true apocalyptic vision is a discontinuous universe—a universe where sudden, qualitatively new breakthroughs occur. It is a universe where the notion of a "quantum leap" is at home. Such is 1 Enoch's "new heaven."

Enoch is outside the Old Testament canon. However, millennial prophecies may also be found within canonical Old Testament prophecy. For example, in Amos 5:18 (Amos lived during the eighth century B.C.), the idea of the "Day of Yahweh" occurs for the first time. According to Amos, a time is coming when God will transform human society on earth. For Amos this will be a day of darkness, a day of dire vengeance wreaked on a corrupt and deceitful Israel. However, Amos kindles a spark of hope in looking forward to the salvation of the House of Jacob (Amos 9:8). Amos was the first prophet to use the expression remnant, recurrent in the history of millennialism. The survivors are the saving remnant, the people who will lead the lost and defeated to a new age.

In the writings gathered under the name of Isaiah, we find a brighter image of the day of Yahweh. Isaiah, too, hopes that a remnant will be spared and sees that remnant ruled by a king-Messiah. Isaiah's images of the future are engraved on the Western imagination—for instance, the image of utopian peace:

> The wolf will lie down with the lamb, the panther lie down
> with the kid, calf, lion, and fat-stock beast together, with a
> little boy to lead them. . . . The infant will play over the den
> of the adder; the baby will put his hand into the viper's lair. No
> hurt, no harm will be done on my holy mountain (Isa. 11:6).

A new principle will infuse the cosmos, a principle of "no hurt, nor harm." Nature will be tamed. The natural basis of conflict and aggression will be abolished. Isaiah spells out in greater detail the discontinuity, the idea of evolutionary breakthrough implied by 1 Enoch's "new heaven."

The idea of invulnerability to danger, the baby putting his hand into the viper's lair, will return in several forms. For example, Jesus is recorded, after the resurrection, as saying that certain signs will reveal the presence of true believers: "They shall take up serpents; and if they drink any deadly thing, it shall not hurt them" (Mark

16:17–18). Snake-handling, drinking poison, and exposure of oneself to fire thus become ways of testing the power of the spirit to vanquish evil. Snake-handling cults have been reported in twentieth century rural America.[10] The psychiatrist Berthold Schwarz has investigated these danger-defying cults among members of The Free Pentecostal Holiness Church and observed some remarkable phenomena.[11]

The belief in one's invulnerability, resulting from states of religious exaltation, may inspire reckless behavior, sometimes with destructive consequences. An example that comes to mind is the late nineteenth century Indian Ghost Dance; practitioners thought their sacred shirts would protect them from all danger. As Schwarz's observations show, people in exalted states of consciousness sometimes in fact do things that seem impossible (drink deadly poison or expose oneself to a blowtorch without injury); on the other hand, exalted states can inflate the ego and cause one to make fatal mistakes, as happened to the Indians whose sacred shirts were no match for American military technology at Wounded Knee.[12]

According to the Millennium Myth, supernormal powers are going to proliferate at the end of history. The union of wolf and lamb, child and viper, evokes an image of supernormal peace. The prophet Joel, writing about 400 B.C., is responsible for a famous image of supernormal inspiration. The words of Joel:

> After this I shall pour out my spirit on all humanity. Your sons and daughters shall prophecy, your old people shall dream dreams, and your young people shall see visions. Even on the slaves, men and women, shall I pour out my spirit in those days (Joel 2:28–29).

Joel's new age pictures a kind of mystic democracy, a time of free and open access to inspired dreams, visions, and prophecies. Yet Joel's vision, however exalted, was still mired in tribal exclusivism. He cannot help seeing the climax of history as the triumph of Israel and the annihilation of all nations opposed to Israel.

However, the very short Book of Jonah does contain a universal prophecy. It tells of Jonah's mission to preach to the Ninevites, his success in teaching them the fear of God, and his displeasure in his success. Yahweh rebukes Jonah for his lack of sympathy for the people of Ninevah. With this little document, humankind takes an important step forward toward the ideal of a truly human consciousness, uncolored and unrestricted by the tribal mentality.

Zoroaster

We began this chapter with the most influential text in the history of the apocalyptic, the Book of Revelation. From there we worked our way back through the Gospels and some Jewish and Christian pseudoepigraphical[13] texts. After these apocryphal writings, we glanced at highlights in the Hebrew prophetic tradition. A supernormal and more universal image of human potential began to emerge there.

The prophecy appears that nature is subject to a higher force of transformation; the lion and the lamb can change their nature. The quality of human consciousness can change. The violent and discordant agencies of the world can be overcome. This complex of ideas, part of the Millennium Myth, anticipates modern evolutionary cosmology. Strip away the religious symbolism, and a picture emerges of a nature that is a process in time, capable of novelty and qualitative transformation. Although modern cosmology derives from the ancient Greeks, the Jewish prophets also enlarged our sense of nature's possibilities.

However, this expansive imagination can be traced to yet older sources. The core idea of the Millennium Myth, that earth is somehow transformable into a heavenly condition, appears in the tradition that stems from Zoroaster. (Zoroaster is the Greek form of Zarathustra—the name, by the way, Nietzsche chose to voice his prophecy of the "superman.") In my opinion, the gospel of Zoroaster is one of the most exalted, one of the purest in the world traditions. It offers what may be the oldest, richest vision of the paradise of human capabilities.

The Iranian prophet Zoroaster Spitama lived in the seventh and sixth centuries before Christ. At thirty he had his first revelation from Ahura Mazda, the Wise Lord. For ten years he sought disciples but found only one, his cousin. At forty he converted King Vishtaspa, launching Zoroastrian history, and at seventy-seven an assassin killed him while at prayer. Zoroaster's thought influenced Judaism, Christianity, and Islam. The Iranian prophet was the first to voice the metaphysical principles of the Western religious faiths. Zoroaster taught the two great opposing principles of the universe, Good and Evil, Light and Dark; he preached transcendent monotheism, revealed to him by the one supreme God, Ahura Mazda. Another staple of the West, Zoroaster championed the power of free will. The capstone of his moral philosophy was clear: we determine our destiny by our own thoughts, words, and deeds. Human nature is defined by a certain divine autonomy.

A great maker of the Millennium Myth, Zoroaster developed a complete eschatology. He preached a Last Judgment, an idea that marked the religions of the West. According to Zoroaster, heaven and hell are states of mind, the product of one's thoughts, words, and deeds: heaven he called the "Best Existence" and the "House of the Good Mind" and hell, the "Worse Existence" and the "House of the Lie."

The Zoroastrian Faith flourished in Iran until the Islamic invasions in the seventh century resulted in converting Iran to a Muslim nation. Zoroastrian eschatology derives from the prophetic writings of the Second (Sassanian) Empire (A.D. 226–651). Under the Sassanians, the doctrine of a final reckoning crystallized, the idea of a last turning point of existence. The Apocalypse of Zoroaster is recorded in later scripture, the Bundahishn, Bahman Yasht, and Zatsparam; allusions to his vision of the End also occur in the first Gathas, the oldest writings of the Zoroastrian tradition.

When Cyrus II, the Iranian King, sacked Babylon in 539 B.C., he released the Jewish people from captivity and helped them restore their Temple and return to their homeland. During this period of contact, Zoroaster's views on the end of time probably seeped into Hebraic culture. However, the Zoroastrian apocalypse differs from the Jewish and Christian in several important ways.

For one thing, no true Mazdean accepted the notion of eternal hell. In one of the sacred scriptures we read, "You are not to consider anyone hopeless of Heaven . . . for in my Religion there is no sin for which there is no atonement."[14] (At once we find ourselves in a different moral climate from that of John of Patmos.) In the Zoroastrian apocalypse, transformation comes through gradual progress and evolution. "Ahura Mazda created the whole material world one home. He created the creatures for progress."[15] Here is a religion that believes in the possibilities of education.

The Biblical apocalypse foresees a virgin-born Savior; the older Iranian tradition foresaw the coming of a third descendent of Zoroaster—Saoshyans. According to some predictions, the Millennium will begin about 2200. As in the Jewish and Christian stories, there will be signs foreshadowing the End. But the signs here seem a little kinder, a little gentler than those we found in the Book of Revelation. One "sign" of the Zoroastrian endtime and coming new age is that human beings will become so skilled in medicine that death itself will gradually be overcome—an idea actively pursued in the contemporary immortalist movement. (See chapter 10 on this.)

Other interesting changes are foreseen. In the Zoroastrian new age, our appetites will spontaneously decline; our animal urges gradually slacken. People will learn to live by the power of the spirit. One taste of consecrated food will satisfy a person for days. People will evolve toward vegetarianism and in the process become less aggressive. Zoroastrian prophecy foresees a time when we shall also outgrow dependence on the vegetable kingdom. We will become waterians. Finally, in the last ten years before the advent of Saoshyans, the scriptures talk of a time when people will begin to mutate into full-scale inediacs, living, without any food or drink, entirely on spiritual energy.

However, such a superlative state of affairs is bound to be resisted by the lower cosmic types. Therefore, a figure, corresponding to the Christian Man of Sin or Antichrist, is obliged to introduce himself on the stage of history. We will have to deal with an unchained Zoroastrian Antichrist, called by some Azhi Dahak; this redoubtable being will temporarily gain strength and "rush into the world to perpetuate crime." It will "gulp down one-third of mankind." As he consumes humans, he "smites the water, fire, and vegetation."

The next move is a showstopper. The blighted seas and vegetation weep; they cry out to the Lord for help. It appears then that this is a nature-centered, not a human-centered, apocalypse. In response to nature's SOS, Ahura Mazda sends one of his "Bounteous Immortals" to set matters straight with Azhi Dahak, the satanic propagandist and wrecker of cosmic harmony.

At the threshold of the great transformation, Saoshyans will "smite the most wicked Lie." The diabolic principle will be mastered; men and women will see through the false consciousness that traps them in everyday life. They will learn to live "in the Spirit." For the Zoroastrian, this meant living free from the compulsions of the lower self, the end of codependency.

Zoroaster saw body and soul united. Unlike soul-fixated Plato, bodily resurrection is part of the supreme goal of history. Ahura Mazda calls upon the dead to rise, giving them new and living bodies. The

34

model for understanding this new species of resurrected organism is the body of the superman Savior, Saoshyans. To the Virgin Eredat-fedhri is born this Savior, whose name is Victorious Helper, and whose title is Body-Maker.

This Savior Body-Maker is a being of light whose "food is spiritual [and his] body sunlike." Zoroaster's resurrected body is a body of radiant energy. Saint Paul spoke of a spiritual or "pneumatic" body; Plato, in his myths, of a "light-body" or "star-astral" body. Comes the Millennium, disease, old age, and death will be no more—thanks to our becoming People of Light.

Zoroaster addressed his prophecies to all humanity. Duncan Green-lees summarizes the revolutionary universalism of the Mazdean apoc-alypse with these words: "So far as we can dig into the past, in no country, in no religion, before the seventh century B.C. had a prophet clearly asserted that before God *all* men are fundamentally spiritual equals."[16]

I have commented on the moral tone of John's Book of Revelation. Whatever one may choose to say about that tone, mirth or humor is not characteristic. In contrast, the Iranian prophet says that in the Millennium "the primal gift of mirth will arise." No gnashings of teeth, no howlings of indignation: the Zoroastrian new age will be tempered by the sound of laughter.

Still, there is more to come—a Last Judgment. At a great assembly everyone gathers; there is a kind of collective panoramic memory expe-rience. People somehow become psychically transparent to themselves; in this detached state, they see through their lives—their thoughts, words, deeds. "In that Assembly everyone sees his own good deeds and his own evil deeds; a wicked man becomes as obvious as a white sheep among those that are black." In short, everyone is seen, and sees, as they really are. The last judgment is really a first encounter; one returns home, as the poet T. S. Eliot says, and "know[s] the place for the first time."[17]

Next, the good and the bad are separated; each person is judged as an individual. In effect, each person judges himself or herself. The good go to the House of Song; the wicked are thrown into a stench-filled abyss. Worse than the stench, says the text, is the pang of sheer "loneliness."

However, this painful process of self-realization is not to be drawn out everlastingly. Compared with Christian John and the Hebrew

35

prophets, Zoroaster is positively lax about punishment. The punished are obliged to suffer for a mere three days and three nights—no inhuman chatter about everlasting torment. Notable is Zoroaster's psychology of hell, which consists of being forced to witness the pleasures of the saved. People are made privy to the goods and delights they missed because of their hard hearts and wrongdoings. Note the contrast with Christian ideas, for with Saint John, Saint Augustine, and even Dante, a significant part of the pleasure of salvation lies in becoming privy to the torments of the damned. Thus says Saint John about the damned on the Day of Judgment: "They will be tortured in the presence of the holy angels and the Lamb" (Rev. 14:10).

Zoroaster also differs from the Biblical tradition in the following way: in the end, evil is destroyed, and all human souls are saved. The traditions after Zoroaster have been content with the idea of excluding large portions of the human community from the supreme good. By contrast, the tradition of Zoroaster seems wealthy in spiritual generosity. Indeed, as the prophet himself is recorded as having said, "For no one is it easier to come into Heaven than the generous."

Nevertheless, all is not effortless at endtime. Before the Zoroastrian Millennium, everyone must endure an ordeal of purification: "Then all men pass into that molten metal and become pure by the cutting and breaking up of the sin-accumulation of the wicked souls." The ordeal is a profound psychic experience. "Good" people who pass through the fiery molten metal feel as if they're wading through warm milk; "bad" people, thanks to their sins and bad consciences, feel the pain of the purgative heat. The inner state is what defines "reality" in Zoroaster's idea of last things.

At the end of the last ordeal, all people emerge and return to *Paradise*—a Persian word, by the way, meaning "a garden-enclosure"—and to the Home of Song. In a grand vision, we are told that Ahura Mazda will save all. Even the Serpent (Azh) is purified and God "brings back the land of Hell to enlarge the world."

To "bring back hell to enlarge the world" is a remarkable image and speaks to the deep psychological need for integration. To integrate hell, the Shadow in Jung's sense, is the Zoroastrian way to enlarge the world. Our hellish propensities, reckoned with and re-integrated, complete and deepen our human world.

With this "the Renewal arises in the universe," pain and deceit vanish, and the "sea becomes sweet again." This contrasts with the image of the sea vanishing in John's Revelation. The sweetening of the sea is followed by a cosmic revel. All of resurrected humanity will gather together to drink the sacred *haoma*—*soma* in the Vedas. *Haoma* is the ambrosia that puts the seal on everyone's immortality. Affection and overflowing joy will abound. The resurrected parade to and fro asking each other questions: "Where have *you* been these many years, and what was the judgment on your soul?"

Myths of Time and Regeneration

I have traced the idea of the Millennium back to the prophecies of Zoroaster. Now it is possible to take another step back and look at the links with myths and rites of time.

Consider the ancient Babylonian New Year festival, known as *ak-itu*.[18] The *Enuma Elish*, or Epic of Creation, was recited annually during the spring and fall equinoxes. The purpose of the rite was to revive the sacred moment of combat between Marduk and the marine she-monster Tiamat. In the myth, Marduk overcomes Tiamat, the primordial oceanic chaos. Marduk creates heaven and earth from the giant corpse of Tiamat.

Tiamat is similar to John's dragon-serpent, but there is a difference. Marduk creates out of Tiamat; John wants to repress, place under lock and key, the ancient sea-monster. John wants to lock up the *kundalini*, or "coiled sexual life force," that boils and slithers at the root of creation. The Christian Millennium is tied to images of imprisonment: the dragon, the primeval serpent, is "chained up for a thousand years." John sees an angel holding "the key of the Abyss in his hand and an enormous chain" (Rev. 20:1–2). The Christian vision is mired in repression; the Babylonian myth makes explicit the whole myth of regeneration, the seamless character of its dark and light, destructive and creative forces.

Marduk, then, creates a new world out of chaos. Thus the core Millennium idea: Out of the corpse of the old world, the old order, a new world, a new order will arise. The Babylonian New Year rite recaptures the power of origins. In Eliade's view, this is done by a "repetition of the archetypes." By reciting the myth, the ritual helps the celebrant recapture a timeless moment of creative power. The world of that creative power is entered through ritual gesture. With proper words and proper movements, demons, diseases, and sins are expelled.

Two groups of actors mimed the struggle between Marduk and Tiamat. Similar ceremonies were also performed among the Hittites and the Egyptians. The experience of regeneration was symbolic; the expulsion of demons and disease took place on the plane of the mythic imagination. In later history, specific people or types of people will be viewed and thus treated as the "demons": the other, the enemy, the heathen, the pagan, the gentile, the Jew, the Catholic, the Muslim. People will learn to project the Millennium Myth onto history.

The Babylonian New Year festival closed with a sacred marriage rite, performed by the king and a prostitute in the chamber of the Goddess; the rite was followed by an orgy. The festival of Dionysos and the Roman saturnalia are classic parallels to the renovative orgy. The orgy offered the ancients a socially sanctioned way to regress to states of regenerative chaos.

In quest of regenerative chaos, the Babylonian akitu inverted the relation of master and slave. According to the Babylonian historian Berossus, the slave became the master and the master the slave during the New Year celebration. Similarly, during the Greek Eleusinian rites, high officials and dignitaries were exposed to scurrilous satire. Note also the parallel to Zoroaster's world-dissolving "primal gift of mirth."

But let me repeat: There is a tendency, which we look at in coming chapters, for these myths to ingress into history, to literalize themselves. This may have creative as well as destructive effects. In later millenarian movements, real social chaos becomes the necessary prelude to cosmic renewal. The poor, the downtrodden, the persecuted will cry out for the literal blood of literal oppressors; John in exile got ecstatic over a vision of society whose power structure was totally inverted. The "saints"—the poor, the marginal, the alienated—become the kings. It is now their turn to "reign for ever and ever." Nietzsche called this inversion of the power structure a "transvaluation of all values."

In the sacred chaos of the New Year rite, the divisions of time are annulled. This has great significance, drawing its energy from the ultimate fear—the fear of extinction. If time can be annulled, if the irreversible relation of "before and after" can be reversed, then may not the dead return among the living? This notion of annulling death at the end of time and history is one that will haunt the millennial imagination. Indeed, as John of Patmos proclaimed, as well as the Native American prophet Wovoka and countless others, a time will come when "death will be no more."

From Vision to History

Given this cursory survey, I hope it is clear that there are a wealth of sources, and that there is much variation even among the first makers of the Myth. There is, for example, a variation in moral tone that is notable. Unfortunately, the most influential early expression of the millennial vision was the harshest and most violent, morally speaking. I do not deny that Saint John had some valid gripes against the oppressive, persecuting Roman empire.

Unfortunately, his ferocious rhetoric of indignation was so powerful and so effective, especially as translated in the King James Version of the Bible, that it is easy to forget how utterly barbaric are the sentiments it expresses. It is difficult, as D. H. Lawrence said, to free oneself of the ponderous spell of that reverberating prose—"For all nations have drunk of the wine of the wrath of her fornication . . ."(Rev. 18:3) and so on and so forth.

Now, the Myth is much greater than John's rendition of it; like all great myths or stories of the human soul, it is a living, many-sensed thing, and as we retell it we are remaking it ourselves. There is, however, in my judgment, a core cluster of images and concerns, common to all the great makers, and common to its meandering (and sometimes exploding) history. I think that these revolve around the idea of rebirth, newness, and regeneration.

This core image is revealed in John's vision of a new heaven and a new earth, and in the closely related ideas that at the end of time the very laws of nature will undergo a vast overhauling in which it may even be possible to defeat death and once and for all liberate human society from injustice, from pain, and above all, from the curse of lovelessness. This undisguised longing for total fulfillment touches the most human part of the Myth.

The marvelous thing about the Millennium Myth, as I see it, is that it taps into the totally unpredictable, creative rage of the human heart and imagination. Just as the history of the Myth is rich and various, so, I am sure, is its future. So let us move on. In the next chapter, we look at how the vision entered into the stream of Western history during the Middle Ages.

Joachim of Fiore:
2 Prophet of the New Age

We shall not be what we have been, but we shall begin to be other.

JOACHIM OF FIORE
The Ten-Stringed Psaltery

Belief in the Millennium, in a new age, is part of an old pattern of mythical thought. The feeling, moreover, of being at a crossroads of history runs high today. One sign of this is the widespread search for a "new paradigm." *New paradigm, new age, revolution of consciousness—* these popular terms have roots in a long tradition of thinking about endings and beginnings. In the minds of many, the signs of the times, ranging from reports of strange phenomena to facts of social unrest and ecological peril, point to impending large-scale transformations.

The last chapter looked at the origins of the Millennium Myth. Beginning with the Book of Revelation, we worked our way back to the Gospels, the Hebrew prophets, the Zoroastrian tradition, and the Babylonian New Year rite. The core notion, I concluded, revolves around the image of regeneration, an image, I am inclined to suggest, that functions as a kind of psychic analogue to DNA.

Since Christian expectations of the Second Coming were not realized, the Church had to modify its view of the Millennium. It now seemed important to deliteralize the whole idea; otherwise, one ran the risk of being discredited. By the time of Augustine, the Church found it had to suppress the belief that a total renovation of human society was possible. "Outside the Church there is no salvation" became the formula for hope.

It was not until the twelfth century and the work of Joachim of Fiore (1135–1202) that apocalyptic theory acquired a new lease on life. But before looking at this new development, let us glance at the status of millennial thought during the first thousand years of Christendom.

The Millennium Among the Early Church Fathers

For the early Church fathers Irenaeus and Lactantius, hope in the Millennium was still strong. But by the third century there was a shift in attitude; for example, Origen now pictured the promised Kingdom of God as an event in the individual soul rather than as a collective mutation of society.

A process of depoliticizing the Millennium had begun, and one can see why. With the conversion of the Roman emperor Constantine to the Catholic faith in the fourth century, Christianity became a great worldly power. Yearning for heaven on earth lost its appeal; in fact, it became downright threatening. Once the Church became the Establishment, it was no longer opportune to focus on the revolutionary side of Christianity.

Saint Augustine dealt with the millenarian question in *The City of God*.[1] The great bishop of Hippo read the Book of Revelation as a spiritual allegory. Why hope for anything more than what the Church could offer? The Catholic church itself was the institution that represented God's Kingdom on earth. No need to talk of social evolution or higher stages of salvation.

Within history, Augustine concluded, no further new age was possible. The resurrection of Christ and the founding of the Church were sufficient. Nothing else was needed to fulfill the divine plan. The next stage of human spiritual evolution would occur at the end of time, and the best hope of humankind lay in the Next World. Our only task here and now is to save our souls and wait for the End. Thus evolved the prevailing view in the fifth century. The visionary impulse that inspired the first Christians was driven underground.

Antichrist and Last World Emperor

By the end of the first millennium, turbulent times were disrupting the lives of Western peoples. Waves of barbarian invasions had ended the rule of Rome, with sprawling human dislocations by 950. The Christian world was under attack from Vikings, Moslems, and Magyars. The Carolingian Empire was in ruins, and barbarian warriors terrorized the land; in those violent times, neither life nor law were respected. Vandal warlords brutalized the lower classes.

Against the background of this fear and anarchy, the abbot Adso of Montier-En-Der wrote his *Letter on the Origins and Time of the Antichrist*. Addressed to Queen Gerberga, Adso's *Letter* became widely known throughout Europe, and remained popular under various pseudonyms until the twelfth century. It popularized two figures of the apocalyptic imagination.

The Antichrist was one. In the days of the Roman Empire, Nero and Domitian were top candidates; Antichrist has assumed many guises down through the centuries. Sometimes whole groups of people were fixed with the label, for instance, the Aryan heretics. The notion of Antichrist was sometimes equated with the sum of all evil doers and unregenerate souls, sometimes with a whole group, the bourgeoisie, or the Communist Party.

Adso focused on a second apocalyptic character. As history nears its climax, and Antichrist steps into the fray, another figure, a countervailing supernatural force, will emerge. He is called the Last World Emperor and represents the good side of worldly power. Rome is pivotal here. Recall that in the Book of Revelation, Rome was the infamous Scarlet-Robed Whore of Babylon. But nothing quite stays the same, and after Constantine's conversion, Rome became the rock of the Catholic church. Sinister Rome assumed a friendly guise. The result, says Bernard McGinn, "was the creation of a potent new apocalyptic myth in the time of the later Roman Empire, the legend of the Last World Emperor."[2]

Although the Roman Empire had fallen, Adso foretold that a messianic Last Emperor would arise among the West Franks, like a phoenix from the ashes of the dead Empire. Antichrist was a symbol of the terrors of the Dark Ages; the Last World Emperor, a symbol of the hope. The stage was set for mutual demonization, a phenomenon repeatedly observed in subsequent centuries. The prophetic imagination was poised to inject itself into the stream of history.

Breakthrough to a New Philosophy of History

This leads us to the main theme of this chapter: the apocalyptic imagination of the Italian abbot Joachim of Fiore (1135–1202).

Joachim was the most important writer on the apocalyptic during the Middle Ages, and the most influential since John of Patmos. Norman Cohn calls him "the inventor of the new prophetic system, which was to be the most influential one known to Europe until the appearance of Marxism."[3] Joachim's three major works were the *Exposition of the Apocalypse*, the *Book of Concordances of the Old and New Testament*, and *The Ten-Stringed Psaltery*.

The abbot of Fiore had two visionary experiences while studying the Trinity that became the basis of his philosophy of history. After wrestling with the meaning of a passage in the Book of Revelation, Joachim had a vision during Eastertide at Casamari in 1183. It was a kind of imageless revelation in which "the fullness of the Apocalypse and the complete agreement of the Old and New Testaments [were] perceived with clear understanding by the mind's eye."[4] In this imageless vision Joachim saw the correspondence between the Old and the New Testaments. To put it another way, he thought he saw that events in the Old Testament prefigured events in the New. This, in turn, seemed to provide a key to prophecy of the future.

In *The Ten-Stringed Psaltery*, Joachim reported a revelation that did contain an image: "Without delay at this moment the shape of a ten-stringed psaltery appeared in my mind. The mystery of the Holy Trinity shone so brightly and clearly in it that I was at once impelled to cry out, 'What God is as great as our God?' "[5] A psaltery is an ancient musical instrument resembling a zither, used for singing the psalms.

The connection between the vision of the psaltery and the Trinity? Again, it lay in the notion of the concordance between the Old and New Testaments. By means of studying the hidden harmonies between the two Testaments, Joachim thought he saw the historical significance of a third epoch of history yet to unfold, an epoch that would unfold under the dispensation of the third person of the Holy Trinity.

Joachim found a secret pattern of correspondences between the contents of the Old and New Testaments. According to the Italian abbot, the two testaments represented two great epochs of human history; Christ was the turning point, the pivot between the two epochs.

So far, all this is compatible with tradition. Joachim, however, carried the argument, followed the logic of the image, a step further. Once he took the Trinity as the paradigm of history, Christ could no longer be the last turning point. Christ could only be the second hinge of history; a third was yet to come. Meditating on the image of the Trinity, Joachim inferred that another epoch of history, divinely ordained, was yet to unfold.

For Joachim the Three Persons of the Trinity became an image of time, of progressive movement. In the Holy Trinity, he saw the pattern of history itself. It was a pattern of progress. The progress of history involved development from the age of the Father to the age of the Son; apparently, the divine reality was progressively unfolding in history. The first age of history was based on the first person of the Trinity; the second age on the incarnate Christ. Tradition stopped here.

But Joachim saw a third age yet to unfold, based on the third person of the Trinity, the Holy Spirit. So a third and therefore new age of history was yet to come. History, as Joachim saw it, was a process with a goal; a self-transcending process. For, just as the epoch of Christ and the New Testament transcended (although it contained and integrated) the preceding epoch of the Father and the Old Testament, so is an altogether new epoch going to proceed out of the first two stages, integrating yet transcending them. Joachim was mounting a full-scale attack on Western patriarchism.

Joachim believed that by studying the correspondences between the two Testaments and the two stages of spiritual consciousness they reflected, he could discern the signs of the times and foretell the shape of the new age, the last great epoch of human history that must arise before the end of ordinary historical time.

Joachim converted the static theological idea of the Trinity into a developmental pattern of spiritual evolution; a dry scholastic symbol became a tool for predicting the course of history. In effect, Joachim historicized the Trinity; he brought it down to earth. Using his analogical imagination, he invented a system of thought that would grip the prophetic imagination of the West and lay the groundwork for the secular ideas of progress, evolution, and revolution.[6]

The progressive idea of the three ages is in the *Book of Concordances*. The chart below depicts the developmental pattern, as Joachim saw it, destined by divine decree to evolve. The three divisions are understood according to the symbolism of the Father, the Son, and the Holy Ghost. The three are aspects or stages of one process, and they exhibit Joachim's law of spiritual development.

The Holy Trinity translated into a scheme
or image of spirit unrolling itself in time:

Father	Son	Holy Spirit
law	grace	greater grace
knowledge	authority of wisdom	perfect understanding
chains of slave	service of son	freedom
exasperation	action	contemplation
fear	faith	love
bondage	freedom	friendship
childhood	youth	maturity
starlight	moonlight	daylight

The general impression one receives from this is that the three persons of the Trinity represent three stages in the progress of history. Thus, for example, according to this schema, the course of history is directed to move from an age of fear to an age of faith. The first moment in the evolution of divine consciousness is fear. The age of fear is the age of the Father, but in the age of the Son we get beyond fear and develop a new attitude of faith. Faith is the state of mind of the order of clerics, the guardians of sacred dogma. But faith, too, will give rise to yet a higher stage of history under the guidance of the Holy Spirit and marked by love, the typical state of monks and contemplatives, according to Joachim.

The course of history is progress from slavery through service to freedom. Under the dispensation of the Father, we find ourselves in chains; under the dispensation of the Son, we step toward freedom. The law of history is thus a law of progress toward freedom. The radical content of this idea for the followers of Joachim was that we are evolving toward freedom beyond the institutions of the Church. Joachim therefore anticipates the Reformation. The philosophy of freedom was developed by Hegel and has recently reappeared in the thought of Francis Fukuyama's *The End of History and the Last Man*, with America leading the world to the promised land.

But for Joachim freedom is not the last word: for, in one of the analogies cited above, we begin in bondage, move on to freedom, but then move further on to friendship. Apparently, Joachim saw friendship as higher than freedom. This strikes me as a very important qualification, and one that modern democratic societies need to pay close attention to. The unfortunate truth is that people may live in a free society but still not know the meaning of friendship. For example, in America today we have the freedom to buy guns but not Joachim's spirit of friendship to prevent us from using them on each other. It is worth stressing the difference here between Joachim's and Fukuyama's view of the end of history: Joachim defines freedom in terms of contemplative friendship, whereas Fukuyama's freedom is defined in terms of the free market, the freedom to produce and consume.

Joachim's stages of historical development are interlocked. The three ages are depicted in the image on the plate "Three Trinitarian Circles" in the *Book of Figures*[7]—three interlocking circles, the third linked with the first two, yet transcending them. Progress is self-enriching, a synthetic process.

As Joachim saw it, the direction of history is beyond aggressive, assertive life styles; the highest type of life style was contemplative. The regeneration of the world will come from the birth of a new order of contemplatives. Joachim's society of contemplatives would, of course, differ sharply from American society, which idealizes productiveness and productivity. The contemplative holds the esthetics of appreciation above the economics of consumption.

According to Joachite theory, human beings are gaining receptivity to *increasing grace*. As spiritual evolution advances, new gifts, charisms, and powers will emerge as part of our normal human equipment. Zoroaster held a similar view: at the end of time, a new spiritual energy will enter the stream of history. Proof will be seen when people begin to learn to live with less food and drink, when they become less consumer-driven, and when they become less exploitative toward nature.

In Joachim's view, the age of spirit began with the rise of the Benedictine monks. The Benedictines preached prayer and manual labor; *ora et labora* was their motto, "pray and work." This orderly pursuit of the contemplative life seemed to the abbot a signal that a new era had begun, a new epoch of social existence.

In Joachim's vision of the new age, there will be no new Bible, no new written testament. Had Joachim's Reformation succeeded instead of Luther's, we would have been spared the literalistic, fundamentalist mentality that has plagued subsequent history with its constant sectarian bickering and warfare. The binding principle of society would have been not creeds or doctrines but the spirit of contemplative friendship. In the Joachite reformation, people acquire a new spiritual intelligence, a new way of understanding scripture that leads beyond slavish adherence to the written word.

The twelfth-century Joachite mind was a far cry from fundamentalist. Dante, for example, in his Letter to Can Grande, described four levels of interpretation of sacred text: the literal or historical, the allegorical or doctrinal, the moral or tropological, and the anagogic or heavenly. Joachim added a fifth, which dealt with "concordance," a type of interpretation in which we read the futuristic, developmental effects of sacred text. In the multicognitive approach to text, text is eventually transcended; text becomes a stepping stone, not a prison, of the spirit.

The Joachite philosophy of reading had existential implications. Bernard McGinn notes that the four (or five) levels of interpretation "were designed to show the gradual transition from slavery to freedom in the course of the history of salvation."[8] Joachim's futuristic-oriented notion of concordance between the two Testaments anticipates modern evolutionary models of consciousness. For the medieval prophet, the next step in human evolution was a step toward greater consciousness.

The Gospel of Revolution

It was a grand scheme, at once pessimistic and optimistic. The optimism, the hope, lay in the belief that God was at work in history. God, for Joachim, was directing what we might call the evolution of consciousness. With obsessive detail, he garnered from the two Testaments the data to help him split the history of spirit into three ascending stages.

Evolution or revolution? It is a question of pacing. Certainly, Joachim's thought was a seedbed for revolutionary thought. For him there was a moment that punctuates the course of history, a decisive turning point, a known locus where a leap in human development occurred. Christ was the juncture in human history where humanity began the process of assuming its "likeness" to God. Christ was the bridge, the original *pontifex*, between the old and the next stage in the evolutionary ascent of humanity.

The next step in Joachim's theory broke new ground. It implied that another stage of development was possible; Christ was not the final human archetype, not yet the acme, the supreme model. It also implied, contrary to Augustine, that the Church was not the last thing in the history of salvation. According to Joachim's trinitarian theory, a social norm higher than the established church was possible on earth. The implication was clear enough: the established church was dispensable, and a new dispensation was forthcoming. The Joachite vision made room for a new age, a new spiritual consciousness, a "New People." These will be People under guidance of the Third Person of the Trinity.

Joachim was vague on specifics, trusting the words of Jesus that the Kingdom will arrive suddenly, like a thief in the night. All the faithful can do is be patient and watchful. The discreet abbot remained in the Church's good graces, although Thomas Aquinas, alert to the dangers, took his ideas to task. Dante, bolder and more reckless, put Joachim in Paradise, calling him a "great prophet."

The Franciscan Spirituals

The radical potential of Joachim's thought remained dormant until the time of Saint Francis of Assisi (1181–1226). Francis's remarkable life seemed a living exemplar of Joachim's vision of the liberated contemplative. This extraordinary man unleashed a tremendous wave of spiritual energy in the Western world, one that touched the Renaissance, as we shall see in the next chapter.

The Franciscan spirit is a living force today. You can see it in the creation-centered theology of Matthew Fox and the liberation theology of Leonardo Boff. The Franciscan spirit, medieval and modern, wants solidarity with the cosmos, as shown in the saint's poem *The Canticle of Creation*. According to the *Canticle*, we are all part of a divine creation; the sun is our brother, the moon our sister, and the earth our mother. We are all kin with the cosmos. Francis's way of thinking about nature speaks to the needs of an age of ecology.

Liberation theologian Leonardo Boff wrote of Francis, "He incorporated the archetype of integration of the most distant links; he historicized the myth of the reconciliation of heaven and earth." Francis was a force of synthesis. Heaven for Francis became something realizable on earth. On earth, as in heaven—in the words of the Lord's Prayer. Again, Boff: "Before Francis of Assisi, we discover ourselves as imperfect and old. He seems to us to be something new and something of the future we are searching for, although he was born eight hundred years ago."[9]

Because they cherish the existential, the revolutionary implications of Franciscan spirituality, Fox and Boff have been censured by the Church. Still, Fox and Boff have hesitated to completely denounce the Church; like their precursors of the late Middle Ages, they seem to agree with Joachim that the new age should proceed (one might say *evolve*) out of the old age, like a flower proceeds out of a seed. Francis was a loyal son of the Church, but at the same time unleashed forces that would shake the foundations of the Church.

For example, some thirteenth-century Franciscans saw Joachim's vision of a Third Age as a call to action. In 1254 a book appeared at the University of Paris titled *Introduction to the Eternal Gospel*, written by a young reader of theology, Gerad of Borgo San Donnino. Gerad, mesmerized by Joachim's vision of a new age, announced that the era of the Holy Spirit was about to begin. And he was specific; in a mere six years the age of spirit would dawn. Gerad's ideas caused a sensation.

The colossal transformation was imminent. There would be a giant step in the evolution of human life and society. A New Christ had appeared in history, a human model for the new age, Francis of Assisi. Francis was cast in the role of the *Dux*, the Leader of a new society of seers, miracle workers, and contemplatives.

In the new society, the old sacraments and theologies would become obsolete. The New People would possess a new inner authority, an esoteric "spiritual intelligence" that would enable them to decipher the occult pattern of politics and history. According to Gerad, a new "Everlasting Gospel" was forthcoming. Had not the Book of Revelation alluded to such a gospel? "And I saw another angel, flying high overhead, sent to announce the everlasting gospel to all who live on the earth, every nation, race, language and tribe" (Rev. 14:6). There will be a new gospel for everybody, for "all who live on the earth," and it will regenerate the world.

The great renewal, however, must be preceded by a great struggle. The forces of evil, and the conflicts they cause, will wax in the last times; the new world order can only come after the old is demolished. Gerad predicted that the "Abomination of Desolation" was soon to appear; according to Gerad, this would occur in the form of an evil pope. Thus, the head of the Catholic church had now become the new Nero, the new "focus of evil." This idea of the Pope as Antichrist would become part of the essential rhetoric of the Reformation.

Gerad of Borgo's book challenged the very existence of the clergy. According to this revolutionary mystic, the sacraments were transitory symbols, their necessity nullified in the Third Age. Instead of the sacraments, gifts of spiritual awareness will flourish. Thanks to a heightened contemplative life, people will effortlessly learn to embody the will of God.

Gerad's most extreme idea was that Saint Francis was the new Christ. The authority of the traditional Christ was therefore supplanted. Gerad, in effect, had discovered the Asian idea of the avatar or boddhisattva, the notion of multiple incarnations of the divine reality, an idea intolerable to the Church.

The clash with Church authorities was inevitable, and Gerad was arrested. Salimbene, a contemporary chronicler, wrote that Gerad, stubborn and unrepentant, "suffered himself to die in prison, and was deprived of the burial of the Church, and was buried in the corner of the garden."[10] According to Salimbene, Gerad rejoiced in prison, unshakable in his belief in the coming *status caritatus*, "the age of love."

The next point is crucial. The New People of the Age of Love and Spirit that Joachim prophesied will have a special relationship to property and wealth. Voluntary poverty was the badge of the new spiritual aristocracy. Accent on *voluntary*. In the new age, spiritually intelligent people will voluntarily embrace poverty. But poverty in what sense? The word usually suggests deprivation or destitution. For the Franciscans it implied a state of grace; poverty, in fact, described an inner state, the precondition for supernatural joy. To espouse Lady Poverty was to detach oneself from created things.

In his *Poems of Praise*, the mystic poet Jacopone da Todi wrote, "Poverty, high wisdom—to be subject to nothing—yet to possess all things in the spirit of liberty."[11] Da Todi's "spirit of liberty," the fruit of voluntary poverty, is Joachite in character, and tweaks the status quo by the nose, for the Church depends on material property for its existence, just as the state needs arms and wealth to sustain its power. Any program that repudiated the economic establishment as uncompromisingly as did the Franciscan spirituals was bound to seem seditious.

According to the *Mirror of Perfection*, Saint Francis "hated money above all else." In one story, a friar made the mistake of touching some money; Francis ordered him to pick it up with his teeth, carry it outside the friary, and "lay it on a heap of dung."[12] In effect, the saint equated money with excreta, thus anticipating psychoanalysis, which associates "anal compulsiveness" with hoarding wealth. Let me note here a sharp difference between the Joachite and the Lutheran Reformation; the former repudiated money and hence capitalism; the latter, as Max Weber[13] has shown, provided the religious psychology instrumental to the rise of modern capitalism.

Voluntary poverty, understood as the conscious repudiation of the values of established life, attracted a type of visionary in whom the pacific and life-affirming instincts predominated. The Franciscan Spirituals belong here, and many of them, like Francis himself, came from wealthy families. By contrast, involuntary poverty, experienced as oppressive humiliation, more often inspires resentment and gives rise to violent revolutionary tendencies. Norman Cohn has underscored this twofold typology, focusing on the violent apocalyptic imagination.[14]

The distinction between the two types is important, though in reality the dividing line is easily blurred. Two kinds of people seem drawn to visions of radical renovation: in one, the aggressive and resentful tendencies dominate; in the other, the pacific and erotic seem to have the upper hand. For centuries Joachim's influence has touched on both poles of the visionary imagination.

Let me highlight a few examples. Angelo of Clareno was a Franciscan Spiritual, a radical disciple of Saint Francis. Like Saint Francis, he was passionate in his betrothal to Lady Poverty. The Spirituals opposed the Franciscan Order as it became more organized; they did not want buildings, libraries, or money. All these things meant entanglement in bureaucratic red tape, time lost from the pleasures of contemplative life.

These radical conservatives wanted to restore the pure life style of the apostles, based on spontaneous trust in God. Guided by the progressive ideas of Joachim, the radicals wished to keep to the strict Rule and Testament of Francis, which forbade private property. Consequently, the orthodox Conventual party of Franciscans often

51

persecuted them. Still, the Spirituals, like Saint Francis, stayed faithful to the Church.

Angelo of Clareno is a case in point. While under house arrest in Avignon in 1317, this excommunicated hermit wrote a *Letter of Defense* to Pope John XXII. Angelo made every attempt to prove his fidelity to the Church, while also making a case for radical poverty. The Franciscan Spirituals of the thirteenth and fourteenth centuries were influenced by Joachim's vision, but not quite to the point of prompting them to sever Church ties.

Joachim's revolutionary theories fascinated many who remained within the Church, for example, Bonaventure, Dante, Ignatius of Loyola. In these men, Joachite ideas pulsate just below the surface of orthodoxy. Take, for example, Loyola's Society of Jesus, the Jesuits. Jesuit elitism is true to the spirit of Joachism. The early Jesuits viewed themselves as an army of spiritual warriors; their job was to regenerate the Church and thus educate the human race. Their at times secret, and some might say, sinister ways are legendary. Thus, even within the Church, forces remain that stem from Joachim's millenarian vision. But the appeal of the vision also reached beyond the Church.

Revolutionary Mystics

"We shall not be what we have been," wrote Joachim, "but we shall begin to be other." To many these words seemed a call to move beyond established institutions. Many fringe groups seized upon the revolutionary implications of the doctrine of the Three Ages, and not all were afraid to sever their ties with mother Church.

These were the *heretics*, the ones who (from the Greek) literally "chose for themselves." Hounded, persecuted, imprisoned, and sometimes burnt alive, many Joachite-inspired heretics believed they were the elect, the new saints, the new martyrs; intensely confident in their vision, they endured trial and tribulation. The Church of Rome thus became the new Whore of Babylon, the Antichrist and Mother of All Oppression.

In the fourteenth century two women conceived the idea that in the last world epoch the Holy Spirit will incarnate as a woman. Prous Boneta lived in Montpelier, Provencal, where the heretical Beguines were busy undermining the status quo with their ideas of perfectionism, elitism, and antinomianism (which I define below).[15] In 1325,

Prous confessed she was the incarnation of the Holy Spirit, and thus the New Female Christ; her incarnation was to launch the new age of spirit. Marjorie Reeves writes of Prous Boneta, "For [according to her confession] she had been chosen to be the abode of the Trinity and the giver of the Holy Ghost to the world. . . . As Eve had been the downfall of human nature, so Prous would be the instrument of all men's salvation. . . . she herself was the angel with the keys of the abyss."[16] The new age of spirit, as conceived by Prous of Provencal, can be taken as a forerunner of the current "return of the Goddess" movement.

Another heretic, Giugliema of Milan, appeared in history about 1271. She died in the odor of sanctity in 1282 and was buried in a Cisterician monastery where a cult grew up around her. By 1300 the Inquisitors decided that Giugliema was a dangerous heretic, disinterred her bones, and burnt them to a powder. And just in case her influence was not entirely expunged, they put to death the two living leaders of her cult, a woman Manfreda and a man Andreas, and also a third, unnamed woman. All were burned at the stake. They were all from wealthy families. Not the disoriented, poor millenarians that Norman Cohn describes, they were a different breed of visionary.

According to testimony of Manfreda and Andreas, Giugliema was the incarnation of the Holy Spirit, was going to rise from the dead, ascend into heaven in the presence of her disciples, and shower her divine self upon them in the shape of tongues of flame. Giugliema had announced that Pope Boniface VIII lacked true authority and proclaimed that Manfreda was the new pope. To her credit, Giugliema planned to take over the Holy See peaceably. In an ecumenical spirit, the new pope intended to baptize Jews, Saracens, and all infidels. A new world order would arise, she foretold, led by the Healing Spirit of the Goddess. Such was the diabolic doctrine that riled the Inquisitors to burn these heretics.

Joachim's Trinitarian dialectic spawned many mystical insurrections against the established order. Sometimes the influence was covert. Such was the case with the fourteenth century Beghards. Also known as Beguines, they got their title from a word that means "beg." German authorities tried to exterminate these mystic rebels whose heresy was to believe that perfection was possible in this life. A harmless enough phantasy, one might suppose, but subversive if *perfection* implied outgrowing dependency on the Church. True to Joachim's philosophy of history, Beghards were claiming it possible to surmount the rule of law and fear that was characteristic of the reign of the Father.

Another type of heresy that grew from Joachim's philosophy of history is known as *antinomianism*. The word literally means "against the law," and it implies the repudiation of all moral norms. Some groups, who cultivated that "spirit of liberty" lauded by Jacopone da Todi, proclaimed they were beyond good and evil. One relatively harmless interpretation of this was based on Saint Paul's idea that people at one with God no longer need the law because they are no longer inclined to sin.

But there was a more radical interpretation. In this scenario, once you reach spiritual "perfection," you can do things customarily thought "wrong" by everyone else. Being perfect, you are "beyond good and evil." A Beghard under interrogation professed that in seducing a woman, he had really restored her virginity![17] Here is a mentality known to us in its extreme form in Charles Manson and his followers. Manson, alias Jesus Christ, was a true twentieth-century antinomian. According to Susan Atkins, a disciple of Manson, the motive for the Manson family's killings was "to instill fear into the pigs and to bring on judgment day which is here now for all."[18]

An antinomian cult known as the Free Spirit emerged around 1200 and spread across Northern Europe, lasting for five centuries in a recognizable form. This cult of mystic individualism exalted a way of life unrestricted by human conventions. The Free Spirit adepts were inspired by a philosopher from the University of Paris, Amaury of Bene. Whether on their own or at the beck of Joachim's ideas that were beginning to be known, the Amaurians arrived at the same three-stage philosophy of history. They announced that the incarnation of the Holy Spirit was taking place *in each of themselves*. Each adept therefore transcended Christ. The Amaurians believed they had started all humankind on a path to god-realization.

The Amaurians, like the Beghards and Beguines, the Euchites and the Adamites, and other millenarians down the centuries, glorified sexual anarchy, a protest against patriarchal domination. An impulse periodically vented among the Greeks in the cult of Dionysos was made into a revolutionary social program. Recent times have witnessed a revival of "Free Spirit" ideas on sex in Marcuse's theory of the perversions; the German philosopher recommended erotic anarchy as a way to destroy the nuclear family. For the erotic anarchist or revolutionary mystic, the oppressive nuclear family is the social cement of established society, and deserves to be destroyed.[19]

By 1320 the movement of the Free Spirit was driven underground. Homeless wandering heretics formed a secret ring of mystic conspirators, an invisible church. Bound by a vision of a new society, a new age, a new erotic freedom, the conspirators excoriated the Church's greed, luxury, and power. We can, to a degree, sympathize with the Brothers of the Free Spirit, a catch-all term for a medley of movements, especially with their anger against the injustice, materialism, and hypocrisy of state and church. And we can sympathize with their yearning for original experience, their desire for an experimental knowledge of what nowadays "New Agers" call higher states of consciousness.

The problem seems to have been with the extreme inflation of their egos. However we label it, the records show that adepts of the Free Spirit espoused a philosophy of pure amoralism; their reasoning, in brief, was: "Because I am God, I can do no wrong." Some recorded pronouncements of the Brethren of the Free Spirit: "Nothing is sin except what is thought of as sin." A dangerous idea, if someone does not think it a sin to smash your skull for your money. Another example: "One can be so united with God that whatever one may do one cannot sin." But what if I am mistaken about being "united with God?" Understandably, the Inquisitors found talk like this disquieting. Can anybody ever be so right, so perfect, that they can do just what they feel like doing, with divine disregard for everything else? The antinomian temptation is one of the riskier features of trying to live the Millennium Myth.

Millennial fever broke out in a strange way in 1260, the year that Gerad of Borgo expected to see the *viri spirituali*, the New People, rise to global power. In 1260 the Flagellants took to the roads of Europe. People left home, gave up their everyday lives, and went on great marches; poor and repentant, they traversed Europe, whipping, lashing, and making themselves bleed. During the Middle Ages, in the Low Countries and all over Germany, this masochistic movement ended, as Norman Cohn put it, "as a militant and bloodthirsty pursuit of the Millennium." The flagellant impulse reappears from time to time, recently, for example, among some Shi'ite Moslems.

Some forms of mystic revolution were strange indeed. Take an example from the seventeenth century. The Camisards, French Huguenots at war with the Catholic church, traded in supernatural warfare, or, if you will, psychic warfare. In 1685 Louis XIV revoked the Edict of Nantes, thus depriving all Protestants of their religious and civil liberties. Subsequently, a Protestant pastor, Pierre Jurieu, published pamphlets based on his reading of the Book of Revelation predicting the fall of the Catholic church in 1689.

A follower of Jurieu, Du Serre, disseminated the apocalyptic message and trained children to become seers. Known as the "little prophets," the children went from town to town announcing the reign of Antichrist and the imminent Second Coming of the Lord. Many adults were seized by the infectious enthusiasm. One of the children, known as "the Fair Isabel," became a prophet who helped inspire the revolt of the Camisards. The Camisards fought with the conviction that they had divine support. Strange lights in the sky guided the Camisards during battle; bullets fired at them were said to turn to water. But in spite of their daring exploits and the heavenly aid they received, their struggle ended in defeat.

An interesting millenarian mystic was Thomas Müntzer, an educated contemporary, and enemy, of Martin Luther. Müntzer's career has caught the attention of Marxist writers. Müntzer, who regarded Joachim highly, was convinced that the Last Days were near. The part of the apocalypse that especially interested him was the extermination of unbelievers. "Harvest time is here," he declared, "so God himself has hired me for his harvest. I have sharpened my scythe, for my thoughts are most strongly fixed on the truth, and my lips, hands, skin, hair, soul, body, life curse the unbelievers." One feels here a throwback to John of Patmos, a falling off from Jesus and Francis.

With Luther, the target for apocalyptic rage was the Roman Church. With Müntzer, it was the rich and powerful lords of Bavarian society. Müntzer was converted to his millenarian convictions in 1520 by a man schooled in the Free Spirit Brethren *and* the Flagellants. (A potent mix, to be sure!) Like many makers of the Myth, Müntzer spoke of himself "becoming God" and preached against the political establishment on behalf of the poor miners and weavers of Zwickau. The proletariat would inherit the Kingdom of God, and the rest would be damned. Scholars are divided in their estimate of this strange man: Ernst Bloch saw him as a forerunner of the Marxists, Norman Cohn as having a mentality destined to reincarnate in Adolf Hitler's Germany.

The Heresy of Self-Transformation

Let me conclude with some thoughts on what seems to me the legacy and significance of Joachim's visionary philosophy of history. Joachim was preeminently a prophet of the new age.

Joachim's prophetic vision was a bridge between ancient and modern social thought; the key to the linkage is the historicizing of the archetypes. The Millennium Myth became the basis for a philosophy of history; prophetic vision evolved into social theory and practice. Joachim, moreover, provides us with a "dialectic"—to use Hegel's term. Or, we could say he anticipated Vico and Marx by providing us with a genetic law of historical evolution. This genetic law involved dynamizing and concretizing the archetype of the Holy Trinity.

Joachim's ideas, as they filtered into the stream of European intellectual history, excited a series of social movements and secular theories that were progressive, evolutionary, and revolutionary. As these visionary speculations became detached from their religious moorings, they became increasingly heretical, increasingly divisive and incendiary.

In my view, Joachim unwittingly gave rise to what is perhaps the chief "heresy" of the modern outlook—the heresy of self-transformation. By this I mean the heresy that humanity must free itself from the authority of organized religion to pursue the outer limits of self-development. Independent of dogma and theoretical presupposition, humanity takes responsibility for its own project to become God. As I interpret this, Joachim's vision of a new species of spiritual humanity laid the groundwork for later secular theories of evolution and superhumanity.

As Carl Löwith has shown, the progressive philosophy of this medieval thinker reincarnates repeatedly in the secular worlds of science, philosophy, and education.[20] It would be a large task to trace these influences in detail, but let me finish with a few examples.

In his *Education of the Human Race*, Lessing describes a three-stage evolution of human consciousness; Lessing explicitly compared his last age with Joachim's age of spirit. The heretical shift is from reliance on revelation to reliance on education. The purpose of higher education, according to the German thinker, is to free us from immature dependence on outmoded institutions. Kant's idea of *Aufklärung* or enlightenment was similar to this; in 1784 Kant wrote, "Enlightenment is the transcendence of man's self-imposed immaturity."[21] In line with the bold freedom of Joachim's "Spiritual Men" was Kant's motto: *Sapere aude*, "dare to know!" The Joachite-born heresy is just this, a daring aspiration to gnostic freedom, a daring will to know all, experience all, be all.

Auguste Comte was the great philosopher of positivism; yet beneath his secular garb, he too was shaped by the Joachite image of three ascending stages of human development. Hegel, Schelling, and the Russian philosophers all thought in terms of consciousness evolving, developing, and ascending through progressive stages. The trappings of revealed religion are cast aside, but the evolutionary dynamic of Joachim's vision endures.

Nietzsche's philosophy displays several Joachite themes: the repudiation of conventional Christianity, the talk of going beyond good and evil, and the will to create the superman. Nietzsche died in 1900, at the threshold of the twentieth century. Conscious of himself as a prophet, he used the figure of Zarathustra as the mouthpiece for his most inspired ideas. Zarathustra, another name for Zoroaster, was one of the original makers of the Millennium Myth. In his manically conceived book *Ecce Homo*, Nietzsche identified himself with the crucified Christ and, like the French revolutionaries, proclaimed it the Year One.

Nietzsche saw himself as starting a new era. Thus he dated his autobiography *Ecce Homo*: "On the first day of the year one (September 30, 1888) of the false chronology." "Man," said Nietzsche, repeating the words of John of Patmos, "is something to be overcome." Man is a "rope stretched between Beast and Superman." "He that overcomes," was the refrain of John of Patmos. For John of Patmos humanity is also a rope, but one that is stretched between the Beast of worldly power and Christ the God-man.

We could say that the heresy of self-transformation represents the will to redefine human essence through science, art, and technology. Mary Shelley's Frankenstein monster story was a powerful articulation of this heresy. Frankenstein is obsessed with creating life, surely an old divine prerogative.

When we look closely, the old religious ideas of a new heaven, a new earth, and a new humanity are still with us; the only change lies in the mythical hardware. Instead of believing all things are possible through God, we moderns assert that all things are possible through human art, ingenuity, and technology. We are going to track some of the twists and turns of this titanic will. Let us then move on to one of the boldest social and artistic experiments in the theory of self-transformation—the Italian Renaissance.

The Renaissance: World Renovation Through Arts and Sciences

3

Golden is the age, a terrestrial paradise,
And here the first times are renewed.

LORENZO DE MEDICI

The word *Renaissance* is used by historians to mark the dawn of the modern world, the break with prescientific medieval Christianity. Historians agree there have been several renaissances or rebirths of Western culture; in this chapter, I discuss the best known, the Italian Renaissance. In Renaissance Italy, the Millennium Myth took the form of a cultural revolution and expressed, in my view, the first great secular turn of the Myth.

The Renaissance Millennium aimed, through the arts and sciences, to push the limits of human achievement toward their godlike potential. This grand hope for world-renovation through art, science, and technology was guided by several leading ideas. I am going to focus on five:

1) Leaders of the Renaissance joined two strands from Western utopian thought, the Biblical and the pagan, and, in effect, created a new wave of change, pointing toward a humanistic Millennium.

2) The humanists, scholars, and magi of the time forged a new image of human potential, an image rooted in hermetic, Biblical, and Platonic sources that pictured the future of humanity in terms that were truly godlike.

3) During the Renaissance, the Millennium Myth, through the influence of magic, lent inspiration to the birth of modern technology—the handmaid to the godlike potential of humanity.

4) Artists, architects, and other new-tech seers conceived, planned, and actually attempted to build visionary cities on earth.

5) Finally, the times produced a prophet, Girolamo Savonarola, who, despite his lingering medievalism, preached a democratic Florence as the earthly locale for the new age. Here, thanks to the inspiration of millennialism, we see the beginnings of an idea that would become one of the major forces in modern history, an anticipation of the European Enlightenment. At twentieth century's end, we are still living out these Renaissance sea changes in the ancient Myth.

A Humanistic Millennium

Let us begin with the first contribution of the Italian Renaissance to millennialism. During the Renaissance, two strands in the Western utopian legacy converged, the Biblical and the pagan. In words of the great Renaissance scholar, Jacob Burckhardt:

> Echoes of medieval mysticism here flow into one current with Platonic doctrines and with a characteristically modern spirit. One of the most precious fruits of the knowledge of the world and of man here comes to maturity, on whose account alone the Italian Renaissance must be called the leader of modern ages.[1]

It is to the echoes of medieval mysticism that I want to call attention here: the mystic revolutionaries, the new age Joachites and Franciscans, the people who carried on the millennial dream and the fantastic hope that the world could be changed radically and decisively for the better. According to Burckhardt, the Renaissance led to the "discovery of the outward world" and the "full, whole nature of man."[2] The Millennium Myth, which is a vision of the full, whole nature of human existence, helped free the energies of renewal that found so many new outlets during the time.

A major figure in the synthesis of pagan and Christian culture was Marsilio Ficino (1433–1499), one of those hard-to-classify figures of the Italian Renaissance. Founder of the Florentine Academy, humanist and Neoplatonist, magus and ordained priest, translator of Plato and the *Corpus Hermeticum*, codifier of Platonic love and exponent of the perennial philosophy, Ficino is attracting growing interest.[3]

The times were ripe for synthesis, the late fifteenth century being an age in ferment. As historian Marjorie Reeves says, in the Italian culture "despair and exaltation were strangely mixed."[4] In Florence, Savonarola was sounding the alarm that judgment day was nigh, while Marsilio Ficino and his long-haired Platonist friends were musing on the fullness of time and the imminence of great change.

Ficino, a short hunchbacked man with a gift for friendship, blended pagan aspirations and Biblical images of rebirth. The key text for our purposes is a letter he wrote, in that fateful year 1492, to the German astrologer-humanist, Paul of Middleburg. In this letter, Ficino announced that the Age of Gold (*seculum aureum*) had arrived; a sign of this was the great revival of the arts and sciences presently occurring. In a feverish outpouring of energy, "grammar, poetry, oratory, painting, sculpture, architecture, music"[5] had come to life and suddenly were flowering. These ancient *liberales disciplinas* were reviving, awakening, and directing the energies of men and women in new channels. There were rumblings of a new astronomy, and most of all, said Ficino, there was the invention of the art of printing.

The liberal arts achieved new significance, said Ficino, thanks to the invention of printing. For now it was possible to "recall from darkness into light" the *Platonicam disciplinam*, the rich and fascinating world of the Platonic imagination. It was now possible, through print technology, to spread the gospel of a pagan revival, the gospel of a new humanity. For Ficino in his time, as for Marshall McLuhan in ours, a revolution in communications technology was the key to cultural apocalypse. New information and the increased ability to communicate that information were leading thinkers in Ficino's time to a Christian-Pagan ecumenism, as they have in our times to a postmodern global village.

For Ficino the revived "liberal disciplines" were signs of the *seculum aureum*, "the Golden Age." Ficino's daring equation (liberal arts=golden age) was an idea afloat in the zeitgeist. Florentine humanism was shaped by Greek scholars who had brought utopian ideas with them from Constantinople. One such inspired devotee of pre-Christian antiquity, Plethon, is said to have prophesied "that the whole world would become susceptible to the true religion." There would be a global awakening of consciousness, according to Plethon, a new mode of being, pervaded by "*uno animo, una mente, una praedicatione*"[6]—"one soul, one mind, one teaching."

For Plethon, the revival of learning promised the peace of ecumenism, a world-spiritual community. Cynical about medieval scholasticism, Plethon believed that Greek thought had the potential to unify the whole of human consciousness. For this learned Greek, the task of education was millenarian. "Platonism was the instrument of a total renovation of theological thought and morals which would open a magnificent stage in human history."[7] Plato and the medieval revolutionary mystics here converge. The higher source of unity of the liberal arts, the unifying thread of the whole cultural enterprise, lay in the transcendent aspirations of humanity. What enflamed Plethon with hope in the power of the humanities was his belief in the existence of an underlying, unifying soul, mind, and teaching.

The Renaissance vision of the *una mente* that lifts us beyond the petty discords of culture leads to the next point. Ficino was a spokesman for the idea of a universal or perennial philosophy. Prompted by Cosimo de Medici, Ficino translated the dialogues of Plato, a project he began in 1463 and finally published in 1484. But Ficino did something else. By 1471, he had translated, published, and placed in circulation the works of the legendary Hermes Trismegistus.

Ficino and his fellow humanists cultivated the myth of this Trismegistian data bank of hermetic wisdom, thought to be coeval with Moses and prophetic of Christ; these writings, however, were actually written around the third century C.E. Believing they were awesome and sacred because of their antiquity, they made a powerful impression on Ficino and his circle of soul-searching scholars. However, their chief interest was not historical accuracy but mythmaking and the care of the soul, as the American Thomas Moore has so nicely shown in his study of Ficino's astral psychology.

In the Introduction to his translation of Plato, Ficino offered a letter of dedication to Cosimo and spoke of the perennial philosophy. The eternal Word, the Logos, he wrote, was the basis of *pia*, "peaceful or sacred," philosophy. Peaceful, sacred, eternal, perennial philosophy is the secret stream of vital light, the time wave of wisdom, which has been flowing down the centuries from the ancient poets and the Hebrew Bible on through those Grecian peaks of human intellect, Pythagoras, Plato, Plotinus, Pseudo-Dionysius the Areopagite, and on to the seers of present times. At the heart of *pia philosophia* was a gnostic enterprise; in Ficino's church of eternal truth, the only savior was the savior within.[8]

But the Millennium Myth is not just about going within, as Saint Augustine had proposed; there is a more radical bent at work here, which stems from the Joachite tradition we discussed in the last chapter. The Millennium Myth is not just about gnosis and illumination but action and social regeneration. Ficino's perennial philosophy was a vision of social regeneration; the liberal arts were roads to a new and golden age of human creativity. For the Renaissance humanist, education became a tool of eschatology, a way of exploring the divine limits of human achievement on earth.

The Renaissance Image of Human Potential

The period of Western history we are looking at rethought, reimagined, reevaluated what it means to be a human being. Looking at the ideas of Renaissance humanists, philosophers, and artists, what stands out is their conception of human potential.

It is a conception that celebrates—indeed, that deifies—human potential. Such an exaltation of what people can do is thoroughly millennial; you find it repeatedly in a wide range of chiliastic movements. Closest to the Renaissance were the radical Franciscans and revolutionary Joachites who foretold the coming spiritual people who would transform human society.

But the Renaissance developed its own secular version of a new age of spirit. The Renaissance Millennium pictured itself coming about through a renovation in the arts and sciences, the humanist prophets promoting a new age of cultural transformation. This was very different from the medieval visionaries who still imagined the New People as a contemplative monastic order.

However, before the Renaissance could break free from medieval restraints, there had to be a rethinking of the human image. Renaissance remakers of the Millennium Myth drew on many sources to carry out their project: pagan, Biblical, patristic, hermetic, gnostic, and cabalistic. A key source lay in this saying from the Book of Genesis: "And God said, let us make man in our own image and likeness" (Gen. 1:26).

Renaissance visionaries seized upon these words with a vengeance. I think it fair to say that the genius of the Italian Renaissance was to take this sentence from the Book of Genesis and exploit it to the absolute secular hilt. They used it to exalt the image of human potential as never before, fashioning for humankind a vision of its unlimited creative potential.

In this effort, Ficino was pivotal. With Ficino, a religious myth of external salvation turned into a myth of evolutionary self-deification. In the last chapter, I referred to this turn as the heresy of self-transformation. Even if Ficino, and Pico della Mirandola who followed him, managed to avoid official condemnation, the genie was out: a new image of human potential had emerged, and this new image was to undermine the theology of human submissiveness. The heresy of self-transformation centered, in fact, on human will power.

To glorify the will was, I note in passing, at odds with the Reformation zeitgeist. Reformation leaders like Luther and Calvin echoed Augustine in stressing human sinfulness, the belief that the divine image is tarnished, the likeness to God grown pale and remote, the human will weak and corrupt. These men played up the gap between human depravity and divine potential. Our human image is so stained by sin, said the northern reformers, that we can *do* nothing to save ourselves. Our rational minds, our free wills are, at bottom, useless; by faith alone, *sola fidei*, are we saved. (Accent on the passive voice.) As Protestant theologian Friedrich Schleiermacher said, the essence of religion is a "feeling of dependency."[9]

Among Renaissance humanists, the "likeness" to God was played up, not the "fallenness" of humanity. Not the distance from God but the nearness, the possibilities for intimacy, not the sinfulness but the dignity of being human, were loudly and proudly trumpeted.

Perhaps the most powerful statement glorifying humanity occurs in Ficino's *Theologica Platonica*. In this book, according to Charles Trinkaus, "Ficino's central purpose as a philosopher was to demonstrate the immortality and divinity of the human soul."[10] This harmonized with Genesis on the human likeness to God but went far beyond it.

For according to the Bible, the soul is not naturally immortal; at best, scripture offers the hope of resurrection, an outcome that depends on the will of God. Salvation lies outside, in a transcendent power, and hangs on the thread of faith. Matters were worse with Calvin, for whom salvation was predetermined and divinely arbitrary. All this contrasted sharply with Ficino, who built his case for human potential on the very different Platonic doctrine that the human soul is *intrinsically* immortal.

The revolutionary idea is this: if the human soul is intrinsically, naturally immortal, *it contains its own divinity within itself*. A crucial link in the chain of dependence on an external God is destroyed. Ficino's case for human immortality—so distinct from the belief in resurrection—set the groundwork for a new conception of being human, a conception we could call evolutionary humanism. This disturbing move follows upon the synthesis of several sources: the hermetic influence was, as Frances Yates has shown, strong; the Biblical, as Charles Trinkaus has pointed out, even stronger, but the central influence, in my opinion, clear in the *Theologica Platonica*, was Platonic. Plato's metaphysics was naturalistic; indeed, the early Greek philosophers were the first to grasp the very idea of nature as an autonomous reality.[11]

The secular turn in Ficino's eschatology of human potential was thus based on his affinity to Platonic naturalism. In the Biblical Millennium, the consummation of history is imagined as coming about by divine agency; we are at the mercy of divine forces outside ourselves. With Ficino the picture changes radically; since the soul is naturally immortal, the source of transformation shifts to the field of consciousness, to human will, intellect, and imagination.

Ficino is clear on this: There is an immanent drive to realize the godlike potential of human beings. It derives from an *appetitus naturalis*, "a natural appetite," to become godlike, to push toward the limits of being. Thus, in the *Theologica Platonica*:

> The entire striving in our soul is that it become God. Such striving is no less natural to men than the effort of flight is to birds. For it is always in men everywhere. Likewise it is not a contingent quality of some men but follows the nature itself of the species.[12]

This is a remarkable statement about the potential to transcend the human condition. Earlier, at the dawn of the Renaissance, Dante had invented the word *trashumanar*, "to transcend humanity." For Ficino this deific appetite is the defining trait of our species. Human nature is just that, a nature, a *nascimento*, "a coming to birth." Our nature is to be reborn as gods, to reorganize and transcend ourselves. Ficino offers an evolutionary perspective on human reality.

This perspective undermines the static hierarchy of being. If all of life, especially human life, is striving for self-transformation, tranquility in the world order becomes impossible. Nietzsche, who knew Burckhardt's work on the Renaissance, took this idea of godlike striving and called it "the will to power." For Ficino and Nietzsche, striving to "become God" is as natural as the flight of birds. Worshiping divinity is as natural as "horses neighing." In the Renaissance turn, the divine is naturalized, the natural divinized.

Ficino invites us to feel the full girth of our being. The gnostic project, that bold hope of reaching the heights and depths of consciousness and the limits of experience is, in Ficino's world, not something embarrassing or anomalous, sinful or heretical, but as universal and commonplace as the will to live. Ficino's eschatology, his philosophy of the End, is thus based upon a theory of human theogenesis: to be human is to be evolving toward godlikeness. From Ficino's angle, the godlike soul manifests in two ways: first, in its relation to the body and second, in its relation to the world.

In relation to the body. The soul knows itself to be the master of the body by introspection. I know that I can eat more or less, yield to discomfort or will to detach myself from it, and so on. I can detach myself from my body and immerse myself in my inner world.

Turning inward is the way to our divine potential: "And they will learn that the unique way not only of attaining but of possessing the incorporeal is to render themselves incorporeal."[13] In other words, defixating oneself from the passive side of bodily life. Ficino's eschatology points to overcoming the limitations of normal embodied existence. People may choose to "withdraw the mind from movement, sense, affect and corporeal imagination as far as they are able." As in Patanjali's system of yoga, this capacity to withdraw our attention from external impressions opens the way to gnostic liberation. Detaching oneself from external and internal events, recollecting one's soul, one becomes an *angel*, "a pure disembodied intellect"; one may learn to enjoy "the infused light of truth."

The soul, says Ficino, is a guest on earth, a traveler in the night of eternity, and it ought to be called "a god or a star surrounded with a cloud or a daemon." But this does not lead to outright denial of the body or repression of pleasure. On the contrary, the human soul surpasses the animal soul because it "feels more sharply," and proof of this is that people enjoy eating, drinking, and sex more than other animals do. These activities, then, are signs of our divinity, not vices about which we need feel guilty. In Ficino's humanistic Millennium, earthly pleasures recover their pagan innocence.

In Ficino's eschatology, the body has a psychic future. In a great concentration of will, the soul can abstract itself from the body;

Socrates and his legendary trances bore witness to this. The poets, as Plato said in the *Ion* and the *Phaedrus*, experience divine rapture; poetic possession is proof of the soul's divinity. Pythagoras and Zoroaster withdrew from their bodies and went on prolonged out-of-body excursions lasting years, it was said. Epimenides, an old Greek shaman-philosopher, was said to have gone on an astral-voyage for fifty years. Instances of bi- and tri-location are cited as proof of the soul's autonomy and divinity. Ficino also wrote a book on Saint Paul's rapture, a celebrated out-of-body case of high strangeness.

The divinity, the evolutionary potential, of the soul is due to its peculiar nature. The soul for Ficino is a mediate reality; it has an affinity for the lower orders of intelligence as well as for the highest. In a way, then, Ficino's soul is void of individuality and is like the Buddhist *anatta*, or "no-self." This notion will reappear in Pico's philosophy of the omnipotentiality of human nature.

The soul "is above fate through mind, . . . in such a way that it imitates its superiors, and together with them governs inferior beings." The power of the soul is to create order out of chaos, which it does when it works in harmony with a higher intelligence called *providence*, literally, "the foreseeing."

Once in tune with this "model of divine governance," the soul is able to rule itself, build home and community, master arts and animals. In short, the soul's divinity is shown by the quality of the civilization it produces and the manner, harmonious and fruitful, in which it governs nature and the forms of natural life.

The following sums up Ficino's eschatology (in secular terms, his theory of evolution):

> Certainly the empire of the mind is great which is freed from
> the fetters of the body by its own power. Great is the riches
> of the mind for as often as it desires precious treasures of God
> and nature, it draws them from its own breast and not from
> the bowels of the earth.

The soul's divinity is affirmed in two ways: First, the soul transcends the limits of physical existence. Second, and more startling, the data-treasure-trove of God and nature is available to us through our own souls; everything lies within, the whole of existence, the divine and the natural. In sum, the soul's autonomy proves its divinity; its ability to access all the powers of the universe through the world of the imagination.

In relation to the world. The metaphysical End of Ficino's Neoplatonic soul is to renovate the world through arts and sciences. "Human arts make by themselves whatever nature itself makes, so that we seem not to be servants of nature but competitors." Ficino would no doubt be amazed if he could see just how competitive with nature human beings have become. Human arts mimic the divine order, we are told: thus Appeles painted a dog that caused real dogs to bark and a statue of Venus by Praxiteles drove men wild. "Man at last imitates all the works of divine nature and perfects, corrects and modifies the works of lower nature."

We humans create worlds more comfortable than any nature has to offer; Ficino notes with pride that human beings invent new and subtle pleasures for their refined senses, which he approvingly calls "food for the phantasy." You find food for the phantasy in the industrial arts, where, according to Ficino, we "utilize all the materials of the universe." The human being, we are told, is the god of the animals, indeed, of all the elements and all the materials of the physical universe.

In the pursuit of our godlike potential, we utilize the natural world; Ficino, of course, living in a pre-ecological age, was not conscious of the risk of destroying or polluting nature, as we are today. The idea was to compete with and perfect nature, not, as Bacon said, put her to the "rack" and exploit her to death.

We need to learn to govern *ourselves* in preparation for the end of history, and it is within this context that we pursue such abstract arts as music and mathematics. How do these weave into the picture of the End? The abstract arts, like music and mathematics, are meant to prepare us for a time when the soul "begins to live without the aid of the body." For beyond the body an aetheric existence awaits us.

As God is creator, Ficino's soul dreams of creating heaven and earth anew, to suit its new aetheric mode of being. For Ficino science is the handmaid to eschatology; a man of genius like Archimedes peers into the mind of the cosmic Author so that "man would be able to make the heavens in some way if he only possessed the instruments and the celestial material." Ficino thus saw science as imitative of God's power to create the very heavens. This phantasy of creating the heavens anew, of restructuring the forms of nature, anticipates the spirit of modern science and technology. For Ficino the power to restructure physical reality was proof of the soul's immortality, thus its divinity and apocalyptic potential.

Another sign of the soul's immortality, and hence its divinity, is the ability to perform miracles, seen by Ficino in terms of human control of the earthly and cosmic environment. "Here we marvel that the souls of men dedicated to God rule the elements, call upon the winds, force the clouds to rain, chase away fogs, cure the diseases of human bodies." Yet even these miracles, which Ficino admits are rare although part of our natural psychic potential, do not exhaust the soul's godlikeness.

Our divine future has a bright subjective prospect. Our likeness to God is the basis of our soul's deep capacity for living in joy; the soul is inherently happy, and so, as the American Declaration of Independence will state, we have a natural right to pursue our own happiness. Moreover, says Ficino, the soul's divine pedigree accounts for its propensity to worship itself, so that even egoism and narcissism somehow refract the light of divine glory! Clearly, there is more here of Ficino's pagan than his Christian self.

A sign of apocalyptic human potential is what Trinkaus calls the "multipotentiality [of man] . . . to become everything." Emotionally and intellectually, human beings strive to become and know all things; they are impatient with servitude, for there "is hidden in us something of I do not know what grandeur which it would be wicked to violate." Our natural love of freedom is another indication of our divinity. This conforms with remarks I will make about the millennial roots of the Enlightenment, which also celebrates our inalienable right to freedom.

Even the will to power in human behavior is proof of our divinely implanted appetite for the infinite, as in this curious argument: "Thus man wishes no superior and no equal and will not be permitted anything to be left out and excluded from his rule. This status belongs to God alone. Therefore he seeks a divine condition." Or, in a similar vein: "He is content with no frontier. He yearns to command everywhere and to be praised everywhere. And so he strives to be, as God, everywhere."

Ficino's whole philosophy of humanity is thoroughly eschatological and points to the mechanism propelling us toward the end of history. Human existence is driven toward overcoming the limits of history. Discontented with bodily limitations, driven by divine energy and love of freedom, the divine appetite in us wants to consume everything and transform everything in a fire of joy and Blakean "eternal delight."

However, the soul's built-in discontent with death and limitation does not imply flight into disembodiment. On the contrary, soul-doctor Ficino believes there is a need for a new "temperate immortal celestial body."[14] This would be a body but with new powers and attributes.

> The condition of the everlasting soul which seems to be in the highest degree natural is that it should continue to live in its own body everlastingly. Therefore, it is concluded by necessary reasoning that the immortality and brightness of the soul can and must at some time shine forth into its own body. . . .[15]

The immortal soul creates its own body; it wants to incarnate and transfuse itself into the colors and textures of space-time worlds. Given that history is heading toward celestial embodiment, one sees why Ficino sanctifies the arts and sciences. The arts and sciences are means to incarnate the dreams of the Golden Age; they are the way to make them real, practical, particular, sensible—in short, livable. The arts and sciences, then, are pathways to a kind of celestial incarnation, to sensible and sensuous ways of renovating human life.

Pico Della Mirandola's Superangelic Humanity

In Ficino's Neoplatonic circle of friends was a young visionary of human potential. Author of a famous paean to what Shakespeare called the "paragon of animals," Giovanni Pico della Mirandola wrote the *Oration on the Dignity of Man* in 1486. Pico's *Oration* echoes Ficino's theology of human potential but adds a few twists.

Medieval theology put humans below angels; Pico put humans above angels. His reasons are intriguing. Unlike angels and all other beings, whose essence, nature, or archetype are forever fixed and thus unfree, human nature is an open and fluid concept.

The "Supreme Maker," declares Pico, set the human "creature of indeterminate image" in the center of the world and said:

> We have given you, Oh Adam, no visage proper to yourself, nor any endowment properly your own. . . . The nature of all other creatures is defined and restricted within laws which

71

we have laid down; you, by contrast, impeded by no such
restrictions, by your own free will . . . trace for yourself the lin-
eaments of your own nature. . . . We have made you a creature
neither of heaven nor of earth, neither mortal nor immortal,
in order that you may, as the free and proud shaper of your
own being, fashion yourself in the form you may prefer.[16]

What a bold statement about the power of human beings to take
command of their lives! Being human is a gift that consists of not being
a prisoner in a fixed hierarchy of being. Humans surpass the worth of
angels because they can shape their own reality; they can soar beyond
their limitations; they can even aspire to union with godhead. Human
existence is an open, a free project.

This is the uniquely liberating side of being human. Thanks to this
marvelous freedom and openness to reality, human beings can learn
to assimilate, and thus transcend, all the archetypes; all types, forms,
and patterns of being can be taken into ourselves and thus mastered.
Instead of a fixed hierarchy, a static icon, the universe dissolves into
time waves of transformation, a place where novelty is possible. In
short, an image of human evolutionary potential emerges.

For Pico, as for Ficino, the function of the liberal arts is to liberate
our God-potential. "The dignity of the liberal arts," said Pico, "and
their value to us is attested not only by the Mosaic and Christian
mysteries but also by the theologies of the most ancient times." The
idea of a common or perennial tradition was strong in Pico and Ficino.
The humanistic Millennium encouraged an ecumenism of spirit, a
happy unity of spirit that would safeguard what we nowadays call
"multiculturalism."

For Pico it was the job of philosophy to pacify civilizations, to give
voice to the healing unity of cultures. Religious and cultural conflicts
are caused by inner conflicts. The philosopher, said Pico, should be a
soul doctor, a healer of the fractured world.

For it is a patent thing . . . that many forces strive within us,
in grave, intestine warfare, worse than the civil wars of states.
Equally clear is that, if we are to overcome this warfare, if
we are to achieve that peace which must establish us finally
among the exalted of God, philosophy alone can compose and
allay that strife.[17]

The deification of humanity is thus linked to the pacific task of philosophy. The peace of the human race lies in the prospect of working out the unity of the great traditions. This means trying to touch the human center of the great mass of world faiths. We touch this center by touching the human center of ourselves. What we need is an "inviolable compact between flesh and the spirit." The aims of the spirit and the needs of the flesh must come together in holy matrimony; for Pico the point of philosophy and the liberal arts was to harmonize the interests of flesh and spirit, in search of a higher civilization.

Like Ficino, Pico was fascinated by hermetic magic and began his *Oration* with the Trismegistus phrase about the miracle of being human. In Pico's view, as I said, human beings are unique because no *archetype*, no "defining or determinate structure," dominates them. Here, in fact, lies the miracle of being human. To be human, for this Renaissance philosopher, means to be open to the infinity of possibilities that nature offers. Pico quotes a Chaldean oracle to clarify his idea of protean humanity: "Man is a living creature of varied, multiform and ever-changing nature." (Pico, by the way, rejected astrology as incompatible with free will. Astrology was a noose around the neck of multipotential man.)

The philosopher, in Pico's view, is a magus. Magic is the will to exploit the forces of the universe. But in the *Oration*, Pico distinguishes two kinds of magic: the dangerous kind that leads to "monstrous" slavery, bondage to dark forces, and the kind that leads to freedom and knowledge of the "secrets of nature." Pico likes earthy comparisons. "As the farmer weds his elms to the vines," he writes, "so the magus unites earth to heaven, that is, the lower orders to the endowments and the powers of the higher."

Pico rejects dualism, the habit of mind that divides the forces of life—the above from the below, good from evil, heaven from earth. Pico's Neoplatonic "magic" wants to merge these opposites, in harmony with the Millennium Myth, which also longs for the marriage of heaven and earth.

Magic and Technology: Making The Millennium

The Renaissance exalted the image of human potential. It did so by validating the will and by validating magic, which, together, prepared the way for modern technology.

At a conference on consciousness, I once stepped into an elevator with Joseph Campbell. Pressing the button for our floor, I said jokingly, "Look, magic!"

"It's *all* magic," replied the great mythologist.

Campbell was referring to technology. Technology is magic. But in what sense? Frances Yates, in her book on Bruno and the hermetic tradition, pinpoints the link between magic and technology:

> . . . the real function of the Renaissance Magus in relation to the modern period (or so I see it) is that he changed the will. It was now dignified and important for man to operate; it was also religious and not contrary to the will of God that man, the great miracle, should exert his powers. It was this basic reorientation of the will which was neither Greek nor medieval in spirit, which made all the difference.[18]

Classical and medieval ideals of life were indeed more contemplative than active. The receptive, not the voluntary or creative powers, were prized. "Life," said Pythagoras, "is like a festival; just as some come to the festival to compete, some to ply their trade, but the best come as spectators (*theatai*)."[19]

Theatai relates to the word *theoretical*—and *theater*. The Greeks were at ease reclining in the theater of theory. The Greek pursuit of knowledge never became experimental, at least in the modern sense. The overfondness for theory, so classically Greek, was also the Achilles heel of Greek science. The world had to wait for the Renaissance and Galileo before the next, the experimental, step in the evolution of science.

Ancient "science" was theatrical and theoretical, not practical or experimental; the eye had yet to marry the hand. How remote from the American way! Work, manual labor, was regarded as bad, almost subhuman, by the ancient Greeks. Aristotle called slaves "living tools." The Greeks had a special word, in English *banausic*[20], which meant "menial, mechanical, workaday." Another Greek word for toil, *ponos*, meant "pain, punishment, sorrow." Nor does the Bible hold work in high esteem; the Lord punished Adam by expelling him from an Eden of pure ease; the fall of humankind was the fall into the sweat of the workaday world.

In modern times, the hermetic or magical tradition encouraged a different view of work. We should recall that Egyptian magic permeated the Hermetic texts adored by Florentine Neoplatonists. In these books, translated by soul-doctor Ficino, the Renaissance learned to entertain the idea of coercing divine forces by means of magic. The *Aesclepius*, an important hermetic text, explains how to invoke the God-powers by talismanic magic. Talismanic magic involved the marriage of hand and inner eye; for a talisman is a magical image you make with your own hands, talismanic magic an operation you perform to produce results.

The shift toward the modern was a shift from the contemplative life to the active life. The new guiding word was operate not contemplate. For the classical thinkers the supreme goal was the vision of God; in the new magico-eschatological view, the great goal was no longer just to see God but to make or do something godlike. Operative magic stimulated the active, experimental life.

Other influences churned this new active, Faustian soul. For example, the early Italian communes developed accounting and banking, the beginnings of Western capitalism. Here the shift toward the active life involved a different kind of magic—the "magic" of making money. If you could make money, you could, as eight generations of Renaissance Medici did, make history; you could patronize the arts and sciences, expand and consolidate power, revise the very art of living. It was the wealthy Cosimo de Medici who hired people to search for rare manuscripts and enlisted scholars like Ficino to translate and artists like Botticelli to illustrate them.

Another Renaissance influence in revisioning the human enterprise came from the mechanical arts: mapmaking, the compass, the printing press, the telescope, ballistics, and fortifications. All gave fresh scope to active life. All provided tools for actively exploring nature.

In the humanistic Millennium, knowledge promotes wholeness of self and is practical and esthetic. Fifteenth-century Italian artists valued constructive knowledge, evident in their many-sided pursuits. Filippo Brunelleschi was an architect, sculptor, goldsmith, watchmaker, fortress builder, and hydraulics engineer. Piero della Francesca was a great painter and leading mathematician. I could fill pages with examples. Above them all, towers the multifaceted Leonardo da Vinci.

The paradigm of knowledge as construction came to a head in the new physics of Galileo. In the Preface to the Second Edition of the *Critique of Pure Reason* (1786), Kant explained the shift which linked the magic of the will to technology:

> When Galileo caused balls, the weights of which he had pre-
> viously determined, to roll down an inclined plane; when
> Torricelli made the air carry a weight which he had calculated
> beforehand to be equal to a definite column of water . . . a light
> broke upon all students of nature. They learned that reason
> has insight only into that which it produces after a plan of its
> own. . . .

The new scientists went beyond the observation of nature; they took the lead, forcing nature to reply to *their* questions. From this it is a short step to Bacon's program of putting "nature to the rack." A new and fateful conception of science was emerging. The new magic of scientific technology will change planetary life, and Bacon's phrase about putting nature to the rack would acquire apocalyptic overtones by the late twentieth century.

What began as a Renaissance revival of talismanic magic will lead to atomic arsenals, biotechnology, virtual reality, and all the rest. Technology increasingly is going to play into the hands of a Promethean will to revolt against the tyranny of nature. Prometheus, let us recall, stole fire from the gods and taught the arts and sciences to humanity.

Promethean technology, gaining power over the centuries, plays to the god-emulating imagination. Ficino said an inventive soul rivals nature in the power to create. Mary Shelley's fable of Frankenstein's monster shows the mad man-god competing with nature. Who can forget the Hollywood image of Victor Frankenstein shrieking with psychotic joy, "It's alive! It's alive!" Frankenstein's passion, like Ficino's, was to rival God in remaking nature. The Frankenstein story reveals the secret eschatology of science. To want to create new life exemplifies the heresy of self-transformation, the secular ambition to crash the gates of heaven. Frankenstein, forerunner of artificial-life enthusiasts, the "new Prometheus" (the subtitle of Mary Shelley's novel *Frankenstein* was *The Modern Prometheus*) and arrogator of God's omnipotence, used science to deify humanity. A renewer of the cabalistic golem phantasy, he becomes a modern maker of the Millennium.

Visionary Cities: Intimations of New Jerusalem

Ficino listed architecture as a sign of the Age of Gold. Architecture, in a way, is the capstone of the humanities, combining the arts and sciences. Architecture figures in the apocalyptic imagination; the New Jerusalem is pictured as a real place, a physical edifice set in a definite locale on earth.

The house, the temple, the city, in ancient times were built on celestial archetypes.[21] Puritan millenarian John Winthrop spoke of building "a city on a hill," a shining archetype for all nations to admire and emulate. In the Book of Revelation, the jeweled architecture of New Jerusalem is prominent. "And I John saw the holy city, new Jerusalem, coming down from God out of heaven, prepared as a bride adorned for her husband."

The Book of Revelation features a symbolic architecture of the city of God; in the practical Renaissance, artists and builders designed actual visionary cities. At best partially realized, their visions of the *città felice* (the "happy city") point to potentials for the future.

Plans for building visionary cities appeared in the works of Leon Battista Alberti in *De Re Aedificatora* (1485), of Filarete in the *Sforzinda* (1461), and of Francesco di Georgio in the *Trattato di Architettura* (1481). "As a corpus," wrote Frank Manuel, "the ideal cities graphically depicted in Italian architectural treatises from the mid-fifteenth to the mid-sixteenth century represent one of the grand moments of independent utopian creativity."[22]

Several points merit mention; first, the stress on the marriage of function and beauty. Take Alberti's Neoplatonic idea of designing cities that harmonized *commoditas* and *voluptas*, "practical function" and "esthetic pleasure." Functional efficiency in the new Renaissance age was not enough; the city must embrace *voluptas*, "divine pleasure." Thus, the reason for curving streets: "I ask you to consider how much more pleasant the view will be if at every step you see new forms of buildings."[23]

Renaissance visionary cities united esthetic appeal and practicality with radial, star-shaped, and mandala-like designs, designed to be hygienic, defensive, and symbolic. The radial design evoked the idea of mystical unity. One could never get lost in the city; no matter how far one wandered, there was always a signpost, an indicator, pointing back to the mystic center.

The city was regarded as a spiritual mnemo-technic construction. In Tommaso Campanella's utopian *City of the Sun*, all knowledge is translated into symbolic images that adorn the principle concentric-city palaces and chambers, mnemonic aids meant to teach children and remind adults of the healing wisdom of solarian culture. Campanella's visionary city harmoniously combined art, science, and spirit.

Giulio Camillo's memory theater was a strange but perhaps prophetic venture into visionary architecture.[24] Camillo's thought world overlapped Pico's and Ficino's, and his memory theater, a quaint wooden structure that two people could enter, was famous in the sixteenth century. The idea behind his contraption was based on Ficino's astral magic and Pico's philosophy of omnipotential humanity.

Camillo's memory theater was semicircular, made of tiers, boxes, and panels, and arranged with archetypal images and magical talismans. What the purpose of this video display was we may gather from a letter written by Viglius Zuichemus to Erasmus in 1530:

> He calls this theater of his by many names, saying now that
> it is a built or constructed mind or soul. . . . He pretends
> that all things that the human mind can conceive . . . may
> be expressed by certain corporeal signs in such a way that the
> beholder may at once perceive with his eyes everything that
> is otherwise hidden in the depths of the human mind.[25]

Camillo's memory theater was an attempt to construct an object that both expressed the contents of the mind (a "constructed mind or soul") and provided the symbolic means of entering the total timeless pattern of human knowledge ("everything that is otherwise hidden in the depths of the human mind"). The purpose was to induce in the experiencer a kind of panoramic memory of his complete inner and historic world. Camillo's theater was designed to enable citizens in an ideal community to achieve a kind of species self-knowledge.

Camillo, along with Pico, Ficino, and other hermetic soul engineers, believed that by arranging certain images in certain patterns, one might 1) draw down, through the talismanic, strange attractors—the ethereal energies of the cosmos, and 2) bring the images, paintings, sculptures, or icons, to psychic life within oneself. The memory theater was, in short, conceived as a technical device for an enormous expansion of consciousness.

Camillo's video-gnostic theater was made for the user to access the entire culture, a device for speeding up the information flow of history. Have we already begun to enter Camillo's memory theater? Using machines to access vast stores of information is a prominent feature of our culture. The virtual electronic world community that is presently forming, like a growth girdling the planet, seems to me a contemporary development of Camillo's hermetic memory theater.

Unlike John's puritanical New Jerusalem, the unifying principle of Renaissance visionary cities was *voluptas*—not an easy word to translate. One might approach it via the Sanskrit *ananda*, "divine pleasure." Renaissance *voluptas* also relates to Platonic *Eros*, that seductive energy that attracts the sensory imagination to ideal beauty.

About being an architect, Filarete wrote, "Building is nothing more than a voluptuous pleasure, like that of a man in love. Anyone who has experienced it knows that there is so much pleasure and desire in building that however much a man does, he wants to do more."[26] Extrapolate this remark to a utopian city populated by workers in love with their work; such a city would be truly *felice*. As I show in the last chapter, it is a hope of the Millennium Myth to unite love and work, which were sundered during the "fall of man."

Lorenzo Valla's *De Voluptate*, more than any Renaissance work, celebrates the healing power of pleasure. In Valla, the opposition between pagan and Christian, body and soul, intellect and imagination, earth and heaven, is overcome, through the healing power of pleasure. Valla builds a bridge for opposites to meet, a way of being that heals the broken self. *Voluptas* is the unifying principle.

Valla attacked Stoic, Aristotelian, and Platonic ethics for their pretensions to independence; they call their virtue *honestas*, but Valla had misgivings about the stress on cold-blooded emotional self-control. Humans are part of a great throbbing life. What drives our behavior, according to Valla, is a pleasure instinct, a force that rational virtue can neither master nor understand. It was planted in us by a divine intelligence, and our duty is to venerate, explore, develop, and refine its potential.

The will comes into play in the universe of pleasure. But it must be the affirming will of the artist, not the repressive will of the moralist. If the artist wills restraint, it is to multiply, sublimate, and play with the infinite pleasures of life. The moralist, according to Valla, is seduced by the illusion of control but thereby cuts himself off from God's power, which is revealed in our divinely insatiable love of pleasure. To Valla, our job is to go with instinct and trust our divine appetites. Valla, one of the forerunners of modern scientific Bible criticism, makes the case for the value of divine pleasure.

Valla's philosophy of pleasure is a guiding ideal of the humanistic Millennium. *Voluptas* brings us down to earth. We do not have to deny our humanity or postpone our heavenly pleasures till the next world. The beyond begins here and now. Valla likes the Platonic image of the step, the ladder. There is a golden thread that connects the lower and the higher steps called divine pleasure. Not the virtues of the controlling ego, says Valla, "not virtue but pleasure must be desired for itself," that is, if you "wish to experience joy both in this life and in the life to come".[27] Through the golden thread of pleasure we learn to weave together opposing forces; with Valla the Freudian id is sanctified, and the logic of pleasure becomes the logic of God.

Valla counseled respect for pleasure and preached the end of repression, especially the end of all repressive philosophies of education. This fastidious scholar argued for a Blakean gratification of desire, a celebration of our animal nature. In ratifying pleasure, Lorenzo Valla ratified another facet of the Renaissance will to deification. Unlike Pico, Valla sees the divine in the animal, the godlike in the pleasure instinct. His humanistic Millennium was a pleasant place.

In the humanistic Millennium, cities are beautiful, embody the wisdom of the ages, and are clean, healthy, and efficient. The Renaissance utopian city was a divine pleasure dome.

Savonarola, Apocalypse, and Democracy

Lorenzo Valla is not an easy figure to place. Is he a pagan in Christian disguise or an eccentrically evolved Christian? Similar questions arise with another maker of the Renaissance Millennium Myth. I mean Savonarola, a man whose name evokes images of a wild-eyed prophet of doom.

Renaissance thought broke centuries of psychic domination, dissipating the repressive spell of the Christian myth and allowing highly developed individuals to emerge, monuments of self-culture, rare geniuses, unrepeatable personalities. On the other hand, the period failed to produce a new collective myth, new guidelines for everyday living. John Addington Symonds, commenting on Renaissance paganism, wrote:

> The study of the classics and the effort to assimilate the ancients undermined their Christianity without substituting the religion or the ethics of the old world. They ceased to fear

God; but they did not acquire either the self-restraint of the Greek or the patriotic virtues of the Roman.[28]

Individual self-culture was paramount. Petrarch's vanity was matched only by his passion for fame. Leonardo's uncivic-minded motto was, "Fly before the storm." Cellini bragged in his autobiography about the artful way he escaped prison and killed his enemies. The highest Church officials were depraved on a grand scale. Italy led Europe in the decline of religion, while magic, astrology, and crude superstition thrived. Machiavelli complained that Italy lacked patriotism and relied on mercenaries. Crime was raised to a fine art; the luxury of the rich was extravagant.

All this roiled the apocalyptic imagination. Sienese prophets wandered about barefoot wailing "Woe!" Florentine diarists recorded omens and miracles. Roman astrologers proclaimed the End was at hand. The learned Landino drew a horoscope for religion and argued from the conjunction of Jupiter and Saturn that on November 24th, 1484, a rebirth of Christianity would commence. Rumors of Antichrist were rife, hope in a coming Angelic Pope ran high, and Joachite prophecies rumbled in the underground.

Against this lurid mental landscape appeared the darkly brilliant figure of Girolamo Savonarola. While Florentine Platonists saw a Golden Age dawning, a revival of pagan thought humanely wed to Christian values, Savonarola saw Biblical catastrophe, and foretold old-style, God-sent scourges. In the midst of cultivated Florentines, Savonarola spouted dire prophecies and proclaimed his visions of Christ, sightings of the Virgin, and meetings with the Devil.

Yet, in spite of his medievalism, the Renaissance prophet's endtime phantasies assumed significant secular colorings. In the *Compendium of Revelations*, for example, Savonarola appears as a forerunner of democratic ideas. He favors a "popular regime" for reasons similar to Montesquieu's theory of government checks and balances. The people should govern themselves, said the friar, not as a mob but through a Great Council. Councils prevent corruption and temper the extremes of individualism. "To corrupt so many would be difficult and in a way impossible, especially because the judgment and examination of other prudent and proven citizens will have been invoked before the Council takes up anything."[29] This is a fine statement of democratic feeling.

Perhaps due to his democratic leanings, Savonarola won respect from the religiously indifferent (and equally misunderstood) Machiavelli, who wrote:

> The Florentines do not consider themselves either ignorant or rough, nevertheless they were persuaded by Fra Girolamo Savonarola that he held speech with the Almighty. It is not for me to decide whether this was true. . . . But I will say that infinite numbers believed him, without having beheld anything extraordinary to compel their credence, and merely because his life, his teachings, and his text sufficed to win their faith.[30]

Savonarola's model of a democratic government flowed from his millenarian vision. The millenarian, remember, is a person in a grand hurry, weary of waiting for heaven. Millenarians want to bring heaven down to earth. The Dominican Friar also wanted to bring the New Jerusalem down to earth, and he chose a particular city, Florence, where he thought it could happen.

Since Florence was a corrupt city, it would first have to undergo a purifying tribulation. The doom phase of apocalypse had to be worked through, but Savonarola foretold that eventually the New Jerusalem would descend into Florence. In the prophet's words: "Florence, the city God chose as the beginning of the reformation of Italy and the Church."[31] Savonarola saw visions of the Virgin Mary, and in one of them, she said, "May the city of Florence become more glorious, more powerful, and richer than it has ever been before."[32] Here was a revelation that validated the idea of sacred prosperity and sanctified the passion for glory, power, and wealth.

Between 1482 and 1486, he preached that a terrible scourging of Italy was imminent, albeit a prelude to the day of glory. He was called back to the city in 1490 where he resumed preaching and increased his popularity, even among learned Neoplatonists.

One prophecy, in the air for a century, was that a French king would attack, burn, and destroy Florence. In 1494, Charles VIII of France approached Florence with a powerful army. Piero de Medici fled in terror, making cowardly concessions to the invader. Meanwhile, Savonarola met with the French king and succeeded in halting the siege and sack of the city; the Florentines managed to throw out the Medici without shedding a drop of blood. Savonarola returned a hero, took steps toward founding a republican form of government, and converted many anxious and grateful souls.

But not everyone was pleased with the new Florence; many of the citizenry were reluctant to renounce the gorgeous pageants and colorful festivals the Medici customarily underwrote. Italian joviality took offense at the strictures against art, fun, and song. Lorenzo, nicknamed the "Magnificent," may have died in 1492, but his *Song of Bacchus* still echoed in people's minds, now godspelled by the preacher of apocalypse:

> Sweet ladies and young lovers, come,
> Long live Bacchus and long live love,
> Let everyone play and dance and sing,
> And fill your hearts with joy.
> Do not toil and do not grieve,
> What's to be will come anyway.
> Be happy, if you will, today,
> Tomorrow is unsure.

Against this honest pagan affirmation of life, Savonarola enacted a bonfire of the "vanities." Children marched in bands through Florentine streets singing hymns; they knocked on the doors of rich and poor, demanding they renounce their "vanities," or *anathemae*: their carnival masks and costumes, their books and pictures, anything that smacked of indecency or wantonness. The items collected were heaped up, seven layers on a giant octangular pyramid in the Piazza, and stuffed with combustibles. In the morning, after Savonarola said a splendid stentorian Mass, the pyramid was torched, to cries of holy delight.

While some no doubt thrilled to this holocaust of cultural elitism, burning the vanities also hardened opposition to the friar. Those opposed to him were known as *Arrabbiati*, the "Angry Ones." The angry ones called Savonarolans *Piagnoni*, "Snivellers"—a name that stuck.

Snivelling, wailing, railing—the doughty prophet inveighed against corruption in high places, giving no quarter to Alexander VI. The old corrupt pope did not take kindly to this. Savonarola, who seemed to know yet relish his fate, was indicted for heresy. It was 1498, nearing century's end, a time of high anxiety. Savonarola's enemies closed in. First, he was excommunicated, then he was tortured, then he was hanged, and then he himself was made into a bonfire of vanity.

Awaiting execution, Savonarola wrote two meditations that circulated widely in Europe. Martin Luther reprinted them in 1524. Luther called the Italian friar a martyr to the Reformation. "This man was put to death," he wrote, "solely for having desired that someone should come to purify the slough of Rome. It was the Antichrist's—the Pope's—hope that all remembrance of this great man would perish under a load of malediction."[33]

Savonarola's personality impressed many distinguished contemporaries. In the *Oracle of the New World* of 1497, Giovanni Nesi hailed him as the prophet of the Millennium. At first even Ficino was charmed, although Ficino finally joined the Arrabbiati and decided that it was *Savonarola* who was the real forerunner of the Antichrist. (It can change at a moment's notice, the personnel in the Antichrist-projection-game.)

Pico's devotion to Savonarola was more enduring. Savonarola, in turn, wrote of Pico as "a man unique in our times for his talent and broad learning," adding that Pico told him he was "terrified" by Savonarola's prophecies, and that on hearing them, "his hair stood on end."[34] Pico died in 1494, the friar at his deathbed.

Savonarola was no fire-and-brimstone philistine. He had cordial relations with thinkers like Ficino and Pico and artists of the rank of Michelangelo and Botticelli. Botticelli, whose greatest paintings were produced under Lorenzo de Medici's pagan patronage, ended his days in mystic silence and gloom-filled solitude, bewitched, perhaps, by the nay-saying spirit of Savonarola.

What was the friar's appeal? For one thing, Savonarola personified the primitive eloquence of the Millennium Myth. He brought conviction to a vision that, in traditional religious garb, was hard for critical humanists to accept. Ficino retreated, I believe, because his sense of the Golden Age was grounded within himself, based on a more confident Renaissance feeling of competence. The sight of books, masks, and paintings reduced to cinders—even the second-rate and obscene ones—must have grieved a man who made a religion of imaginative learning.

Ficino understood the tremendous challenge of the Renaissance, a challenge we still face today, the unsettling discovery that we have to find our own way, nurture our own divine spark, or, as Keats would later say, be our own soulmakers. Later on, around the time of the American transcendentalists, Ralph Waldo Emerson called it "self-reliance."

Another Renaissance man, the wild utopian Tommaso Campanella, who spent twenty-eight years in Spanish prison dungeons, said we must find our own way, use what is at hand, above all, learn by trying. Columbus was a fine example:

> Christopher Columbus, the Genoese, saw more with his eyes and experienced more with his body than did with their minds the poets, philosophers, and the theologians Augustine and Lactantius. . . . Our age . . . has in it more history within a hundred years than all the world had in four thousand years before![35]

Campanella here suggests that the experience of time is changing because of the quickening rate at which the modern world is forced to absorb information. Experience is becoming more and more condensed and complex. And yet, a new experience of time is to be expected in apocalyptic times, times of accelerated change and creative synthesis. I believe there is a resonance across time between the Renaissance and what is happening today in our heightened experience of time. The Renaissance looks forward to the present information age.

In those days when Michelangelo was painting the *Last Judgment*, it appeared that a world was coming to an end. In historical retrospect, the period did go through a fateful turning point. In face of Renaissance future shock, one can see the appeal of Savonarola. Here was a man who showed a moral conviction that Renaissance originals like Pico and Michelangelo may have sensed was uncomfortably missing in themselves. In the new world that was opening up, the old faith, its comforts and antique enchantments, may have pulled wistfully on their heartstrings, but, in the last analysis, it was shaken by the doubts that were beginning to arise all about them, doubts that were the pangs of a rebirthing consciousness—the inevitable price, one might say, of progress.

But Savonarola's contribution had another side. The progressive view of government, wealth, art, and industry as human blessings was part of a new discovery of what human beings could do, in a world that was still ecologically innocent. The politics of Savonarola supports the idea, central to this chapter, that the millennial mind turned secular during the Renaissance; for even in this extreme prophet of traditional apocalyptic, we find a foreshadowing of the modern world, a new spirit of democracy, a warm embrace of material wealth, and a sympathy for the arts and sciences.

A Place In the Landscape of the Possible

Let us summarize our look at the Renaissance makers of the Millennium Myth. For a moment in history, different traditions came together in a voluptuous embrace, giving birth to a revolution of culture, a humanistic Millennium. The idea of a humanistic Millennium, of life transformed by the arts and sciences, speaks to us. During the Renaissance, as in our times, old paradigms were breaking up from the impact of rapid historical change. Just as Pletho and Lorenzo and Ficino and others saw themselves as part of a great renewal of spirit and culture, many of today's visionaries believe passionately that a new age is dawning or about to dawn.

The Renaissance speaks to any culture in the throes of major transition. It was a period that owed its creative élan to a spirit of synthesis. Artists, scientists, and humanists converged in new and unpredictable ways: pagan and Biblical, Platonic and Christian, body and soul. Botticelli, who gave us *The Birth of Venus* also painted the apocalyptic *Saint John on the Island of Patmos*. Michelangelo painted the *Last Judgment* on the Sistine Chapel, yet his imagery shows a titanic humanity straining toward godhood.

A polytheism of the imagination characterized not only the artists but the thinkers of the day, who had not yet learned to dissect and disenchant reality in the style of modern scientific materialism. Ficino saw humanity as nascent divinity; in the same year that Columbus made landfall in America, he saw the Biblical prophecy of a new heaven and earth come together with the pagan vision of a golden age. But for Ficino the new arts and sciences were signs of this new age. Meanwhile, Pico was promoting the peace of the perennial philosophy, the belief in a secret unity of the human spiritual adventure. In our present age of ethnic and cultural wars, this spirit of tolerance, this ideal of a polytheistic imagination that embraces all forms of human culture, is one we might emulate with profit.

Another point where the Renaissance speaks to us concerns the exaltation of human potential. In the tremendous challenge of transformation that we face, we need to focus on the full range of our creative powers. Needless to say, there is plenty of evidence that we are more enamored of our destructive powers—all the more reason why we need to cultivate the better angels of our potentials. The Renaissance hope that we may learn to realize our divine potential speaks to all who believe in the value of education.

In the Renaissance paradigm of culture, technology is still close to the arts, still infused with a spirit of esthetic humanism. The idea of technology working in harmony with human needs, esthetic values, and the environment seems especially germane to us who are witnessing runaway technological growth.

Renaissance artists, philosophers, and architects were builders of a cultural New Jerusalem, fond of planning and building visionary cities. Once again, the visionary spirit behind such exercises seems one that we in our increasingly overcrowded, noisy, and polluted world might profitably cultivate. The big difference is that today the unit calling for visionary rethinking and replanning is not the city but the entire globe.

For people facing an uncertain future, the Renaissance pursuit of the Millennium is an interesting place in the landscape of the possible: a geography of great individuals, a theater of novelty and synthesis, a station on the way toward the End that eternally draws us on. For us who are poised on the edge of a new millennium, the Renaissance is proof that breakthrough is possible, that a culture can be reborn, and that human transformation happens.

The Enlightenment: 4 Progress and the Millennium

To the future the philosophers therefore look, as if to a promised land, a new millennium.

Carl Becker
The Heavenly City of the
Eighteenth Century Philosophers

Eighteenth-century Europe witnessed the birth of a new climate of opinion, a visionary philosophy destined to shape the consciousness of the modern world. Historians talk of the Age of Enlightenment; so our next venture is to look at the millennial underside of this great pulsation of human thought. It was an age in which the prophecy of the Millennium mutated into the secular ideal of progress.

As a cluster of recurrent obsessions, the Millennium Myth is, perhaps, part of the collective groundplan of human consciousness— hence, broadly speaking, a shaper and driver of human history. Now we look at this shaping power as it shows itself in:

- the core metaphor itself of "Enlightenment"
- progress and human perfectibility as slow apocalypse
- education as a surrogate for grace
- the spirit of invincible optimism
- the unheard-of right to the pursuit of happiness
- the notion of the elect as noble savage
- regeneration as rechristened revolution

Despite the scientific and secular veneer that marks eighteenth-century rationalism, there remains a drive, religious in drift, toward radical social regeneration, a vision of progress in the shape of a secular eschatology. In the undulations of history, the millennial imagination flares up, bodying forth new forms, searching out new niches where it can incubate and reinvent its forms.

The century of reason and regicides saw disturbing developments in physics and astronomy, new anthropological data trickling in from explorers, and the fraying of the mental ancient regime; it also brought unfair taxation, the fracturing of the class structure of Europe, Reformation-spawned religious wars, and after Copernicus, Nicholas of Cusa, and Giordano Bruno, cosmological and decentering angst. And yet, still steeped in the archetypes of Christianity, unconscious remakers of the Myth rebound from the abyss with new affirmations, in shiny secular disguise, of soaring hope and transcendent aspiration. Despite the conscious attempt at repudiation, the enchantment of the archaic dream persists. So Blake, catching the paradox:

> Mock on, Mock on Voltaire, Rousseau:
> Mock on, Mock on: 'tis all in vain!
> You throw the sand against the wind,
> And the wind blows it back again.

"Light," the Core Metaphor

The religious undercurrent of the Age of Enlightenment is first of all evident in the core metaphor of "light" it used to define itself. From the Hindu *Upanishads* and Plato's Allegory of the Cave through the Fourth Gospel of John and the Book of Revelation, light is a constant metaphor, a transcultural symbol of gnosis, of "higher consciousness." Shamanism, comparative mysticism, the near-death experience, all attest to a core encounter with inner light. The Enlightenment can be seen as a philosophical offshoot of the experience of what Eliade called the "mystic light."[1]

The psyches of the most acute rationalists could not escape the power of this archetype, which is grounded in a universal human experience. Thus, in eighteenth-century Europe, the great mathematician and co-founder of the *Encyclopedia*, D'Alembert, spoke of *l'age des lumières*, the English philosophers used the word *enlightenment*, the German progressives spoke of *Aufklärung*.

There is, however, a difference. The "enlightenment" of European thinkers was not the intuitive illumination of mystics, saints, or shamans. Shed, rather, by reason, common sense, science, mathematics, it was a "light" rooted in the rational *clartè* of Descartes' *Discourse on Method*, not in the noetic luminosity of Plato's mystical Idea of the Good. The light of the age was the light shed by the mind of Newton, as in Alexander Pope's 1730 epitaph for Sir Isaac Newton:

> Nature and Nature's laws lay hid in night:
> God said, *Let Newton be!*, and all was light.

Nevertheless, the metaphor of light does signal a hidden continuity; for the key motifs of Enlightenment philosophy, both in content and in the manner in which they were upheld, still echo a general mystical zeal.

It was the passionate zeal with which visionaries of the "age of lights" pursued their aims that betrays their religious origins. The ideals of the Enlightenment, insofar as they fly in the face of fact and reveal a visionary faith and hope, show their affinity to the tradition of the Millennium Myth. Historian Carl Becker has vividly described the missionary enthusiasm of the *philosophes*:

> . . . they were conscious of a mission to perform, a message to deliver to mankind; and to this messianic enterprise they brought an extraordinary amount of earnest conviction, of devotion, of enthusiasm. We can watch this enthusiasm, this passion for liberty and justice, for truth and humanity, rise and rise throughout the century, until it becomes a delirium, until it culminates, in some symbolical sense, in the half admirable, half pathetic spectacle of June 8, 1794, when Citizen Robespierre, with a bouquet in one hand, and a torch in the other, inaugurated the new religion of humanity by lighting the conflagration that was to purge the world of ignorance, vice, and folly.[2]

The Slow Apocalypse of Progress

As makers and proselytes of the Millennium Myth, the philosophers rallied around the idea of progress and human perfectibility. The idea of progress—the belief that humanity was destined to improve as a species, indeed, to rise to remarkable heights of perfection and well-being—was an idea that matured in human consciousness in eighteenth-century Europe.

The idea of human perfectibility was part of the Christian tradition: "Be ye perfect, as your father which is in heaven is perfect" (Matt. 5:48). To the men of the eighteenth century, however, there were several obstacles to the ideal of human perfectibility. One was the theory that the Golden Age lay in the past. If perfection lies in the past, hope in the possibilities of the future is hobbled. If, as Marcus Aurelius said, a well-educated man of forty has seen all there is to see of life and knows all the essential permutations of history, hope for progress is dashed. For the ancients, who pictured history as a cyclic phenomenon, human life was, in essence, a scene doomed to repetition compulsion.

What had to be overcome was the theory of history as repetition—the monotony of history. This theory saw civilizations as analogous to living organisms that are born, mature, grow old, and die. The analogy is tempting. The early phases of a culture do often seem more vital than the later. The later poets of Greece seem, by contrast, to crawl in the monumental shadow of Homer; Racine seems puny compared with Aeschylus.

How to overcome the burden of the past? It was not easy. Part of the story was a one-hundred-year controversy that engaged the best minds of Europe known as the Quarrel between the Ancients and the Moderns. Swift's *Battle of the Books* was perhaps the most famous product of the Quarrel.

Some said the ancients were supreme in works of the imagination. One might hope to match but not to surpass Homer or Cicero. In the domain of science, however, the philosophers did think that progress was possible. Pascal, for instance (not, by the way, a sanguine *philosophe*), suggested that we think of the entire human species as one person. That one great person, in the course of generations, absorbs the experience and knowledge of the race. We the living are really the ancients, for we are able to stand on the shoulders not only of giants but of all people; we inherit the whole of human experience and knowledge, and are therefore bound, in the long run, to evolve and progress.

The idea of progress rested on making a case for the Moderns. The Moderns had to shake off the yoke of the past before the way was paved for human perfectibility. A vision was needed that offered hope to future humanity. Ironically, the Biblical view of time was more consistent with the idea of progress than the pagan, since Biblical time was linear, not cyclic. The world, according to the Bible, was created, had a beginning; if a beginning, it also had an end, a purpose, a climax. Thus, as Blake said, the wind blew the sand back in their faces, and the advanced thinkers of the age slipped, willy-nilly, back into the lap of the mother culture's idea of time. The mother culture was Christianity, and Christians looked forward to the Millennium, a golden age of peace and perfection. Freedom from repetition of the past was essential to the idea of progress; but the best ally of the eighteenth-century Myth makers in pursuit of perfection was science. Science was the way the human race acquired the potential for indefinite progress. Newton's mechanistic universe opened the door here. Newton showed that by one law one could explain, and thus predict, the behavior of things as diverse as an apple falling from a tree and the planets moving in their orbits. The universe seemed orderly after Newton. The idea of order suggested the idea of progress.

The scientific enterprise suggests a model of progress, even per-fectibility. With Galileo, Newton became possible. It was Newton who said he saw far because he sat on the shoulders of giants. Once the march of science begins, it never stops. Now, to the extent that science can usefully be applied to human life, it becomes a model of human progress itself. Knowledge is cumulative. Empirical obser-vations increase; theories, through testing, improve. Science, subject to the checks and balances of observation and theoretical critique, offered to eighteenth-century thinkers a model for collective human improvement.

But now, what warrant had the philosophers for supposing that scientific advance would bring about moral advance? Clearly, they were taking a leap of faith as big as any millenarian hopeful. The idea of progress through science was deeply tinged with religious feeling. Condorcet, who is discussed in detail below, had a vision of progress, for example, that was millenarian in its totalistic atti-tude toward reform. Just as the medieval mystic revolutionaries and Joachites dreamed of one ecumenical Pope who would spread the true religion over the whole planet, so did Condorcet with equal missionary fervor yearn to reach out to Africa and China and reeducate all humanity to conform to a universal standard of scientific rationality. "One happy day," says Condorcet—we could translate "the Day of the Lord"—the nations will all gather together in peace, at the feet of the Goddess of Reason.

The dream of progress went much further. A sure sign of the millennial mind at work was the Enlightenment dream of enlisting science for that eschatological goal of goals: the gradual elimination of death. Thus, Condorcet could write that it is not absurd "to suppose that a period must one day arrive when death will be nothing more than the effect either of extraordinary accidents, or of the slow and gradual decay of the vital powers; and that the . . . interval between the birth of man and this decay, will itself have no assignable limit."[3] Since the prophet Daniel this has been one of the great obsessions of the Myth.

The Book of Revelation tells us the transformation of nature will be sudden. Science holds out the hope of a slower, more progressive mastery of nature. On April 22, 1780, Benjamin Franklin wrote enthusiastically to Joseph Priestley on the theme of scientific progress:

> The rapid Progress *true* science now makes, occasions my regretting sometimes that I was born so soon. It is impossible to imagine the Height to which may be carried in a thousand years, the Power of Man over Matter. We may perhaps learn to deprive large Masses of their Gravity, and give them absolute Levity, for the sake of easy Transport. Agriculture may diminish its Labor and double its Produce; all Diseases may by sure means be prevented or cured, not excepting even that of Old Age, and our lives lengthened at pleasure even beyond the antediluvian Standard.[4]

Franklin, like Condorcet, hoped for the eventual conquest of death.

In 1792, Joseph Priestley, another man of the Enlightenment who believed that the power of knowledge was indefinitely extensible, wrote these remarkable words:

> Nature, including both its materials, and its laws, will be more at our command; men will make their situation in this world abundantly more easy and comfortable; they will probably prolong their existence in it, and will grow daily more happy, each in himself, and more able (and, I believe, more disposed) to communicate happiness to others. Thus, whatever was the beginning of this world, the end will be glorious and paradisaical, beyond what our imaginations can now conceive.[5]

Here, the Biblical and hence the millennial conception of time is suddenly in our face; at the "end" of the world is not the end but a detour to paradise.

In the European Enlightenment, the tree of knowledge, unlike in the Bible, does not cause the fall but the rise of humanity. With Priestley, Franklin, Condorcet, and the others, there seems to have occurred a definitive break in attitude toward the power of knowledge. The Enlightenment makes no bones about the wisdom of the serpent; we must eat from the tree of knowledge and leave the garden of Eden. It will be a long journey before we ever come back. Progress is a slow apocalypse.

Education as a Surrogate for Grace

In the old Myth, especially in that dark Calvinistic strain, the ultimate felicity is sheer gift; we are predetermined by God to salvation or damnation. A situation that has sent a shockwave of anxious uncertainty through Western history. For how does one ever know if one is saved? What a queasy speculation that the game is over for us before it even starts!

The Enlightenment Myth holds out the carrot of education. In trusting to the power of education, it hearkens back to the Renaissance humanists and the Platonic believers in the power of *paidea*, literally, "child-rearing." Remember Plato. In his masterpiece *The Republic*, he put his whole hope of human happiness in education. To the eighteenth-century makers of the Millennium Myth, education alone had the power to usher in the new age.

Progress through education remains one of America's most precious ideals. In this we are indebted to the eighteenth century, which was very much the education century; an age of great and innovative educators, Fontanelle, Turgot, Condorcet, and Lessing, who all argued that education was the key to the progress of humanity. Lessing, in particular, modeled his vision of progressive education on Joachim's idea of the three ages of humanity. For Lessing, Joachim's Age of Spirit became an Age of Progressive Education. Auguste Comte, heir to Enlightenment idealism, also used the threefold aeon-table, with positive science filling in for the Age of Spirit.

The philosopher John Locke produced a theory of mind that cleared the way to higher education. Locke's denial of innate ideas was a blow struck for higher education. For generations the Christian world believed people were born stained by a kind of depravity called "original sin." Original sin, the belief in our flawed nature, bodes ill for the dream of education. Original sin is a blot on the chances of educating the human race.

True, the Christian story provides at least one dogma that is conducive to the ideals of education and human perfectibility. This is the dogma that people are made in the image and likeness of God. The Renaissance humanists took this part of the Christian story and used it to launch a full-scale deification-of-humanity project. Unfortunately, the Protestant Reformation focused on a different part of the story, dwelling on original sin and the depravity of the species. We are, as Jonathan Edwards said, "sinners in the hands of an angry God."

Then along came the philosophers with the good news. For people oppressed by the myth of original sin, John Locke's gospel that the human mind is born a *tabula rasa*, "a blank slate," offered a bracing change of perspective. The doctrine of mind as blank slate implied a rejection of innate ideas. Without innate or inborn ideas, people could no longer be said to be born tainted by original sin or by any inherently bad dispositions.

If human nature is not tainted, it becomes easier to think about educating people to their superior potentials. If we are born blank slates, it follows that the influence of environment can write itself on us. All that is needed to improve people is to improve their environment; people can be "revised" for the better. Thus, the blank slate image of human nature inspires hope in the power of education. Locke offered a philosophic rationale for overcoming Protestant pessimism with regard to the education of humankind. We need no longer tremble before an inscrutably sovereign God who, for all we know, has already consigned us to perdition. Instead of praying at the divine lottery, we can enroll at the college of enlightenment.

The last great Enlightenment visionary of human progress was the Jesuit-trained Marquis de Condorcet (1743–1794). Condorcet lived through the Revolution, his enthusiasm high to the end. It is worth noting that the Jesuits carried on the tradition of Joachim's idea of a spiritual èlite who would usher in the new age by propagating the faith. Condorcet himself had something of the pluck and fervor of the medieval mystic revolutionaries. By 1793 he had become an outlaw and fugitive from Robespierre. Without benefit of books or friends, he wrote his great work on human progress, the *Outline of an Historical View of the Progress of the Human Mind*.

Condorcet was intoxicated by the idea of using science to educate and improve the lot of humanity. He embraced the vision of human perfectibility through science and education with the passion of a martyr. "Such is the aim of the work that I have undertaken, and its result has set no term to the perfection of human faculties; the perfectibility of man is truly indefinite."[6] For Condorcet two things opened the way to the progress of the human mind: one was the discovery of the New World, the other was the invention of printing. Ficino, too, we recall, hailed the invention of printing as a sign of the Golden Age. For Condorcet printing was the way science and philosophy could shake off the yoke of authority. " . . . in this instrument the conspirators of evil were confronted with an invention which could spread scientific truth over so vast an expanse of territory that suppression became virtually impossible."[7] Faith in education, a rational distillation of the Millennium Myth, has persisted to the brink of the twenty-first century. Its latest incarnation is the Information Highway, the logical extension of the eighteenth-century *Encyclopedia*.

The Spirit of Invincible Optimism

Are there any grounds for optimism in this world? The Millennium Myth, surrealistic in its take on all the obstacles, holds out for a view of invincible optimism. Consonant with this yea-saying spirit, the philosophers were optimistic to a fault.

Enlightenment optimism was based on the dream of human educability. For after all, if, at least in principle, the education of humankind is a progressive venture, there is reason to be optimistic. And if we and our mastery of nature are going to steadily improve, we are entitled to look to the future with great expectations. But like faith, optimism is of things unseen. Given the harsh truth about ordinary life in eighteenth-century Europe, the optimism of eighteenth-century thinkers was clearly an article of religious faith.

The roots of this optimism lie deep in the Western psyche and are the basis of the continued life of the Millennium Myth. Marjorie Reeves, concluding her massive study of prophecy in the Middle Ages, singled out optimism as the chief abiding motif. "The outstanding impression which remains from these studies is the significance of the motif of optimism," she wrote. "This unites the medieval and the Renaissance periods in an unexpected way."[8] The optimism shared was directed toward a vision of political and religious unity. The Enlightenment was also a period of optimism directed toward a vision of unity, based on toleration and the ideals of reason and natural rights. Optimism in the benign drift of the world is the connecting thread between these great periodic bursts of sometimes creative, sometimes destructive, enthusiasm.

The basis for optimism in the middle ages was religious; the forces of regeneration would emerge with the coming of the new dispensation, the third *status*, the age of spirit. Progress—if that is the right word— was conceived as a form of grace. With the Renaissance, the idea of progress was stepped up a grade to include human ingenuity, the Italian notion of *virtú*, which relies on individual exploitation of God-given talents. With Enlightenment thinkers, the hope of progress is detached from all ideas of grace or providence and is based on the free exercise of human reason.

Of course, this world-historical optimism went beyond the warrant of reason; for one thing, it ran against the grain of the mechanistic bias of the new physics. Had not the new science of Galileo, Descartes, and Newton banished the idea of plan or purpose from cosmology? If the new physics dispensed with the need for final causes, what grounds did the *philosophes* have for believing that history has a goal, a "final cause" or Eschaton of progress? There were no rational grounds for such a belief at all.

Something else was at work prodding, igniting the imaginations of the sanguine thinkers of the age. Call it the deeply felt urge all decently vital human beings have to improve the world. It is an urge that finds its archetypal expression in the family of visionary aspirations I am calling the Millennium Myth.

The Millennium Myth is a myth of linear time. Optimism presupposes a linear notion of historical time; the long struggles of history have a *telos*, "an end and purpose." Optimism seems impossible without the inspiration of religious emotion; it is religious in spirit because only a transcendent outlook justifies such radical hope in the future. Of course, the *philosophes* of the Enlightenment consciously rejected the transcendent outlook, as formulated by traditional Christianity. Condorcet, who dreamed of an Elysium of progress, was rabidly anticlerical.

If one looks closely, however, there is an unconscious translation of religious into secular symbolism. Sometimes, as in the following apostrophe from Diderot, the translation, hence the underlying religious content, is transparent. Diderot, like other visionary thinkers of the age, was fond of personifying abstractions:

> O posterity! Holy and sacred! Stay of the unhappy and the oppressed, thou who art just, thou who art incorruptible, who avengest the good man, who unmaskest the hypocrite, who draggest down the tyrant, may thy sure faith, thy consoling faith, never abandon me! *Posterity is for the philosopher what the other world is for the devout*.[9] (My emphasis.)

In the sentence I have emphasized, Diderot has made things easy for us; he demonstrates, as it were in a clear equation, the translation of the religious into the secular. Instead of the "other world," the philosopher puts all his hope in "posterity." Without progress toward eschatological fulfillment in "posterity," there is no redemption from the nightmare of history.

For Diderot, the inveterate compiler of that great monument of eighteenth-century rationalism, the *Encyclopedia*, three ideas blend into each other: a Biblical-born but now rationalized notion of linear time, a spirit of transcendent optimism, and a hopeful vision of progress based on the endless extension of human knowledge. Seen in this broader perspective, Diderot's *Encyclopedia* is not merely a vast compendium of knowledge, a tool for universal education, it becomes an instrument of salvation, the new bible for a rationalist Millennium.

The Unheard-of Right to the Pursuit of Happiness

One of the few humanly appealing promises of the Book of Revelation is the promise of transcendent happiness. God is going to wipe away all tears and do away with human sorrow, says John of Patmos. At the end of the tunnel of the Millennium, the light of happiness at last!

I believe that one of the great contributions of Enlightenment political philosophy was to have codified and legitimized for the modern world this deeply human, deeply millenarian aspiration for happiness; it did so in the language of basic human rights. The dumb yearning for happiness that animates the common soul of humanity here found a voice.

Let us step back a moment and ask about the goal of progress. To what end does progress point? There was, to be sure, the progress of getting rid of negatives: fear, want, ignorance, intolerance, inequality, injustice, and oppression. But was there a positive content to the goal of progress? The answer lies in the American Declaration of Independence. This historic document, drafted by John Adams, Benjamin Franklin, and Thomas Jefferson, was adopted by the Second Continental Congress on July 4th, 1776. A supreme expression of Enlightenment thought, it was written by Jefferson:

> We hold these truths to be self-evident, that all men are created equal, that they are endowed by their Creator with unalienable rights, that among these are Life, Liberty, and the pursuit of Happiness.

Here we meet the *faith* of the Enlightenment. For there is nothing "self-evident" about the assertions cited above; they are, in fact, riddled with questionable assumptions. Notions of equality, of a Creator, and of unalienable rights are "self-evident" solely to the heart of religious faith. Biblical, not Greek, are their origins; for no Greek took equality or a creator-deity or any "unalienable rights" on faith or as self-evident. The Greek sophists, for example, argued that in nature, might made right; and never did Aristotle doubt that slavery was natural. The roots of Jefferson's vision lie deep in the millenarian religion of Christianity. "Neither sorrow nor crying, neither shall there be any more pain," says the Book of Revelation (Rev. 21:4).

The most visionary aspect of the Declaration—the most positive content of the goal of progress—is the "pursuit of happiness." The phrase was Jefferson's. Locke, in *The Second Treatise of Civil Government* wrote of the right to property, possessions, estate—not, explicitly, to happiness. Making it explicit was an American contribution.

No one can say precisely what Jefferson's source for the phrase "pursuit of happiness" was, nor exactly how to interpret its meaning. Happiness was certainly on Locke's mind: "It is a man's proper business to seek happiness and avoid misery," he said. But he said nothing about the *right* to seek happiness, although the notion was certainly in the air. Aristotle discussed the pursuit of happiness as part of the rationale of government in *The Politics*. A more immediate influence was probably George Mason, who wrote of the "inherent right" of "pursuing and obtaining happiness and safety" in the 1774 Virginia Declaration of Rights.

Whatever the background for the phrase in question, its originality is uncontested. The Declaration of Independence says that we have a right to *pursue* happiness; pursuit is a positive idea. If we are looking to the end or purpose of the progress, the linear movement of history, then Jefferson makes more sense than Locke in claiming it to be happiness, not merely property and possessions. For both the Greek philosophers and the Biblical prophets, property and possessions were at best means to an end.

In making happiness—the religious counterpart would be bliss or beatitude—central to the ideal of the new nation, Jefferson underscored the progressive, linear, and consequently millenarian spirit of the Enlightenment philosophy of history. There is an end of history, a why and a wherefore to all the suffering—and it is something human, called happiness.

The ideal of the pursuit of happiness, inscribed in the American Declaration of Independence, is unprecedented: no government had ever explicitly pronounced it a *right of all human beings to pursue their own happiness*. Of course, this right does not appear in the Constitution as law, no doubt because of the open nature of the concept of happiness; it remains an overarching ideal, a visionary promise regulating the purpose of government in the United States.

The German Enlightenment philosopher Kant wrote of the inherent vagueness of the concept of happiness:

> . . . the concept of happiness is so indeterminate a concept that although every man wants to attain happiness, he can never say definitely and in unison with himself what it really is that he wants and wills.[10]

There is a reason for this vagueness about the ideal of happiness: happiness is an ideal that must be "borrowed from experience." In other words, different people have different experiences of happiness; there are no a priori rules to guide us in our pursuit of happiness. Happiness remains an open concept.

However—and this I believe is crucial—there is one restriction: the pursuit of individual happiness must be consistent with the happiness of society as a whole. Here an important millennial note is sounded, for the pursuit of the Millennium is a pursuit of *collective* felicity. Kant and Locke agree that the right to the pursuit of happiness is not a license for egoism but is restrained by the Golden Rule. Thus, even anti-Christians like Condorcet are punctilious in matters of morality.

In his study of the Declaration of Independence, Garry Wills underscores this point about the public nature of the happiness people are entitled to pursue. Wills traces the idea of general welfare in the writings of moral philosophers like Adam Smith, Adam Ferguson, David Hume, Voltaire, and Francis Hutcheson with his 1725 formula for "the greatest happiness of the greatest number." Wills observes that "public happiness was a secular and scientific term for men of the Enlightenment, a 'heretical' displacement of man's hopes from the hereafter. . . ."[11]

This displacement, of course, is characteristic of the Millennium Myth, which lobbies for a collective transformation of *this* world and *this* society. The heresy lies not in the "displacement" to the here and now, which was an original feature of apocalyptic-creationist Christianity, but in the will to autonomy and self-transformation. What marks the revolution of modern thought is not the shift from heavenly to secular concerns but the shift from a God-imposed to a human-invented perspective.

In the Jeffersonian revolution, it is asserted that we have a right to pursue our own happiness. This remarkable statement of the American dream should be seen against the background of the European view of human dignity. The Biblical tradition, as the Renaissance thinkers and artists affirmed in their provocative way, honors the idea that human beings are made in the image of God.

If we are made in God's image, humanity's eschatological horizons open up enormously. Our Biblical-sanctioned status as God-imitators ratifies the Jeffersonian myth of the universal right to the pursuit of happiness. If we are made in the image of God, then surely it is our lot to be happy. The divine prerogative is to be happy, for what could be happier than to be a wellspring of infinite power, knowledge, and benevolence? The Declaration of 1776 was, on this reading, a project for human deification.

Here, in this phrase of the Declaration, American idealism links up with the vaulting aspirations of the Renaissance magus. Clearly, this linkage has been muted in public consciousness; perhaps we might think of it as the occult meaning of America—the first country in the   **101** history of the world to make the pursuit of divine happiness a constitutional ideal. Our medieval gnostic forebears were more receptive to this, perhaps the most subversive feature of the Millennium Myth.

Against the background myth of the Fall, of original sin and Greek fatalism, the Enlightenment-born pursuit of happiness was truly an extraordinary idea. It was in harmony with the Renaissance idea of conscious self-culture. Thomas Jefferson himself was a man of Renaissance versatility: architect, scholar, inventor, botanist, and statesman. The Declaration says that we are entitled to take responsibility for our own happiness and well-being. Acknowledging this right has been enshrined in a now-famous phrase of myth-gatherer Joseph Campbell: *Follow your bliss*. The phrase has reached the status of a cliché and hence has become a target of ridicule.

Yet Campbell lines up with Jefferson on this point, inviting us to take seriously, to act upon, our right to pursue our own happiness— to become, as it were, ambitious for bliss. Pico, who exalted human potential, spoke of cultivating "a certain divine ambition." This idea of a divine command to expand our consciousness—so consistent with the spirit of the Myth—is one that practically defines the phenomenon known as the American New Age. But on that, later.

The Elect as Noble Savage

The Enlightenment, like the Italian Renaissance, sought to renew itself by returning to ancient sources. The Renaissance went back to pagan antiquity. The Enlightenment refreshed its spiritual imagination by meditating on the myth of the noble savage.

In general, the Millennium Myth nurses the idea that there are special types of human beings, people gifted, evolved, inspired, whose job it is to lead humanity into the new age. In the Joachite tradition it was the *viri spirituales*, the "Spiritual Men"—an army of enlightened monks—who were to inaugurate the Age of Spirit. The eighteenth century saw the myth of a regenerative elite in the guise of the noble savage.

The noble savage was promoted by that convoluted genius, Jean-Jacques Rousseau. Lionized as an apostle of primitivism, Rousseau used the noble savage as a figure to attack everything he hated about the civilization of his day.

Rousseau's thought is more subtle than the slogans he is known by. His conception of the noble savage may be seen in his 1755 *Discourse on the Origin of Inequality* and his earlier, prize-winning *Discourse on the Arts and Sciences*. Rousseau held that the more evolved a culture was, the more refined its arts and sciences and the more degenerate its morals. The worst vices wax like weeds in the lushly manured soil of advanced civilization. People are at their best in the springtime of their history, wandering in the liberty of nature.

The "savage" serves as a device for reflecting on the genesis of inequality. In Rousseau's view, the evils of human society result from developing and then learning how to exploit our higher faculties. We become entangled by "different accidents which may have improved the human understanding while depraving the species, and made man wicked while making him sociable." Improved human understanding leads to depravity for the species; wickedness necessarily accompanies advances in sociability. Understanding and depravity, wickedness and sociability are tragically wed; you cannot have one without the other. Culture exacerbates egoism.

For Rousseau, civil society began when the first man marked off some land and said, "This is mine." This act sets into motion the dialectic of private property, which Rousseau deplores as the original imposture and declaration of egoism, and thus, infecting everything, the ultimate cause of all social evils.

Every advance in civilization entails a setback—for instance, population. "In proportion as the human race grew more numerous men's cares increased." As cares increased, people responded by inventing new tools for the convenience of life. The new tools that made life convenient and gave people more leisure time become for "man the first yoke he inadvertently imposed upon himself, and the first source of the evils he prepared for his descendants." Labor-saving devices enervated the body and "degenerated into real needs." People became dependent on their technology, but technology failed to make people happy.

Rousseau's argument: To excel, to distinguish oneself in any way is to create inequality. Merely to do well in something, to stand out, to surpass another is to lay the groundwork of pride, vice, and cruelty. These, in turn, lead to class warfare, oppression, and all the miseries of civilization.

As civilization progresses, Rousseau contends, people forget their "original wildness" and, as a pale surrogate, learn to covet public esteem, cherish extravagant but useless wealth, and pursue other tokens of satisfaction. In the process, they lose the simple pleasures early people enjoyed in their free, untrammeled, solitary existence. "The example of savages," wrote Rousseau, proves "that all subsequent advances have been apparently so many steps toward the perfection of the individual, but in reality towards the decrepitude of the species."

The way to revive the species from decrepitude, and thus accomplish the Millennium, is to liberate the noble savage. Other eighteenth-century philosophers cultivated the Millennium Myth by cultivating the myth of the noble savage. Diderot, for example, in his dialogue on the *Voyage of Bougainville*, used the noble savage as a foil to attack European corruption:

> Savage society is so simple and our societies are such complicated mechanisms. The Tahitian is near the origin of the world, the European near its old age . . . He understands nothing of our laws and customs or only sees in them impediments disguised in a hundred forms, impediments which can excite only the indignation and contempt of a being in whom the sentiment of liberty is the deepest of all.[12]

The important point here is that the "savage," in this case the Tahitian, is "near the origin of the world." The European, on the other hand, is "near its old age." For Diderot the *philosophe*, as for the typical millennialist, regeneration requires a return to sacred origins. For the Romantics, who worshiped the purity of feeling over the depravity of reason, as Rousseau did, rebirth and renovation lay in the return to primitive culture.

The quest for revival, for return to our mythic origins, is a recurrent quest in Western history; in the Age of Reason, the phantasy of the noble savage seemed to attract the best minds—a backlash from the excesses of rationalism. Or consider Nietzsche's "blond beast," a nineteenth-century take on the noble savage which, in Adolf Hitler's demonic hands, turned into a monumental nightmare.

More currently, the American interest in shamanism is, in part, a renewal of interest in Rousseau's noble savage. Shamanism, as Eliade tells it, is a return to our paradisaical origins, a reconnecting with earth and heaven, a remembering of the universal language of animals. Shamanism is the pursuit of renovation, an attempt at revival of the archaic: Native America, drumming, vision questing, psychedelics,

Tantrism, wicca, cults of Gaia and of Mary, earthlights and ley lines, aboriginal dreamtime, and matriarchal archeology—these, and a whole swarm of related phenomena, are part of a growing Timespirit we will discuss in a later chapter.

For the moment, I'll say this: the noble savage is having a comeback today in American New Age pursuits. And the call to follow our bliss seems an effort to rekindle our connection with the makers of the American Declaration of Independence. The Millennium Myth has a way of bringing us together across time and culture.

Revolution as Regeneration

Is there a way to bring about the regeneration promised by the Myth? The Enlightenment hit upon two possibilities. Education is one we have discussed. A second is more radical: in extreme situations, there may be legitimate recourse to revolution.

Voltaire introduced John Locke to a receptive France. Locke's *Second Treatise on Civil Government* (1690) made the case for revolution. People renounce the liberty of nature and enter into society to preserve their property. The power of government thus comes from the people and is based on a trust. If a government commits a "breach of trust" with the people, if there are "arbitrary disposers of the lives, liberties, or fortunes of the people," the people have a right to "dissolve" the government. The people may "resume their original liberty" and establish a "new legislature."

If all attempts to educate a corrupt society fail, we may be driven to wipe the slate clean by purging corrupt institutions through the use of revolutionary force. Indeed, the Enlightenment climate of opinion, as shaped by Locke, Rousseau, Voltaire, and others, furnished the background for two of the greatest revolutions of modern times.

Needless to say, the causes of the American and the French Revolutions were very complicated. In this book, we are following the spoor of the Millennium Myth. I just want to point out that there were signs in revolutionary France of the Myth at work, signs of millennial passions jolting the collective imagination. In those catastrophic times, the millenarian mind was roused to activity. What I want to bring out here is the totalistic, hence religious nature of the inspiration that inspired so many revolutionaries of the time. There is no better example than Thomas Paine.

The religious, the chiliastic passion of Thomas Paine was evident in his brilliant rhetoric. Paine's rhetoric worked. Paine, wrote philosopher Sidney Hook, "inspired two of the greatest revolutions in human history."[13] It was Paine's *Common Sense* that awakened the Colonies to full consciousness of their rights in the dispute with King George. When disagreement led to war, the English-born Paine fought with the Americans.

In *Common Sense* he wrote these words—words, in my opinion, that draw on the powerful vision of the Millennium Myth:

> We have it in our power to begin the world over again. A situation similar to the present hath not happened since the days of Noah until now. The birthday of a new world is at hand, and a race of men perhaps as numerous as all Europe contains are to receive their portion of freedom from the event of a few months.

In this pamphlet, notes historian Christopher Dawson, we find two things that mark the revolutionary temper of the future:

> One was the conception of political revolution as part of a universal and almost cosmic change which far transcended the local and historical circumstances of any particular state. The other, which is closely related, was the note of messianic idealism, which looked forward to a social millennium and the birth of a new humanity.[14]

Cosmic change and messianic idealism—clearly, the spirit of the Myth has been rallied. Paine, the friend of Condorcet, wrote a series of pamphlets to encourage Washington's army in the darkest hour of the revolutionary war. The *American Crisis* was written on a drumhead by the light of campfires. Washington had Paine read before the soldiers the pamphlet that began with the famous words, "These are the times that try men's souls." The men, after the reading, rallied with a successful counterattack against the English.

What can we say about this uncanny power to inspire? Remember Paine's outcry: "These are the times that try men's souls." It is a power that appeals to soul. The present crisis was not, as Paine himself said, merely another colonial dispute that had to be resolved, but rather a declaration to all humanity, a revolutionary act that would purify and regenerate the whole human race. Paine's rhetoric reached toward universal imagery and transpersonal aspiration, drawing its power from a source beyond politics, a source deep within the soul. Look at the words he used to stir the depths of Washington's troops.

December 23, 1776: "Tyranny, like hell, is not easily conquered." In this sentence, Paine read the politics of the day in light of images of eternal significance. It resonates with the core dualism of the Millennium Myth: heaven and hell, Christ and Antichrist.

What is at stake is the soul's struggle for a piece of heaven on earth. And so we read, "Heaven knows how to put a proper price upon its goods; and it would be strange indeed, if so celestial an article as FREEDOM should not be highly rated." There will be no cheap victory in the fight to secure the "celestial article" of freedom.

In a surprising reference for Paine the freethinker: " . . . in the fourteenth century the whole English army, after ravaging the kingdom of France, was driven back like men petrified with fear; and this brave exploit was performed by a few broken forces collected and headed by a woman, Joan of Arc. Would that Heaven might inspire some Jersey maid to spirit up her countrymen. . . ." By evoking an archetypal image of the inspired warrior, Paine suggested that the ability to resist the foe was latent in every one of Washington's troops. If a French peasant girl could perform such mighty deeds, anything in the present crisis was possible.

Anything is possible as long as America is committed to the right cause. In Philadelphia, on Sept. 12, 1777, Paine wrote in *The Crisis*, "It is not a field of a few acres of ground, but a cause that we are defending, and whether we defeat the enemy in one battle, or by degrees, the consequence will be the same." Two points here, in line with the messianic zap of Paine's rhetoric: First, the war is portrayed as an event of universal significance; second, the outcome is thought inevitable, the right cause absolutely destined to win.

In Philadelphia, April 19, 1783, after the war, Paine wrote of "the greatest and completest revolution that the world ever knew, gloriously and happily accomplished." Why, one would like to know, the "greatest" and "completest"? Paine's answer is consistent with Jefferson's declaration of the human right to pursue happiness. The American revolution, said Paine, has given the world the "art" of happiness. "To see it in our power to make a world happy—," he writes, "to teach mankind the art of being so—to exhibit on the theater of the universe, a character hitherto unknown—and to have, as it were, **107** a new creation entrusted to our hands, are honors that command reflection. . . ." A new creation, a character hitherto unknown? Clearly, it is an exalted, a messianic view of the task of government. At the heart of the Millennium Myth, as noticed many times, is a vision of a "new creation." The American revolution, as Paine's words show, was animated by the yearning for a "new creation."

The French Revolution, a turning point of the modern era, had, in many respects, the character of a religious revival. Wordsworth, in his poem "French Revolution: as it appeared to enthusiasts at its commencement," caught the exalted mood of the time:

> Bliss was it in that dawn to be alive,
> But to be young was very heaven!

The Revolution loosed an orgy of expansive emotion; much more was involved than what Locke called the dissolution of a legislative body, a reaction to a breach of trust, a failure to live up to a bargain. The French Revolution was a solemn ritual, a healing spasm of purification, a raid on the energies of regeneration.

Again, Tom Paine is our witness to the spirit of millennial religiosity. To Paine, and his French cohort Lafayette, the revolution transcended matters of finance and constitutional reform. Of towering magnitude, it was about the Rights of Man. The French ideologues who galvanized the end of the century believed with Paine that in the

> Declaration of the Rights of Man we see the solemn and majestic spectacle of a nation opening its commission, under the auspices of its Creator, to establish a government, a scene so new and transcendently unequalled by anything in the European world, that the name of a Revolution is diminutive of its character, and it rises into a Regeneration of Man.[15]

The word *Revolution* "is diminutive of its character"; the enfolding scene is "transcendently unequalled." The people were baptized in a rush of revivifying emotions; they were co-creators and witnesses of the collective rebirth of a nation.

The Millennium Myth plays on calendar magic. Millennial phantasies have roots in mystic numerology, in old beliefs of cycles of renewal, in the myth of the new year and of the expulsion of the demons of the past. Locke, the theoretical ancestor of the Revolution, provided the image of the human mind as a *tabula rasa*, a blank slate.

The republican zealots of the French revolution thought they were wiping the very slate of time clean.

Thus they proclaimed the founding of the Republic on September 22, 1792: *the first day of the first month of the Year One.* The old Gregorian calendar was canceled. In the spirit of renewal, the republicans abolished slavery in the French colonies. They abolished debtor's prison. They proclaimed a new faith in public education. They instituted a critique of classist language. (It ceased to be politically correct to address a woman as Madame—my lady.) The Year One inaugurated a cultural and spiritual revolution, as well as a political and economic one. A republican decree read, "The French nation . . . wishes its regeneration to be complete, in order that its years of liberty and glory may betoken still more by their duration in the history of peoples."[16]

The new religion of humanity displaced the Christianity that Voltaire and Condorcet had savaged. Anti-clericism prospered. Secular heros were sanctified, churches turned into temples of reason. The church of Sainte-Geneviéve, for example, was turned into a national pantheon that housed as holy relics the ashes of Voltaire. Statues of the Virgin Mary were demolished and in their place erected statues of the Goddess of Liberty. By 1802, however, Napoleon managed an agreement with the Pope, and Church freedom was restored. The end-of-the-century spirit of revivalism had spent a good deal of its force. By the time it was all over, the world would never be the same again. Another pulsation of the Millennium Myth had passed.

Dissent Against Enlightenment

Every pulsation that proceeds from the Millennium Myth rises and falls, waxes and wanes, depending on outcomes and circumstances that heighten expectation or lower hope. Yet, no matter what the circumstances, the core Myth endures and periodically stirs the cauldron of enthusiasm, leaving the landscape of history dotted with new monuments of meaning and scattered debris of old institutions.

The shockwave of Enlightenment passed, and before long the Goddess of Reason fell on bad times. A reaction set in against the Enlightenment ideals of optimism, rationalism, and belief in progress. After all, the French Revolution led to the Reign of Terror, indulged in its own fanatical intolerance, and wound up with Napoleon's dictatorship. **109**

Voltaire, the wit of the new "age of lights," scorned the facile optimism of Alexander Pope, who worshiped Newton and uttered the foolish line, "Whatever is, is right" (in *The Essay on Man*). In 1755, Voltaire dashed off a poem on the Lisbon earthquake: "Philosophers are deceived who cry 'All is well,' " it ran. He laments the "fantasies of pundits," their "profound chimeras." Voltaire saved his best barbs for *Candide*, a satire on the then "new age" belief that everything happens for the best in the best of all possible worlds.

Edmund Burke, a friend to the American Revolution, was appalled at the sweeping destructiveness of the French Revolution. He hated the hard heart of what he called the "thoroughbred metaphysician." Burke argued against tampering with religious instincts, the cement of civil society. He opposed the idea that societies and governments could be remade by intellectual fiats.

The case against linear progress was made in Vico's *New Science* of 1744; Vico showed that when reason increases, imagination declines. For Vico it was clear that cultures need living myths. Without living myths, cultures lose cohesion, the *sensus communus*[17] breaks down; people slip into a "malicious barbarism of reflection." Mythical imagination grows feeble, and the culture starts to die from inner depletion. Only briefly and rarely is it possible for a culture to keep its prosaic and poetic forces in balance. For Vico linear progress was an incoherent idea because no culture can remain "young" and "old," vital and wise, at the same time. Not for long, at any rate.

Other thinkers had different reasons for attacking Enlightenment ideals. Rousseau attacked the religion of progress on the basis of his genetic principle that advances in the arts and sciences lead to egoism and the evils of civilization. (There are similarities to Vico here.) In extolling sentiment above knowledge, Rousseau undermined the rationale of progress. What people need is to return to lives of natural simplicity, not to increase their knowledge; regress, not progress, is the road to Eden.

And do not forget Malthus, who attacked Diderot on the first page of his masterwork. According to Malthus, the population explosion of the human species will eventually tax to death the resources of the planet; this argues against the Enlightenment dream of limitless progress. Overpopulation enters the eschatology equation, a problem we still have to face.

Worse, there may be an incurable streak of perversity in the human will. In Dostoevsky's *Notes From Underground* lurks the quintessential anti-Enlightenment hero. The character in this novel resents the tyranny of logic and insists that sometimes, "twice two equals five!" Jefferson declared our right to the pursuit of happiness; Dostoevsky's underground hero declares our right to the pursuit of unhappiness. Dostoevsky hated Western ideals of comfort, culture, contentment. The Dostoevskian soul wants more than the happiness of the contented "ant-heap."

Another Russian, Count Tolstoy, had worse to say about Enlightenment optimism. In the eyes of the great novelist, the new civilization was going to ruin the whole planet. Europe was going to "spoil" India, Africa, China, and Japan with its "electricity, railways, and telegraphs." Like Dostoevsky, Tolstoy felt that this new world was going to perish from spiritual starvation, rot from meaninglessness. He decries the loss of purpose in the new philosophy: "Machines—to produce what? The telegraph—to despatch what? Books, papers—to spread what kind of news? Railways—to go to whom and to what place? . . . Hospitals, physicians, dispensaries to prolong life—for what?" What has any of this to do with "true enlightenment"?[18] Misgivings for contemporary Data Highway enthusiasts to ponder.

Finally, by way of easing out of the "age of lights," let us listen to yet another saboteur of the dream of a rational Millennium. The poet Baudelaire started to write a piece titled "The End of the World," of which parts appeared in 1851 under the title of *Fusées*. Progress is going to kill us, wrote Baudelaire, and America is going to ruin the world.

> We shall perish by the very thing by which we fancy that we live. Technocracy will Americanize us, progress will starve our spirituality. . . . Universal ruin will manifest itself not solely or particularly in political institutions or general progress or whatever else might be a proper name for it. It will be seen, above all, in the baseness of hearts. Shall I add that this little left-over of sociability will hardly resist the sweeping brutality, and that the rulers in order to hold their own and to produce a sham order, will ruthlessly resort to measures which will make us, who already are callous, shudder.

It is interesting to contrast Condorcet the optimist with Baudelaire the pessimist; the millennial imagination is obviously a creature of violent mood swings. Black despair oscillates with manic exaltation. What began in confident affirmation of human potential ended with the gloomiest forebodings. The science the philosophers hoped would regenerate humanity had for Baudelaire become the tool for ultimate human degradation.

So Where Are We Now?

The Millennium Myth causes spiritual explosions in the landscape of human experience; after an explosion, one looks around, dazed at the repercussions.

One thing Enlightenment thinkers had right: the indefinite power to extend human knowledge, the belief in scientific progress, has been proven correct. Science is a steadily expanding enterprise, and quite marvelous, as anyone in the late twentieth century can see. The philosophers, for instance, believed in the new art of printing, which they saw as the basis for an information and communication revolution. Fontanelle said human knowledge would progress. He was right. We have gone from the printing press to cyberspace. What would Fontanelle say if he knew we could store Diderot's thirty-six volume *Encyclopedia* on the head of a pin?

Franklin and Priestley and other eighteenth-century remakers of the Millennium Myth predicted that science would emancipate us from the limits of nature. On this score, too, the philosophers were right; more and more we find the power to bend nature to our will.

But the problem remains. What to do with all this power? With the incredible amounts of information? What do we really need? asked Tolstoy. The old Myth codified our true needs in transcendent Christian images. But those images are presently under attack. The new Enlightenment of the twenty-first century will have to renew the Millennium Myth, provide a new home for its transcendent needs, and a new set of tools for crashing the gates of the heavenly city. One place the Myth has veered toward in a big way is called America. So let us move on; our next stop is the Yankee New Jerusalem.

Yankee New Jerusalem

*We Americans are the peculiar, chosen people—the
Israel of our time: we bear the ark of the liberties of
the world.*

HERMAN MELVILLE

My father emigrated to America from a hamlet near Naples, Italy; word
was that the streets of New York City were paved with gold. That tall
tale was a little piece of the Millennium Myth; my father was not the
first to see America from a distance painted as a Yankee New Jerusalem.

The philosopher George Berkeley, Bishop of Cloyne, spent three
years in Rhode Island, fifty years before the American Revolution.
Berkeley wrote a poem about America vibrant with millennial sentiment called "On the Prospect of Planting Arts and Learning in America." In America, wrote Berkeley,

> There shall be sung another golden age,
> The rise of empire and of arts,
> The good and great inspiring epic rage,
> The wisest heads and noblest hearts.
>
> Not such as Europe breeds in her decay;
> Such as she bred when fresh and young,
> When heavenly flame did animate her clay,
> By future poets shall be sung.
>
> Westward the course of empire takes its way;
> The four first acts already past,
> A fifth shall close the drama with the day;
> Time's noblest offspring is the last.

America has recaptured the youth and "heavenly flame" that once
animated old Europe, and the course of empire is westward; the final

act of history—hearkening back to Daniel's prophecies—will be played out in America. "Time's noblest offspring is the last" sums up the essence of linear time: the last is the best.

The American dream, the New World, el Norte, the Great Frontier, the city upon a hill, God's country. Something about the ocean-bounded vastness of North America excites the imagination, so that in some ways America is more a psychic condition than a country, a place where the prophetic imagination found a home, a giant lab for utopian experimentation. North America has also become a world power whose visionary origins may seem quite forgotten. The modest aim of this chapter is to recollect some significant moments in American history that suggest the influence of the Millennium Myth. That influence is a part of the American collective unconscious; its creative potential is by no means spent, as I hope to show in the last five chapters.

Here I want to dwell on the fact that the influence of the great visionary Myth we are tracing is present in several defining moments of American history: in, for example, the discovery of America; in the Puritan colonizers; in the ideology of the American Revolution; in the motives for the abolition of slavery in the Civil War; and very practically, in the many utopian communities and new religions that makers and remakers of the Myth have formed. But let us go back to the beginning.

Columbus and the Millennium Myth

America, from the time the Europeans first saw its shores, has been a land of dreams. Indeed, I think it right to say that the American dream began with Columbus. The great Admiral of the Ocean Sea died, his dream intact, thinking he had found a new route to the Indies. Four voyages, and he never had an inkling of what he had stumbled upon.

Evidence, ignored by historians until recently, reveals how the land discovered by Columbus served as a prop for his millennial phantasies. Christopher Columbus saw himself as an agent of world history, a man gifted with spiritual intelligence, as he himself said, God's "messenger" to a new heaven and earth. In late 1500, he wrote a letter to Doña Juana de Torres, a confidante of Queen Isabella. "Of the new heaven and the new earth which the Lord made," he wrote, "and of which St. John writes in the Apocalypse, as the Lord told of it through the mouth of Isaiah, he made me the messenger, and he showed me the way." Here, for the first time, and before the Puritans, America appears to the Western imagination as the gateway to the New Jerusalem, one of the great phantasies of the Western world.

Columbus wrote this letter after his third voyage and after he had been discharged as viceroy of Hispaniola. It was a letter filled with bitter complaints. "None would believe me," he wrote, "but to my Lady the Queen He (the Lord) gave the gift of understanding, and great courage, and made her the heiress of all." Columbus here invents the idea that Spain has a divine right to the New Land. The Lord made the Queen his prophet, gave her the gift of second sight, so she could become the "heiress of all." That "all" includes quite a bit. And yet, laments Columbus, after securing for Spain "another world," after spending his youth in the enterprise, the honors due him were denied.

Was a wily Columbus just catering to the religious prejudice of the Spanish Queen, hoping to recoup revenues denied him, or were there real prophetic interests that motivated him? What, in short, really drove the Genoese to make his epoch-making voyage? Writes John Noble Wilford, "It may be, on closer examination, that spirituality, which fed his apocalyptic view of history, lay at the heart of the man and was the dominant force in his life and actions."[1]

The importance of prophecy in the explorations of Columbus may be known from a remarkable manuscript known as *Libro de las Profecias*, the *Book of Prophecies*.[2] He wrote this compendium of prophetic lore with the help of a Carthusian monk, Gaspar Gorricio, in 1500, while waiting to meet with Ferdinand and Isabella. The *Book of Prophecies* opens with a letter to the Spanish King and Queen, stating that God had favored Columbus with the "spirit of intelligence," and that it was this intelligence, not the maps of Toscanelli or the books of scholars, that inspired his great adventure.

This clashes with the traditional view of Columbus as a pioneer of the new scientific spirit. "All the sciences," he wrote, " . . . were of no use to me." What moved him to "press forward with great haste" was the "Holy Spirit" and, in the words of the mystics, "a radiance of marvelous illumination." In view of these remarks, the Renaissance explorer begins to look more and more like a medieval visionary.

Medieval millennialism pervades the *Book of Prophecies*. In talk of his "spiritual intelligence," Columbus brings us back to the prophecies of Joachim of Fiore, discussed in chapter 3. The people of the new age, Joachim had foretold, will possess a new spiritual intelligence, a faculty above ordinary reason. Columbus, in fact, took to heart the words of Joachim. Thus he wrote:

> Not undeservedly or without reason, I call earnestly to your attention, most noble sovereigns, some very important things that are to be observed, since indeed we did read that Joachim the Abbot of Southern Italy has foretold that he is to come from Spain who is to recover again the fortunes of Zion.

Columbus apparently saw himself as the one from Spain destined to recover the "fortunes of Zion." In this phrase we note the happy conjunction of fortune hunter and millenarian prophet. The myth that a man from Spain would recover the New Jerusalem did not, by the way, come from Joachim, but from one of Joachim's radical followers, Arnold of Villanova. It was a prophecy that had been circulating for over a hundred years.

In the *Book of Prophecies*, Columbus said that the voyage to the Indies was a step on the way to financing a crusade. Crusade? To recover the Holy Sepulcher in Jerusalem. The discovery of the "Indies," then, in the mind of Columbus, was part of a much bigger agenda— namely, the global expansion of Christianity. For Columbus such an expansion implied the preamble to the end of history, for the prophet Isaiah (Isa. 25) had foretold salvation for all people. Mass conversion, which Columbus would promote, was part of the divine plan.

But woe to them who resist the divine plan. In his letter to the Spanish sovereigns, Columbus recalls the chilling words of Augustine: "God will prevail, it is said, against them, and He will wipe out all the gods of the peoples of the earth, and they will adore Him." The Millennium Myth is here invoked to justify the destruction of the indigenous cultures of the New World.

At turns, in the dream-haunted mind of Columbus, America appears as the terrestrial paradise, as evidenced by the guilelessness and innocence of the natives and the fabulous flora and fauna of the new land; then as the new heaven and earth of the Book of Revelation; finally, as a waystation and source of revenue to finance the recovery of the Holy Sepulcher and hasten the end of history. "I believe that there is evidence that our Lord is hastening these things," he wrote to Ferdinand and Isabella, with the urgent tones of the true millennialist.

Columbus was influenced by radical Franciscans, those revolutionary mystics who believed that Francis of Assisi was the New Christ who had launched a new age of spirit in history. The American scholar John Leddy Phelan, in his *The Millennial Kingdom of the Franciscans* (1956), studied the millennialism of Columbus. According to Phelan, Columbus's chiliastic phantasy was in his mind since 1493, when he began to sign all his letters and documents *Christoferens*—"Christ-bearer."

Columbus took his name as a clue to his purpose in life. The signature he used, and instructed his heirs to designate him posthumously, has puzzled scholars. Above "Christoferens" he made a pyramid of letters:

$$. \; s \; .$$
$$. \; s \; . \; a \; . \; s \; .$$
$$x \qquad m \qquad y$$

No one has been able to decipher the meaning of this, although medievalist John V. Fleming thinks it is an "acrostic of considerable complexity committed to a more or less learned and hermetic mystical theology."[3] Hermetic ideas were in those times woven into seafaring lore and reflected, Fleming suggests, in this "acrostic." Whatever the exact meaning of the signature, it tallies, in a general way, with Columbus's mystical persona.

This persona was visible in his journal of the first voyage of 1492. He wrote on December 26 of obtaining gold in "such quantity, that the sovereigns, before three years are over, will undertake and prepare to go conquer the Holy Sepulcher." The lust for gold, which possessed Columbus, was directed toward the conquest of Zion. Columbus's greed was tied to his apocalyptic ambitions. In whatever garbled and devious way, it seems then that the Millennium Myth played a part in the inspiration that led to the "discovery" of America—a case of prophetic phantasy leading to historic serendipity.

The Puritan Colonizers

The English Reformation, born of protest against intrigue and corruption in church and politics, set the stage for the Myth of the Yankee New Jerusalem. To the Puritan makers of the Myth, America became the "new Israel," as Melville and countless Protestant preachers would later say.

117

The Puritans lived in light of what they thought were Scriptural prophecies yet to be fulfilled. Thus, in 1641 Thomas Goodwin wrote in *A Glimpse of Sions Glory* that "there is a glorious Time a coming." Goodwin saw abundant signs that "the Time is at hand." The sense of millennial excitement was equally intense ten years later, when, in Edward Johnson's revealingly titled "The Wonder-Working Providence of Sions Savior in New England," the author wrote, "I am now prest for service of our Lord Jesus Christ, to re-build the most glorious Edifice of Mount Sion in a Wildernesse."

"The Puritan colonists, nurtured in the providential assumptions of the English Reformation, brought to these shores an acute millennial consciousness," writes historian James A. Moorhead.[4] These assumptions, part of America's national unconscious, have surfaced and resurfaced periodically in the form of crusades, revivals, social experiments, psycho-spiritual epidemics, political ideologies, and, more recently, New Age beliefs and practices. Whether this millennial consciousness erupts spontaneously, as, for example, it did in the early eighteenth century in the Great Awakening, or in the early nineteenth century, which climaxed in Millerism, or whether it manifests in response to a crisis as it did in the Civil War or the First World War under President Woodrow Wilson's messianic leadership, the consciousness of having a world-pivotal destiny has been part of the American Myth.

Puritan, like *gothic* and *quaker*, began as a term of reproach. The Puritans were reformers of the Reformers, people who felt the Church of England had not gone far enough in purifying itself of the trash of "popish" worldliness. "God's people" is what the Puritans called themselves, which is how America came to be called "God's country." America owes a lot to these extremists of prophetic imagination: the Massachusetts Pilgrims founded the first of the northern Colonies and fathered the American Revolution; they established majority rule and the town meeting, the first tax-supported schools, the first college, and the first public library in the Colonies.

In December 1620, about a hundred persons, led by the "Puritan Fathers," sailed across the Atlantic in the *Mayflower* and established the first successful colony at Plymouth Bay. The historian of that pioneer effort was Governor William Bradford. The opening paragraphs of Bradford's history of the colony *Of Plymouth Plantation* reveal the millennial mentality that was to make its mark on the new American society. The colony made its debut in history as a theocracy, as firm and sometimes as cruel as the Ayatollah Khomeini's Islamic revolution. Before the century ended, Puritans would be expelling free-thinkers like Roger Williams, hanging Quakers, and burning witches.

Still, the Puritan's conviction that their pilgrimage to the New Land was overseen by Providence inspired them to survive the hardships of what to them was an unknown wilderness. The prophetic imagination was the invisible ally of the pilgrims.

England, according to Bradford, was the "first of nations" that witnessed the "first breaking out of the light of the gospel" after "the gross darkness of popery which had covered and overspread the Christian world."[5] The struggle against this gross darkness is described as a war fomented by "Satan" against the "saints"—a Biblical (non-Catholic) usage meant to designate God's chosen people. After continued persecutions from the Church of England, the Puritans or Separatists (as they sometimes called themselves) resolved to emigrate to the Low Countries "where they heard was freedom of religion for all men."

In Bradford's mind, the providential hand of God was at work everywhere. He recounts, for example, a story of "a special work of God's providence," about "a proud and very profane young man," a robust sailor who mocked the poor seasick pilgrims. Not a wise thing to do, for "it pleased God . . . to smite this young man with a grievous disease, of which he died in a desperate manner."[6] Bradford coolly observes that it was "the just hand of God" that caused the sailor's death. But how did Bradford really know this was true? He didn't, of course. Bradford was just inventing, indulging in a bit of American mythmaking.

Commenting on the safe arrival at Cape Cod, the Puritan father vents amazement at the poor pilgrims' mighty achievement; after all their hardships, "they had now no friends to welcome them nor inns to entertain or refresh their weatherbeaten bodies." Bradford then reminds the reader of a passage from Acts of the Apostles about how the Apostle Paul and his shipwrecked company were aided by barbarians.

"But these savage barbarians," says Bradford, referring to the Native Americans and comparing the pilgrims landing in Cape Cod to the shipwrecked Apostles, "were readier to fill their sides full of arrows."[7] Native Americans were not as nice as Paul's barbarians, inclined, as they were, to fill the sides of the poor pilgrims with arrows. The point: The Puritans were equating themselves with "saints" who were living out God's plan of salvation. Thus living and embracing their myth, they were no doubt heartened to perform feats of great fortitude in their colonizing adventure. Here, where the odds against success were so great—the first Jamestown settlement in 1605 had failed—the Millennium Myth served a hard and indispensable purpose.

Seeing themselves as chosen, as "saints," the Puritans upheld an ideology of self-righteous severity, as testified by Bradford's gleeful mention of the "profane" sailor's death. The myth of chosenness and saintliness provided a convenient rationale for pigeonholing the natives, whose land they had appropriated, as "savage barbarians."

John Winthrop was one of the great civil leaders of the Bay Colony, a man of impressive intellectual skills but also one who reminds us of the dangers of the Millennium Myth. Winthrop it was who uttered the famous remark about building a "city on a hill." America was to be a model for all to admire and emulate. A theocrat, however, and for that reason leery of popular rule, Winthrop thought there was no basis for democracy in Scripture and that "among nations it has always been accounted the meanest and worst of all forms of government."[8] Fellow Puritan John Cotton concurred: "Democracy I do not conceive that God did ever ordain as a fit government. . . . He (God) setteth up theocracy as the best form of government."[9] Under Winthrop's theocratic dispensation, adultery was punishable by death.

The Puritans came to America in quest, as Governor Bradford said, of "freedom of religion for all men," but they denied that freedom to people outside their faith. The Massachusetts leaders required of every voting man that he be a member of the church, but only the clergy could decide who was a member of the church. Cotton Mather wrote:

> Mr. Cotton effectually recommended . . . that none should be electors, nor elected therein, except as were visible subjects of Our Lord Jesus Christ, personally confederated in our churches. In these, and many other ways, he propounded unto them an endeavor after theocracy, as near as might be, to that which was the glory of Israel.[10]

However, it is a mistaken impression that the early Puritans were monolithic in their opinions. Right from the beginning there was dissent, and it came from their own ranks and from the more extreme millennialists. Roger Williams was a Puritan who rejected the ministry of the Boston Congregation because it had not fully separated from the Church of England; he balked, in short, at the abortion of true millennial rebirth. Locke's "slate" was not sufficiently wiped clean. Williams moved to Salem, his "strange opinions" causing controversy everywhere. Among these strange opinions, Williams believed that the land belonged to the Indians; he also denied that the government should impose religious laws on the people.

The Massachusetts General Court expelled Williams, who fled to the Indians on Narragansett Bay. In 1636, he founded Rhode Island, a haven for heterodoxy, publishing in 1644 *The Bloudy Tenent of Persecution*, a classic text in defense of religious freedom. Williams eventually joined the Seekers, a millenarian group that, Krishnamurti-like, was opposed to all sects and creeds. This highly original Puritan was one of the first Americans to become an activist on behalf of Native America; the Cambridge-bred radical studied Native linguistics, in 1643 publishing *A Key to the Language of America*.

A continuity of mystic dissent revolved around the notion of spiritual intelligence and its practical consequences. This may be seen in the career of another radical Puritan. In 1634, Anne Hutchinson emigrated with her husband to Massachusetts. An articulate woman, learned in the Bible, she denied that conformity with religious law was proof of godliness. True godliness came from *gnosis*, "an experience of the indwelling Holy Spirit." Once again we note the Joachite emphasis on the Holy Spirit—the Third Person of the Trinity and the experiential basis of the new age.

In Anne Hutchinson's "covenant of grace," we can know God directly, which she took to be the real meaning of the end of days. This deliteralization of the Millennium was also evident in her gloss on the resurrection, which she interpreted as a meeting with the indwelling Christ.[11] The congregation found this offensive and branded Hutchinson an *Antinomian*—the millenarian conviction that true Christians are not bound by the law. Antinomians were people who felt themselves so immersed in the Holy Spirit that they no longer needed established institutions for their salvation. Found guilty of sedition and contempt by the ecclesiastical synod, the Boston Church excommunicated her in 1638. Hutchinson joined Roger Williams in Pocasset, Rhode Island, that hotbed of mystic revolutionary sentiment.

Rhode Island attracted other Antinomians. These were the overflow from the Antinomian Controversy that swept through the Bay Colony between 1636 and 1638. The Antinomians expressed in extreme form the ancient millennial impulse to immediately appropriate the Heavenly Kingdom. They were sworn enemies of reality as it is with all its tidy distinctions, segregations, and compartments. Given the high anxiety induced by Calvin's unpredictable God, many chose the "left hand" path to immediate realization; among the most radical, like George Fox and Anne Hutchinson, the pursuit of paradise was abetted by visions, revelations, and "contactee" experiences of various sorts.

These early American Millennium Myth makers were a menace to the status quo, and many of them were not treated kindly. The affronts against them were fueled by Puritans who insisted on the stark dualism between future Heaven and immediate lust. Thus, one Puritan complained that the opinions of the extremists were a cover for "distempers and lusts lurking in men's hearts." What unforgivably drove the Antinomians was that "it pleased nature well to have Heaven, and their lusts, too."[12]

The Antinomians wanted their paradise now and in the definite shape of love's body. As the English Levellers insisted, the experience of the indwelling Christ obliterated all distinctions between heaven and earth, spirit and lust; it also wiped out the artificial separations between people. The Antinomians were people who chose "the faire and easie way to heaven."

Samuel Gorton was an Antinomian whose ideas found a temporary home in the Rhode Island settlements. Gorton believed that rebirth in Christ implied an egalitarian society, justifying revolt against all hierarchy and authority. Justice, he said, "belongs only to the Lord" and "men make themselves Gods . . . by ruling over the bodies and estates of men."[13] Gorton was accused of being a "mortalist" because he had claimed that if one is touched by the Holy Spirit, one already is in eternity. "There is no other heaven," he said, "than what is in the hearts of good men; nor no other hell than what is in the hearts of bad men."

In my last example of New England prophets of the new heaven, we can see, as in other examples to be cited in what follows, the power of the Myth to sweep men away in passions of revolution and confrontation. Thomas Venner was a wine cooper who later led bloody Fifth Monarchy uprisings in London. Venner, like David Koresh and Jim Jones, stockpiled weapons in preparation for the battle of New Jerusalem. This Yankee-inspired prophet built a reputation of extremism, till early in 1661 he and a ragtag gang of fellow believers went on a rampage through the streets of London, crying "Live King Jesus," murdering innocent bystanders on the way. After further bloody rampages, Venner was arrested and tried; he defended himself by raving incoherently and grandiosely about Scripture, claiming, like Charlie Manson and Adolf Hitler, that the indwelling Christ was acting through him. The Court hanged, drew and quartered him, and had his head impaled atop the city gate. It was meant to show disapproval of Thomas Venner's gloss on the Millennium Myth.

Not all prophets of the New Light were so violent. Some, in fact, were peaceful to a fault. The Quakers belong to the tradition of serious celebrators of the Inner Light. Although the early Puritans of Massachusetts hanged a few members of the "Society of Friends," there was eventual rapprochement. George Fox started the Quaker movement during the Civil War in England in the seventeenth century. Again, as with the medieval visionaries, the stress was on experience of the Inner Light. Fox claimed independence from all intermediaries, since "that of God in every man" rendered external rites and the professional clergy superfluous.

Pennsylvania became a refuge for Quakers, and, led by William Penn, became a "holy experiment" in religious laissez-faire. The Society of Friends became active as reformers and lobbied for Indian rights, prison reform, the abolition of slavery, improved education, and the rights of women. It is interesting to note that the experience of Inner Light—whatever that may quite be—may lead to consequences as diverse as the violent rantings of Thomas Venner or the constructive reforms associated with Quaker history. The power of the Millennium Myth is highly volatile and unpredictable as to concrete outcome.

In the long run, the antidemocratic sentiment of the Pilgrim fathers was countered by the natural love of liberty characteristic of most Englishmen. Nevertheless, they did leave behind a legacy, not all the time merely latent, of intolerance and anti-intellectualism. The Puritan fathers were learned men, but evangelical Protestantism and fundamentalism, ever harping on the inerrancy of Scripture, lends itself to contempt for what in the 1950s was dubbed "eggheadism" or nowadays "cultural elitism."[14] It was not only Savonarola and the Nazis who lit bonfires of the vanities; attempts to exclude certain books from home and library are still reported in America today.

The American Revolution

In the last chapter, I talked of Paine and Jefferson whose political philosophy contained secular echos of millennial aspiration. As Jefferson said, he meant the Declaration to "express the mind of America." A feature of that mind, I argued, which claimed the right of all human beings to pursue their own happiness, is resonant with deep millennial longings. Paine's voice was no less resonant with millennial longing, evoking in the American and French Revolutions themes of transcendent import.

I want to look a little further into Paine's prophetic rhetoric, as it served to inflame the psyche of the American Revolution. Paine's *Common Sense*, which made the case for independence, was a runaway bestseller; the author gave away all his profits for the Cause. It has been called the most successful political pamphlet of all time; it taught George Washington to despise kings and rallied the army that threw off the yoke of the British empire. The American Revolution, which Paine's prophetic rhetoric kindled, itself became the paradigm for a wave of revolutions across Europe, a wave whose force is unspent even in current times.

America has not quite been able to approve of Tom Paine, a "free-thinker" and general despiser of all irrational authority. In my judgment, however, Paine was a deeply spiritual man, if by *spiritual* is meant sensitivity to the suffering of other human beings, hatred of injustice, love of truth, and the courage to do something about it all. I would go a step further and say that Paine was a prophet of the new age, a maker of the American Millennium Myth.

Like John of Patmos, there wells up in Paine tremendous hatred of power that oppresses. He knew poverty and the "insolence of office" first hand, being forced to grovel for a living before the rich as a corset-maker. But for Paine, whose father was a Quaker, the true bane of humankind was the King, the abominable patriarch and living embodiment of oppressive power. Paine plied all his rhetoric to unmask what was objectionable in kingship. "*Common Sense* killed the concept of kingship in America," wrote historian Robert Leckie.[15] In this, Paine parts company with John of Patmos, for Paine struck a tremendous blow against the Oppressive Father archetype, the ancient principle of patriarchy. It was a blow struck against the Western psyche. John of Patmos, on the other hand, had no wish to end the reign of kings; not at all—he wanted to make the oppressed into little new kings, new oppressors who would "rule with a rod of iron."

John of Patmos and Tom Paine hated cruelty, injustice, oppression; but the one seems deficient in compassion and the other, amply endowed with it. Consider what Paine said in a piece called *African Slavery in America*, published in *The Pennsylvania Journal* in 1775, shortly after he arrived in America with a letter of introduction from Benjamin Franklin: "Too many nations enslaved the prisoners they took in war. But to go to nations with whom there is no war, who have no way provoked, without farther design of conquest, purely to catch inoffensive people, like wild beasts, for slaves, is an height of outrage against humanity and justice, that seems left by heathen nations to be practiced by pretended Christians."

Unlike John of Patmos, who seems, like Saint Paul, to have accepted slavery, Tom Paine's rage wasn't against "unbelievers" but against injustice; his indignation was for all humanity, not just for the members of a private cult. Paine spoke for the rights of blacks, and he spoke for the rights of Native Americans.

In the next passage, he picks at the King archetype while alluding to Christian hypocrisy. "And when I reflect on the use she (Britain) has made of the discovery of this new world—that the little paltry dignity of earthly kings has been set up in preference to the great cause of the King of kings—that instead of Christian examples to the Indian, she has basely tampered with their passions, imposed on their ignorance, and made them the tools of treachery and murder— . . . I hesitate not for a moment that the Almighty will finally separate America from Britain."[16] The American Revolution, as Paine painted it, was a holy war against "the little paltry dignity of earthly kings" for the sake of the *whole* of humanity.

The energy of Paine's rhetoric, the ability it demonstrated to set into motion the revolt against Britain, siphoned itself from the massive discontent, the general outrage against patriarchal power, at that moment of history, concentrated in the English Crown. Dehumanized blacks, betrayed Native people—Paine spoke for another sector of humanity whose plight John of Patmos also ignored—women.

In his *Letter on the Female Sex*, he bewails the "lot of women over the whole earth. Man, with regard to them, in all climates and in all ages, has either been an insensible husband or an oppressor. . . . When they are not beloved they are nothing; and, when they are, they are tormented." (I will return to Paine's incendiary views on marriage later in the book.)

I bring out these points not to demonstrate Paine's precocious political correctness, but to demonstrate that the underlying passion that drove him in support of the Revolution was a global and religious passion, one that was directed against a type of social existence—the epoch of the dominator patriarch, the epoch that Joachim of Fiore said was destined to pass away in the coming new age of spirit.

The next passage of Paine I want to quote shows quite clearly the way the overthrow of patriarchy is viewed as the basis for restoring paradise. "Society in every state is a blessing," he wrote in *Common Sense*, "but government, even in its best state, is but a necessary evil. . . . The palaces of kings are built upon the ruins of the powers of paradise." Do away with kings, with government itself, and the powers of paradise may be restored.

The appeal to the universal longing for paradise—along with the outrage and mockery of kings—got to George Washington. Paine dedicated *The Rights of Man* to Washington after the latter had become the first president of the new United States of America. Whether the American or the French Revolution, the millenarian sentiment was the same. To Washington he wrote, "That the Rights of Man may become as universal as your benevolence can wish, and that you may enjoy the happiness of seeing the New World regenerate the Old, is the prayer of Your much obliged, and obedient humble servant." The American Revolution is here cast in the millenarian role of "regenerating" the "old" world.

Around the figure of George Washington hangs a haze of legend. One thing clear was his sense of destiny. He saw the Revolution and the birth of the nation as nurtured by Providence. It is part of the Millennium Myth to imagine that history is guided by the invisible hand of God; it is here that the Biblical view contrasts with the pagan. In Washington's First Inaugural Address of April 30, 1789, for example, he spoke clearly from the heart of the Biblical zeitgeist:

> It would be peculiarly improper to omit, in this first official act, my fervent supplications to that Almighty Being, who rules over the universe . . . No people can be found to acknowledge and adore the invisible hand, which conducts the affairs of men, more than the people of the United States. Every step by

which they have advanced to the character of an independent nation, seems to have been distinguished by some token of providential agency.

Tokens of providence he may have found in his own life and military adventures. Washington was known to feel a kind of magical immunity to bullets. It happened once that his troops became confused in the dark and began firing on each other; Washington threw himself in the midst of the melee and sought to disarm his men. After the exchange of "friendly fire" was over, fourteen of his men were killed, twenty-six wounded; Washington was unscathed.[17]

One wonders about the mental makeup of such an extraordinary man, especially the source of his near-supernatural courage and determination. I will mention two facts—usually ignored or played down—that may have helped to form the great man's mind, and both have curious millennial resonances. Notions of spiritual elitism and secrecy have always been leitmotifs in some forms of reformist societies. Two examples that come to mind are the Jesuits and the Freemasons. Oddly enough, there is reason to believe that in the background of Washington's mind flowed streams of influence from these two quite different but often-supposed sinister societies.

According to military historian Robert Leckie, "the literary work that had the utmost influence"[18] on Washington was a pamphlet called *The Rules of Conduct and Politeness*, a popular Jesuit-style manual, written in 1595 by the Jesuit fathers of La Fleche, on how to win friends and influence people. The Jesuits, of course, were the elite guard of the Catholic Counter Reformation and were dedicated to a subtle form of spiritual guerilla warfare. It is, moreover, incontestable that George Washington, along with other major makers of the American Revolution, was a Freemason. Freemasonry was a secret brotherhood of Enlightenment illuminati, and it is a fact that George Washington was Master Mason of his Lodge when he became the first President of the United States.

I will return to the possibility of Masonic influences at work among the Fathers of the Revolution in a moment. Right now I want to give another example illustrating converging prophetic influences in John Adams, another great Founding Father of the Revolution. With Adams the influence of the Millennium Myth is operative both through the Enlightenment and the Protestant Reformation.

In 1765, Adams published *A Dissertation on the Canon and Feudal Law*. This work was immediately published abroad where it was retitled *The True Sentiments of America*. According to Adams—and here he repeats Fontanelle and Condorcet—history involves a progressive increase in knowledge and benevolence. Optimism, as stressed in the previous chapter, was a heady value of Enlightenment philosophers. The common people aspire toward independence, Adams wrote, because of the growing consciousness of human rights: "Rights," he said, "that cannot be repealed or restrained by human laws—rights, derived from the great Legislator of the universe."[19] The great Legislator, of course, is the God of the Bible.

Unfortunately, notes Adams, the dream of progress meets with obstacles on the road of history. What has slowed the progress of history is the canon law of the "Romish clergy," a system that has served as an ideology for the oppression of humankind. As historian of millennialism Ernest Tuveson notes, the real obstacle to progress, in Adam's mind, was spiritual evil and "religious corruption."[20]

Adams, it turns out, was a full-blown dualist, with an outlook in some ways comparable to that of John of Patmos. For Adams the union of canon with secular law is proof positive of Antichrist: "Thus was human nature chained fast for ages in a cruel, shameful, and deplorable servitude to him, and his subordinate tyrants, who, it was foretold, would exalt himself above all that was called God, and that was worshiped."

In Adam's view, all was foretold by the Book of Revelation: Antichrist enlists the aid of worldly powers to exalt himself above God and the godly. But, in unison with the Book of Revelation, Adams believed that God's will must—in the end—triumph in history. To this end, Adams favored the separation of church and state. People would be allowed to meet God on their own terms. So, ironically, under the influence of the savagely theocratic Book of Revelation, Adams presses home for the separation of church from state.

In his dissertation on mental progress, Adams seemed to attach little importance to the Renaissance revival of learning or to the Scientific Revolution. It was the Reformation and its passion for returning to the pure message of the Gospel that moved him most. The Rights of humanity are derived from the divine architect of the universe. The New England colonies were to establish a new world, free of the "Romishness" that yet tainted the Church of England.

Adam's diary, February 1765, reads, "I always consider the settlement of America with reverence and wonder, as the opening of a grand scene and design in Providence for the illumination of the ignorant, and the emancipation of the slavish part of mankind all over the earth." Such words—reverence, wonder, grand design, illumination, emancipation—come straight from the lexicon of the millennial mind. The American sense of mission was in the minds of the Founding Fathers at the birth of the nation.

The religious roots of the American Revolution are clear from words of the theologian and chemist who discovered oxygen and anticipated the discovery of photosynthesis, Joseph Priestley. Priestley was an apostle of the American Revolution whose house was bombed by enraged adversaries and who fled from England to America at the end of his life. Having witnessed revolutions in France and America at century's end, he wrote in his commentary on the Book of Revelation:

> Indeed, some of the most interesting parts of this prophecy are, at this very time, receiving their accomplishment . . . It is, indeed, sufficient for us, and affords us much consolation, that the great catastrophe is clearly announced, and such indications of happy times, as lead us to look forward with confidence and joy. These prophecies are also written in such manner as to satisfy us, that the events announced to us, were really foreseen.[21]

Priestley was reading the history of the great eighteenth-century revolutions through the spectacles of the Millennium Myth. Like his fellow-Protestant John Adams, Priestley dualized and demonized the drama of history:

> The blasphemy of the beast, of which the papal power was a part, consists in the Pope's usurping the authority of God, setting up other objects of worship besides him, and persecuting his true worshippers, and in all the kingdoms represented by the ten horns concurred.[22]

The Papacy is not merely a dangerous and corrupt human institution; it is part of a diabolical conspiracy—the Antichrist in institutional form.

The Dollar Bill as Millennium Museum

We backtrack now to the Masonic factor in the founding of the nation. Here, the evidence I invoke is available for all to inspect in the Great Seal imprinted on the American dollar bill. The symbolism of the Great Seal is a memorial to the influence of Masonry on America. Masonry is an international brotherhood of mystic freedom-fighters, among whose ranks are listed many illustrious names: in addition to George Washington—Voltaire, Lafayette, Franklin, Lincoln, Roosevelt, and so on. The Masons were Enlightenment-educated men with an aristocratic taste for secrecy and symbolism, for the idealism of sacred traditions, without their superstition and authoritarianism. The imagery on the dollar bill perhaps contains information about the spiritual origins of America, as Robert Hieronimos contends in his *America's Secret Destiny*.[23]

In 1776, four men were given the job to design a seal that expressed the meaning and destiny of the new nation: Thomas Jefferson, Benjamin Franklin, John Adams, and Pierre Eugène DuSimitiere. The Great Seal is thus a record of the visionary origins of America.

On the reverse side is a mandala containing a broken pyramid with a radiant eye enclosed in a triangle. The triangle points back to the evolutionary trinity of Joachim's philosophy of history. The pyramid points back to the Egyptian dawn of civilization. It is, however, an unfinished pyramid, as the work of civilization is unfinished. America's mission is to finish the pyramid, suggests Hieronimos. (Robert Hieronimos runs an extremely open-minded show called 21st Century Radio, a place somewhere at the mental antipodes of Rush Limbaugh.)

I invite the reader to meditate on this curious icon, born of the American Revolution. Reading the image on the seal, I see that the challenge is to connect the massive base of the pyramid, symbolic of the people, with the all-seeing, radiant wisdom of the divine seer. I read, in Roman numerals, 1776, the year of the birth of the nation. Above the radiant triangulated eye, the words in Latin read, *Annuit Coeptus*. He—the deity with the radiant eye—favors our venture. He bids our undertaking prosper. What does *Coeptus* refer to? What venture or undertaking? Clearly, it can be nothing less than the birth of America, which is why the numerals read the year of the birth of the nation. According to the seal, the radiant Eye of Providence presides over this new nation, exactly as Washington said in his Inaugural Address. Beneath the pyramid we read *Novus ordo seclorum*, "New Order of Ages." In other words, the founding of America was the founding of a "new world order." This is how the Founding Fathers understood the meaning of the birth of the American nation.

It was a nation conceived in the spirit of liberty, a spirit that guaranteed unalienable rights—free from the arbitrary power of monarchs, free, as Adams had said, from canon or religious law. Clearly, in the minds of the Founding Fathers, the birth of America was associated with the dawn of a new age.

On the obverse side of the Seal, we find another mandala, another image of American wholeness. Although Franklin's choice for the national animal was a turkey, here we see an eagle with outstretched wings, on its chest a shield of red, white, and blue. In one talon, which the eagle's head faces, is an olive branch; in the other, thirteen arrows. The eagle holds in its beak a sash, on which is written the metaphysical motto: *E pluribus unum*, "Out of many one," meaning that thirteen states are united in one nation.

America, as portrayed in the Great Seal, appears to be an instrument of military power. Jung once observed that the eagle, America's national symbol, is a bird of prey. However, under the auspices of the Radiant Eye of Providence, the secret destiny of America is to create unity out of diversity, peace out of conflict.

The eagle looks to the talon of peace. Peace, then, becomes the national goal. There we have one part of the message. The arrows in the other talon announce to the world another message: America is prepared to use its military might to realize its goal. America has abundantly proven in blood this part of the seal's insignia. The sense of being guided by a righteous destiny is as deep in the American psyche as it is clearly symbolized in the American dollar bill. Speaking of the American dollar bill, I am led to the next point.

American Materialism and the Millennium

The Millennium Myth was from the start a Myth of sacred materialism, a vision of heaven coming down to earth, of nature rendered docile and amicable. The Myth's evolution in America is certainly in this direction. Indeed, for many Americans, a none-too-sacred materialism marks the last lingering vestige of the Myth, the Great Shopping

Mall being all that remains of the Temple of Sion. The trend toward a coarser Yankee version of the New Jerusalem began among the makers of the Revolution, whose practical penchant was to blend the secular and the spiritual.

The happy combination of the secular and the spiritual, a trait of Adams and Priestley, was evident in other American Protestant millennialists. However, it is here where the secular and the spiritual join that the character of the American dream begins to change, the puritanical cast of mind begins to melt, and a profaner materialism starts to emerge. Samuel Hopkins illustrates the transition.

In 1793, Hopkins, founder of the New Light theology, published *A Treatise on the Millennium*. Hopkins was convinced that history must come to an end to redress the shame and reproach of Christ's crucifixion. The cause for which Christ suffered must "prevail and be victorious in this same world, where he suffered and died." The words to underscore here are "prevail" and "in this same world." Not to worry, though; it is not Henry Kissinger speaking. Hopkins is not talking Realpolitik but about a victory of "disinterested benevolence toward man, including ourselves." In the Millennium to come, grace and the influx of new light will give rise to a universal benevolence. Hopkins still conceived of the new age as a substantially supernatural affair.

But now note a new focus, reminiscent of the Renaissance Golden Age: "And great advances will be made in all arts and sciences, and in every useful branch of knowledge, which tends to promote the spirit and eternal good of men, or their convenience and comfort in this life." Placing side by side, "the spirit and eternal good of men" with "their convenience and comfort in this life" heralds a shift in the meaning of the American dream. Glancing back at our Puritan forebears and then at the world around us at the end of the twentieth century, the movement of the Myth has been from theocracy to democracy, from frugality to consumerism, from severity to comfortableness, from communitarian self-sacrifice to a preoccupation with the Gross National Product. In other words, when people talk about the American dream nowadays, they are thinking more of comfort, convenience, secure jobs, homes with manicured lawns, and all the rest of modern life's amenities.

With Samuel Hopkins, however, the accent was still on the search for spiritual light. Real prosperity for Hopkins two hundred years ago wasn't measured by the size of one's bank account but from "such benevolent and fervent charity in every heart, that if any one shall be reduced to a state of want by some causality, or by inability to provide for himself, he will have all the relief and assistance he could desire." Hopkins' Millennium is a welfare state, rooted in the generosity of grace.

Thanks to the influx of grace and benevolence, Hopkins' millennial America will banish war, "which has been a vast expense and scourge to mankind in all ages, by which poverty and distress have been spread among all nations." Comes the Millennium, moreover, another radical obstacle to human happiness will be snuffed—not quite death itself, but at least the fear and pain of dying. Hopkins, who believed in the power of the Inner Light, could see a time when we will all know death as a painless exit from the body, an effortless passage of reunion with our divine origins.

Hopkins sounds another millennial theme, the coming of a universal language, a time when people "shall all become as one family in affection." The search for a unifying language is a theme we observe addressed, perhaps a little unconsciously, in many so-called New Age pursuits. In the chapter on the New Age, I will try to show that New Age interest in such esoterica as Tarot, I Ching, astrology, runes, and Crop Circles, are part of the quest for such a unifying language, a language needed to relearn "affection" in the human "family."

Moreover, predicts Hopkins, the art of printing, along with this universal language, will speed the circulation of "useful" ideas and "all kinds of intelligence, which may be a benefit to mankind." Hopkins, I suppose, is talking about what we today call the information revolution, predating Marshall McLuhan's "global village" and Peter Russell's electronic "global brain."

Less affably, Hopkins foresaw a prolonged Armageddon beginning in the late 1990s—before the Last Wrap Up. The prognosis of a final conflict of global proportions puts Hopkins back in the ranks of traditional apocalyptic; for, despite his vision of a comfortable and convenient American Millennium, he foresees an unavoidable bloodbath, vast purgative conflicts before the nation settles down to its secret destiny. In Old Time apocalyptic, catastrophe always precedes renewal—as the saying goes, no pain, no gain. Indeed, Samuel Hopkins foresaw a moral catastrophe coming even sooner, a confrontation of apocalyptic significance.

The Abolitionism of Slavery

Many Americans, caught up in the spirit of Paine's rhetoric, had viewed the Revolution as a historic turning point, the dawn of a new world order. Yet all was not well in the New Israel.

There remained a great stumbling block—the ugly specter of enforced servitude. The abduction and enslavement of millions of blacks, upon which a good deal of the early economy of the Colonies was based, was blatantly at odds with Jefferson's Declaration of Independence. How could you reconcile slavery with liberty and equality? The nation was sick with moral cancer and had to be healed.

The Millennium Myth allowed many Americans to see in the Civil War the healing of the nation. The Myth makers saw the war to abolish slavery as a holy war and fought it in the shadow of millenarian hopes. Just as Paine saw American emancipation from British rule as a new epoch in human history, northern Protestant evangelicals saw Civil War as a step toward the rebirth of the New Israel.

By 1787, the churches were calling for an end to slavery. Before the millennial age could dawn, the abomination of slavery had to go. Listen to Samuel Hopkins:

> Thanks be to God! He has assured us that all these works of the devil shall be destroyed, and that the time is hastening on, when all the people shall be righteous and benevolent . . . and there is reason to conclude that this light and conviction, and these exertions, will continue and increase till the slave traders shall be utterly destroyed.[24]

The idea that "all the people" are going to be "righteous and benevolent" when slavery is abolished is redolent of millennialism.

Millennial ardor grew in the years up to and during the Civil War. On Thanksgiving Day in 1862, for example, Joseph P. Thompson preached a sermon in the Broadway Tabernacle Church in New York City. Thompson spoke of Lincoln's recent proclamation:

> The Proclamation of Emancipation has challenged the powers of darkness to defeat it. Unclean spirits, like frogs, seem to swarm out of the mouth of the dragon, and out of the mouth of the beast and the false prophet. But we cannot be dismayed. We will still march on with the psalter in our hand; for soon the seventh seal shall 'pour out his vial into the air, and there

shall come a great voice out of the temple of heaven, from the throne, saying, IT IS DONE.'

Once again the travails of history are seen through the eyes of the Millennium Myth, the preacher depicting Lincoln's move to emancipate the slaves as the prelude to the end of history.

Soon after at Gettysburg, Lincoln himself evoked in unforgettable Biblical cadences an image of apocalyptic rebirth. "Four score and seven years ago our fathers brought forth upon this continent a new nation. . . ." Garry Wills, in *Inventing America*, comments: "Lincoln is talking about generation on the spot. The nation is rightly called new because it is brought forth maieutically, by midwifery; it is not only new, but newborn. The suggested image is, throughout, of a *hieros gamos*, a marriage of male heaven ('our fathers') and female earth ('this continent')."

In giving us a vision of national rebirth, Lincoln became one of our Millennium Myth makers. Even in the worst-case scenario of total national conflict, as the Civil War was, the resources lay within us to rally and rebirth ourselves. One of the great messages of the Myth is that we have the resources, the power to reinvent ourselves and forge a new national identity, even when it seems we have hit bottom. We can always go back with Lincoln to Gettysburg, regenerate, and bring ourselves forth again.

The Civil War was the nation's crucifixion. "The country set apart by miraculous birth undergoes its supreme test and achieves—resurrection: 'that this nation under God shall have a *new birth* of freedom.' "[25] Garry Wills notes the flattering charm of this vision of America, a vision so flattering and so seductive that at certain times in our history we revert to it to justify acts of imperialism and self-interested interventionism.

The myth of America as the redeemer nation was imprinted on the collective mind from the experience of the Civil War. It happened when Northern soldiers were exposed to the hypnotic rhetoric of evangelical preachers. One day in October 1862, for example, a company of Union volunteers about to head for the front listened to a sermon by William L. Gaylord:

Oh! what a day will that be for our beloved land, when carried through a baptism of fire and blood, struggling through this birth-night of terror and darkness, it shall experience a resurrection to a new life, and to a future whose coming glory already gilds the mountain tops. . . . The day of the Lord is at hand![26]

It is easy to imagine young men thrilling to these words, as they polished their boots and cleaned their rifles. The preacher's rhetoric calls to mind the words of Julia Ward Howe's millenarian "Battle Hymn of the Republic," which inspired thousands to think their eyes were seeing "the glory of the coming of the Lord." Published in the *Atlantic Monthly* in 1862, the American Myth sang through Howe's "Battle Hymn." It will happen many times—bloody confrontations wrapped in the rhetoric of supernaturalism. For those who may have forgotten the opening lines:

> Mine eyes have seen the glory of the coming of the Lord:
> He is trampling out the vintage where the grapes of wrath are
>   stored;
> He hath loosed the fateful lightning of his terrible swift
>   sword;
> His truth is marching on.

As Howe and many American evangelicals saw it, the Civil War was the great test for the final birth—or rather rebirth—of the nation. The war is a "fiery gospel writ in burnished rows of steel," wrote Howe, a gospel, a piece of good news. The "Hero," the Northern soldier, is going to "crush the serpent with his heel." This crushing, or imprisoning, of the serpent, as we know from the Book of Revelation, is supposed to signal the approach of the end of days.

From Civil War to Social Experimentation

Dreams of the end of days sometimes take the form of social experimentation. The Revolution and The Civil War were national dramas through which Americans lived the Millennium Myth. Other ways have been tried, less violent and grandiose. Some have retreated from the nation at large and tried to create their own little patch of paradise, somewhere off the beaten track of God's country.

A prominent feature of Yankee millennializing has been the willingness to engage in social experimentation. American history is rife with radical groups of every stripe, trying to build the New Jerusalem somewhere, here and now. It started with the Pilgrims. America is a gigantic womb. No other country in history has been so consciously designated as a place to sow the seeds of new forms of social existence. From Puritan colonies to hippie communes, Americans have been passionate about reinventing the art of sociability; it was very American for Ken Wilber to write a book called *A Sociable God*.

I can, of course, only offer a few examples. There is a rich and fascinating history here, and the literature is growing. So, to focus as clearly as possible on the power of the Millennium Myth, consider three groups that were based on three different interpretations of the same statement of Jesus about marriage in the Kingdom of Heaven. In all three of these utopian experiments, ordinary social life was completely subverted, and people attempted to taste a little bit of love as they imagined it may be as we come toward the end of time.

In 1840, R. W. Emerson wrote to Carlyle, "Not a reading man but has a draft of a new community in his waistcoat pocket."[27] The fact is that American millenarians have used the Bible to sanction some pretty bold social experimentation—in particular, in the area of sex and family life. The passage they used comes from the New Testament, at first glance, not a text known for subversive sex philosophy. And yet, asked about what marriage would be like in the Kingdom of God, Jesus replied:

> The children of this world marry, and are given in marriage;
> but they that shall be accounted worthy to obtain that world,
> and the resurrection of the dead, neither marry nor are given
> in marriage. Neither can they die anymore; for they are equal
> unto the angels; and are the children of God, being the chil-
> dren of the resurrection (Luke 20:34–36).[28]

Thus, comes the consummation, there will be no marriage at all; people, in some way like angels, will not even die. Here, I suppose, is a key passage for this book, which explicitly links the end of sex and death, as we ordinarily understand them, with the end of time and the coming of the Kingdom of Heaven. These were powerful words for people who felt, or wished to feel, they were God's chosen people. What could they mean for people eager to see ordinary time and history come to an end?

Three American prophets of the Millennium—all from a stretch of land west of the Catskills and the Adirondacks—took the remarks of

Jesus about marriage in heaven very seriously indeed. Each thought the words of Jesus had radical—but, as it turned out, quite different—implications for the way folk should conduct themselves in matters of sex and family life.

For Ann Lee, the founder of Shakerism, the remark of Jesus was taken as a call to get rid of sex *in toto* and to embrace celibacy. Yale-educated John Humphrey Noyes saw it another way. Noyes was more logical. The end of marriage, he said, by no means implies the end of sex. Noyes felt that in the Millennium, sex itself would not be finished, only a certain kind of selfish, exclusive sex. After much soul-searching, he came out in favor of what he called "complex marriage."

The Shakers, celibacy; Noyes's Oneida Perfectionists, group marriage. The Mormons, yet another prophetic group hailing from antebellum New York State, came up with a third take on the same Bible quote. Joseph Smith, whose story is very strange indeed, took the words of Jesus as proof that we should revive the polygamous practices of the Hebrew patriarchs. Polygamy in the Old Testament was popular from the time of Lamech (Gen. 4:19) and was not even forbidden by Scripture.

The Americans were extremely practical millenarians; by their actions, they hoped, perhaps by a kind of sympathetic magic, to bring on the end of history. In each of our examples, the prophet votes to destroy the nuclear family, the social fabric that sustains the old earth and its sin-begotten society. The traditional family must go, before the Millennium can come. Traditional "family values" are in for a surprise, come the end of days.

For the Shakers, renunciation of sex was the first step toward bringing about the Millennium. The idea, not foreign to Catholic priest or Hindu renunciant, was to free all one's energies, to focus single-mindedly and with purity of heart, on the supreme goal of spiritual transformation. Instead of squandering spiritual energies in unhappy sexual relationships, the Shakers decided on a communal life style where worship through manual work and ecstatic dance became the center of social life.

Noyesean Perfectionists made sex the basis for communal worship but followed a path of affirmation, not denial. Noyes thought—as do some Tantrics and Taoists—that sex has its higher or "angelic" dimension. If in the resurrection we become like angels, then our divine job is to learn somehow to make love like angels. Sex becomes a way of worship, a way of opening oneself up to the divine bounty.

This may seem far from the mainstream, but I believe that Noyes's optimism about the true purpose of sex reflects Western creationist metaphysics, according to which the earth and our bodies and their pleasures are created by an all-good God and so are good themselves. The idea of the sacredness of sex has been all but lost in the Western tradition, but visionaries like Noyes, and more recently the renegade Catholic priest, Matthew Fox, may be more attuned to one of the forgotten and mystified messages of Christian tradition.

So let us look more closely at these movements, which, for all their diversity, shared a common revulsion for ordinary civilization and its discontents.

The Shakers

The Shakers called themselves the "Church of the Last Dispensation." They saw the "Last Dispensation" as a revival of Pentecostalism, which covered five principles 1) celibacy, 2) common property, 3) nonresistance to evil, 4) a government distinct from worldly government, and 5) "power over physical disease."[29]

On the last point, the Shakers were largely vegetarians and enjoyed unusually good health and long life. They saw themselves as striving to restore the "virginity" of the first Adam—the androgynous human who flourished before the Fall. Virginity, in the sense of androgynous wholeness, was the answer to love and death.

The Shaker philosophy of celibacy began with a woman who had nasty experiences with sex. Ann Lee had four painful childbirths, losing all her offspring in infancy. Her last delivery almost killed her, and she ended up refusing to have sex with her husband. To escape her problems in bed, Ann Lee took to the life of revivalism, so widespread in those transitional times. She entered these activities with so much zeal that on one occasion she got herself arrested for "disturbing the peace."

While she was in jail at Manchester, Ann Lee had an awe-inspiring vision of Adam and Eve in carnal embrace. Ann saw that carnal desire was the true cause of the fall of humanity. She saw Eve's curse: "I will greatly multiply thy sorrow and thou shalt bring forth children." Seeing all this so clearly, Ann Lee decided to live in communal celibacy. By uprooting lust and living a life of "virgin purity," the human race could be restored to God's good graces. Celibacy could only help to expedite the end of history and hasten the Millennium.

A small band of followers gathered around the prophet. In 1772, one of her associates had a vision of the tree of life planted in America; Ann Lee became convinced that America was the place to sow the seeds of the new society that would witness the Last Dispensation. She and her seven disciples emigrated to New York City in 1774; it was the eve of the American Revolution.

Members of the new church, who were growing in number, came to believe that Ann Lee was the second Incarnation of God. An apostate later wrote: "Some of them say, that the woman called the mother (Ann Lee), has the fullness of the God Head, bodily dwelling in her, and that she is the Queen of Heaven, Christ's wife: and that all Christ's elect must be born through her; yea, that Christ through her is born a second time."[30]

In Ann's ecstasies, she spoke of Jesus as her Lord and Lover. Once more we meet with the idea of *hieros gamos*, in this context, of becoming the spouse of Christ. Most people viewed the claims about Ann as "enthusiastic"—crazy or inflated. This claim, by the way, of being a female incarnation of God is a rerun of medieval heresies when Prous Boneta and Giugliema of Milan proclaimed themselves incarnations of the Holy Spirit.

Rapt by their visions, the Shakers danced ecstatically. The Shaker dance was a kind of voluntary surrender to possession. Historian Lawrence Foster believes[31] that the function of the dance was to mollify by fatigue the sting of frustrated sexual desire. The Shakers shook, shrieked, sang, sobbed, and spoke in tongues; they whirled, stamped, sighed, and rolled on the ground.[32] However, the revivalist orgy, like the whirling Dervishes, was more than just a way to let off sexual steam; it was also a way of refining sexual fire.

Ecstatic dance worship may well have aroused what in the East is known as kundalini, a sense of the sacredness of sexual energy. Calvin Green, an early Shaker theologian, put it like this:

> And when the soul is baptized into its life it is a spiritual recreation to all the feelings of soul and body; an employment far superior to any natural recreation, or carnal pleasure. In no earthly pursuit whatever have I ever experienced such

delightful feelings or such as would bear any real comparison to what I have felt in sacred devotion.[33]

More, in short, was involved than a mechanistic blowing off of sexual steam. Not only did they claim to have a transcendent experience, but later disciples claimed contact with the deceased spirit of Ann Lee. (Shakerism is a forerunner of Spiritualism.)

To outsiders, these spiritual orgies must have seemed crazy, possibly dangerous and frightening. To themselves, the believers "knew perfectly what those things (the wild behaviors) meant, and felt, therein, the greatest possible order and harmony, it being both the gift and the work of God for the time then present: and which bore the strongest evidence that the world was actually come to an end . . . and the day of judgment commenced."[34] Dancing for the Shakers, then, was a sensuous way of "ending" their bondage to ordinary reality, a way of regenerating themselves.

The Oneida Perfectionists

John Humphrey Noyes, as I said, saw sex in the Millennium not as something to be abolished, but fulfilled. Like Ann Lee, personal experience launched Noyes on his millennial odyssey. A deeply sensitive man, he became distraught when Abigail Merwin, his first supporter and idealized love, dropped him to marry another man. Many people find rejection intolerable, but Noyes's response was probably unprecedented. In a letter to a friend, he declared his intention to inaugurate the age of the resurrection on earth. He would do this by abolishing marriage and founding a divine love-feast. "In a holy community," he wrote, "there is no more reason why sexual intercourse should be restrained by law than why eating or drinking should be."[35]

Noyes revolted against the society he felt was holding back the Millennium, which, in his view, had begun with the resurrection of Christ. In the mind of Noyes, the general resurrection was already under way, which meant there should be no more marrying and no more marriage in the old style.

It is remarkable that this scholarly, at first self-effacing, New Englander managed to keep intact what was perhaps the most audacious social experiment in American history. To create a new society in which everyone was encouraged and allowed to enjoy sex with one another

141

is quite an achievement for a community still living in the wake of New England Puritanism. (Noyes himself came from Puritan stock.)

In the Heavenly Kingdom, there is no marriage or marrying; there is only the untrammeled bliss of love. "The secret history of the human heart will bear out the assertion that it is capable of loving any number of persons, and that the more it loves, the more it can love."[36]

Noyes built the Oneida community around the idea of a divine family; he did not promote irresponsible libertinism. The issue for Noyes was control. Self-control, he said, is an earnest of the Kingdom of God. By self-control, we sublimate our animal nature into our divine.

To free our amative nature demands control of the sexual impulse. Noyes enjoined "male continence," also known as *coitus reservatus* or *maithuna* in the Eastern tradition, and it means that although a man may enjoy sexual congress with a woman, he abstains from consummating the act as determined by nature. This was the chosen method of birth control at Oneida; surprisingly, it worked rather well. Not more than twenty accidental births were reported for some thirty-odd years.

From Noyes's prescriptions, it is clear that violent sexual emotion was discouraged; instead, the model seems to have been similar to what the modern Tantric philosopher Bhagwan Shree Rajneesh called a "valley orgasm."[37] The Perfectionists sought to spread an amative halo of harmony on all the practices of daily life.

Noyes was convinced that ordinary sex life was a burden, a source of torment, conflict, and economic bondage. His list of the ills that flow from what he calls the "law of marriage" is notable:

> It provokes to secret adultery, actual or of the heart. It ties together unmatched natures. It sunders matched natures. It gives to sexual appetite only a scanty and monotonous allowance, and so produces the natural vices of poverty, contraction of taste and stinginess or jealousy. It makes no provision for the sexual appetite at the very time when that appetite is strongest.[38]

The law of marriage must therefore be transcended. This can only be done by recovering the true meaning of sex. Toward that end, Noyes distinguished between the amative and the propagative function of sex. He argued that the amative is the primary, the true function of sex; for God first made Eve as Adam's "helpmeet." For Noyes, this meant something roughly equivalent to "divine playmate."

It was only after the catastrophe of the Fall, as part of the curse inflicted by God upon humankind after original sin, that humankind was expelled from the Eden of amative light and bliss into the dark cycle of procreation and human bondage. Existence was originally recreative, not procreative. Procreation causes economic burden, and the greater the burden, the more we stray from the amative purpose of sex.

In the resurrection, we return to the amative play, the pleasant society, of original sexuality. (Radical Freudians speak of "polymorphous perversity," sexuality not constrained by specialization or the "reality principle.") The Oneida Community pursued the Millennium through sexual evolution. Noyes wrote:

> Reconciliation of the sexes emancipates woman, and opens the way for vital society. Vital society increases strength, diminishes work, and makes labor attractive, thus removing the antecedents of death. First we abolish sin; then shame; then the curse on woman of exhausting child-bearing; then the curse on man of exhausting labor; and so we arrive regularly at the tree of life.

It was a complete system of thought. There is a whole chain of institutions that has to be broken, but the root is false sex, alienated sex, and violent, selfish, painful sex. The answer to our problems, sexual and economic, involves an expansion of our God-given amative potential. Noyes used the words "free love" with great trepidation. "Free Love with us does *not* mean freedom to love to-day and leave to-morrow; nor freedom to take a woman's person and keep our property to ourselves; nor freedom to freight a woman with our offspring and send her downstream without care or help . . ." The Oneidan was responsible, not promiscuous. "The tie that binds us together is . . . permanent and sacred, . . . for it is our religion."

Noyes was a great American dreamer. He dreamt of an America whose entire unregenerate system of social and metaphysical reality was "abolished." Subjection to fallen sex and subjection to death are two sides of the same coin. Did not Jesus associate the end of marriage with the end of death? Complex marriage thus points the way to liberation from death.

Noyes expected the entire scaffolding of ordinary reality to fall to pieces. The End will and must be total and systematic: "The sin-system, the marriage-system, the work-system, and the death-system, are all one, and must be abolished together." The Oneida Community, which thrived economically for more than a quarter of a century, was based on this vision of the end of ordinary social reality. In its place, Noyes contended, something new will arise: "Holiness, free love, association in labor, and immortality, constitute the chain of redemption, and must come together in their true order." It was, in my opinion, one of the boldest and most attractive versions of the Millennium Myth. It sure beats Saint John's rod of iron.

Is it really possible to reorganize human society on such a utopian basis? Noyes wrote a 678-page book *The History of American Socialisms*, which tried to answer the question. He concluded that the religious—we might say *transpersonal*—factor was the essential ingredient in every successful communistic experiment. (Noyes would not have been surprised by the collapse of Soviet communism, which suppressed, rather than cultivated, the religious factor.) Without the religious principle active in a social group, the "general depravity" or selfish part of humanity dominates, he said.

To radically renew society, we need radical spiritual powers; a new kind of people will have to emerge. As Noyes put it: "The men who are called to usher in the Kingdom of God will be guided, not merely by theoretical truth, but by the Spirit of God and specific manifestations of his will and policy, as were Abraham, Moses, David, Jesus Christ, Paul, &c." In other words, social and political revolution, for it to be positive and enduring, requires people to be in touch with nonordinary powers and consciousness.

In the eyes of the rational establishment, these ushers of the Kingdom are likely to appear as fanatics. "This will be called a fanatical principle," writes Noyes, "because it requires *bona fide* communication with the heavens, and displaces the sanctified maxim that the age of miracles and inspiration is past." Noyes understood the possibility of human perfection as depending on supernormal abilities. From there we may proceed to the social, the economic, the physiological—and to the sexual. In the absence of such a supernormal creative spiritual principle, social and economic experimentation is doomed to failure.

The Mormons

The Mormon experiment differs from Shakerism and Perfectionism; for one thing, it has survived, resulting in one of the fastest-growing religions in the world. From Utah to New Zealand, Mormon Missionaries have built temples round the globe. In some ways, Mormonism is the American dream come true, the most earnest pursuit of the Yankee New Jerusalem—a true "upbuilding" of the City of God on earth.

The Church of Jesus Christ of Latter-day Saints—so these millennialists call themselves. *Latter-day* refers, of course, to "last day." At its roots, Mormonism was a Church of the endtime. Millennium madness, some might say, was in the air in the 1840s. In the Northeast, thousands followed the farmer-prophet William Miller, in preparation for the Second Coming, the Rapture, and the New Jerusalem. The press had a field day. Despite all disappointments, prophecy continued to thrive; doomsday kept getting rescheduled. Millennial phantasies boiled up from an area of Western New York State said by historians to be "burned over" from the fiery preachings of tireless revivalists.

One man who emerged from this era of anomie and economic dislocation had more than a touch of the charming trickster in him, a Burt Lancaster-Elmer Gantry type. Joseph Smith, a handsome, visionary, and self-proclaimed "amative" young man from Palmyra, upstate New York, started out a crystal-gazer and treasure hunter and ended up a prophet, murdered in Carthage, Illinois, by a mob of vindictive rednecks.

Joseph Smith was what is nowadays called a "channeler." Joseph—or "Joe" as indignant monogamists dubbed him—"channeled" the revelations of the angel Moroni. The story, as Jacques Vallee[39] has pointed out, is very UFOish; Moroni seems like a typical "space brother" (replete with glowing light) who plays tricks with Joseph, showing him phantasmal plates of gold and a new bible (the Book of Mormon) engraved in hieroglyphics. No one has ever found any golden plates, but somehow the "hieroglyphic" Book was translated, becoming today's Book of Mormon.

The early Latter-day Saints ruffled the monogamous conscience of America; they preached and practiced, at first secretly, then openly, that infamous hangover from primitive times, polygamy or plural marriage. Polygamy was crucial to the Mormon's version of the Millennium Myth. Having plural wives, in the Mormon scheme, was sanctioned by the practice of the Hebrew patriarchs, and to practice plural marriage was to revive the age of prophecy.

According to Joseph Smith, the call to polygamy came in an overpowering vision. On July 12, 1843, Smith dictated a revelation

concerning the doctrine of "celestial marriage." According to this doctrine, a "new and everlasting covenant" was dawning; a new conse-
cration was being offered to humanity, a new way of relating to one
another. It was a way that would prepare us for eternal life. It involved
imitating Abraham and Isaac and Jacob and Moses, who were allowed
concubines, so they could "multiply and replenish the earth."

Let me quote some exact words from Smith's Contact at Large. The
reason God wants his elect to take many wives is "to multiply and
replenish the earth, according to my commandment, and to fulfill the
promise which was given by my Father before the foundation of the
world, *and for their exaltation in the eternal worlds. . . .*"

Polygamy is a step taken in accordance with a divine plan, a plan
meant to culminate in "exaltation." The exaltation promised by the
Book of Mormon is an exaltation to godhood; for according to Smith's
evolutionary theology, that is the plan of the universe. The universe
is a stage for the evolution of humans into gods.

But back to polygamy. Polygamy, for the Latter-day Saints, was part
of an attempt to restore sacred time. Plural marriage was an attempt to
recreate the original prophetic spirit of the patriarchs, those aboriginal
prophets who lived in close contact with angelic and divine agencies.
Based on his own psychic experiences, Smith simply claimed that
power for himself.

Joseph Smith and the patriarchs took their wives sacramentally, not
profanely. They took seriously the Biblical command to be fruitful,
and Smith would do his best to bring on the millennial Kingdom by
sowing his seeds with holy lavishness. Thus, to enlarge the Kingdom
of God, the Mormons took many wives.

But they took them, says the Book of Mormon, *in the spirit*. They
took their pretty wives, not as lusty unregenerate men do, but as co-
builders of the City of God; plural marriage, to the Mormons, was
Eternal and Celestial Marriage. The Mormon Priesthood sanctioned
and ratified these divine families, as networkers for the emerging Millennium. It was the ritual of sacred "sealing" that made the difference;
by performing a magical gesture, the marriage was made over into
something capable of enduring beyond the grave.

The Egyptian kings went to the next world, their psychic dou-
bles gaily provisioned with their wives. The Sumerian kings claimed
the right to the bride before the bridegroom. The Hebrew patriarchs
took their concubines in the bosom of Yahweh. In the wild and vast

landscape of America, it seemed the right thing for dashing underdog Joseph Smith, and his followers, to revive these ancient customs.

Scholars remain puzzled by this venture into plural marriage, which was so contrary to the old Puritan stock of most Mormons. Some unfriendly witnesses say that Joseph Smith was a lecher whose talk of celestial marriage was just a trick to follow his inclinations with women under cover of religious sanction.[40] Polygamy, in this view, is the perfect badge of ultra male-chauvinist individualism.

There was no question in Smith's mind about the subservient role of women in his millenarian scheme. There was certainly no precedent for polyandry in the Bible. In the "Revelation on the Eternity of the Marriage Covenant, including Plurality of Wives," given to "Joseph the Seer" in 1843, there was a message for Smith's wife Emma: "And I command mine handmaid, Emma Smith, to abide and cleave unto my servant Joseph, and to none else. But if she will not abide this commandment, she shall be destroyed, saith the Lord."

Smith, not long before being murdered in 1844, declared himself a candidate for the presidency of the United States. In *An Address to the American People*, we get a sample of his visionary platform:

> Abolish the cruel custom of prisons, penitentiaries, court-martials for desertion; and let reason and friendship reign over the ruins of ignorance and barbarity; yea, I would, as the universal friend of man, open the prisons, open the eyes, and open the ears of all people, to behold and enjoy freedom— unadulterated freedom.[41]

This passage, indistinguishable in spirit and almost in phrasing, from many transcendental outpourings of Walt Whitman, is an American exaltation of freedom. It is full of the optimism and progressivism of Enlightenment philosophers; it wants to break free from the last remnants of original sin. Indeed, this was a Mormon doctrine—quite in line with John Locke—that rejected original sin. It is safe to say that Smith's idea of penal reform would not go over in contemporary politics.

Perhaps the most powerful idea of Mormonism is one we met in the Renaissance and labeled the deification project. Mormon metaphysics is a strange mix of evolutionary materialism and crass supernaturalism. Mormons teach an evolutionary philosophy, summed up in a famous pronouncement: "As man is, God once was; as God is, man may become." Divine and human are orders of reality on the same continuum. Gods were once people; people may become gods. The mentality here is curiously akin to Renaissance self-deifiers like Pico and Ficino. A link between Renaissance humanists and American Mormons? It may sound odd to speak of it, yet the common source for these clearly diverse currents of thought is the Biblical idea that people are made in the image and likeness of God.

The Book of Mormon offers a startling image. God, it is said, literally has a human form. God, in fact, is a highly evolved human being; thus, any one of us humans might become a God. As we become gods, plural marriage becomes a necessity. As Gods we humans must create our universes. In Missouri and Illinois, and in the wild otherworldly land-scape of Utah, the Mormons imagined they were evolving into gods, sealing and building up their patriarchal seraglios for the wonders of "celestial marriage."

The dream of deification that fills the imagination of Mormonism is related to the dream of abolishing death. Abolishing death, for all of the founders of experimental communistic societies we have mentioned, depended on the reorganization of human sexual energies. The original Biblical idea had linked the end of marriage with the conquest of death and evolution to angelhood. Shakers thought that by abolishing sex entirely it would be possible to hasten the conquest of death. The Perfectionists were also opposed to propagation, which they regarded as a curse and stumbling block to the restoration of our Edenic potential. Finally, in sealing sacred polygamy the Mormons thought it possible to speed the evolution of humanity to godhood and immortality. This leads me to comment on another episode in the history of millennialism.

Spiritualism

In the spiritual ferment of New England and New York State, the forms of millennial consciousness multiplied. An aspect of the Millennium Myth, as I have noted, is that the dead are revived and rejoined in the Kingdom of the Saved. The Zoroastrian prophets saw this awakening from death occurring at the end of history.

For the Mormons, the coming of the Millennium was linked to the practice of the Latter-day Saints baptizing the dead. According to this Mormon doctrine, it is possible to sanctify and resuscitate dead souls.

The Millennium signifies the period when progress toward enlarging the divine family has begun, the dawn of the resuscitation of the species. This, in effect, implies increasing traffic between the world of the living and the world of spirits.

Perhaps, then, it is no accident that modern Spiritualism also had its origins in Western New York. Spiritualism began in 1848 with the Fox sisters in Hydesville, New York. Table raps and other unaccountable phenomena were reported to occur in the presence of these girls, which were taken to be communications from the spirit world. From this beginning a vast movement spread from Hydesville to Europe and South America, a type of religious revival based on alleged contact with discarnate intelligences.

John Humphrey Noyes spoke of "the Age of Spiritualism," which showed "that the world is full of symptoms of the coming of a new era of spiritual discovery."[42] Noyes, who counted himself an empiricist, took the new phenomena as signs that a new age of the spirit was dawning. Nordhoff, an investigative reporter who wrote about the Shakers and the Perfectionists, observed in 1875, "They (the Shakers) are pronounced Spiritualists, and hold that 'there is the most intimate connection and the most constant communion between themselves and the inhabitants of the world of spirits.'" Nordhoff adds, quoting a Shaker autobiography, that such things as "spiritualism, celibacy, oral confession, community, non-resistance, peace, the gift of healing, miracles, physical health, and separation from the world are the foundations of the new heavens."

American Spiritualism was not an isolated phenomenon. The new receptivity to the spirit world was part of a general awakening in nineteenth-century America of the millennial imagination. Spiritualism was one of several patterns of sign and symptom that a new world was emerging. The notable feature of American millennialism was its tendency to converge with ideas of science and empiricism. The tendency toward union of science and spirituality was evident as early as John Winthrop, whose contributions to millennialism were well matched by his contributions to early American science. And so with American Spiritualism we note that effort toward the empirical, an effort that found fruition in the work of the British founders of psychical research. As with Joseph Priestley and the French *philosophes*—not to mention some New Age writers—we encounter the dream of uniting modern science and ancient spirituality.[43]

An Evolving Dream

The American dream of the Millennium keeps evolving. It began with Columbus's medieval quest for the land of Eldorado, the terrestrial paradise thought to be somewhere in Asia, the hope of refurbishing a New Jerusalem. It proceeds to John Winthrop's city on a hill and transmogrifies into the temples of Mormonism. Somewhere along the line there is a decided shift from Hopkins' pursuit of spiritual happiness to Locke's preoccupation with real estate.

This shift, which is a shift in values, a coarsening and literalizing of the dream, clashes with Native America, which, as Sitting Bull said, was not "crazy for gold or possessions." It turns out that the millennial lust for real estate, the unalienable right to possess "property" and undertake its economic development is not environment-friendly. The "conquest" of the Western frontier is, geographically speaking, complete, and America, in a true spirit of Baconian hubris, has succeeded in putting the land to the rack and turning the earth into a gigantic factory. World history, as a conquest of this Protestant messianic assault, has entered the dark age of toxic proliferation, which, we might say, is the direct offshoot, the successful enactment, of John Winthrop's city on a hill. The hills and valleys have mushroomed with cities, with the numberless tentacles of a driving technology reaching out and squeezing the life out of the land.

American expansionism is rooted in visionary thinking. America, deep in its historical consciousness, is driven by powerful psychic forces, seen, for example, in the Mormonist, neo-Renaissance, self-deification project. Mormonism, as I said, is a growing religion; it appeals to deep parts of the American psyche.

Mormonism was born around the time of the myth of Manifest Destiny, which also appeals to deep parts of the American psyche. In 1845, a New York editor, John L. Sullivan, coined the phrase when he wrote that it was "the fulfillment of our manifest destiny to overspread the continent allotted by Providence for the free development of our expanding millions." At the time, the issue was the annexation of Texas. Manifest Destiny was again evoked in the dispute with Great Britain over Oregon; it was used to justify the Mexican War (1846–48), to rationalize the Alaska Purchase (1847), and to instigate the Spanish-American War in 1898. Manifest Destiny was spawned from the Millennium Myth and gave America's "expanding millions" the confidence to master the continental frontier.

During the twentieth century, the myth of Manifest Destiny evolved into the myth of America as "leader of the free world." Woodrow Wilson, dreamer of an enlightened League of Nations, is a central figure here, a man who conceived the destiny of America in messianic terms. And there is no doubt that the messianic spirit lives on in American politics, even if it manifests itself in uninspired sloganeering, and even if the purity of its origins has been sullied by crass economic interest.

I think we should remember the deep idealistic strain that slumbers in the American soul. However, the old consciousness of America as the Redeemer Nation is on the wane, especially after the mighty binge of the Cold War. In these the whimpering nineties, eroding economic opportunity, crime and moral muddle, the specter of uncanny disease, and creeping ecological disaster have become the new obsessions. The old myth that America should be the guardian of the "free world" begins to seem more like a fossil from a burnt-out age of prophecy.

The American dream has evolved from puritanical frugality to pagan consumerism. It must be said that the old version of the dream, when the Millennium Myth was in full force, was an incentive to extraordinary deeds. In sum, the Millennium Myth has been a guiding force at critical junctions in American history: the discovery of America, the founding of the first colonies, the territorial expansion from "sea to shining sea," the birth of the nation, the healing of the nation in the Civil War, and in the twentieth century, the leadership, of "the free world."

Does the original power of the myth still live in the people? Our leaders seem little inspired by the old rigorous puritanical vision of godliness and high destiny. The rhetoric is still present, to be sure, but one senses fatigue, hollowness, shrillness. The American dream is still alive, but for the most part, the dream has lost its spiritual content.

From an informal survey of college students, I culled these associations from the phrase "American dream": The American dream represents a "freedom to pursue your own goals, whether it is to own your own business, to have a loving family, or to indulge in your own fantasies." "The American dream is to entertain, feed, and fulfill everyone's life." "All the good things that America can offer, a house, a good-paying career, family, peace, and harmony."

At the same time, there are revivals of the Millennium Myth in its more extreme, more potent, more transformative forms. A steady

stream of oldtime evangelicals and fundamentalists is more than no-
ticeable. You have a fair share of Elmer Gantry types haunting the new
electronic churches, trickster types who know how to exploit the confusion and anxiety that troubles so many Americans. The Millennium
Myth also lives on through the tradition of American Spiritualism and
Transcendentalism and is related to much that goes under the rubric
of "New Age" ideas and practices. In coming chapters we look more
carefully at this sprawling development of twentieth-century America,
noting its links with more ancient tributaries.

But first a detour into the extreme shadow-side of our subject. The
twentieth century has been a century of apocalyptic upheavals. So let
us turn from the twilight of the American dream to the darkness of
the millennial nightmare. There are two grim exemplars. Let us begin
with Soviet Communism—the now-shattered dream of the proletarian
paradise.

The Proletarian Paradise

6

*This is our vocation: to become the Templars of this
Grail, to gird the sword about our loins on its behalf,
and joyfully to risk our lives in this last holy war that
will be followed by the millennium of freedom.*

FREDERICK ENGELS

T his chapter describes the apocalyptic climate of thought in the Russian Revolution. A sign of this is the extremism, and at times, the fanatical intensity with which nineteenth- and early twentieth-century Russian ideas were pursued. In religion, in philosophy, and in art, that wonderful bugbear the Russian "soul" repeatedly takes things to apocalyptic extremes.

Apocalyptic extremism feeds thoughts of revolution. The Russian philosopher Nicolas Berdyaev put it like this in 1931:

> Apocalyptic feelings, connected with the awaiting of Antichrist, are very strong among the people, and they come to light also in currents of religious thought among the cultured classes, in Russian writers and thinkers. And these tendencies remain as psychological forces, but in a secularized form, in movements which are divorced from Christian religious consciousness. Thus a schismatic and eschatological disposition is the fundamental psychological fact of the Russian nineteenth century; it will express itself both in a religious way and in an anti-religious way.[1]

Berdyaev observed that apocalyptic ideas may express themselves in antireligious ways. Instead of hating the Devil, one hates the bourgeoisie; instead of adoring the Savior, one adores the leader. In the twelfth century, they worshiped Mary the Mother of God; in the eighteenth century, they built altars to the Goddess of Reason.

Wipe the slate clean, said Locke, and renew society; throw off the chains of a decadent civilization, said Rousseau. The metaphors of philosophers turn into bombs tossed at the Russian Czar. Russian nihilists, populists, and anarchists thought in sweeping, finalistic terms; they wanted to erase the past, start the world over again. Up until, and even after 1917, the painters Malevich and Kandinsky, the poets Blok and Mayakovsky, and the dancer Nijinsky, exemplars of Russian soulfulness, were artists who trafficked in apocalyptic extremes. Or look at Karl Marx as millenarian. His ideas were like firestorms that swept across twentieth-century history. What kind of ideas? Why such a powerful influence? I believe much of the answer lies in the deep, prophetically deep, righteous indignation that Marx's critique of the bourgeoisie stirred up.

Traditional Spiritual Extremists

Berdyaev said the Revolution was a religious phenomenon. The cause of this goes back a ways. Russia's sense of its messianic mission may be seen as far back as the teachings of the fifteenth-century monk Philothey. Philothey believed that when Byzantium fell, Russia inherited true Christian Orthodoxy, and that world renewal was destined to come from this pure Christian wellspring, not from the soiled runnels of Roman Christianity. Philothey preached a coming rebirth of the spirit to take place under tutelage of Moscow, which he dubbed the "Third Rome."[2]

In general, Russian Orthodox Christianity is highly apocalyptic. Consider, for example, the tradition of icons. The art of the icon is a sacred art, a form of prayer, a ritual effort at communing with the Transcendent. In the Orthodox tradition, icons or holy images symbolize the Incarnation; the icon is a visual sign that God is becoming human, or that humanity is becoming godlike. This is very much in the spirit of the Millennium Myth, which sees the end of history as involving the transformation of humanity.

According to Leonid Ouspensky, the Incarnation shows "that the image is inherent to the essence of Christianity, since Christianity is the revelation of God-Man."[3] The God-Man was a staple of Renaissance humanism, whose catchphrase was "man is made in the image and likeness of God." Russian iconology also teaches that the image is the root of transformation. Saint John the Evangelist wrote, "We shall be like him [the Lord]; for we shall see him as he is" (1 John 3:2). By seeing, we become. The iconographic tradition, which meditates on the visible image of divine power, is thus part of "the living experience of the deification of man."[4] In other words, the icon is a blueprint of history as eschatology; a window on the future of humanity.

Certain images from the New Testament are especially venerated; for example, the Transfiguration: Christ stands on the summit of a mountain, speaking with Moses and Elias. The face of Christ shines "like the sun," his raiment "white as the light." And, we are told, a "bright cloud overshadowed" the disciples (Matt. 17:2, 5). The image is futuristic, for, according to Saint Basil, the Transfiguration was "an anticipation of His glorious Second Coming."[5] Iconology represents the tame side of Russian apocalypticism. The Russian Orthodox tradition encouraged more extreme endtime pursuits. The Khlysty, for example, practiced flagellation; an ascetic enclave initiated by Danila Filippov, they sought the gifts of the spirit through self-mutilation, strict vegetarianism, and abstention from carnal relations.

Here is a widespread motif: the belief that you can awaken spiritual energy through the mastery of sex. It fascinated Russian thinkers like Fedorov, Solovyov, and Berdyaev. Nietzsche described the ascetic as somebody burning with the will to power, which applies to the Russian Khlysty who thought that by mastering their carnal natures, they would transcend human laws. We are familiar with the type, the so-called "Antinomians"—weird progeny, I suppose, of Jesus who healed, contrary to Jewish law, on the Sabbath.

The Russian Nihilists, who were forerunners of the Revolution, were antinomian rebels against conventional morality. The most famous fictional antinomian was Dostoevsky's Raskolnikov of *Crime and Punishment*. Raskolnikov—the name means "schismatic"—was possessed by the idea that he had the right to kill an old landlady because he fancied himself above the law. Raskolnikov has a touch of the old Orthodox believer—stubborn, fanatical, nihilistic. Like the old Orthodox believer, he wants to destroy the established order. At the same time, of course, he dreams of creating a new and exotic order.

A fanatical zeal to crash the gates of heaven was evident in a group that grew out of the Old Believing Flagellants—the Skoptsy. The Skoptsy, if anybody, illustrate Russian apocalyptic extremism. *Skoptsy* means "eunuch." Remember (Matt. 19:12): "And there are eunuchs, who have made themselves eunuchs for the sake of the kingdom of heaven." Skoptsy were Russian extremists who took the remark about eunuchs literally; they castrated themselves, hoping thereby to hasten the coming of the Kingdom. In the same spirit, Origen castrated himself in the third century.

In 1757, the founder of the self-mutilation cult, Kondrati Selivanov, a Khlyst, announced that 144,000 human souls converting to Skoptsy would launch the Last Judgment. Selivanov, like Shaker Ann Lee, believed sex was the cause of human bondage; the key, then, to the Kingdom of God was to master sex. The Russian solution: Remove the offending sex organ. Control the *ophos archaios*, the "ancient serpent power," which, according to John of Patmos, was literally the key to the Millennium. Master this vital force, and we might unleash a renaissance of spirit—call forth the New Jerusalem, bring down to earth the Kingdom of Heaven. So ran the logic that drove so many Russian fanatics.

The practice of self-mutilation continued through the Russian Revolution; in 1927, during forced collectivization, the sect was two thousand strong.[6] Old Believers mutilated themselves when they were persecuted, or burnt themselves to death, making a cult of "self-burners." Individual self-immolation, it was ardently hoped, was a means of igniting apocalyptic ekpyrosis, a world-renewing conflagration. The self-burners were literalizers of Biblical metaphors. They thought they could hasten the Day of the Lord, which "will come like a thief, and then with a roar the sky will vanish, the elements will catch fire and melt away, and the earth and all that it contains will be burned up" (2 Pet. 3:10).

Thinkers of the End

Nineteenth-century Russian thinkers carry on the spirit of apocalyptic extremism, casting powerful influences on the tangle of events that led to the Russian Revolution. These influences may be difficult to discern, confounded with the secular; still, there were telltale signs of chiliasm on the move.

Take, for example, Russian antireligiousness. Again, let us recall Berdyaev, who lived through the Revolution of 1917 and watched the antireligious psychology in action. Berdyaev calls the Russians a "people of the End." People of the End are prone to schism, to thinking divisively; their mode of thought involves the principle of "either-or," or "all-or-nothing."

An affinity for schism, for becoming schismatics (*raskol* or *raskolniki*), is a feature of Russian history, notable among the so-called *intelligentsia*, intellectual schismatics. The intelligentsia argued a great deal about the end of time, the end of History, and the end of "man." Philosopher of history Benedetto Croce put it like this: "What are our histories of civilization, of progress, of humanity . . . save the form of ecclesiastical history in harmony with our times?—that is to say— . . . of the strife against the powers of darkness, of the successive treatments of the new evangel made afresh with each succeeding epoch?"[7]

The messianic impulse, Croce's "new evangel made afresh," was evident in the transposed religious psychology of the Russian intelligentsia. The basic phenomenon, Berdyaev said, involved:

> a transposition of religious motives and religious psychology into a non-religious or anti-religious sphere, into the sphere of social problems, so that the spiritual energy of religion flows into social channels, which thereby take on a religious character, and become a breeding-ground for a peculiar form of social idolatry.[8]

When an unconscious religious psychology dominates a secular culture, people tend to invest finite ideas and institutions with absolute value—a kind of delusion some call "idolatry." Perhaps the most obvious example was the ritual preservation of Lenin's waxed face and embalmed corpse on display in Moscow, becoming an object of state cult, worship, and pilgrimage.

Russian thinkers of the End were attracted to anarchism. Modern anarchism is a revival of the antinomian will to power, the mystic-revolutionary idea that conventional morality is dispensable on the road to true freedom. For the anarchist this means rejection of irrational authority.

Although the word *anarchism* typically suggests chaos, violence, and terrorism, anarchists like Godwin, Tolstoy, and Kropotkin generally opposed violence. They rejected authority to affirm ideals of natural justice and community. They were more pacific in their anarchism and, like Chinese Taoists, preached the return to a form of social life of Edenic spontaneity. Historian George Woodcock defines anarchism as "a system of social thought, aiming . . . at the replacement of the authoritarian state by some form of nongovernmental co-operation between free individuals."[9] It was an ideal at odds with the irrational authority of established society.

William Godwin, father of Mary Shelley, was a notable anarchist, whose great poet-disciple was Percy Bysshe Shelley. Shelley evoked the anarchist dream of returning to a golden age:

> The earth's great age begins anew,
> The golden years return,
> The earth doth like a snake renew
> Her winter weeds outworn . . .

Shelley's poetic anarchism, which traffics in images of ecological renewal, was also unsympathetic to violence.

Violence, however, was more popular with some of the Russians, where the negative side of the creed seems to have gotten the upper hand, and the passion to destroy authority became an end in itself. The best example of this was Michael Bakunin, an aristocrat turned anarchist, a monumental eccentric with gargantuan appetites, and a man with a taste for cabals and conspiracies. Less a thinker than a doer, Bakunin fled czarist society to Berlin, where he met the Young Hegelians. The Young Hegelians, who believed that history was constant change, took revolution, not reaction, as the byword of the avant-garde. The revolutionary tone of Bakunin's influential *Reaction in Germany* was blatantly apocalyptic:

> There will be a qualitative transformation, a new living, life-giving revelation, a new heaven and a new earth, a young and mighty world in which all our present dissonances will be resolved into a harmonious whole.[10]

In this sentence, two influences are seen to blend: the Biblical, evident in that all-enchanting phrase, "a new heaven and a new earth"; and the Hegelian, where we are told that "dissonances will be resolved into a harmonious whole."

Bakunin fixated on the dissonances, sticking grimly to the negative side of the Hegelian dialectic. According to Hegel, contradiction is the force that moves things; first, there is negation—then, affirmation. Bakunin rang all the changes of his Russian soul on the creative power of destruction. Bakunin, whose ideas, life, and legendary prison escapes kindled revolutionary enthusiasm, had little to say about the positive side of revolution. His main idea was that a perfect society should be free of government; the top priority was getting rid of oppressive government—the negative phase of Hegel's dialectic.

Here are the words Bakunin is most remembered for: "Let us put our trust in the eternal spirit which destroys and annihilates only because it is the unsearchable and eternally creative source of all life. The urge to destroy is also the urge to create." Bakunin's phrase "the eternal spirit which destroys" is a lift from Goethe's *Geist der stets vereint*, "the spirit that perpetually negates." That spirit, of course, was Mephistopheles. As with other nineteenth-century Romantics, Bakunin's heros were Goethe's Mephistopheles and Milton's Satan. Romantics and anarchists of the nineteenth century were inclined to join forces with Antichrist, raising his Satanic Majesty to a principle of creative freedom.

To bring about the new heaven and earth, the old heaven and earth must be destroyed. Bakunin dwelled passionately on this destruction. Exiled in Paris in the 1840s, he described how he felt fighting with the working class: "I breathed through my senses and through all my pores the intoxication of the revolutionary atmosphere. It was a holiday without beginning and without end."[11]

In 1848, he wrote his *Appeal to the Slavs*, now calling for destruction of the Austrian Empire and for a federation of all Slavs, foretelling a messianic destiny for the Russian nation and proclaiming the Russian people were the hope of the world. In Bakunin's rendering of the Millennium Myth, the Russians were the chosen people. Bakunin's prophecy was half-right: "The star of revolution will rise high and independent above Moscow from a sea of blood and fire, and will turn into the lodestar to lead a liberated humanity."[12] He was right about the sea of blood and fire, wrong about it leading to a liberated humanity. The Myth is totalistic; so was Bakunin's anarchism:

> The anarchist promoted social and cultural revolution. We must first of all purify our atmosphere and transform completely the surroundings in which we live, for they only corrupt our instincts and our wills, they constrict our hearts and our intelligences.[13]

The anarchists aimed to overthrow society *in toto*, to tear up the cultural roots of consciousness. Bakunin, obsessed with negative dialectic, agitated all his life for revolution.

One can become enchanted by glowing archetypal images of power and renewal but lose sympathy for real people. Isaiah Berlin put it like this:

> The fate of individuals did not greatly concern him; his units were too vague and too large; 'First destroy, and then we shall see.' Temperament, vision, generosity, courage, revolutionary fire, elemental force of nature, these Bakunin had to overflowing. The rights and liberties of individuals play no part in his apocalyptic vision.[14]

In 1869, Bakunin met a younger man more inclined to act out the darker phantasies of mystic revolution. Sergai Nechayev, a student from Moscow University, a master of intrigue, conspiracy, and disinformation, flitted nefariously through revolutionary circles, preaching extreme nihilism. His formula for revolution was simple: "Total Annihilation."[15] Nechayev was Dostoevsky's model for Peter Verkhovensky in *The Possessed*. Bakunin was drawn to this strange man as someone he sensed had the demented courage to turn his reckless ideas into deeds.

The two collaborated on several unsigned, highly inflammatory, highly extremist pamphlets. The most extreme was titled *Revolutionary Catechism*, which was found in Nechayev's possession when he was arrested in 1870 by Swiss officials. The *Catechism* describes the duties of the revolutionary; he must renounce his individuality and become a kind of exterminating monk:

> The revolutionary is a man under vow. He ought to occupy himself entirely with one exclusive interest, with one thought and one passion: the Revolution. . . . He has only one aim, one science: destruction. . . . Between him and society there is war to the death, incessant, irreconcilable.[16]

Nechayev was an apocalyptic nihilist. He reveals his transposed religiosity with his talk of being "under vow." Nechayev vowed to serve the nihilistic god of death and destruction. What we can call the Nechayev mentality helped smooth the way to the Bolshevik power grab of 1917, finding its supreme expression in Joseph Stalin who, like other Russian nihilists, began in the seminary.

Nikolay Chernyshevsky, one of the founding fathers of Russian nihilism, hated slavery and injustice and became a martyr to the religion of rational egoism. He began in the Eastern Orthodox church and ended in a fanatically serious pursuit of the Millennium, spending over twenty-five years of his life in the prisons of Siberia and the Peter and Paul Fortress.

What drove Chernyshevsky and his compatriots was the need to sweep away the old world and create a new and radically better one. The Russian Revolutionaries shared a single myth, says Isaiah Berlin: "that once the monster was slain, the sleeping princess—the Russian peasantry, would awaken without further ado and live happily forever after." This was populist sentiment in high gear. Chernyshevsky struck a chord of sympathy with many disenfranchised souls, the alienated and the uprooted, whose numbers continued to multiply, to be finally seduced en masse by Lenin's promise of the proletarian paradise.

Deep in the world memory is a vision of cosmic transformation. Among the Russian Old Believers, it took the form of expecting apocalypse. The Russian nihilists, anarchists, and populists were as taken by this vision as the Old Believers. Again, to quote Sir Isaiah: "All these thinkers share one vast apocalyptic assumption: that once the reign of evil—autocracy, exploitation, inequality—is consumed in the fire of the revolution, there will arise naturally and spontaneously out of its ashes a natural, harmonious, just order."[17]

The apocalyptic assumption is that it is possible to end history, to leap over fundamental barriers, and to enter a new phase of socio-cosmic evolution. The leaders of the Revolution drew charismatic power from playing on this apocalyptic assumption, buried deep in the Russian Orthodox mentality.

In 1863, Chernyshevsky published a novel *What Is to Be Done?*—whose title was picked up by a later fan, Vladimir Lenin. Not known for its literary merit, the novel was a testament to the revolutionary creed of the New Men (this expression came from Turgenev's novel about nihilists, *Fathers and Children*). It was a tract on feminism. Chernyshevsky felt that since women have been oppressed for so long by men, the men of today owe their wives plenty of latitude for self-development, especially in matters of sex. Chernyshevsky practiced what he preached, marrying a pretty and vivacious lady from his hometown Saratov, who, it must be said, took full advantage of her emancipation.

Dostoevsky joked about the compliment a nihilist pays his wife: "My dear, hitherto I had only loved you," says the nihilist, after finding she has taken a lover; "Now I respect you."[18] Like the Shakers and the

Oneida Perfectionists, the Russian nihilists took to heart the words of Jesus about the abolition of marriage in the Kingdom of Heaven.

Though a rich man, the main character of *What Is To Be Done?* gives his possessions away, shuns wine and women, goes on eighty-hour study sprees, and sleeps on a bed of nails. Rakhmetov, an updated Khlyst or Skoptsy, is an apocalyptic masochist.

Religion, in fact, bristles just below the surface of these Russian extremists. Most nihilists were university students and professed atheists, yet they often admired Christ as a great revolutionary. And so before Dimitry Karakozov shot the Czar, he made a pilgrimage to the Monastery of the Trinity and Saint Sergius.

The term *nihilist* was popularized in Turgenev's novel *Fathers and Children*, many of whose characters were modeled after real people: usually young university dropouts; children of poor gentry, of priests; affected in behavior, hair long, blue spectacles, furious smokers, titanic tea drinkers, sporters of walking-sticks—they mixed wild idealism with furious resentment.

Dostoevsky's *The Possessed* recreated the feverish apocalyptic mindset of these revolutionary Russian extremists. They protested against the established order, hijinxed bourgeois mores, and, above all, armed themselves with heavy theory about the ills of society. In some ways, the Russian nihilists were similar to the hippies and yippies of the 1960s, though the sixties had LSD and the Beatles to temper its violent leanings.

Extreme Russian Nihilism led to acts of terrorism. The culminating Russian act of terrorism in the nineteenth century was to toss an assassin's bomb at the feet of Czar Alexander II on March 1, 1881, killing him. In killing the Czar, the young male and female assassins were acting out Nechayev's gospel of terror and destruction.

The yearning to smash the establishment fed populist sentiment. Populism sanctified the proletariat, around whom the Russian intelligentsia placed a halo of divine chosenness. Populism tended toward *Slavophilism*, which exalted Russia for lofty historic purposes. Even now, after the downfall of Soviet communism, Slavophilism and xenophobia are rising in Russia. The satanic adversary in the Slavophile scenario was Europe. Decadent, rationalistic, disgustingly bourgeois, Europe, it was thought, would sink in the battle that was coming at the end of history.

Anarchists, nihilists, populists, Slavophiles—each in their own ways—thinkers of the End. Government had to end, the bourgeoisie had to end, Europe had to end—everything had to be swept away before the heavens could open and the Russian New Jerusalem descend to earth.

However, not all extremism took a nihilistic form; some Russian makers of the Millennium Myth had more pious obsessions. Such was Fedorov's dream of resurrection. Nikolay Fedoravich Fedorov was preeminent as a thinker of the End. Solovyov, Dostoevský, and Tolstoy all admired him, a man who merged science and apocalyptic imaginings. The big issue for Fedorov was the scientific resurrection of the dead. Saintly and ascetic in daily life, he could not bear the idea of the death, the irrevocable loss, of loved ones. Death sickened this master of metaphysical agitprop.

Fedorov, librarian and polymath, believed in the mystical unity of the human family and that science should wage final warfare against the "dis-unity" of society. The secret to unifying the human race lay in retrieving the dead. How could this happen? Fedorov thought it possible to reconstitute the body's material components. "Put together the engine," he said, "and consciousness will return to it."[19] A crude speculation, Fedorov had not a clue to *how* this might be possible; all he knew was revolt against death. Fedorov's passion is alive and well in America today in the "immortalist" movement.

Fedorov was scientist and mystic, social critic and global activist. In 1891, while Russia was suffering from crop failure and famine, he heard of American engineering efforts to control the weather. Fedorov immediately put the American experiments in an apocalyptic framework. The human race, he declared, should employ itself in building a technology to resurrect its deceased ancestors. The use of explosives to change weather patterns and deal with the food problem inspired him. In *The Question of Brotherhood*, he wrote:

> At the present time everything serves war. . . . If armies were charged with the duty of adopting everything which they now adapt to war to the control of the forces of nature, the task of war would in fact be converted into the common task of the whole human race.[20]

Fedorov's common task was to resurrect the dead. To accomplish this called for a revolution of life style. In particular, it called for a revolution in our attitude toward work. Remember, Fedorov was driven by the apocalyptic urge to restore our lost "relatedness." Fedorov, who slept on bare boards and was too modest to be photographed, was a sworn enemy to work that was unrelated to meaning. "The separation of thought from work is the greatest of all misfortunes, incomparably worse than the separation into rich and poor."[21] The Marxists called it alienation, labor for mere wages. Fedorov's message: Bring thought into our work, meaning into our lives. But what gives meaning? For Fedorov it was the apocalyptic goal of restoring the dead. This ultimate goal would regulate technology. Thus, for Fedorov the true purpose of technology was to reconstitute the atoms of all the human beings who have died, somehow to recollect and to put them back together again. Fedorov preached the eschatology of Humpty Dumpty, a heroic phantasy that flouted the Second Law of Thermodynamics.

Fedorov insisted that reconstitution was our duty and that to be content with progress, at the cost of forgetting our ancestors, was unconscionable. Use technology to hasten the resurrection, said the Russian thinker; the material improvement of life is just the first step. Grander prospects are before us. Technology, for Fedorov, had an eschatological agenda—to resurrect the dead and thus bring on the end of history.

We saw the Millennium Myth looking for scientific support in the Renaissance and the Enlightenment. Fedorov also looked for scientific support, but he was strangely focused on restoring the deceased rather than improving the present or the future. As the Hebrew prophets imagined the End, the violent elements of nature are pacified, the lion and the lamb learn to play together. Although Fedorov was a Biblical patriarch, he was not afraid to question the patriarchs of science or to ask for their help in the pursuit of the Millennium.

Fedorov takes his place among the scientific eschatologists such as Joseph Priestley and Samuel Hopkins. He wanted to apply meteorology to the control of harvesting and thus solve the food supply problem. Fedorov called the new regime he imagined a "psychocracy." The guiding ideal: Convert the blind, destructive forces of nature and make them serve humankind. Fedorov dreamed of harnessing solar energy and speculated on ways of exploiting the electromagnetic energy surrounding the earth as a medium for colonizing other planets.

Nevertheless, all these grand enterprises were just warm-up exercises for the main job—the physics of resurrection. Like Zoroaster, Fedorov wanted to reconstitute and reunite the entire human family.

Some of Fedorov's phantastic ideas influenced Soviet thinkers such as N. A. Setnitsky, who said in his book *On the Ultimate Ideal* (1932) that, in Soviet Russia, science has "a peculiar mission of expert men for carrying out the task of studying the blind and deadly forces of nature"[22] and for putting them to work on behalf of humanity.

In 1932, the Soviet press echoed some rather Fedorovian ideas when they talked of diverting the Gulfstream to warm Siberia and (less Fedorovian) of diverting icebergs toward England to freeze the cold-hearted capitalists to death! Thus, in the Russian finale of history, technology rearranges the forces of heaven and earth, destroying the capitalist Antichrist.

Artists of the Russian Millennium

The Revolution produced great painters, sculptors, poets, and dancers. A tremendous discontented energy had been building up all through the nineteenth century that boiled over into millennial imaginings.

Consider, for example, Vaslav Nijinksy, the great dancer, who was said to play tricks on gravity when he curveted through space. In 1918 and 1919, while Russia was at war, Nijinsky lived with his wife in St. Moritz, Switzerland, where he was declining into what the world calls "madness." During this transition Nijinsky painted, dabbled in music, and wrote his diary.

The Diary of Vaslav Nijinsky is a rare book. It takes the reader on a journey into a rare soul. The book is a bubbling stream of outcries, childlike and disarming, short choppy sentences that jump from peak to peak with the logic of the Mad Hatter. Here is a sample:

> Many people think about money, I need some to carry out my plans; we all have our plans and aims, and we earn money to realize them, but our problems are different. I am God's problem, not Antichrist's. I am not Antichrist. I am Christ. I will help mankind.

Nijinsky begins by noting that people think about money (a sane enough observation), and from there rushes to the idea that he is

Christ and plans to save the human race. Now, messiahship is a motif of the Millennium Myth, and Nijinsky lapsed into messianic delusions.

"I suffered more than any one else in the world," he wrote at the start of his diary. But thanks to his suffering, Nijinsky found a certain intimacy with God. "The fire inside me does not go out. I live with God. I came here to help—I want paradise on earth. At the moment earth is an inferno." Indeed. The world was at war in 1918. In the midst of the hell of human war, Nijinsky dreams of paradise on earth.

Nijinsky rants against commerce and science, obstacles to paradise, causes of war. "I know what starts wars . . . commerce, (which) . . . is the death of mankind. I would like all factories to be destroyed . . . The earth is suffocating, therefore I am asking everybody to abandon factories. I know that this is necessary for the salvation of the earth . . . I am the Savior . . . all the scientists must abandon their books and come to me."

Jungian John Perry has studied the interplay between archetypal Messiah phantasies and psychosis. Many of Perry's psychotic patients underwent a type of inner apocalypse, a disintegration and renewal, dominated by symbols and archetypes of the Millennium Myth. Perry was intrigued by Nijinsky's messianic ravings.

Perry found that he had to "transliterate" the images of his messianic schizoid patients. "For the statement 'I am called by a special election to save the world,' one reads instead, 'There's an image appearing in my psychic world representing a redeemer, a messianic hero.'"[23] The image, according to Perry, has a valid psychic function; problems result from getting too literally entangled in the image. The "psychotic ego identifies with each archetypal image or process," which, says Perry, chokes off the archetype's creative potential. The Millennium Myth furnishes matter for the creative self as well as for the psychotic ego.

If in Nijinsky himself we find the madness of messianic inflation, in poet Vladimir Mayakovsky the messianic impulse takes a different turn. Mayakovsky projected messiahship onto a specific historical personage, the great Lenin.

In 1917, Mayakovsky was twenty-four and had a record of revolutionary antics that had gotten him into trouble with authorities. In 1912, he was one of four who signed the Russian Futurist Manifesto *A Slap in the Face of Public Taste*. (The Italian founder of Futurism, Marinetti, had made a successful tour in Russia; Futurism ceremoniously spat on the past and chiliastically exalted the "modern"—speed, violence, the machine.)

In 1914, Mayakovsky wrote the iconoclastic poem "The Cloud in Pants," originally "The Thirteenth Apostle." Berdyaev's transposed religiosity fired this would-be Saint Paul of the Russian Revolution. "The Thirteenth Apostle" consisted of four parts, summed up by Mayakovsky under four slogans: "Down with your love!" (Mayakovsky, like John Humphrey Noyes and other millenarian rebels, agonized over rejected love, turning sour grapes into apocalyptic visions.) "Down with your art!" "Down with your system!" And finally: "Down with your religion!"

"The Cloud in Pants" is an amazing poem, full of wrath, menace, and tenderness; for a taste, consider this—an aside to his mother, a comment on himself:

> Mother!
> Your son is beautifully sick . . .
> Every word,
> be it even a joke,
> that his scorched mouth belches out,
> leaps like a naked whore through the smoke
> out of a burning brothel.

A prophet calling for a total renovation of human life, Mayakovsky cannot resist assimilating his prophecy of revolution (off by one year!) to crucifixion imagery:

> Crowned with the thorns of revolt,
> the year 1916 draws nigh.

When the Revolution came, Mayakovsky welcomed and called it "my revolution."[24] He then turned to spreading the new communist gospel in the popular media, writing for magazines and newspapers, making political posters, and writing a dozen screenplays.

When Lenin died on January 22, 1924, the hyperbolic bard vented the national grief in a long poem called "Vladimir Ilyich Lenin." Mayakovsky called it "the most important piece of work I have ever done."[25] Mayakovsky, poet of the Revolution, invested Lenin with the attributes of a messiah. Nijinsky's messianic madness has now mutated into Mayakovsky's messianic revolution. All at once, we are back with

the medieval mystic rebels who put their hopes in the Angelic Pope.
Here are some snippets:

> He took in all the planet with his mind,
> saw things out of reach for the common eye.

Lenin, says the poet, was the clairvoyant eye of the human race. Like
the Angelic Pope or Last World Emperor of the Middle Ages, Lenin
fought fiercely against the evil principle—Capital:

> a human, working-class dictatorship arose,
> to checkmate Capital and crush its prison-castle.

Mayakovsky feels strongly about Lenin:

> Then why is it, no kin of his, I'd welcome death,
> crazy with delight, would gladly perish
> so that he might draw a single breath.

Here, it seems to me, we hear the echoes of ancient martyrs, people
who believed that a new spirit had begun to blow across history and
were willing, often with disarming readiness, to give up their lives to
prove their beliefs. Mayakovsky says any decent Russian would do it:

> Not a single soul of us, I reckon,
> in all the mines and mills from East to West
> would hesitate to do the same at the slightest beckon.

Mayakovsky carols the camaraderie of martyrdom, wants to unite with
the great soul of suffering humanity, and treats death with apocalyptic
bravado.

The great soul of humanity was embodied in the Messiah; Lenin
had led humanity in the last war with "Capital, His Majesty," the evil
force that:

> pumped gold into the bellies of banks,
> while at the workbenches, lean and humped,

the working class whispered and closed ranks. The poet reminds the
people, a great leader is coming:

> But remember: he is coming, he is nigh,
> The Man, the Champion, the Avenger, the Fighter.

In a word, the Messiah.

> And the call came rumbling from shack and slum,
> covering the whimper of kiddies:
> Come protector! Redeemer, come!
> And we'll go to battle or wherever you bid us!

To Mayakovsky, the word *proletariat* sounds "like mighty music that'll rouse the dead to get up and fight." This music that promises to raise the dead reminds me of the Native American Ghost Dance of late nineteenth-century America, Native Americans believing, against all reason, that by means of the dance—hyper-Nijinsky—it was possible to resurrect the dead.

Like Fedorov, Mayakovsky wants history to come to an end, wants the dead to rise, and wants all the old accounts settled. The end of history is possible, chants Mayakovsky, because the Messiah is coming:

> He is coming—sage and leader—to declare
> war on you, to end war for all time.

Like Woodrow Wilson, whom Nijinsky also adored, Mayakovsky believed it possible to fight a war that will end all wars—a quintessential apocalyptic dream. To end war for all time—this is a way of talking about the end of history. For Mayakovsky the end of history was at hand, a new wisdom set free:

> I knew a worker—he was illiterate
> yet he had listened to a speech by Lenin
> and so knew all.

Lenin, by sheer force of spirit, transmits a revolutionary gnosis to an illiterate worker. Lenin was no ordinary human thinker; his thought-word was a lightning rod, sent to dispel the darkness of millennia:

> Slashed by the lightning of Lenin's pamphlets
> his leaflets showering on surging crowds.
> The class drank its fill of Lenin's light
> and, enlightened, broke from the gloom of millennia.

Lenin's tomb was for seventy years a shrine for pilgrimage. Lenin was a saint, an avatar, a boddhisattva:

> Raise the banner of holy war
> against the world-wide bosses!

Despite the grand words, Mayakovsky shot himself in 1930, his messianic mania exploded by disappointed love and the onset of Stalinist Russia.

Another revolutionary poet, Alexander Blok, died in 1921; Blok was spared Stalin. In Blok, who started as a Symbolist and was seduced by the Revolution, we also see some robust messianic imagery frothing up; here, instead of making Lenin messiah, the proletariat is outright sacralized. The proletariat becomes the new vehicle for turning history into eschatology.

Blok called his greatest revolutionary poem "The Twelve"—echo of the Twelve Apostles. In "The Twelve" we catch the dirt, sprawl, and thunder of the masses en route, the irresistible rush of human forces:

> Foreward, foreward, foreward,
> Working-People.

It is a war of the gods:

> What did it ever save you from,
> The icon framed in gold?

So smash the icons! The world is in the toils of rebirth. All the old images must be broken and room made for new images. All this is very perplexing, and freaked-out capitalists scurry for cover:

> Wind the slasher
> Frost no better!
> The bourgeois at the crossroads
> Tucks his nose into his fur.

Blok ends this hymn to the proletarian masses in a surprising way. In a metaphorical twist, he equates the suffering proletariat with the old image of the Christian Messiah:

> Oh they march with sovereign tread . . .
> in advance with flag blood-red . . .
> crowned in wreath of roses white—
> Jesus Christ walks on ahead.

Old archetypes never die; they just pop up in queer places—like revolutions.

The revolutionary zeitgeist inspired the Russian poets; it also inspired the painters and sculptors. Fedorov used science to talk up his apocalyptic obsessions; Russian revolutionary artists used art. For Gaubo, Malevich, and Kandinsky, art was metaphysics in action. Art was the pursuit of a new reality, a systematic rejection of the old heaven and the old earth. Art was the creation of a new heaven, as they said, each work possessing its own "inner necessity." For these Russian artists, art became a pursuit of the Millennium.

Wassily Kandinsky painted the first completely abstract painting. In 1910, seven years before the political revolution, he began his own artistic revolution. Kandinsky renounced the imitation of nature and aimed instead to create new artworlds, new reality specimens. Kandinsky's thought, which fed on theosophy and occultism, was meant as an all-around slap in the face of the establishment. Nonobjective art was Freud's discontent with civilization announcing itself in a new way; a call to arms against the prevailing view of things. Let there be new realities, beyond the furniture of pedestrian "things"—new creations of form and color.

Influences on Kandinsky were many. Friendly to his native Russian Orthodoxy, he was also a science watcher. More keen on the poetics of science than science itself, Kandinsky found eschatology in quantum mechanics, which he thought proved how insubstantial the material world was. When he heard that the atom had been split, he rushed to the apocalyptic conclusion: "The destruction of the atom seemed to me to be the same as the destruction of the world."

Kandinsky meant this metaphysically; material things are phantoms of a more elusive, a more subtle reality. One thinks of the atomic bomb. Splitting the atom meant that a new—indeed, an apocalyptic power—had entered history. In the lexicon of current times, nuclear apocalypse remains a live metaphor.

Kandinsky's apocalyptic esthetics borrowed from Rudolf Steiner. According to Steiner, Western civilization is riding the rails of history toward self-destruction; only spiritual revolution can save us. Steiner, as in Kandinsky's Orthodox iconic tradition, said art should serve the spirit: " . . . anyone who immerses himself in the hidden internal treasures of his art is an enviable co-worker on the spiritual pyramid which will reach to heaven."[26]

Art thus becomes a vehicle for apocalypse, and Kandinsky's abstract improvisations become epiphanies of heaven on earth. His art wants to graduate from the role of imitator of objective nature—the object is the enemy and must be destroyed. Echoing Bakunin, for Kandinsky every act of destruction was an act of creation.

Kandinsky's art was honed by Russian Orthodox imagery. He painted Saint George four times, the Last Judgment several times, and the Resurrection of the Dead. Saint George, whose business is to slay dragons, is a surrogate messiah; Resurrection and the Last Judgment are apocalyptic themes. In his *Autobiography*, Kandinsky expressed his chiliastic intent:

> In many ways art is similar to religion. . . . Its development consists in sudden illuminations, similar to lightning . . . this illumination shows with blinding light new perspectives, new truths. Was the New Testament possible without the Old? Could our time, that of *the threshold of the 'third' revelation*, be thinkable without a second?[27]

I have added the emphasis because I want to focus on the fact that in the twentieth century the medieval Joachite expectation of a third age, a third revelation, a third manifestation of spirit, was still very much alive. Kandinsky related the radical nonobjective art he was creating to a new age of spirit—*a third revelation*.

Kasimir Malevich was another Russian founder of nonobjective art with new age preoccupations. Like most millenarians, Malevich wanted to rebirth the world. To that end, according to Malevich, natural forms must be dominated and destroyed. "Things have disappeared like smoke," he wrote in 1914, "to gain the new artistic culture, art approaches creation as an end in itself and domination over the forms of nature."[28]

In 1913, Malevich called this ideal of pure art "Suprematism" and painted the most abstract painting yet, a black square on a white ground. The extreme intent of Suprematism is clear: "Only with the disappearance of a habit of mind which sees in pictures little corners of nature, madonnas and shameless Venuses, shall we witness a work of pure, living art." Suprematism, or nonobjective art, is an attempt to purify art by destroying a habit of mind. Malevich's examples tell; he objects to "shameless Venuses." Malevich shows an old nihilistic revulsion toward pagan sensuousness.

Malevich and Kandinsky differed on three points in their esthetic millennialism. I see these points as clues to a deeper breach in the millennial mind. First, consider the attitude toward compatriots. Is it inclusive or schismatic? Inclusive Kandinsky felt rapport with the Orthodox iconographic tradition; he was also receptive to Cubists, Symbolists, Futurists, Dadaists.

Malevich was anti-past and snarlingly ungrateful toward the present. "Clean the squares of the remains of the past, for temples of our image are going to be erected." Malevich absorbed the ideas of the Futurists, then turned against them. "We have abandoned Futurism; and we, the most daring, have spat on the altar of the past." Spitting on the altar of the past—it was itself the pose mastered to perfection by the Futurists. The Futurists smashed every icon of the Muses; before John Cage, Russolo advocated a philosophy of music as noise. Malevich was behaving like the typical Russian *Raskol*, a professional ingrate and backbiter.

Second, Kandinsky retains color, the complete freedom of the formal imagination, including the right to play with the forms of nature; Malevich, in a puritanical frenzy, wants—to use his word—to "dominate" nature. So he eliminates color—a rich dimension of human experience. Malevich created the first black and white painting, the first colorless painting. The assault on the ecology of the imagination is extreme; Malevich reduced his forms to the square. He gushes over a bleak, mechanical mandala, a kind of icon of resignation.

The third way the two artists differ was in their attitude toward religion. Kandinsky was interested in his grandmother's folktales, respecting his ancestors' faith. Malevich repudiated the old orthodoxy for Bolshevism, dogmatic as any religion.

During the Revolution, Kandinsky returned to Russia, where he and his co-avant-gardists were for a while hailed by the Bolsheviks. This state of grace, however, lasted as long as Trotsky was in power; once Lenin took over, Russia's greatest artists were forced to leave. The schismatic intolerance of Malevich became a harsh political reality under Lenin, and the revolutionary artists went into exile.

Kandinsky and Malevich reveal two ways the Millennium Myth may go: inclusive or exclusive, colorful and life-affirming or colorless and rigidly restrained, creatively attuned to one's religious past or angrily at odds with it. This bipolarity is a running theme in the history of the Myth.

The Marxist Millennium

The eschatological overtones of Marxism have been noted by several writers. The epigraph for this chapter from Engels reeks of millennialism; here we have talk of the Grail, holy war, the millennium. Engels and Marx were more than political scientists; they were prophets, latter-day minstrels of the Millennium Myth.

First, there is the notion that history as a whole has a meaning and that history is a movement toward final consummation. Faith in the inevitable forward march of history is typical of millennialism. The idea that history will end when class consciousness ends is a secular doctrine of last things, an eschatology full of Berdyaev's transposed religious passion.

Second, there is the dualism of Marxism, the penchant to demonize the bourgeoisie as the last obstacle to the proletarian paradise on earth; this too reflects a gambit of the millennial mind. Another gambit is the Antichrist. Along the way we have noted various candidates for Antichrist. During the Reformation and in early American history, the Romish Church was a favorite. With Marx the target becomes money, or rather a certain inhuman way money is used as an instrument of power. Marx called this device of demonic human abuse "capital."

The ultimate evil is the conspiracy of capital, a force that infiltrates every aspect of society. Marx quickly gets to the point in the *Manifesto*:

> Our epoch, the epoch of the bourgeoisie, shows this distinctive feature: it has simplified the class antagonism. Society as a whole is splitting up into two great hostile camps, into two great classes directly facing each other: *bourgeoisie* and *proletariat*.

And so the stage is set for Armageddon, Marxist style.

Marx's communist revolution, like the Biblical apocalypse, is total and worldwide. A revolution of mind, culture, and society—a holy war. In the opening words of the Communist Manifesto: "A specter is haunting Europe—the specter of communism. All the powers of old Europe have entered into a holy alliance to hunt down and exorcise this specter."

Third, in this dialectic of jihad roams Antichrist. Here is how Marx sees history unfolding:

> In all history up to now it is certainly an empirical fact that single individuals, with the expansion of their activity to a world-historical scale, have become more and more enslaved by an alien power.

Called Antichrist in the Millennium Myth, Marx called it "capital," money power and the mentality it promotes; the cement of social systems that work on principles of class warfare. Capital is a power that the genius of history will let pass unchallenged; social forces must evolve, Marx assures us, out of these conflicts of society. People will overthrow the capitalist Antichrist. It is, says Marx:

> empirically grounded that through the overthrow of the existing social order, through the communist revolution, i.e., the abolishment of private property, this power—the alienating power of money—will be dissolved, and then the emancipation of every single individual will be achieved to the same extent that history transforms itself into world history.

The fact that Marxism wears the garb of materialism makes it no less millennial-minded; truth is, there are materialist as well as spiritual millenarians. Marx, of course, gave no reason why history should come to an end with the proletarian conquest; according to his view of history as class warfare, the proletariat should generate a new class antagonist. But Marx drops his realism and embraces the faith that history is coming to an end.

The Marxist ideology provided a new myth of chosen people—the proletariat; a new focus of evil, a new Antichrist—capitalism, the bourgeoisie; a new vision of heaven on earth—the classless society, the death of alienation. In the end, the Russian Revolution fell into the hands of a monster, the incarnation of the will to power—that fearsome man with the beady eyes, Joseph Stalin.

The God That Failed

The reason all utopian schemes are doomed lies in a fatal proneness to being seduced by spiritual counterfeits, believed Dostoevsky and Solovyov.

Dostoevsky's "Legend of the Grand Inquisitor," as told by Ivan in *The Brothers Karamazov*, hinted obscurely of the coming Stalin reign of inhumanity. A bitter tale of the Second Coming, Ivan Karamazov tells his saintly brother Alyosha how Christ returned to Seville, Spain, in the sixteenth century; at first unrecognized, Christ appears in the city, only to be promptly arrested by the Grand Inquisitor.

The Grand Inquisitor? Well, he is the Pope, he is Antichrist, he is a cynical symbol of worldly power that exploits the spiritual weakness of humanity. The Grand Inquisitor, a man "with bloodless aged lips," hauls a silent Christ into a small prison cell and harangues him.

Christ, complains the Inquisitor, failed to understand what people really want. The basic error, due to a cruel overestimation of human capacity, was to expect freely given love from the average frightened, disoriented human being; what the average person really wants is bread to feed the body, and to feed the spirit—mystery, miracle, and authority. Ivan's Legend is cynical. The Pope, the Inquisitor, the State—they are all in cahoots with the "the wise and dread spirit, the spirit of self-destruction and non-existence."[29] They are on the side of Satan—the very one who tempted Christ in the wilderness.

Christ, you recall, resisted the Devil's temptations. He refused to create bread miraculously and refused the mantle of pride, power, and authority. For man lives not by bread alone but by the word of God. But to think like this was a grotesque mistake, says the Inquisitor.

Human beings are weak, "impotent rebels," and would rather be fed than free; they hate the burden of freedom and responsibility and are happiest when herded together into servile communities of animal contentment. Christ was a fool to expect so much from people. Dostoevsky's Inquisitor, who believes neither in God nor in afterlife, is the reluctant shepherd to freedom-fearing humanity, "for nothing has ever been more insupportable for a man and human society than freedom."

Dostoevsky's Antichrist is the social system that exploits the weakness of human nature—the fear of freedom, the preference for comfort, for security, for ignorance. Stalin, one might say, like Dostoevsky's Grand Inquisitor, exploited the cowardly "craving for universal unity," the readiness to sell one's soul for bread and creaturely comforts. The irony, of course, is that neither bread nor creaturely comforts were forthcoming for the Russian people under Stalin.

Vladimir Solovyov may have been Dostoevsky's model for the saintly Alyosha, to whom Ivan tells his Legend. Solovyov's book *War, Progress, and the End of History* contains a chapter called "A Short Story of the

Antichrist." The author takes us inside the mind of a cold-blooded egotist, a soul devoured by envy and conceit. The Antichrist, after we eavesdrop on his musings, appears a monstrous caricature of tendencies in ourselves. Solovyov's Antichrist, not unlike Dostoevsky's, is a kind of spiritual cancer that gorges on the base instincts of humankind. Solovyov, like many older chiliasts, identified the Antichrist with the power of deception and pseudo-goodness.

He warned against "the world-unifying power of the Anti-Christ, who 'will speak loud and high-sounding words,' and will cast a glittering veil of good and truth over the mystery of utter lawlessness in the time of its final revelation."[30] Like Dostoevsky's Grand Inquisitor, Solovyov's Antichrist embodies the human capacity for self-deception.

Dostoevsky and Solovyov prophesied a time of inhuman concentration of power in one human being. They probed Russian submissiveness to power, holding that the most insidious evil in the world, the true Antichrist, consists of lack of spiritual energy. Stalin's "demonic" power, on this interpretation, would be a product of the moral failure of humanity; in other words, the Antichrist is us.

Berdyaev, who lived through the Stalin era, finished deliteralizing the Millennium. The "End" of history for this Russian thinker meant the end of a form of consciousness; the End pointed toward inner transformation, not toward external events or visitations from beyond. Deliteralization frees us from the spell of chronology. For if the End is a transformation of consciousness, any time may be the end of time. The Day of the Lord becomes our day, a question of inner time and inner timing. The Daniel-spawned timetables of fundamentalists become irrelevant—worse, they become obstacles.

In Berdyaev's world, everyday life is an apocalypse, a journey to the end of history. The End will come when we are freed from what the Russian thinker called the "objective point of view." Berdyaev put it like this: "The metaphysical and epistemological meaning of the end of the world and of history denotes the end of objective being and the overcoming of objectification."[31] This is Berdyaev's clumsy way of talking about honoring the uniqueness of every human being, celebrating our Renaissance "dignity". The apocalypse is an individual moment, a personal epiphany, an end of the "world of necessity."

The Russian artists also tried to "overcome" the objectivity of the world by creating nonobjective art. Malevich wrote his manifesto *The*

Nonobjective World in 1927. Kandinsky freed art from bondage to objects and natural forms. Berdyaev thought Soviet Communism was a ghastly triumph of objective thinking and believed it would probably continue to cause mischief in ever new and more subtle ways.

The Russian Revolution shaped twentieth-century history, with appalling results: a catastrophic waste of precious planetary resources, gratuitous pain and death for millions; the rise of enormous collective paranoias; wrenching geo-political convulsions; a dangerous, monumentally wasteful arms race; prolonged distortions of human priorities; and in 1962, the Communist attempt to impose its idea of heaven on earth brought the world to the brink of thermonuclear holocaust. The Russian visionary imagination, as far as its political consequences, must be judged a tragic failure.

But then, in the words of George Kennen, a "miracle" happened—Mikhail Gorbachev. Wrote Gary Hart, "Mikhail Gorbachev has, virtually single-handedly, ended the Cold War." Hart calls Gorbachev a "mystery." "We do not know why he has chosen to alter fundamentally and often universally the policies, practices, doctrines, and precepts of his own vast and troubled nation."[32] Gorbachev introduced *glasnost* ("openness") and *perestroika* ("restructuring")—policies that have, like the 1917 Revolution, shaken the world. *Glasnost* and *perestroika* are ideas with a distinctly millennial ring. Mikhail Gorbachev ended his book *Perestroika* (1985) with a summons to all humanity to work toward the "Golden Age."

Golden Age aside, Gorbachev's *glasnost* and *perestroika* have unleashed tremendous forces. Under the leadership of Boris Yeltsin, democracy is struggling to be born. On the other hand, alcoholism, divorce, crime, anti-Semitism, Slavophilism, and nationalism are rising in a country at the edge of economic chaos. And, *glasnost* has unleashed violent anarchy in Georgia and inhuman wars of ethnic cleansing in Bosnia.

Many old and sinister forces, held in check by seventy years of Communist domination, have been set free. The world was startled when Vladimir Zhirinovsky performed so well at the polls in December 1993. The new openness has proven a vacuum; Western liberal capitalism has not been automatically embraced. With the KGB off the back of the Russian people, the Mafia have leaped in their place. The result is worsening conditions for the majority of Russians; it turns out that Western values are not magical nostrums.

No wonder so many Russians are drawn to neo-Hitlerian Zhirinovsky and talk of the good old days of czarist expansionism, Slavic brotherhood, and anti-Semitism. True to the formula, economic suffering and social dislocation breed negative millennialism: racism and scapegoating, for example, as seen by the popularity of a man who stated on CNN that Bill Clinton was "sexually impotent" because Clinton snubbed him!

Restructuring—the end of the known world—in this case, the end of the Soviet Union. This restructuring—as Saint John pictured it in his classic vision—lets loose the dark satanic forces and creates conditions for mass social conflict. Restructuring the Soviet Union has also revealed something about the durability of the religious imagination. A tremendous religious revival is underway in Russia today. The Russian Center for Public Opinion Research in Moscow polled thousands in 1991, and found that mass religious conversions were occurring at a rate unknown since the Middle Ages. Sociologist Andrew Greeley's conclusion: "St. Vladimir has routed Karl Marx."

Russia is in the midst of a Great Awakening of Christian Orthodoxy, along with its apocalyptic proclivities. Meanwhile, Boris Zaladov, a blond New Age Rasputin, is wooing the ladies with his healing vibes and saying the only way to head off Armageddon is to liberate "psychic energy." In Russia, New Age ideas are attracting a lot of attention. UFOs, holistic healing, white magic, and other New Age topics are big in Moscow. Says Aleksandra Yakovleva, publisher of the Moscow New Age magazine *Inward Path*, "We find ways that people can change their lives by changing their consciousness" (quoted in the *New York Times*, December 6, 1992).

From Slavophilism to New Ageism, *glasnost* has triggered a pandemonium of possibilities for the Russian future. At the moment, everything is up for grabs. "The old order is dead, the new order is not yet born, and in the interregnum there is much morbidity," said Antonio Gramsci.

Russia seems unable to muster her old visionary zeal for the tasks ahead, nor does she seem fit or inclined to adapt to the ways of the West. The Russians, at the moment, are a people in need of a new myth. (This seems increasingly to describe people everywhere in our interregnum world.) They have yet to realize their rendering of the Millennium Myth, without enslaving or destroying themselves.

Nobody knows if Russia—perhaps dragging Europe and the rest of the world with her—is about to plunge us all into a New Dark Ages. In building the New Russian Paradigm Gary Hart speaks of—and Gorbachev made possible—one hopes the more amicable side of the Russian soul emerges: not Malevich's truculent geometry, but Kandinsky's sociable palette; not Bakunin's lust to destroy, but Fedorov's passion to resurrect; Nijinsky, not Nechayev; Solovyov, not Stalin.

But let us move on; it is time to descend even deeper into the shadowy depths of the millennial imagination.

The Messianic Third Reich

Things fall apart; the centre cannot hold;
Mere anarchy is loosed upon the world,
The blood-dimmed tide is loosed and everywhere
The ceremony of innocence is drowned;
The best lack all conviction, while the worst
Are full of passionate intensity.

WILLIAM BUTLER YEATS
The Second Coming

O n July 15, 1940, the *New York Herald Tribune* gave an account of a mortally wounded Nazi soldier being approached by a priest. The young Nazi rebuffed the priest: "The Führer is my faith," he said. "I don't want anything from your church. But if you want to be good to me, get my Führer's picture out of my breast pocket." The youth kissed the picture, a beatific look on his face, murmuring before he died, "My Führer, I am happy to die for you."

This story offers a clue to the nature of German National Socialism. The dying soldier was in the grips of a profound religious emotion. I think it can be shown that the nation that followed Adolf Hitler through the Holocaust and to its own destruction was in the grips of deep religious emotion. As Nicholas Goodrick-Clarke, who has written about the occult roots of Nazism, notes, "something more . . . than fear had been needed to keep a large majority of the German people loyal to the Nazi Third Reich through thick and thin, displaying remarkable courage and endurance almost to the bitter end."[1]

Mass unemployment, inflation, and the humiliating Versailles Treaty undoubtedly shaped the Hitler movement. But was there something else that needs to be taken into account to explain the Nazi nightmare? That something has been called "meta-political"[2] by Peter Viereck in his study of the romantic roots of the Nazi mind. The *meta-political* refers to the romantic antimaterialism and anticapitalism, the mysticism of the Volk, and the mythic racism that propped Nazi ideology.

C. G. Jung thought that psychic possession was the key to the meta-political side of National Socialism. In his 1936 essay "Wotan," he wrote, "The impressive thing about the German phenomenon is that one man, who is obviously 'possessed,' has infected a whole nation to such an extent that everything is set in motion and has started rolling on its course towards perdition."[3] The one man was, of course, Adolf Hitler.

But by what was he possessed? In part, as Jung contends, by the imagination of pagan deities like Wotan. One thinks of Heine's 1834 prophecy: "Thor, leaping to life with his giant hammer, will crush the Gothic cathedrals." In my view, the Nazi seizure involved an odd blend of Germanic paganism and millennialism. The Nazi cultural unconscious harbored a mix of pagan and Christian symbols and archetypes. To anticipate my main points: In the Nazi version of the Millennium Myth,

- Hitler appears as an Aryanized messiah
- the figure of Antichrist assumes the colors of the racist imagination, as in Alfred Rosenberg's *Myth of the Twentieth Century*
- the apocalyptic idea of chosenness is reduced to a category of biomyth
- the expectation of a Biblical Armageddon turns into a Teutonic twilight of the gods
- and, the most spectacular distortion, the Kingdom of Heaven is reduced to the Nazi Third Reich.

In the Nazi venture, the emotional force of the Millennium Myth was bolstered by magical, romantic, occult, and racist ideas. The Christian cross and the Nazi swastika were diametrically opposed in what they represented; however, in the deep unconscious of the Nazi Teuton, the two symbols seem to have played off each other, creating a potent brew of psychic force.

Several scholars have remarked on Nazi millennialism. Carl Löwith points to the medieval Joachite tradition with its visions of a coming third age, which became the Nazi Third Reich.[4] Norman Cohn found similarities between the Hitler movement and medieval mystic rebels like Thomas Müntzer. In *Warrant for Genocide: The Myth of the Jewish World Conspiracy and the Protocols of the Elders of Zion* (1967), Cohn argued that insecurity, widespread anomie, and demonization of the Jewish people were features common to Nazis and medieval millennialists. Eric Voegelin (1952), James M. Rhodes (1980), and Nicholas Goodrick-Clarke (1985) have studied these parallels and their possible significance. It might be useful, then, to say something about one of Hitler's millenarian forerunners.

A Medieval Forerunner of Hitler

In the Biblical tradition, God's righteous people long for divine rescue; they hope for a messiah who will destroy the wicked and exalt the elect. Hope in divine rescue lived on in Western consciousness; in medieval times, for example, it nurtured the belief in a coming Angelic Pope—a Führer or leader, pure in righteousness and great in power.

In the sixteenth century, it produced Thomas Müntzer, a German mystic rebel whose fanatical messianic pretensions qualify him as a forerunner of Adolf Hitler. Müntzer was a learned humanist scholar before he fell in with Niklas Storch in 1520. The two men embraced old Taborite teachings, claiming direct communication with the Holy Spirit; they were, as people say today, "channels."

Their mission was to form a League of the Elect, which attracted the uneducated, the disoriented, and the poor. Prepare for the Millennium by force of arms was the message: "The sword is necessary to exterminate them," said the inspired prophet, "for the ungodly have no right to live, save what the Elect choose to allow them."[5] This righteous readiness to kill the other was a trait shared by Adolf Hitler. Müntzer, like Hitler in his romantic ravings, was fond of speaking of the Elect "becoming God." Inflated with a sense of occult power, the League of the Elect, like the Nazi military juggernaut, were daring and reckless of human life.

Müntzer became involved in current peasant uprisings, exploiting social unrest, and mobilizing the poor in a holy war against the establishment; in the end, millenarian mania was crushed by superior artillery, and Müntzer was captured and beheaded.

Some Marxists have shown their affinity for the inhuman by hailing Müntzer as a forerunner of the Communist creed.[6] (Müntzer and his disciples smashed some priests and landlords and were therefore on the side of good, truth, and history.) Müntzer, as Norman Cohn says, cared little for the fate of his followers, but mainly for the "mass exterminations" that must precede the Millennium. Müntzer had become, as John Perry would say, psychotically identified with a fragment of the messianic Myth.

How does a humanist scholar turn into a bloodthirsty millenarian? Or, to put it another way, how does a myth dehumanize a human being? The Russian Berdyaev gave part of the answer: by so hardening oneself as to see the world, especially other people, as ciphers, abstractions, objects. Müntzer's own words tell us something about his priorities. In his pamphlet *The Explicit Unmasking of the False Belief of the Faithless World*, he waxes poetic on his hatred of princes—"for they have spent their lives in bestial eating and drinking, from their youth onwards they have been brought up most delicately, *in all their life they have never had a bad day.*" (My emphasis.)

With "in all their life they have never had a bad day," Müntzer betrays his deeply malignant resentment. Hatred and resentment seem behind his bloodthirsty cry for apocalyptic justice; the claim to messianic leadership becomes a warrant for his brutality and aggression. This was true of Müntzer and other medieval fanatics, and it is true of fanatics of the twentieth century.

The Messiah in Jackboots

Invoking a messianic warrant for brutality and aggression was a prominent feature in the career of Adolf Hitler. To begin with, National Socialism was committed to the *Führerprinzip*, "the leadership principle," a political echo of the idea of messiahship, which scorned democracy and enjoined absolute obedience to one leader. A caption under Hitler's portrait at Nazi headquarters in Munich read: "Nothing happens in this Movement, except what I wish."

The *Führerprinzip* was an irrational concept whose roots were in Romanticism and German philosophy. The Nazi leadership principle was linked to Rousseau's mystical general will—the Leader embodying the general will. The principle had an affinity with the notion of the *daemonic*, as in Socrates' *daimon* or "spirit guide," and with genius, an infallible inner leader. The Nazi leadership principle grew from Nietzschean superman poetics and Wagnerian hero worship.

Three Hegelian ideas tie in with this: first, that the State is the divine Idea incarnate on earth; second, that the Germanic world represents the highest unfoldment of the divine Idea; and third, that there are "world-historical individuals."[7] The world-historical individual is an agent, often unconscious, of the "will of the World-Spirit."[8]

Like the antinomian mystic rebels of the Middle Ages, and like Nietzsche's superman, a world-historical individual is "beyond good and evil." As Hegel put it, "But so mighty a form must trample down many an innocent flower—crush to pieces many an object in its path." I do not say that Hitler consciously modeled himself after Hegel's philosophy, but his leadership principle is in line with the Hegelian zeitgeist. Like the Catholic Apostle's Creed, the Nazi party, as Hermann Rauschning reported, had a Hitler creed: "We all believe, on this earth, in Adolf Hitler, our Führer, and we acknowledge that National Socialism is the only faith that can bring salvation to our country."[9]

Hitler saw himself as a messiah, so did others—I began this chapter with the last words of a dying Nazi soldier, showing how Hitler had become a Christ-surrogate. Note now the observations of an American reporter. Hitler had entered Nuremberg one September day in 1934, and thousands of Nazis waving swastika flags were cheering hysterically "We want our Führer!" The reporter remarked:

> I was shocked at the faces, especially those of the women. They reminded me of the crazed expressions I saw once in the back country of Louisiana on the faces of some Holy Rollers who were about to hit the trail. They looked up at him as if he were a Messiah, their faces transformed . . .[10]

The nocturnal torchlit rallies in Nuremberg and other public meetings took on the air of religious revivals, and Hitler's appearances were orchestrated like epiphanies. "It was not long before the German people were prepared to take the short step of seeing Hitler, not as a man, but as a Messiah of Germany,"[11] wrote Walter Langer, who collected data on Hitler's messianic phantasies.

At a Nuremberg Nazi Rally in 1937, a huge photo of Hitler was captioned: "In the Beginning was the Word." According to the Mayor of Hamburg: "We need no priests or parsons. We communicate directly with God through Adolf Hitler." Painted in black on a giant white canvas in Odenwald were the words: "We believe in Holy Hitler." Reichmaster for Church Affairs, Hans Kerri, said: "Adolf Hitler is the true Holy Ghost." An American from Chicago had witnessed a Passion Play at Oberammergau. "These people are crazy," he said. "This is not a revolution, it's a revival. They think Hitler is God. Believe it or not, a German woman sat next to me . . . and when they hoisted Jesus on the Cross, she said: 'There he is. That is our Führer, our Hitler.' "[12] Even the great philosopher Martin Heidegger believed for a while that Hitler embodied the coming of the "Holy."

Architect Albert Speer spent twenty years in Spandau prison at Nuremberg. Hitler charmed Speer, an intelligent, sensitive man. Speer's candid self-observations help us understand something of Hitler's seductive appeal. Evil, apparently, works its most potent magic by appealing to the "higher" self.

"Today, in retrospect," wrote Speer of his first meetings with the Führer, "I often have the feeling that something swooped me up off the ground at the time, wrenched me from all my roots, and beamed a host of alien forces upon me."[13] Jung had written of Hitler possessing the German people. According to Speer, Hitler knew how to appeal to people's lofty romantic side. Hitler's routine pep talk was, "The higher he aims, the more a man grows."[14]

Hitler appealed to transpersonal ideals: "The Aryan is not greatest in his mental qualities as such," declared the Führer, "but in the extent of his willingness to put all his abilities in the service of the community." People have a need to serve the greater community; the Nazis exploited this need and seduced the Germans by sweet-talking their better angels. The Millennium Myth makes seduction by idealism easy.

If others saw Hitler as the Messiah, Hitler paid himself the same compliment. In private and public life, he revealed his pretensions to messiahship. In 1923, he spent a night in a pension in Obersalzberg, where Dietrich Eckart watched the Führer-to-be strutting up and down, swinging his rhinoceros-hide whip, boasting of his ambitions to the wife of the pension manager. Prophetlike, he denounced Berlin:

> . . . the luxury, the perversion, the iniquity, the wanton display and the Jewish materialism disgusted me so thoroughly that I was almost beside myself. I nearly imagined myself to be Jesus Christ when he came to his Father's Temple and found the money-changers.[15]

While celebrating the publication of *Mein Kampf* at the famous Hofbräuhaus in Munich, Hitler mused on the real meaning of Christ's ministry: "Christ," he said, "was the greatest early fighter in the battle against the world enemy, the Jews." Then he said: "The work that Christ started but could not finish, I—Adolf Hitler—will conclude."[16]

According to James Rhodes, Hitler's infamous *Mein Kampf* ("My Struggle") is "probably is the best available key to the mind of a millenarian 'messiah.'"[17] The opening sentence of this strange book betrays the author's fantastic conceit: "Today it seems to me providential that Fate should have chosen Braunau on the Inn as my birthplace." At once, grand notions of fate and providence. Fateful was the fact that Hitler's birthplace was located on the border of Austria and Germany. But "one blood demands one Reich," that is, Germany and Austria must be united; Hitler's birthplace thus becomes "the symbol of a great mission." For more messianic rhetoric turn back a page to the dedication, which speaks of the "resurrection" of the German people. The Nazis relished talk like this. Fate, providence, mission, resurrection—this is the language of the Millennium Myth.

Mein Kampf sets out the terms for one of "the greatest revolutions of the world," a struggle of eschatological proportions. By 1925, Hitler had come to see himself as fated to play a central role in that struggle. That struggle, like all millenarian struggles, was conceived as totalistic and dualistic; in Hitler's mind, an absolute evil had to be absolutely eliminated. As Müntzer, Hitler's medieval forerunner, thought, the ungodly had to perish by the sword. This and only this was the way to usher in the Millennium.

Hitler believed that Providence assigned him the task of rescuing the German folk from a cruel relentless foe. Referring to himself, he said, "Fate some day bestows upon it (the oppressed people) the man endowed for this purpose, who finally brings the long yearned-for fulfillment." Hitler thought of himself as the embodiment of German yearnings for liberation—the incarnation of Rousseau's general will.

Hitler was not the only Nazi who indulged in world-historical messianic phantasies. Other Nazis were steeped in them—for example, Propaganda Minister, Joseph Goebbels. Goebbels had a Ph.D. in Romantic literature and wrote a novel, *Michael: A German Fate in the Pages of a Diary*. Rhodes calls *Michael* the "best extant self-portrait of an apocalyptic messiah."[18] In this thinly disguised self-phantasy, the hero Michael becomes a sacrificial savior for a "new Reich." He cries: "I am a hero, a god, a redeemer." Michael decides that his "salvific word" will "resurrect" the people. He goes on:

> I arise, I have power
> To wake the dead . . .
> The ranks fill up, a host arises,
> A *Volk*, a community.
> Purpose binds us.
> We are united in the faith
> In the strong will . . .
> And so we will form the New Reich.

Goebbels, like Fedorov whom we met last chapter, wants to raise the dead and feels a call from the folk soul. Savior Goebbels, with Goering and the Führer himself, was one of the three most powerful figures in the Nazi movement. However, it was Hitler who assumed the status of ultimate sanctity for Goebbels, as may be seen from his sycophantic diary. An early sample, July 6, 1926: "Weimar. Hitler spoke. About politics, the Idea, and organization. Deep and mystical. Almost like a gospel. One shudders as one skirts the abyss of life with him. I thank Fate which gave us this man."

Enough of this. The German people, the German soldier, leading German intellectuals, Hitler's closest associates, and Hitler himself shared the phantasy of Hitler's messianic status in National Socialism. Moreover, it sometimes happens that the play of external events serves synchronistically to bolster and temporarily sustain our delusions. Such seems to have been the case with Adolf Hitler, whose lucky escapes from death on several occasions served to strengthen his delusion that "Fate" had chosen him for a special task.

A sign of the strength of the Hitlerian messiah phantasy is that, as with James Dean and Elvis Presley, some people still refuse to believe that Hitler is dead and think he escaped Berlin at war's end or even absconded into another dimension where he continues to carry on his work. Since messiahs are divinely sent beings, they do not die that easily, and so the Hitler survival myth has waxed in the psychic underground.[19]

For example, the erudite Chilean Ambassador Miguel Serrano, author of *C. G. Jung and Hermann Hesse: A Record of Two Friendships*, was a strong believer in the Führer's supernatural status. As late as 1984, Serrano published a six-hundred-page tome with the shocking title *Adolf Hitler, el Ultimo Avatara* ("Adolf Hitler, the Last Avatar"). Serrano argued that Hitler was the Tenth Avatar of Vishnu, whose incarnation was meant to end the *Kali Yuga* ("the Dark Age") and thus to bring about the New Age. Serrano thought Hitler escaped Berlin in 1945, in a German flying saucer.

Apparently, the Führer vanished at the South Pole, entering an invisible realm, from whence he still wages esoteric war against the Demiurge. Ambassador Serrano thinks this war is about the purification of Hyperborean blood, a substance said to come from condensations of "the light of the Black Sun, of the Green Ray."[20] Pure blood obsessed other Aryan supremacists. The tenacity of such fantastic ideas in the mind of a learned, worldly man, thirty years after the Führer's death, says something about the spell of the Messiah archetype that gathered around Adolf Hitler.

The Jewish Antichrist

In the core dualistic scenario of the Millennium Myth, the Messiah is pitted against the Antichrist. On this point, the Nazi movement was also true to the Myth. For just as Hitler played the part of the Messiah, so were the Jewish people cast in the role of Antichrist. Millennial phantasies helped shape the form that anti-Semitism took in National Socialism.

To read *Mein Kampf* is to see how central anti-Semitism was to Hitler's ideology. Hitler never lets up on the "Jewish question." As Hitler described it, the task of dealing with the Jews was comparable to regenerating a living thing by killing a "bacillus," an agent of disease and infection. The point cannot be understated: The Nazi phantasy of a millennial Third Reich demanded the destruction of the Jewish people, just as John's vision of the Kingdom demanded the destruction of Antichrist.

Although the Antichrist is a shadowy figure with a complicated history, several of his features stand out. The Antichrist is the universal foe of humankind and represents pure, unalloyed evil. Deceptively Christlike, Antichrist is a liar and a deceiver and hides behind a mask of good; the New Testament links him to false prophets. The war he wages is total. He may be a particular personage in history, have many minions, cast many shadows, and have many forerunners. Or he may appear as a group of people; to the Nazis, the Antichrist was the Jewish people.

Struggle with Antichrist is inevitable, but struggle will usher the Kingdom of God. Antichrist is a foil to the Second Coming of Christ, a spur to the consummation—in Nazi parlance, part of the "final solution."

Hitler projected the image of Antichrist on the Jewish people in *Mein Kampf* for all the world to see. What is so strange is that this book, rather than serve as warrant for Hitler's confinement, became a bestseller and made him a rich man. The following quotes are all from *Mein Kampf*[21]. They illustrate Hitler's Jewish Antichrist projection.

Musing on the question of "social democracy," Hitler said, "I was overcome by gloomy foreboding and malignant fear. Then I saw before me a doctrine, comprised of egotism and hate, which can lead to victory pursuant to mathematical laws, but in so doing must put an end to humanity." This doctrine that threatens to "put an end to humanity" is connected with "the nature of a people." But only "a knowledge of the Jews provides the key" to understanding this world-destroying doctrine. According to Hitler, the Jews were responsible for a way of thinking that promised to "put an end to humanity."

He then explains how he became an anti-Semite, bizarrely stating how in the course of centuries the Jews "had taken on a human look." Since Antichrist is a nonhuman principle, Hitler felt obliged to see the Jewish people as essentially nonhuman. Once the Führer grasped the "key" to the menace, he looked around with fresh alertness. "Wherever I went, I began to see Jews, and the more I saw, the more deeply they became distinguished in my eyes from the rest of humanity." What was this menace that Hitler saw lurking everywhere?

The Jewish people were part of a conspiracy in the "world press," they were behind every skulduggery from prostitution (which obsessed Hitler) to the Marxist conspiracy. In "Marxism," Hitler wrote, "(the) . . . goal is and remains the destruction of all non-Jewish states." The "scales" fell from his eyes, his insights "accelerated," and he saw through the "diabolical craftiness of these seducers." Note: Diabolical craftiness is the trademark of Antichrist.

Hitler was horrified by the unlimited "fertility" of Jews, their "tremendous numbers," the "spiritual pestilence" they constituted, "worse than the Black death," an "infection" that threatened to "poison men's souls like germ-carriers of the worst sort." The Nazis were health freaks; the war against the Jewish Antichrist was perversely holistic. The Jewish Antichrist was a medical as well as a spiritual peril.

For Hitler it was total war. German society was threatened by Marxism, "a Jewish doctrine." Marxism, like Antichrist, was an international menace, a threat to all humanity. Nature itself was under siege. "The Jewish doctrine of Marxism rejects the aristocratic principle of Nature and replaces the eternal privileges of power and strength by the mass of numbers and their dead weight." So deadly is the principle of Antichrist that it threatens "the aristocratic principle of nature." (Whatever that is.)

In Hitler's view, the satanic Jewish principle was the enemy of personality, race, culture, and humanity. Hitler exploited the fear of the satanic. He understood that what is needed to mobilize the people is a spiritual principle. Again, I want to underscore the peculiar danger of the Millennium Myth; taken literally, it turns the world into a theater of spiritual war. The war against Jewish international Marxism was more than economic and political; it was a spiritual war and as such was capable of rousing the deepest emotions.

Hitler saw it was necessary to put a spiritual mask on brute force. "The application of force alone, without the impetus of a basic spiritual idea as a starting point, can never lead to the destruction of an idea . . . except in the form of a complete extermination of even the very last exponent of the idea. . . ." The last sentence contains a chilling prophecy of the "final solution," an idea that stinks of chiliastic craziness. Hitler understood the psychology of holy war. "Any violence which does not spring from a firm, spiritual base, will be wavering and uncertain. It lacks the stability which can only rest in a fanatical outlook." Hitler thus equates the spiritual with the fanatical.

The menace of the Jewish people means "destruction for the inhabitants of this planet." Such a menace, supernatural and total in scope, is the old menace of Antichrist. Hitler, the messiah in jackboots, could therefore write: "Hence today I believe that I am acting in accordance with the will of the Almighty Creator: by defending myself against the Jew, I am fighting for the work of the Lord."

Hitler demonized and dualized the Jewish people. He wrote, "There is no making pacts with Jews; there can only be the hard: either—or." In a sly ploy, he distinguished between race and religion, insisting that the Jewish problem was unrelated to religion. To say that the Jewish people are a "religious community" is a "great lie." Hitler was opposed to *religious* persecution. If the problem were merely a matter of religion, it might be possible to convert the Jews. To maintain **191** absolute confrontation, the hard "either—or" attitude, Hitler argued that the Jewish people were a biological entity, a race. As a race their nature was unalterable, and so the essential antagonism remained, and Hitler could preach jihad against the Jewish Antichrist. Antichrist means the unalloyed will to power. And so: "Today it is not princes and princes' mistresses who haggle and bargain over state borders; it is the inexorable Jew who struggles for his domination over the nations."

Chosen People, Master-Race

It is one of the ironies of history that the Nazis twisted the Jewish idea of chosenness and used it as a weapon of mass destruction against the Jewish people. In the Old Testament, God elects the Jewish people to serve his will and purpose, not to confer advantage upon them. Chosenness is a burden, a challenge, an obligation; not a badge of merit or a sign of superiority. Israel's election was meant to show God's glory to the world (Isa. 40:20). Election implied a strict judgment of national sins (Amos 3:2). Moreover, the blessings of election were always in danger of being forfeited through unbelief and disobedience. Isaiah foretold that only a faithful remnant would be saved to reap the benefits of a golden age, after the judgment of Israel's sins (Isa. 10:20–22; 4:3; 27:6).

Nazi resentment of Jewish chosenness, so evident in Mein Kampf, was therefore based on a malicious misunderstanding. Moreover, the prophets applied election to the individual, not to the people as a whole, and had begun to back off from the idea of a covenant exclusively with the Jewish people. The Nazi view of chosenness, therefore, was a caricature of the prophetic.

Somehow, the prophetic idea of chosenness mutated into Aryan racism. The Nazis turned the idea of moral election into a racist biomyth. Mein Kampf concludes with this thought: "A state which in this age of racial poisoning dedicates itself to the care of its best racial elements must some day become lord of the earth." Racist myth here serves to justify making a bid for world power. It was all laid out, the roadmap to the Nazi Millennium, in Mein Kampf: purify the race, and become lord of the earth.

The Führer's testament contained lengthy discussions of race and culture, with much talk of the "culture-founding Aryan." Aryans were not only the founders of culture but of "humanity" itself. "All human culture, all the results of art, science, and technology that we see before us today, are almost exclusively the creative product of the Aryan." This leads to the "inference" that "all higher humanity" and the very notion of "man" are an Aryan by-product.

The Aryan master-race therefore has the right to use non-Aryans to build the millennial future culture. "Without this possibility of using lower human beings, the Aryan would never have been able to take his first steps toward his future culture." The supreme obstacle to fulfilling this sublime destiny is the "poisoning" of "blood." Hitler obsessed over preserving Aryan "blood" from poison, infection, and contamination.

Hitler's pseudo-scientific opinions came from older racist traditions. One of the most powerful was the Romantic philosophy of Richard Wagner. In 1881, Wagner was absorbing Count Gobineau's *Essay on the Inequality of the Human Races*. Thereafter Wagner wrote articles expounding his views on the "purification" of the Aryan race. Wagner wanted to awaken and purify "unconscious race-force," which he thought was the answer to Germany's problems, specifically, democracy, materialism, and, of course, the Jews. The mystic force that Wagner wanted to purify sprang from the divine origins of the Aryan race. Non-Aryan stock have prosaic Darwinian origins "from monkeys"; the Nordic race "trace back their origin to gods" and consequently "are marked out for rulership." Wagner conceived a program of purification, based on vegetarianism, antivivisectionism, and anti-Semitism. A program dedicated to the "regeneration of the human race."

Nietzsche eventually split from Wagner,[22] whose music had inspired Nietzsche's first book, *The Birth of Tragedy*. In fact, Nietzsche despised anti-Semitism, racism, and German nationalism; still, the poetics of the "blond beast" in which he couched some of his insights was co-opted by the Nazis and reduced to savage literalism. The German thinker was fond of talking about the "master-race," as well as the "superman" being "beyond good and evil." He distinguished master morality from slave morality and spoke with contempt of Christian "slave" morality, pegged by Nietzsche as a symptom of declining vitality. However, Nietzsche's *Übermenschen* were closer to Joachim's Spiritual Men, aristocrats of a new inner dispensation, than to SS Nordic storm troopers.

Nazi race ideology drew from a Frenchman, Gobineau, whom I mentioned above and, from the English-born Houston Stewart Chamberlain. In 1908, Chamberlain married Wagner's daughter Eva, became a German citizen in 1915, and, by 1923, met Hitler with whom he became enraptured. He explained his racist convictions in a book called *The Foundations of the Nineteenth Century* (1912). In Chamberlain's phantasy, the principle of race is said to oppose "chaos," echoing the Babylonian apocalypse in which Marduk fights Tiamat, the Goddess of Chaos.

The Teutonic race, Chamberlain tells us, bears the "soul" of modern culture, and must avoid dilution in the chaos of Latins, Mongolians, and Semites. The "splendid (Teutonic) barbarians" must "force their way with untold toil out of the night of this Chaos toward a new dawn." The entrance of the Germanic people into world history is thus an event of apocalyptic significance. Mysterious powers guide German history, we are told: "The guardian angel of his lineage is ever at his side, supporting him where he loses his foothold, warning him like the Socratic Daemon. . . ." According to Christian angelology, entire nations have their guardian angels, an idea here transposed to race mythology, muddled with Platonic daemonology.

The Ex-English Wagnerian describes the intoxication of group consciousness—the ecstasy of losing oneself in a larger psychic entity:

> Race lifts a man above himself; it endows him with extraordinary—I might almost say supernatural—powers, so entirely does it distinguish him from the individual who springs from the chaotic jumble from peoples drawn from all parts of the world.

To heighten the religious exaltation of race consciousness, Chamberlain advocated eugenics, noting that the best Irish sporting dogs were products of artificial selection. From dogs he leaps to the conclusion that the Teuton is "the very greatest power in the history of mankind." However, now threatened by sinister inroads of racial chaos and blood contamination, the future is looking bleak; so Chamberlain can promise nothing but "a struggle for life and death." And in this he was prophetic. The Third Reich did indeed enter into murderous struggle with the "chaos" of non-Aryan "races."

Chamberlain's ideas, a strange mixture of myth and pseudoscience powerfully influenced the Nazi mythmaker Alfred Rosenberg, author of

The Myth of the Twentieth Century, first published in 1930. Rosenberg edited the official Nazi paper *Der Voelkische Beobacter* ("The Folkish Observer"). With Rosenberg, we come closer to the living psychic forces that inspired Nazi brutality and fanaticism. In 1934, Hitler created for Rosenberg the office of Director of Party Education and *Weltanschauung*. The essence of that *Weltanschauung* ("worldview") may be seen in the blurb on the back cover of *The Myth of the Twentieth Century*: "The myth of the twentieth century is the myth of blood, which under the sign of the swastika unchains the racial world-revolution. It is the awakening of the race soul, which after long sleep ends the race chaos."[23]

This book, second in influence only to *Mein Kampf* as Nazi holy writ, reveals the German hunger for a new myth to live by; myth, as Viereck says in his keen study, is an honorific term, meaning something like "necessary faith, or inspiration, or unifying mass yearning, or folktale truer than truth."[24] An essential point about Rosenberg's myth: Only the race, never the individual, has soul. The nation expresses the race soul, the Nordic Atlantean being the highest on earth, the cause of all that is superior in world history. The greatest danger to Germany is contamination from inferior race souls. "The job of Nazism is to build a golden age by repurifying race soul."[25] Rosenberg's *Myth* reveals the secret of history: "Nothing can change the one fact that the meaning of world-history, shining out from the north, has passed over the whole earth, borne by a blue-eyed blond race."[26]

The illusion of chosenness, of master-racism, called for the creation of secret guards and elite conclaves. Thus the phantasy incarnates itself. Heinrich Himmler's SS was an elite organization dedicated to training the ruling class and eliminating all opposition to it. The SS used the S sigil, which was an ancient rune. The SS ran the concentration camps; these were designed to purify and to preserve the master-race from its foes.

Runes are an old Germanic sign language, a language of sigils that speaks to a pre-rational level of mind. The most powerful rune used by the Nazis was the swastika, the sun wheel or cross in motion. As we will see in the next chapter, the American New Age is also enamored of runes. (There are other notable parallels.)

Jung said that Germany was possessed by the archetype of Wotan, the God of War, magic, and poetry; Wotan also invented runes. Runes, in early times, were Nordic hieroglyphs, the "mute" language of Vico's giants, used by diviners, poets, weathermen, warriors, lovers, and wizards. The Germanen Order, founded in 1912, was a runic society. Members signed their names in runes. Runes meant protection in battle. They were a little like the talismans used in Renaissance magic, psychotronic devices for manipulating the subtle energies of the universe.

The Nazi myth of the Nordic master-race—their version of the idea of chosenness—had complicated roots. In addition to romantics and race thinkers like Wagner, Chamberlain, and Rosenberg, there were occult influences. One example will have to do. A renegade Catholic monk, Lanz von Liebenfels, was obsessed with *theo-zoology*, "the zoology of gods." Religion with this writer was reduced to biology; for, according to Liebenfels, there were at first two kinds of people, Aryan heros and animal apemen. Aryans, of course, embodied light, health, solarian blondness, and leonine courage, not to mention audacity and superlative creativity. Apefolk, on the other hand, are the pathetic embodiments of our Shadow selves: dark, deceptive, cruel, greedy, lustful, ugly, and lavishly stupid.

Because of the weakness of women (sexually enchanted by apeman animality), the two kinds of people began to interbreed. With miscegenation, the races became a Babel of inferiorities. Fortunately, in a few mongrel species, there remains—thank Thor—a preponderance of Aryan *blood*. Liebenfels, like the Wagnerians, phantasized much about blood. The shape of skulls also prompted Nazi phantasy life. Because their skulls were said to have certain fiendish properties, Jews were judged to be akin to apemen. Liebenfels had an inclusive mind. He thought the female sex was as ape-oriented as the Jewish people. Thus, according to Liebenfels, "the soul of the woman has something prehuman, something demonic, something enigmatic about it." According to this visionary, most Marxists were also "prehumans." As fate would have it, Adolf Hitler visited Liebenfels in 1909, when he was down and out in Vienna.

Armageddon and Twilight of the Gods

The Millennium Myth trades on visions of last wars; those elected for triumph win perfect bliss. In the Book of Revelation, Armageddon is the place of the last war. Armageddon, the battle of all battles, must come. That is the frightening side of the Myth. But there is also a hopeful side: after the battle of battles comes the world's rebirth—happy times, the Millennium.

Hitler exploited transcendent hope, only to use it for his own miserable purposes. Give them a cause to fight for, and the people will fight to the death. An anxious sense of impending Armageddon, the sense that a final conflict was imminent, infused the Nazi mind. In his fascinating account of the Hitler movement, James M. Rhodes refers to the German bent for "ontological hysteria." Ontological hysteria consists of prolonged fear of imminent annihilation, panic over the insecurity of existence. People experience it in disastrous, disorienting times.

Michael Barkun[27] studied the social settings conducive to millenarian reactions. Disaster, says Barkun, is one of the key variables. When the world around them is falling apart, human beings reach for straws. Desperate for orientation, their attention is drawn to archetypal images, which fascinate and soothe their troubled souls. And for the literal-minded and the brutal, images help focus action—violent, dehumanizing action. This was true for many in the Germany between the wars.

At that time a popular word in the Nazi lexicon was *collapse*. Things started to collapse in November 1918. First, the crippling Versailles treaty and the shock waves that followed: the Spartacus uprising, the communist insurrection in Munich, the French occupation of the Ruhr, troubles at the Polish border. German life was in a shambles: unemployment, inflation, bankruptcies, strikes, riots, high sexual weirdness, homelessness, widespread hunger, murderous gangs on the prowl, shootings, corpses in the street, and so on. The world seemed indeed to be collapsing. The feeling of collapse led to ontological hysteria. Germans were primed to listen to a seductive messiah—to Adolf Hitler, a romantic dreamer and failed artist who discovered he had "a voice."

In the midst of postwar disaster, the dreams of a Nazi Millennium were born. Studying the speeches, the overblown rhetoric, the apocalyptic word *resurrection* often appears. Hitler, the voice of the fanatic hopefuls, repeatedly used this religious term. In February 1935, he said: "We celebrate the proud *resurrection* of Germany." In September 1935: "Through us and in us the nation has *risen again*." And two years later: "Today Germany has in truth *risen again* and *risen again* as our work." In October 1938: "It is like a miracle that in so few years we should be able to experience a new German *resurrection*." And in

November 1940, Hitler declared he had led *"a new resurrection"* of the German people.[28]

The core chiliastic vision is bipolar; that is, resurrection presupposes Armageddon. There must be a final confrontation. The Nazi elect would do battle with the Jewish Antichrist. But final battles call for final solutions, which leads to the practical eschatology of SS boss Heinrich Himmler. It was Himmler who ordered the commandant of Auschwitz to prepare for the "final solution" in August 1941: "The Führer has ordered that the Jewish question be solved once and for all. . . . Every Jew that we can lay our hands on is to be destroyed or the Jews will one day destroy the German people."[29] Here you have the Armageddon myth literalizing in the gruesome politics of the Holocaust.

Armageddon—the term occurs once in the Book of Revelation—is a symbolic place; a locale where the battle of battles takes place, the prelude to the new age. Armageddon, the motif of a final war of cosmic liberation, appears in northern mythology. Icelandic storytellers tell of Ragnarok, "the fatal destiny of the gods," the final battle that precedes the end of the world. In the twelfth century, Norse bards changed the word *Ragnarok* so that it now meant "twilight of the gods"—which, in Wagnerian opera, became *Götterdämmerung*.

An old poem of the Edda, *Voluspa* ("what the prophetess says") narrates the twilight of the gods. The story is similar to the Book of Revelation. In a great final round of storm and cataclysm, gods and giants clash, earthquake and flood sweep over humankind. Wotan is the first casualty of the cosmic slaughter. After the twilight, however, new gods arise in a new, a peaceful world—thus, the core image of the Christian Millennium, albeit slightly skewed. For, according to the prophetess, "The black dragon has fled far away and the shining serpent has left the depths of the pit." Unlike John's revelation, the serpent is unbound at the end of time. In a new Valhalla, "I see a hall, as bright as the sun and covered in gold; there the valorous nations will live, they will live in joy for as long as one can foresee."[30] As usual, after frightful destruction, visions of renewal and abundance.

Heine had mused about the Germanic pagan past awakening from a thousand-year sleep. The hammer of Thor would rise, said the poet, and smash the cathedrals. Nordic mythology, since the Romantic Schlegel brothers, had been stirring uneasily in German dreams and phantasies. It had spilled from the academics to the fringes by early twentieth century. The Germanen Order, for example, active from 1912 to 1922, peddled the myth of a Nordic master-race of magical warriors. But myth can take strange detours into reality. Initiates to the Berlin Germanen Order had their skulls measured with a "planometer" to certify their pedigree; by 1942, Himmler was applying the planometer to Russian prisoners.

Images of Armageddon and Ragnarok mingled in the agitated consciousness of the German underground, enchanting hooligan poets like Dietrich Eckart and Bohemian nomads like Hitler. In the history of the Millennium Myth, there have been similar cases of cross-cultural influence. During the Italian Renaissance, for example, the Millennium Myth crystallized around images from the Greco-Roman golden age and the hermetic tradition. Similar mythic time bombs entered the Nazi mental environment; but again there were differences. Instead of Aesclepius, the hermetic God of Healing, Wotan, the runic God of War and ecstatic Destruction, sprang huffing and puffing onto the stage of history. Germany was awash in occult delvings.

Pamphleteer Guido von List mixed *voelkish* ideology and occultism. Along with Lanz von Liebenfels, he helped to create the myth of an Aryan master-state. List, raised a Roman Catholic, converted to Wotan. This came about because of a strange psychic experience. In a catacomb under Saint Stephen's cathedral in Vienna, List became convinced he stumbled on a ruined pagan altar, a place of worship of old Wotan; he was overcome by feelings of an awesome presence.[31] It was one of those bizarre transformative experiences, such as we often hear reported nowadays in America. Rosenberg, in the *Myth of the Twentieth Century*, was right when he wrote, "Wotan, as the primeval mirror of the eternal soul-forces of the Nordic man, is living today as five thousand years ago."[32]

In the 1936 essay on Wotan, Jung expressed his opinion that the German catastrophe was an example of mass possession. On the psychic plane, National Socialism arose because of nothing less than an invasion from pagan archetypes. The alien energy of the old berserkers was suddenly afoot. Instead of Christ, Guido von List imagined Wotan was returning, the German God of War and Runes, the arouser of the Beast, the new berserker of the Nazi Millennium. The prospect of Armageddon was received with enthusiasm by National Socialism. The Nazis demonstrated the force of spiritual perversion. Hitler imagined he was the Messiah but acted like a psychopath. And the Kingdom of Heaven? What was there to speak of but the death camps?

Kingdom of Heaven: Nazi Millennium

Jesus spoke of the coming Kingdom of Heaven, and the Book of Revelation of "the holy city, the New Jerusalem, coming down from God out of heaven." The medieval millenarians imagined the coming of new forms of social reality. The Nazis rhapsodized about a "new better Third Reich;" the "thousand-year Reich," the "new Reich," the "new Germany," a "new creation," and so on.

Granted that Hitler was the Messiah of the Nazi Millennium. What exactly was this Millennium going to be like? One is hard put to find an answer to this question. There is scarcely a clue to the positive content of the Nazi golden age. Hitler and Albert Speer liked playing at being architects of the new Reich and fiddled with diagrams and models— mostly of vast marble structures, very monotonous, very cold, very lifeless, like the abstract paintings of Malevich. A world of "stone faces," as Primo Levi once described his Auschwitz security guards.

For a moment let us return to the basic image of the Millennium, as it appeared in John's Book of Revelation. What we see is the serpent under lock and key for a thousand years, an image, at one level, symbolic of repression and rigidity—the enchanting symbol of life force, chained in the bottomless abyss. Here the Nazis were in secret accord with the dark side of the Book of Revelation.

For the Nazis, the "old serpent" became the racially inferior portion of humanity, the infected throw-aways that had to be exterminated. Imprisoning the serpent or generative force is a metaphor that fits with the practice of putting human beings in deathcamps. Thus seen, the Nazi deathcamps were ghastly literalizings of one of the main images from the Book of Revelation. There are, I am afraid to say, uncanny links between the Book of Revelation and the Holocaust. However shocking the idea, there is a connection, a dark continuity, a twisted relationship between that sacred document and the Hitler movement. Like the Book of Revelation, the Nazi movement was drunk with lust for power and inhumanly unforgiving to adversaries. The Nazi Kingdom of Heaven was a gigantic perversion of spirit whose unforgettable trademark is the crematoria, a nightmare of incomprehensible dimensions.

Beyond the Nightmare to Self-Knowledge

There is an apocalyptic undertow to the psychic dynamics of National Socialism. In myth, pageantry, doctrine, ritual, symbolism, and emotionalism, Nazism was a typical religious revival, markedly millenarian.

Of first importance was the fact that the movement had its messianic leader in Adolf Hitler; Hitler, as revealed in *Mein Kampf*, saw himself as the messianic Führer of Germany. So potent was this enchantment that belief in Hitler's messiahship still persists in certain circles, as we saw in the case of Miguel Serrano. More troubling is the growing and worsening Neo-Nazi skinhead movement in Germany today, a movement that is distinguished by a peculiar sort of stupidly brutal xenophobia. In skinhead Nazism, the new demons are the Turks—any, for that matter, foreigners.

In the old apocalyptic scenario, the Messiah squared off against absolute evil, the redoubtable Antichrist; in this regard, too, the Hitler movement exploited yearnings for the Millennium by scapegoating the Jewish people as Antichrist. This deadly paranoid projection turns up over and over again in Western history—this time it did so with truly fatal consequences.

A third Nazi-Millennium connection is the idea of chosenness; the Nazis battened on the fiction that they were the elect; the elite, the founders of civilization, the archetypes of Nordic superhumanity. Throughout history, the phantasy of election has fired the imaginations of millenarians. The Nazis went for this part of the Myth in a big way.

After being elected to purify the world, what next? There is still the job of bringing about the metaphysical convulsion craved, the new mode of being, in short, the real live Millennium.

The formula calls for a final conflict, an Armageddon, a Ragnarok or Götterdämmerung—world-destroying battles of enormous dimensions. The Nazis brilliantly succeeded in realizing this part of the Myth. Needless to say, benefits to none followed; it was all hell, not one jot of heaven.

Nevertheless, the positive yearning for renewal, the hope in a coming transformation, go to the heart of the apocalyptic. Nazi rhetoric, myth, and propaganda catered to this vague but deeply felt yearning; the propaganda machine stirred the masses with garish poster art and pagan torchlit rallies. In a fog of religious yearning, Nazi slogans

201

justified brutish action and created opportunities for discontented souls—they were plentiful—to wreak havoc on imagined enemies.

What is there to learn about ourselves from the Nazi abortion of the Millennium Myth? Perhaps it is that the worst kind of evil operates behind the mask of good. Hitler succeeded by manipulating people's ideals; he heaped contempt on materialism and spoke to the need for community. He despised, as the Marxists do, bourgeois egoism and apolitical individualism. Hitler sensed the spiritual longings of his times and used them to further his own ends. He provided for the needs of the German imagination with clearly defined collective goals, unmarred by ambiguity and gussied up in flamboyant rhetoric.

The great challenge to self-knowledge is blind attachment to our virtues. It is hard to criticize what we think are our virtues. Although the spirit languishes without ideals, idealism can be the greatest danger. It was the fire of idealism that moved Germany to raise the hammer of Thor; the high ideals of socialism were the bloody flags of the Russian Revolution; and some say it was misguided idealism that got America into Viet Nam. Our better angels seem to keep getting us into trouble.

The danger of the millennial mind is its passion to moralize, or rather, its terrifying need to simplify the moral universe. Working at this simplistic level, it is a mind that thinks—that needs to think—in bald contrasts and bulldozing absolutes. In a world of infinite grays, it sees only black and white. The machinelike, the computerlike part of the brain takes over and forces us to see nothing but blood brothers or inhuman foes. The great challenge is to gain self-knowledge—to face the little Hitler who lives inside each one of us.

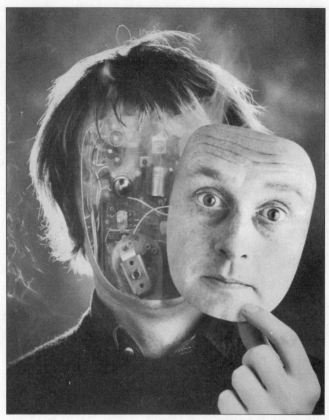

John Brown, Electric Man taking face off

Part II

Futuristic

Part Two: Futuristic

*America is therefore the land of the future, where, in
the ages that lie before us, the burden of the World's
History shall reveal itself.*

GEORG WILHELM HEGEL
Introduction to the Philosophy of History

The Millennium Myth, which was an incentive to the Russian Revolution
and the Nazi Movement, may seem to have discredited itself once and
for all. Besides these obvious failures of the great mythical vision, the
twentieth century has witnessed other movements, rooted in chiliastic
phantasies, end disastrously. For example, mass suicide at Jonestown
in 1978, and mass murder at Waco, Texas, in 1993, stand out in most
people's memories. Nevertheless, the Millennium Myth is by no means
dead nor its energies spent.

The hope, the drive, the dream impelling people to seek an extraordinary future on earth are still forces to reckon with. From here on I
pick up the trail of the great Myth largely as it continues to wend its
way on the American scene.

The role of millennialism in the discovery, settling, and founding of
the United States of America was discussed in chapter 6, "Yankee New
Jerusalem." The hope for a millennial new age lives on in the ideals of
Thomas Jefferson's heavenly city of the Enlightenment philosophers,
specifically in the American Declaration of Independence, and most of
all, I would say, in those world-historical words about the right to the
pursuit of happiness.

Hints of millennialism were evident in George Bush's talk of a "New
World Order" and in Bill Clinton's talk of the "New Covenant." As we
shall see, the urge to millennialize remains a factor in other areas of
American life. In my view, the pursuit of the American Millennium
remains a live option, running deeper than superficial political rhetoric

and more promisingly than in familiar frauds, like Jim Jones and David Koresh. I will try to show this in the remaining chapters of this book.

Hegel On the Future of America

The philosopher Hegel had some interesting thoughts on America—on North America in particular, which he regarded as a place in which "the most unbounded license of imagination in religious matters prevails."[1]

Hegel's own philosophy was eschatological in its core claim that the history of the world is the history of freedom. In Hegel's version of Joachim's chiliastic prophecy, patriarchal fear, and domination will one day yield to an age of spirit marked by love and freedom. However, for Hegel freedom was basic, for without it, there could be no love. For Hegel, as for Berdyaev, the *substance* of history was the *subject*, that is, the "human person."[2] The full development of the free individual, as for the Renaissance humanists, is the *meaning* of history.

In Hegel's *Philosophy of History*, in the section called "The Geographical Basis of History," we read, "America is therefore the land of the future, where, in the ages that lie before us, the burden of the World's History shall reveal itself." America thus becomes the historic theater for the apocalypse, the place where the goal of world history will be revealed.

Contrary to what Marx said, Hegel did have a grasp of the material conditions of history. Thus, for Hegel, geography was destiny, and Europe was old, cramped, and tired; America, young and vast, bordered on two sides by oceans, a natural setting for the further adventures of the species, which, according to Hegel, are driven by an urge toward realizing the end of ordinary history.

Hegel offers a few hints on the psychology of North America, dismissing South America as Catholic and authoritarian. The American psyche is governed by the "principle of confidence," he says. With confidence, America will push toward the limits of freedom on earth. American geography and destiny portend a break with all foregoing assumptions and conditions of history.

"It is for America to abandon the ground on which hitherto the History of the World has developed itself," wrote the German philosopher. A similar idea was suggested by Marilyn Ferguson in her underground bestseller *The Aquarian Conspiracy* (1980). Here are the words that open her book: "A leaderless but powerful network is working to bring about radical change in the United States. Its members have broken with certain key elements of Western thought, and they may have even broken continuity with history."

And lest we be tempted to write off this chiliastic proclamation as New Age hyperbole, we might recall another recent bestseller, State Department official Francis Fukuyama's *The End of History and the Last Man*. Fukuyama argues that history, understood as the struggle to realize freedom, has in essence reached its goal in America, in the sense that the world at large now acknowledges the preeminence of the Western ideals of freedom and democracy. America's messianic consciousness of itself here reflects the goals of the Millennium Myth.

American Self-Inventiveness

America is a millennialist-prone land because it is an ongoing experiment in self-invention. Edmundo O'Gorman has expounded this thesis in his book *The Invention of America* (1961). Columbus, argues O'Gorman, did not "discover" America; there was no *thing* there to be discovered. From the beginning what was there was appropriated, interpreted in light of preexisting ideas, endowed with meaning—in a word, *invented*. America is the country where the idea of the "self-made" man or woman has found its most congenial home.

America is a place where people understand that reality is invented, a kind of conscious dream, as enshrined in the phrase *the American dream*. It is the fate of America to be forever reinventing itself, not only culturally, as, for example, via the Hollywood dream machine, but constitutionally, for a people having the right to emend their own government have in effect institutionalized revolution. One nation, in Lincoln's metaphor, *conceived* in liberty. America, in other words, is an act of the creative imagination, and Americans are still exploring the meaning of Lincoln's words.

This openness as to our very identity as a nation, the readiness to reinvent and transcend ourselves, is what makes America a country ideally suited to millennial longings. So, on the threshold of a new millennium, it seems opportune to reflect on this feature of our history and on the visionary roots of the American experience.

Walt Whitman—Bard of the American Millennium

To see how this spirit wells up from the land, and is, as it were, native to the continent's physiology, hear the words of the bard of the American Millennium—Walt Whitman. Whitman, like Fukuyama and Ferguson, was in his own way a reader, if not a disciple, of Hegel. The poem that begins with the line, "Thou mother with thy equal brood," is full of Hegelian millennial sentiment. (The exalted mood prompts Whitman to talk in *thous* and *thees*.)

America, we are told, is the "ship of Democracy" and stores within its hold the past, the present, and the future of humanity:

> Thou holdest not the venture of thyself alone, not of the
> Western continent alone,
> Earth's *résumé* entire floats on thy keel O Ship . . .
> With thee Time voyages in trust, the antecedent nations sink
> or swim with thee. . . .
>
>
> By history's cycles forwarded, by every nation, language,
> hither sent,
> Ready, collected here, a freer, vast, electric world, to be
> constructed here,
> The true New World, the world of orbic science, morals,
> literatures to come.

Whitman saw in America a place where the entire human enterprise might be recast, discover an infinity of fresh meanings, come home to essential freedom, and thus, in effect, would bring history to an end:

> Brain of the New World, what a task is thine,
> To formulate the Modern—out of the peerless grandeur of the
> modern,
> Out of thyself, comprising science, to recast poems,
> churches, art,
> (Recast, maybe discard them, end them—maybe their work is
> done, who knows?)

The cloud that has weighed on the "mind of man" for millennia, the doubt, suspicion, dread, and decadence—will be lifted forever. A new race of spiritual athletes will arise. Like Joachim, like Blake, like Hegel, Whitman sees in history a movement toward the internalization and transcendence of institutions:

> . . . thee in no single bible, savior, merely,
> Thy saviors countless, latent within thyself, thy bibles
> incessant within thyself, equal to any, divine as any.

Whitman sees a coming race of "sacerdotal bards, kosmic savans." One of his more prophetic productions as "kosmic savan" is the piece called "Years of the Modern." It is, in the spirit of Hegel, a foretelling of a time of complete human freedom and revolutionary democracy. The "average" will be exalted to a new soul life: "Never was average man, his soul, more energetic, more like a God." This godlike American people will spread the gospel of freedom and cosmic consciousness everywhere on earth. And, with a characteristic American flourish, it will do so with the help of technology:

> With the steamship, the electric telegraph, the newspaper,
> the wholesale engines of war,
> With these and the world-spreading factories
> he interlinks all geography, all lands.

Like President Bill Clinton, Whitman wants to eliminate all barriers to world trade. Whitman also foresees Marshall McLuhan's "global village," the new "data highways" that the Clinton Administration wants to put in place; Whitman would have warmed to such global computer networks as the Internet. What an opportunity for humankind to come together and embrace in an ecstasy of electronic cosmic consciousness!

Whitman exalts technology as a means of achieving a millenarian solidarity of the human spirit. Thus he writes, "Are all nations communing? is there going to be but one heart to the globe?"

In a wild burst of democratic expansiveness, he asks, "Is humanity forming en-masse?" *En-masse* is one of Whitman's favorite words. In this line, we find intimations of Teilhard de Chardin's *noogenesis*, the formation of a new terrestrial mindsphere, even of Arthur C. Clarke's end-of-history genesis of the Overmind as portrayed in *Childhood's End*. But the sacerdotal bard senses danger ahead, too, and lapses into fairly explicit apocalyptic imagery: "The earth, restive, confronts a new era, perhaps a general divine war."

Here is an augury of contemporary jihad, of the culture and civilization and religious wars we are witnessing today. No one knows what will happen next, says Whitman, although "portents fill the days and nights," as he reels drunk in a "strange ecstatic fever of dreams" **209** over premonitions of things gigantic and shadowy to come, things that hover in a gray limbo of the yet "unperformed." Clearly, Whitman saw something unprecedented on the horizon of American history.

Whitman's Preface to *Leaves of Grass* qualifies him as poet of the American Millennium. It attempts to redefine the function of the poet, going beyond Shelley's poet as the "legislator of the human race." For Whitman, poet and prophet are one. The new poetry is not a specialized esthetic zone. The new poetry is about the poetics of a new earth, a new humanity. And because this poetics is directed not toward the Byzantium of the imaginal world, as it was for Yeats, but toward the "average" man and woman and toward a specific place, America, it is millenarian in scope and feeling.

America is a locus of vision, the poetic culmination of the history of the human race, not a nation but a "teeming nation of nations," where "the United States themselves are essentially the greatest poem." Millenarian is the phantasy—again foreseen by the Renaissance humanists—that life itself will one day become art, that men and women are the greatest of self-inventions, that art in the future will serve our teeming, sensual, various, turbulent terrestrial life. John Dewey's masterpiece, *Art as Experience*,[3] took up this Whitmanesque stance, in which esthetics merges with life itself, breaking down barriers that enslaved the hierarchical life styles of the Old World.

Whitman's poetry evokes the creative chaos of this marriage of art and life. His free verse, his rolling expansive lines, ("barbaric yawp" he called it), his mixture of slang, foreign words, science words, speech rhythms that combine the commonplace and the ecstatic, his love of lists and panoramic catalogues, his fusion of egotistical rant with democratic mystic-mongering, his androgynous prophetism mixed with raw cliché, produce in the reader a kind of rapture of jingoism.

The common people are exalted in "their deathless attachment to freedom." "The President's taking off his hat to them not they to him—these too are unrhymed poetry." The central millennial phantasy is that America is somehow, in its people and history and geography, the incarnation of a new species of poetry. Hence in the Preface there is much talk about the American poet—a projection and justification of Whitman's poetics, grounded, if we take his Canadian admirer Richard Bucke[4] at his word, in Whitman's experience of cosmic consciousness.

The old millennial phantasy of self-deification arises anew in Whitman's American poetics. The key is a relentless, Dionysian all-inclusiveness. "Exact science and its practical movements," for example, "are no checks on the greatest poets." The "direct trial" of the poet is to "flood himself with the immediate age as with vast oceanic tides."

Again echoing—no doubt unconsciously—the medieval prophet of the new age, Joachim of Fiore, Whitman declares, "There will be no more priests. Their work is done. . . . A superior breed shall take their place. . . . the gangs of kosmos and prophets en masse shall take their place. A new order shall arise . . . and every man shall be his own priest." Here now the superdemocratic message of the "great poets": "Did you suppose there could be only one Supreme? We affirm there can be unnumbered Supremes."

Moreover, the American language is uniquely the language of the new age, the "chosen tongue to express growth faith self-esteem freedom justice equality friendliness amplitude prudence decision and courage. It is the medium that shall well nigh express the inexpressible." The American poet's diction is to be "transcendent and new." He is one who speaks a direct language of soul; he is a seer, a complete and autonomous individual.

Whitman's poetics of the American Millennium contains themes and motifs we will explore in the following pages. Not altogether new to America, they depict continuities in the history of the Millennium Myth.

Certain primordial obsessions keep recurring. Some go back to the master source of world-moving millennial thought, the Book of Revelation; for example, the idea of cosmic and social renewal. Others are offshoots from millenarian movements, rooted in the Biblical tradition but entering history at later dates, during the Middle Ages, the Renaissance, or the Enlightenment.

These offshoots are related to what I call the heresy of self-transformation. So, for example, the idea of a race of new people—spiritual superfolk who live beyond good and evil—the idea of self-deification, keeps coming back. The continuities revolve around a small set of meta-themes. So here is a preview of the remaining chapters.

• Chapter 8 looks at the American New Age through the lens of the Millennium Myth. In the perspective of the Myth, much that appears under this maligned label assumes fresh significance. Even the most frivolous claims look different when seen against the background of the deep structure of the Myth.

• Chapter 9 explores the apocalyptic notion that there will be signs and wonders pointing to the end of the old world. Nowadays we call such signs and wonders *anomalies*, and the fact is, whether delusive or authentic, reports of disturbingly inexplicable phenomena are on the rise. What does all this mean, what transformations are foreshadowed by these omens appearing in the night sky of the future? The Millennium Myth offers a guide for interpretation.

• Chapter 10: Modern technology, rapidly evolving during the twentieth century, is converging with the apocalyptic imagination. Technology is not a purely rational development; it is, I believe, in the grips of an unconscious archetype. What drives Western technology are the future-oriented energies of the millennial mind. The Book of Revelation gives us a clue to what technology is aiming to achieve— nothing less than "a new heaven and a new earth."

• Chapter 11 looks at one of the oldest phantasies of the millennial mind—the abolition of death. What are the possibilities of realizing this, the ultimate dream? In light of the whole range of reported human capacities, can we begin to form a new vision of death?

• Purveyors of the Myth see a time when human relationships will change, transcending the dividedness of heart that troubles unregenerate humanity. Chapter 12 examines utopian ideas for revisioning human love, sex, and social relations.

New Age America

*A leaderless but powerful network is working to bring
about radical change in the United States. Its members
have broken with certain key elements of Western
thought, and they may have even broken continuity
with history.*

MARILYN FERGUSON
The Aquarian Conspiracy

T he American New Age is a complicated phenomenon, without clear
boundaries. In some ways a consumer-driven, publishing artifact,
many of its leading ideas are nevertheless rooted in ancient traditions.
The New Age is a potpourri of pursuits and effects, ranging from the
flaky to the intellectually provocative, the sinister to the spiritually
daring. In this chapter, I look at the New Age through the lens of the
Millennium Myth.

I focus on the American scene, although the phenomenon is not
just American; it is global, with ample signs of life in Great Britain,
Germany, Italy, the Spanish-speaking world, post-Soviet Russia, China,
Eastern Europe, and elsewhere.

The immediate ancestry of the American New Age includes Mes-
merism, Theosophy, New Thought, Spiritualism, Swedenborgianism,
and New England Transcendentalism. Two themes run consistently
through the movement: one is an idealistic revolt against the encroaching materialism of modern life and science; the other, closely related,
is the search for spiritual renewal through sources outside mainstream
religion and bodily renewal outside mainstream science.

New Age concerns may be traced back to the Millennium Myth.
This older dimension of the New Age is what I want to focus on here.
Once that is done, it will, I believe, become apparent in what sense
the New Age is a renewal of ancient visionary hopes. The "New Age,"

as psychedelic eschatologist Terence McKenna has said, is more like an "archaic revival."[1]

Antipathy Toward the New Age

New Age bashing has become fashionable and stems from different persuasions. Among the most bitter are Christian fundamentalists and evangelicals; thus, in Kerry D. McRobert's *New Age or Old Lie* (1989), the author proclaims, "Concerns by some Christian writers that an ominous system, like the New Age, could usher in the reign of Antichrist are valid. . . ." Apparently, some literal-minded Christians have taken Marilyn Ferguson's *Aquarian Conspiracy* at face value, and fancy diabolic conspiracies are afoot. By now, I trust, the reader of this book will have become used to the habit people have of slapping the Antichrist label on their enemies. In the chapter on the Third Reich, it was the Jews; in the chapter on the proletariat paradise, capitalism and the bourgeoisie; now it is the American New Age.

At the other end of the political spectrum one finds a good Marxist like Michael Parenti criticizing the New Age for its "political quietism."[2] Parenti contends that New Age idealism is a coverup for denying the objective ills of capitalist society. Economic inequality, pollution, oppression—all the ills that plague our society—are things we create for karmic or other metaphysical reasons. For New Age quietists, the only remedy is to work on ourselves—and society be damned!

Hardcore secular academics also feel obliged to hit on the New Age. One of my favorites is Harold Bloom's depiction of the movement as "orange crush." Sweet, in short, but without substance. To make the case for Bloom, I turn at random to a page from the *Newlife Expo '93* catalogue and find this bit of apocalyptic kitsch: "The Avatar Course: The End of the Search" is a course that promises to help you redesign your beliefs so you can "create the world that you prefer." Remarkable! Especially when the writer adds, "This technology is simple, fun, and miraculously effective." Miracles may be fun, but such hype is likely to turn off sincere pundits and alarm the false-prophet police.

That said, I must add that even hype has its history and deep structure. At any rate, the way I look at it, the American New Age is a thing nested in the archetypal Millennium Myth, whose meandering course we have been tracing. Far from being a passing fad, American New Age thought is a twentieth-century rerun of very old, very persistent ideas.

According to J. Gordon Melton's authoritative *New Age Encyclopedia*[3]: "The New Age Movement can be defined by its primal experience of transformation." Transformation, as we have been noting all along, is a major theme of the Myth.

A Course in Miracles, the near-death prophecies, the alien-abduction apocalypses, the godmaking rhetoric of the channelers, the declarations of holistic healers, the wisdom of runes, crystals, *I Ching*, Tarot cards, astrology—I could extend the list; the point is that the American New Age is a call to transformation. An exercise of the malcontented imagination, an unhappy consciousness hungering for a new spiritual identity. New Age discontent is deep in our history; it began with the pilgrims. Harold Bloom is right when he says, "Extravagant as the New Age is, it is only the most garish of all the American originals that have expressed our national spiritual exuberance."[4] Let us look at this exuberance, as sampled in some New Age ideas and pursuits.

The Holistic Health Movement

Somewhere in Plato's *Republic*, Socrates mentions with ironical disdain the cult of *somatophiliacs*—literally, lovers of the body. Somatophiliacs outnumber philosophers or lovers of wisdom, groused Plato. In our day, the somatophiliacs also prevail. American somatophilia takes many forms: the cult of youth, fitness, vitamins, and diet. Meanwhile, New Age philosophers are intent on reclaiming the body from sinister Cartesian dualism. Somatophilia is evident in the quest for cryonic (refrigerated) immortality, as we will later see. A prickly awareness of health is in the air, and the media constantly harps on disease, bringing us good and bad "news from medicine" and daily warnings and recantations of warnings about the endless variety of insidious threats to our health.

In fact, there are good reasons for taking an interest in new approaches to health and healing. First of all, new threats to our health do exist: the hazards of processed food, toxins, and pollutants everywhere in the environment; new and hard-to-diagnose diseases of immunodepression; diseases of stress and future shock; and a health care system that can be fatal to one's economic existence. All these are good reasons for taking an interest in preventive medicine, in anything that promises freedom from the medical establishment.

Discontent with the medical establishment is not just a fringe phenomenon. With the inauguration of the Clinton administration in 1993, First Lady Hillary Rodham Clinton began a crusade to reform the American medical establishment. Mrs. Clinton has been derided for airing what are said to be her New Age sentiments.

In a *New York Times Magazine*[5] article, the author referred to the First Lady as "Saint Hillary." In an artist's caricature, her arms are sanctimoniously crossed, holding a sword, and there is a halo round her head. The author took the First Lady to task for talking about the "politics of meaning" and for saying that America suffers from "sleeping sickness of the soul." Not the kind of talk usually heard from inside the Beltway. The *Times* reporter sniffed at the First Lady for stating her misgivings about "the prevailing acquisitive and competitive corporate life," and for the suggestion that we Americans need to work on redefining "who we are as human beings in this post-modern age."

Admittedly, to try to reform our health care system does sound like wanting to launch a millenarian crusade, touching, as it must, on fundamental questions of meaning, values, the nature of the self, and so on. To get to the bottom of our health troubles would indeed demand that we question some pretty basic assumptions about how we think and how we live.

The cynical author of the *Times* article was right when he wrote, "But there actually is, as the mists of New Age mysticism slip away, a clear line to Mrs. Clinton's message. It is, fundamentally, an old and very American message, one that goes purposely beyond the normal boundaries of politics into the territory of religion." A good historical example of this misty mysticism transcending the "normal boundaries of politics" was the Abolitionist crusade against slavery. American apocalyptic fervor was roused during the antislavery crusade among notables such as Harriet Beecher Stowe, author of *Uncle Tom's Cabin*, and suffragette Julia Ward Howe, whose "Battle Hymn of the Republic" voiced the millenarian hope for the end of slavery. The issue of slavery pricked a moral nerve, although not everyone felt it immediately. As the injustice of slavery was slow to penetrate the status quo awareness, so the different but equally systemic injustice of our health care system has been slow to penetrate the American conscience. Just as the Abolitionists saw slavery as an obstacle to national rebirth, it can be argued today that medical materialism and medical capitalism are obstacles to national rebirth.

To see this clearly we have to focus on the deep structure of the Myth. The American holistic health movement reflects the spirit of the prophets who saw a day coming when sickness would be no more and when the human body's divine potential would come into its own. From Iranian Mazdean prophecy, to Saint Paul's Letters, to Neoplatonic philosophy, there has been a tradition of hyper-health, a futuristic yearning for the divine body. In the American Human Potential Movement, this ancient quest has its latest and most comprehensive voice in Michael Murphy's magisterial *The Future of the Body* (1992).

American holistic ideals are rooted in the New Testament. Jesus led a spiritual healing ministry, stressing the value of love and faith.[6] Holistic health teachers also say that love, hope, and spirituality are critical to our health and well-being, forces that can be mobilized to heal people, sometimes in strikingly unconventional ways. Bernie Siegel's *Love, Medicine and Miracles* says it clearly enough: love—the medicine neglected by the medical establishment—can make "miracles." By *miracle* I mean to point to a wide range of possible breakthroughs toward greater wholeness.

The radical side of the holistic vision may be seen in the work of John Humphrey Noyes, whom we met in chapter 5. Noyes insisted on the connection between healing, the resurrection, and social revolution. They were all intertwined—as we say—"holistically."

> The abolition of death is to be the last triumph of the Kingdom of God. Christ cannot save the body until he has 'put down all [present] authority and rule,' and organized society anew. It is true that, since life works legitimately from within outward, the social revolution ought not to be commenced until the resurrection power is established in the heart. . . . Just so the breaking up of the fashion of the world must precede the resurrection of the body.[7]

Thus, before the body can be saved and death itself abolished, society must be organized "anew." Like Marx, social revolution must precede human renovation. But unlike Marx, for Noyes the social revolution is based on awakening the "resurrection power" of the heart.

New Age thought does not spell out these connections as clearly as Noyes did, but they are latent in the idea of holism. In fact, few medical professionals today focus on the *social* dimensions of healing. The emphasis is on healing individuals, reclaiming the inner child, **217** working through dysfunctional family life, and so forth.[8] Broader issues of social pathology are not prominent concerns.

More radical New Age healers who align themselves with millenarian Noyes say there are spiritual forces untapped and unrecognized by the medical establishment; healing must engage all dimensions of the person. Work, economics, environment (inner and outer), relationships (personal and social)—all figure in the healing equation. Thus, to wish to reform the health care system in America is to throw down a very big gauntlet, for it raises questions about governing values and assumptions—for example, about the logic of money versus the logic of need. In the American system, only the rich or the well-insured get good medical care. For the middle class, serious illness or accident can mean economic ruin, while millions are forced to face serious sickness with slight or no resources at all.

Health reform has explosive implications. From a holistic perspective, for example, the idea of environmental pollution would acquire new dimensions of meaning. The dedicated reformer would have to tackle the problem of information pollution, values pollution, and esthetic pollution. A holistic system would focus on the needs of the inner as well as the outer environment. It would have to broaden the concept of environment and deal with the issue of emotional, spiritual, and symbolic ecosystems.

Once the profit motive yielded to the prophetic motive, every institution and every aspect of American life would become subject to critical revision. The automotive industry, the food industry, the entertainment industry, the media industry—all these and more would cry out for critical revision in light of holistic ideals of health. Practical implementation of these ideals would entail overturning many a sacred cow in American society.

The holistic health movement has scarcely made a dent in the medical establishment or the society at large; but *if* its principles were applied, we would be taking the first halting steps toward an American Millennium. The reason is that everything we do, think, and feel, and every aspect of our environment, is related to our health. The repercussions of a real holistic revolution would be indeed "apocalyptic."

True and total health would mean realizing our truly transcendent potentials; from the standpoint of the apocalyptic tradition, what confers our final bill of health is bodily resurrection. Short of being on the path to achieving this, we are all fundamentally sick, and normal existence, as Plato said, would indeed be a disease and ordinary life, a hospital. The First Lady has indeed touched a sensitive public nerve by talking of the "politics of meaning."[9]

The premises of the American holistic health movement go back through idealistic New Thought and the Christian Science of Mary Baker Eddy and Phineas Quimby to early Christian and other prophetic traditions of hyper-health. It is a tradition that denies the necessity of death and disease and declares that to be "healthy" is to realize our "divine" psychosomatic potential.

The holistic health movement thus seems to be riding an apocalyptic time wave. For example, Seventh-day Adventism is a movement that grew from the failure of the Millerite Millennium to materialize in the 1840s. John Harvey Kellogg and his brother Will Keith Kellogg were allied with Ellen Harmon White, known as the prophetess of health[10] and founder of Seventh-day Adventism. Like thousands of other northeast Americans, White and the Kelloggs got caught up in Miller's endtime prophecy.

Perhaps, reasoned the Adventists when Miller's prophecy failed, we were not pure enough to receive the Millennium; let us therefore purify and ready ourselves for the Rapture. But how? Why not eat right and strive for physical fitness? Why not make our bodies perfectly attuned instruments for the Rapture? Thus, an effort to prepare for the Millennium lay at the origins of the health reformation and temperance movement in the United States.[11]

The Kellogg brothers, health food pioneers and founders of the corn flake empire, also led an antimasturbation crusade, but split when Will insisted on mixing sugar with the original health flake, thus yielding to worldly interests and roadblocking the Millennium. White and the Kelloggs sublimated their yearning for the resurrection body into a holistic health program. Like the Great Seal on the American dollar bill, the Kellogg's cornflakes box belongs in a pop museum of the Millennium imagination.

Holism and the Future of the Body

The American New Age is a wide-ranging phenomenon, bound together by deep millenarian longings. It stretches from the anti-masturbation founders of the Kellogg's cornflakes empire to Michael

Murphy, co-founder of Esalen and pioneer of the Human Potential movement. Murphy has written a book that defines a new genre: an encyclopedic-prophetic blueprint of the future of the body.

In *The Future of the Body*[12], Murphy concludes that humanity is on a "path toward extraordinary life, which, I believe, includes types of love, joy, and embodiment beyond our present abilities to conceive." This remarkable sentence sums up a massive marshaling of data from medicine, psychical research, extraordinary annals of sport, comparative religion, and anthropology. Murphy employs what he calls "synoptic empiricism" to deploy his facts and construct his vision of the human body's potential; unlike most specialists, he takes in the whole range of pertinent data. The holistic health movement implies a new conception of embodied existence, traceable to the Neoplatonic, Christian, or Islamic[13] light-, spiritual-, or resurrection-body.

Murphy bridges the prophetic imagination with an evolutionary perspective. He translates concepts like "grace" into empirical frameworks for thinking about the farther reaches of human development. Murphy states, "Reframing Christian vision from the developmental perspective proposed here, doctrines of the Final Days might symbolize a new evolutionary domain, and 'risen bodies of the just' might represent metanormal embodiment."[14] Thus viewing science and prophecy together, Michael Murphy joins the ranks of other American pioneers in scientific eschatology.

Quest for a New Paradigm

In the American New Age, the apocalyptic yearning for a new cosmic epoch is evident in the pursuit of new paradigms. Thomas Kuhn's *Structure of Scientific Revolutions* provided the key terminology, *paradigm* and *anomaly*.

The *paradigm* is the overall socio-mental pattern that defines what is real and researchable in the domain of the real. *Anomaly* refers to events that do not fit in a given paradigm; anomalies are irritants in our epistemic eyes. As such they stimulate the hunt for better, more comprehensive paradigms. Anomalies are the juice of vital science, though in practice, they are often ignored or gruffly dismissed. Anomaly is the scientific term for sign and wonder—words from the prophetic lexicon.

How does the pursuit of new paradigms relate to the pursuit of the Millennium? Think of it like this: The Millennium Myth is a vision of a new reality, a new heaven and earth. A new paradigm is also a vision of a new reality; but the scientist, not the prophet, now speaks. A paradigm shift might indeed be described as a kind of apocalypse. And New Age thinkers say we need just this: a radical shift in our concept of reality, a new paradigm for a new heaven and earth—in scientific language, a new cosmology. The paradigm is an ontological map, a set of guidelines for what we can do and experience or hope to do and experience. It is widely felt today that the old paradigm fails to do justice to the whole of natural fact or to the whole of human potential. Above all, there is a felt need for paradigms that speak to the ecological crisis.

So what is the problem with the old reality maps? Philosopher Alfred North Whitehead offers a diagnosis in his *Modes of Thought*, in a chapter called "Nature Alive." Since the rise of seventeenth-century science, we seem to find ourselves in a universe made of lifeless matter, a place deanimated, mechanized—in Max Weber's word, *disenchanted*. The major complaint against the old paradigm, as far as I can see, is that it destroys animism; in other words, it takes the soul out of the universe, strips it of feeling, meaning, purpose, beauty.

Now, if the universe is dead, the human adventure is spoiled at the core; the shadow of death hangs over all; the possibilities of joy and communion are checked. Hence the need for a new paradigm. Rupert Sheldrake has titled one of his books *The Rebirth of Nature*, which summarizes in a phrase the goal of the new paradigm. I am reminded of Saint Paul's strange remark that the whole of creation is "groaning" to be reborn. Evidently, Paul, Whitehead, and Sheldrake all agree that our view of nature in some sense is dead and wants to be reborn.

So the New Age paradigm quest is a quest for rebirth. In contemporary vocabulary, it wants to overcome a worldview that is mechanistic, Newtonian, Cartesian, dualistic, hierarchical, authoritarian, patriarchal, anti-ecological, and unspiritual. The enemy is Whitehead's dead and deadening nature, that scene of bits and pieces of impervious matter floating atop an unfeeling matrix of space, a nature without redemptive power, bereft of life and color. As historian Edwin Burtt said, after Galileo launched the mechanistic worldview, human beings, reduced to spiritual impotence,[15] became accidental observers in a universe ruled by alien causes.

The new scientific materialism had practical consequences; worst of all, a Promethean man-centeredness was unleashed on what we have recently come to personify as Gaia or Mother Earth. At first the technological rape of the planet was slow. But things have come to a head by the end of the twentieth century: the mounting onslaught against the environment, the runaway decimation of species, the despoiling of eco-rich rainforests, the pillage and plunder of Native cultures, and the general toxicosis of the environment depress our collective spirits with increasing urgency.

The new paradigm that New Agers seek would remedy all this. A paradigm that promises a rebirthing of Gaian ecology, it heralds the return of an animistic cosmology, a more amicable and harmonious relationship between people and nature. This, of course, is very much in the spirit of the Millennial Myth.

The Poetics of New Age Science

The convergence of myth and paradigm leads me to speak of the *poetics* of New Age science.

By the poetics of science I mean something exact. The poetics of science is distinct from the logical or explanatory value of science. What counts in the poetics is the cash-value for the imagination, the ability to promote a significant emotional dialogue between ourselves and nature.

The question for the poetics of science is this: Does a particular theory, law, experiment, observation help me emotionally to inhabit the world? Does it speak to the creative needs of the soul and the imperatives of social and cosmic community?

The poetics of science is its own thing, and we can study it as such. The New Age is a movement in quest of a new poetics of science. In our times of info-glut and info-chaos, people need new metaphysical maps and guides. They need, as Joseph Campbell put it in one of his books, "myths to live by."[16] From this angle, let us glance at a few scientific ideas that have captured the New Age imagination. My comments are restricted to their imaginative value to people groping for paradigms of animistic renewal.

James Lovelock's Gaia hypothesis, which states that the planet Earth is in some sense a living organism, is a perfect example of the new poetics of science. For one thing, it reinstates mythology at the heart of Earth science; it also appeals to seekers critical of "male-dominated" paradigms by invoking an ancient Greek goddess and endowing her with new scientific status. Despite Lovelock's disavowal of teleology as part of his hypothesis, new paradigm seekers talk of Gaia having purposes and even willful responses to the evils of humankind. For example, I have heard it said by zealots that AIDS is Gaia's way of protecting herself from human overpopulation.

Rupert Sheldrake's hypothesis of "morphogenesis" has added an image that appeals to the New Age imagination. Sheldrake has suggested that we might understand the history of religion in light of the hypothesis of morphogenetic fields. Religious geniuses like Jesus and Buddha open up new forms of experience and consciousness; they make it easier for us to imitate their behavior and inner life, thus enriching the "morphogenetic field" associated with Christianity or Buddhism. The Resurrection itself, Sheldrake has suggested, may be viewed in this light.[17]

Sheldrake reenchants nature by seeing her laws as habits that themselves may be evolving. This idea, pregnant in the philosophy of Bergson and Whitehead, has tremendous poetic power. For if the laws of nature are not written in stone, then new laws are possible, and poets and prophets who foresee a new nature coming, ruled by more amicable principles, may be on to something.

For example, the ancient shamanic philosopher Empedocles said there were two principles of cosmology, *Neikos* and *Philia*, "Strife" and "Friendship." If nature is more malleable in the hands of creative time, as Sheldrake has suggested, then it is reasonable to hope that Empedocles and John of Patmos were correct in imagining the possibility of a world radically more friendly than the one we know in the current dispensation. Quite apart from its scientific merits (worthy, in my view, of respect), the hypothesis of morphogenesis that Sheldrake has put on our mental map is rich in poetic significance.

Sheldrake is not alone in mounting a case against established Darwinism. Darwinism is based on the idea that life evolves gradually. The fossil record, however, does not support a gradualistic image of evolving life; on the contrary, according to the fossil evidence, life evolves, as Stephen Gould and Niles Elredge assert, suddenly, like a thief in the cosmic night. Evolution occurs in "punctuated" leaps.

This shift toward an image of sudden evolution is a shift toward an apocalyptic view; sudden, of course, in geological time is not like sudden in apocalyptic time—I am talking about poetic overtones, not literal equivalence. In the apocalyptic view, the new nature, the new heaven and earth, will occur in a way that suggests a miraculous breakthrough, more like a quantum leap or a fractal novelty ejaculated from the swirl of chaos. The new may emerge at any instant, and it may be, as the surrealist poet Lautreamont once put it, "convulsive." Indeed, eschatology is about the convulsions in the history of time.

The physicist David Bohm has become increasingly popular in New Age circles; he has advanced the idea of wholeness and the "implicate order."[18] Bohm is a physicist who speaks out against soul-deadening mechanistic theories of nature. Like Whitehead, he wants to reanimate, reenchant nature. The notion that all the parts of nature are enfolded in some kind of wholeness satisfies a need for belonging—in old Myth talk—to the Kingdom of God. The poetics of Bohm's science is clear; for, according to him, we all emerge from an implicitly holistic ground, so that even in our explicit separation, we remain enfolded in the oneness of being.

Or consider the holographic universe described by gifted science writer Michael Talbot;[19] based on the work of Karl Pribrim and others, it revisualizes reality with congenial effects on the spiritual imagination. The holograph seems to those who peer into its properties to hold keys to new dimensions of self and reality. Like physician and author Larry Dossey's talk of "nonlocal" ESP, the holograph has the poetic value of helping us imagine that we—or at least some deep aspect of ourselves—are capable of transcending time and space. All this resonates with the Millennium Myth. Talbot's holographic universe lifts us out of the old, disenchanted, mechanistic universe by giving us a framework for revalidating miracles, which (see the next chapter) figure in the current reawakening of the Millennium Myth.

Talbot's holographic universe caters to the deep New Age need for connection and community. If all parts are everywhere and everywhere is in all parts, then we are all connected, all enfolded in each other, all part of an invisible community. Like David Bohm's implicate order, the holographic universe reenchants nature by enabling us to believe we are part of a greater whole. In the holographic or implicate order, there is room to imagine mystical oneness; in a mechanistic universe, there is not.

The poetics of new science revolves around images of discontinuity, self-organization, and breakthrough—images that resonate with the Millennium Myth. One new science image suggesting cosmic breakthrough is the image of the "quantum leap." Full of eschatological overtones, the "quantum leap" has made its way into popular culture—into advertising, fiction, and TV sitcoms. Perhaps the best book that evokes the poetics of quantum mechanics is by physicist-educator-shaman Fred Alan Wolf, *Taking the Quantum Leap*.[20] I asked Fred if he would comment on the millenarian or apocalyptic implications of the New Physics and, in particular, of the "quantum leap." He responded by saying, "In its figurative sense a quantum leap is a major unexpected change, a jump in evolution, a leap beyond any previous imagination. Implied in its peregrination is risk, for as we leap we know not what we are about to do." Wolf added the following: "Sometimes the 'leap' leads to personal regrets, even though its ultimate consequences produce a new vision of humanity and the universe."

Wolf notes with irony that even the founders of the new physics—he mentions Planck, Einstein, and Shrödinger—"were sadly upset with their discoveries." The human side of our nature shrinks from the element of risk that pervades our evolving universe. "It seems that whenever a quantum leap occurs, in matter or consciousness, there is something going on that tends to resist it. In matter we call it inertia, in mind we call it prejudice or just plain pig-headedness."

If Wolf is right, quantum mechanics—modern evolutionary cosmology in general, I would say—contains an insight into reality and into our situation as human beings that we have yet to come to grips with. In my view, the millennial zeitgeist prepares us for this insight. The poetics of quantum mechanics draws upon the millennial hope that we are not bound by the old dispensation of a disenchanted mechanistic universe, but that a pregnant uncertainty, a new openness and fluidity fill the universe, and above all, that "reality" is not something fixed or autonomous, but a co-creative shape-shifting partner, a "wave function" whose "collapsible" outcomes depend on human participation.

One more example of new science poetics: the work of Ilya Prigogine straddles physics, chemistry, and biology, and also speaks to the poetics of reanimating our world. In fact, several aspects of the Nobel prize-winning chemist's work translate into poetic support of the Millennium Myth. Thus, in a disenchanted nature, entropy is all.

The universe is running down, like a slowly burning candle. The clock is unwinding on everything. Eventually, as Bertrand Russell lamented in a *Free Man's Worship*, the universe will die a heat death, and the candle of creation will go out. If ever there was a disenchanted cosmology, this is it. Entropy becomes the Antichrist, the enemy who would reduce all to nullity.

But Prigogine brings back the angels of novelty into the big picture and makes entropy over into a source of creativity. For entropy causes fluctuations; the old structures come apart, bits and pieces and elements of a world are tossed about, like confetti in a randomizing machine. But there is good news; the fluctuations allow for certain self-organizing—Mardukian and Apollonian—principles to emerge and give rise to a new order of existence. Prigogine's reality is bipolar: destruction and recreation, chaos and the new heaven and earth, the dark and the bright side of apocalypse.

Prigogine offers new paradigm seekers a hopeful way of looking at time; no longer the enemy, time becomes a friend, an ally in the co-creation of new realities. This creative view of time supports the hopes of the Millennium Myth, which extols the creative power of time.

The Fatigue of History and the Myth of the Wild

Civilization is reborn in the poetic imagination, said Vico. The yearning for a new poetics comes from the "fatigue of history."[21] The old images grow weary, lose their numinous charge, decay into dogmas, turn into clichés. One therefore sets out on a journey for exotic landscapes and magical times, hoping, like Ponce de Leon, to find the spiritual Fountain of Youth in the dank Floridean jungle of the *mundus imaginalis*.

Now, an old image in the American psyche is the image of wildness, the wild West. The pioneer, forever exploring, forever conquering the frontier; the young men, forever going West, gold-rushing and treasure-hunting; pistol-packing cowboys in rough pursuit of the Millennium.

Emmanuel Leutze's mural commemorating westward expansion, painted in the Capitol Building in Washington D.C. in 1863, showed the missionary optimism that earmarks millennialism. Leutze painted his great mural during the Civil War, and it became a source of inspiration for many; Nathaniel Hawthorne wrote that it was "full of energy, hope, progress, irrepressible movement onward," a "good augury" during a "dismal time." Leutze's mural was a beacon of hope during the apocalyptic crisis of the Civil War; its images pointed, after Armageddon, to a new Eden. "Westward ho!" was the cry of the time.

R. W. Emerson said of the wilderness in 1844: "The great continent we inhabit is to be physic and food for our mind, as well as our body. The land with its tranquilizing, sanative influences, is to repair the errors of a scholastic and traditional education, and bring us into just relations with men and things." The American wild West and its "sanative influences" stirred Emerson's millennial imagination; the land itself, said the New England sage, would transform the psyche of the old dispensation.

But by the end of the last century, there were signs of American fatigue; the nation had moved too swiftly, perhaps not thoughtfully or reverently enough, across the "wilderness." The iron horses swept the plains, and men began the great wiring of America: the Pony express, the railroad, the airlines, the data highways, the snooping satellites in space; in short, the disappearance of the wild, and in its place, the rationalizing, mechanizing, and commercializing of Gaia or Mother Earth.

A yearning for the recovery of wildness and wilderness had already set in in the 1890s when Jack London wrote *Call of the Wild*, a Nietzschean parable of primitivism, about a dog named Buck kidnapped to serve in the Klondike gold rush. Buck, a yuppified couch-potato canine, had to suffer savage nature before awakening to his authentic wild powers. Buck heard the call of the wild and recovered his authentic self, a kind of born-again dog.

In late twentieth century, the American New Age is busy exploring what Buck had thrust upon him a century ago—the call of the wild; Robert Bly points the way for men to hunker down, beat their drums, and reconnect with the archetype of the Wild Man. Clarissa Pinkola Estes, en rapport with Buck and Jack London, is teaching New Age women to know the creative wolf in themselves, and, in counterpoint with Bly, to get down and dirty with the archetype of the Wild Woman. The New Age search for wildness and wilderness reveals what Mircea Eliade has called the nostalgia for paradise, a nostalgia that pervades the millennial dream.

The Hundredth Monkey Myth

A myth that has circulated deep in New Age consciousness concerns the hundredth monkey. The story of the hundredth monkey is a comment about the powerful—I would say millennial—need to believe in the possibility of miraculous breakthrough. The story begins with a book by Lyall Watson, *Lifetide: A Biology of the Unconscious* (1979). Watson briefly and tentatively reported an odd phenomenon, possibly involving mass telepathy, said to have been observed in the 1950s. He wrote:

> In the autumn of that year (1958) an unspecified numbers of monkeys on Koshima were washing sweet potatoes in the sea. . . . Let us say, for argument's sake, that the number was ninety-nine and that at eleven o'clock on a Tuesday morning, one further convert was added to the fold in the usual way. But the addition of the hundredth monkey apparently carried the number across some sort of threshold, pushing it through a kind of critical mass, because by that evening almost everyone was doing it. Not only that, but the habit seems to have jumped natural barriers and to have appeared spontaneously, like glycerine crystals in sealed laboratory jars, in colonies on other islands and on the mainland in a troop at Takasakiyama.

Once the critical mass was reached—that is, the hundredth monkey— the behavior seemed to spread through the whole population. Not surprisingly, many seized upon the exciting potentials implied by Watson's story. Might not the hundredth monkey be a model for changing the human world? If, for example, a critical number of human beings could learn to be loving and peaceful, might not love and peace spread to the whole human population? If we worked on reaching the critical mass, could we not, for example, bring about a new age of peace on earth?

In the end, Lyall Watson admitted that his hundredth monkey had little basis in fact. But that did not stop the idea from taking root and becoming a powerful metaphor of hope in the New Age community. The idea of "jumping natural barriers," short-circuiting the limits of nature, evokes the Millennium Myth, which sees a supernatural agent waiting in the wings of human history.

Ken Keyes, founder of the Living Love Seminars, published a book in 1982, *The Hundredth Monkey*, which outlined a procedure for bringing about the New Age by reaching the critical mass of enlightened souls. The story of the hundredth monkey touched a New Age nerve and quickly graduated to mythical status. The hundredth monkey myth, like the Millennium Myth, pictures a moment of history when society experiences a breakthrough by supernormal means to a new mode of being.

The Harmonic Convergence

Millennialists are often tempted to specify the time of the End. Throughout Western history, prophets have announced specific dates, based on somebody's chiliastic calculus, in which the end of the old and the dawn of the new age were supposed to start. I have stopped collecting such dates. Scarcely a decade has passed in the last two thousand years when one group or another has not been swept away in the expectation of the cosmic kaput.

1843 was one of the more famous dates, picked by the Millerites. A more recent example, October 22, 1992, was slated as the day of the Rapture, a date picked by a Korean prophet of shady origins who has since been imprisoned for swindling his followers. Other examples abound. American New Agers have also succumbed to this old temptation.

Now the date was August 16–17, 1987. The alleged event, butt of a good deal of journalistic joking, was known as the Harmonic Convergence and was touted by art historian José Arguelles, author of *The Transformative Vision* (1975) and *The Mayan Factor* (1987). In a curiously flat phrase, Arguelles spoke eschatologically of the "climax of matter." Based on Native American myths, calendars, and prophecies, he predicted that on said days, a collective rebirth of human consciousness would commence—a new era of love, cooperation, and planetary consciousness.

The Wall Street Journal wryly noted the advent of the Harmonic Convergence, a kind of superbenign piece of astrological synchronicity. New Agers seized on it, and people (millions according to Arguelles's reckoning) gathered to hallow the event at sacred power sites round the world: California's Mount Shasta, Peru's Machu Pichu, the Great Pyramids in Egypt, Mount Fuji in Japan, and for the homebound, at whatever ley-enchanted hillock or seashore was handy. The Harmonic Convergence, orchestrated by the art professor turned chiliast, pressed all the buttons of New Age consciousness.

Thus, to bring about the Convergence, at least 144,000 people (that magic number) had to pitch in with their positive energy, thus evoking both the Hundredth Monkey Myth and Biblical numerology. Celebrants came armed with crystals, revved up to focus the requisite good vibes. There was talk of an increase of visitations from "galactic ambassadors"—translate—endtime angels of old-style apocalyptic. A new consciousness of Earth as a sentient being would arise, in tune with the Gaia hypothesis; and finally, (and roughly) in accord with the Biblical pattern, the Convergence would trigger Earth changes, stock-market crashes, and other debacles of industrial civilization—all preludes to the dawning "Age of Flowers."

Clearly, the Millennium Myth influences people other than Christian fundamentalists. However, for this to happen the Myth has to be repackaged, translated from tired, familiar symbols into new or exotic ones. Repackaging the Myth is one device for overcoming the fatigue of history.

Some New Age Fads Via the Myth

The American New Age sports a variety of intellectual curios. Looking closely, one finds links to the Millennium Myth.

Crystal Consciousness. Fascination with gems and crystals earmarks the American New Age. In the eyes of critics, this proves the flakiness of the movement. Is it all not just the frippery of yuppies, spiced with a twinge of existential anxiety? Is the love of gems and crystals not just a refined, spiritually correct mask for consumerism? So a cynic might ask.

My view is that there is a deep structure to New Age fascinations. What about crystals? Is there a deep structure to crystal consciousness? Throughout history people have used gems and crystals as talismans and believed they had healing and protective properties. Their reflective properties stimulate the imagination, even perhaps the nervous system in odd ways. The mystic Jacob Boehme, for example, was glancing at a pewter dish when by chance a ray of sunlight fell on it, reflecting in his eyes. Boehme was suddenly enveloped by dazzling visions, which transformed his life. Pewter, of course, is not crystal, but it functioned like a crystal when it reflected sunlight in Boehme's eyes.

I want to mention two classic texts dealing with last things that refer to gems, crystals, and precious stones. The first is Plato's Myth of the True Earth, described in the *Phaedo*, a dialogue about death and immortality. The Earth we dwell on is not the True Earth, says Socrates. We humans occupy a tiny portion of Earth, a pocket, a cave below the surface, sealed up in the mists and shadows of delusion, remote from the world of sunlight. If we could step out of this dark Earth hollow, up onto the plain of the Whole Earth, we would discover a different world; our perception of things would become *aetheric*. The world around us would appear with extraordinary clarity, and we would commune clairvoyantly with gods and goddesses. We would see the forms and colors of nature with the eyes of painters and poets.

Says Socrates, "our highly prized stones, sards and jaspers, are fragments of those there, but there (the True Earth) everything is like these or still more beautiful" (*Phaedo*, 110e). Here perhaps is a clue to the fascination with precious stones: they are visible "samples" of the higher—Plato calls it *aetheric*—consciousness that we will experience after death and arrival on the True Earth. According to Socrates's story, heaven *is* on earth; we have only to purify our souls to see and know this. And to do that best we must "die," that is, detach the soul from the body and cleanse the doors of perception. For Plato, crystals and precious stones were symbols of consciousness at the end of ordinary time.

The other example is from our master text, the Book of Revelation. The author of that potent psychic talisman chose to build his vision of the New Jerusalem with crystals and precious stones. "The wall was built of diamond, and the city of pure gold, like clear glass. The foundations of the city wall were faced with all kinds of precious stone" (Rev. 21:18). On the list of precious stones: diamonds, lapis lazuli, turquoise, crystal, topaz, quartz, emeralds, pearls, and sapphires.

As in Plato's prophetic True Earth, John saw no temples in the New Jerusalem because God himself was present in place of the temple, neither were there sun or moon because God's radiance lit up the heavenly city. As with Plato, so with John, precious stones symbolize a chiliastic change of consciousness. From this perspective, the New Age attraction to crystals appears to be steeped in the symbolism of the end of time.

Another angle deserves mention. In New Age circles, crystals are sometimes thought of as devices for tuning in to extraterrestrials. I once observed the late Marcel Vogel, an inventor for IBM, enchant a crowd of New Agers with talk of a crystal he held in his hand, a means, he said, for tuning in to intelligent beings from the Pleiades. This is a contemporary and somewhat literalized take on the Myth that people will commune face to face with otherworldly beings. Whatever interpretation we stress, I believe the charm of precious stones and crystals shows a longing for spiritual breakthrough and reflects our millennial longings.

Mute Signs and the Arts of Divination. American New Agers are drawn to the arts of divination: runes, the Tarot, the *I Ching*, astrology, and so on. Whatever else they are, these things seem to me ways of trying to get one's bearing in a world whose traditional signs and symbols no longer seem to speak to us. What runes, Tarot, and all the rest share is what I might call their imaginal magnetism. They stir the imagination in ways that mainline symbols no longer do.

Vico, my mentor in the philosophy of culture, says that in the formative stages of a new civilization, a certain type of language dominates. It consists of "poetic characters," which Vico calls a language of "mute signs" or magical hieroglyphs. Mute signs make up the language of the gods. They stir up heroic feelings, which bind a people together by creating a *sensus communus*, or "shared consciousness." Vico takes seriously the etymology of *religion* as that which *binds* a people together. So the experience of human solidarity is based on the power of mute signs. The cross is an example from Christian history; the spell of the swastika over the Nazi mind is another.

New Age people are drawn to the mute signs of runes, of Crop Circle pictographs, of the greater arcana of the Tarot, of *I Ching* lines and broken lines, and so forth. In current terms, think of these as attentional devices for tuning oneself to the creative unconscious. One begins to understand the charm—and in the case of Hitler, the danger—of these mute signs, potential shapers and energizers of new social movements.

According to Vico, without the primal language of mute signs—so attractive to American New Agers—societies tend to disintegrate, thanks to a runaway "malicious reason." By "malicious" reason Vico meant reason cut off from the mythical common sense of a people.

A modern example of what Vico meant by "malicious reason" is the scientific intellect working on behalf of the military-industrial complex.

The need for a language of mute signs may therefore be seen as signaling the need to rediscover a new *sensus communus*, a new sense of human solidarity. The obscure spell cast by these soul-stirring glyphs plays off the deep need in our culture for "connection" and community, features rapidly disappearing in mainline American life and society.

To some, runes and astrology may seem shallow; but, again, if one probes the deep structure, a different picture emerges. The runes with their obscure Nordic resonance, the Tarot cards with their haunting images of Magician and Fool, the yarrow stalks of the *I Ching*, the signs of the Zodiac may be seen as tools people are trying to use to map and to orient their uncertain futures. If Vico is right, they are signs, mute but eloquent, that a new common consciousness is struggling to be born in American society. They are signals of protest against the fragmentedness of prevailing modes of experience. Such protest is typical of millenarian discontent.

Walk-ins. Take another New Age curio. This one originates from a Washington D.C. journalist turned prophetess. (A reasonable transition, if you stop and think about it.) Ruth Montgomery introduced the idea of "walk-ins" in her book *Strangers Among Us* (1979). According to Montgomery's Spirit Guides, walk-ins are highly evolved, discarnate beings who "have earned the right to take over unwanted bodies." A strange notion indeed, but part of a much bigger message: borrowed bodies are needed to aid humankind in its momentous transition to the New Age. According to Montgomery's Guides, a poleshift is going to occur in 1999 that will wipe out millions while paving the way to the Golden Age. (Again, note that old habit of picking a date for apocalypse.)

Now, a walk-in is a kind of divine zombie. Are we really surrounded by divine zombies, reality conspirators secretly finessing the transition to a New Age? One may suspect that people who warm to the idea of walk-ins are not very happy with their circumstances. If, for example, you have a poor sense of self-esteem, the idea of a superior, well-meaning ET taking over your body might be a welcome prospect.

One's prospects are further improved from a millenarian perspective. Does the Bible not say that strangers may be angels in disguise? And that the End will be heralded by the coming of hosts of angels?

Walk-ins fit neatly with the flattering phantasy that we are angels in disguise, sent to hasten the coming of the Millennium. For the metaphysically oppressed, walk-ins might also seem like allies. Against the background of what is seen by many as a claustrophobic scientism, the idea of walk-ins from dimension X offers an image, a mute sign, that points to a way out. Or one could see walk-ins as symptoms of cosmic loneliness, heralds of a new kind of community.

Walk-ins have been around for millennia, according to Montgomery's Guides. Some prominent examples: Christ, Ben Franklin, and Albert Einstein. At the moment, untold thousands of these extraterrestrial strangers fill our midst, undercover agents for the coming transformation. The Book of Revelation paints cognitive chaos as the setting for cosmic breakthrough; walk-ins add nicely to cognitive chaos. Since none of us quite know who we are anyway in these anomic times, it is no surprise that some folk should be open to the idea of ETs taking over their bodies and giving them an identity.

Belief In a Coming Poleshift

The Book of Revelation sees the End attended by violent Earth changes. So does the American Ecological New Age. Ruth Montgomery is not the only one to predict cataclysmic Earth changes—volcanic eruptions, tidal waves, hurricanes, shifting land masses, and so on. Rosters of prophets foretell the same. Perhaps the best-known poleshift prophet was Edgar Cayce, whose clairvoyant eye saw Japan sinking into the sea, Northern Europe cracked in the twinkling of an eye, California submerged, and even New York City going under. New Agers also invoke Native American prophecy to ratify their Earth change premonitions.

With eco-anxiety on the rise, old prophecies of Earth changes acquire new meaning. UFO contactees repeatedly ring changes on this theme. John White's book *Pole Shift*[22] carefully investigates the literature of prophetic Earth changes. In a recent work,[23] White acknowledges that the psychics who predicted these grave changes were wrong and has come to see the prophecies as symbolic revelations of the unconscious; not literal premonitions, but wake-up calls to a species hellbent on its own destruction. Poleshift thus becomes a symbol of ecocatastrophe:

If a pole shift destroys civilization some people will survive, according to the predictions and prophecies. The great loss of life will open up niches in the environment where new life forms can emerge. Those most deeply attuned to cosmic processes will become the seedbed from which, it is said, a new race, a higher humanity will evolve in accelerated fashion.[24]

Note the Biblical idea of a saving remnant, the hope that an enlightened minority will emerge from endtime and form the "seedbed" of "higher humanity." White regards these prophecies as not about geophysical but psychic convulsion, agreeing with Ken Ring's view of the prophetic visions of his near-death subjects. According to Ring, they are "reflections of the collective psyche of our time, which is generating its own images of planetary death and regeneration for which the sensitive souls of our era serve as carriers."[25]

With Ken Ring and John White, we are at the antipodes of the fundamentalist mindset. And yet, the Millennium Myth lives and finds new voices in these authors, as it does elsewhere in the New Age zeitgeist; Ring's Omega Project and White's Homo Noeticus have added to the images, the mute signs, that are part of the spiritual rebirth struggling to take place in our disenchanted universe.

Making the Best of the American New Age

As Americans, we inherit a powerful mythical legacy. From the beginning, the country served as a place for creating and living out great myths. Something about the landscape—the big sky countries, the otherworldly landscapes of Utah, the California coast, sleeping on a fault line, gazing out at the Pacific toward the Orient; something about the seascapes and the "purple-colored" mountains—invites the imagination to soar. There is something crazy and extravagant about it all, and on that score Hegel was right. But Hegel also said that America was the place where the Idea of history would rise from the grave of the Old World and pursue the adventures of the future.

If my point in this chapter is right, the American New Age is not a foolish fad but the expression of deep spiritual drives in the people, part of an ongoing impulse, rooted in a pilgrim American history and an immigrant Millennium Myth. We have noted the admirable spirit in which American New Agers seek to open up the boundaries of human consciousness, free the body from disease and even death, recreate the mythology of the future, explore ways to unite heaven and earth, and encourage the meeting of science and spirit.

The critics, of course, do have their points. No complex human activity is without its shadow side. I have seen the shadow side of the New Age with my own eyes. In my opinion, the critic of the American New Age is right in deploring the psychic inflation, addiction to clichés—worse, and most irritating, a type of fundamentalism and spiritual correctness. There is also that suspicious prosperity conscious-ness, the transparent commercialism, the ignorance of history, the intellectual primitivism, the dangerous talk about karma and making one's own reality, and the tendency toward political quietism.

On the other hand, one feature of the American New Age is its democratic upsurge; true to the Book of Joel, the young and the old, the housewife and the farmer, are seeing visions and channeling dreams. Now and then we might have to contend with a New Age messiah. But any serious bid for messiahship in America would mean having to face the press. If Gary Hart, Bill Clinton, and countless others have not been able to conceal their less than presidential propensi-ties, neither would any self-proclaimed messiah get very far with our snooping press and paparazzi.

No religious leader, however charismatic, could handle the relent-lessly critical news and law-enforcing industries, as Jimmy Swaggert and Jim Bakker found out. The memory of apocalyptic horror stories, of Jim Jones and David Koresh, are also bound to have imprinted a little skepticism on our nervous systems. Any candidate for messiah would be compelled to sit before the planetary eye on CNN's *Larry King Live*, warts and all.

The New Age is keen on mythology. An increased capacity to recognize myth as myth should also guard us against falling for phoney messiahs. We should be able to quickly spot the symptoms of messiah madness: the racist talk of purification, the odor of anti-Semitism, the habit of dualizing, dogmatizing, and demonizing. There is a good deal of that around, but the likelihood of large-scale success, one hopes, is small.

Democracy is our greatest weapon against the pathology of mes-sianism. One of futurist John Naisbitt's megatrends is movement away from hierarchy to networking. Networking, made uniquely possible in the New Age by telecommunications, is inconsistent, as Marilyn

Ferguson said in the *Aquarian Conspiracy*, with the idea of autocratic leadership, messianic or otherwise.

Still, critics fear that interest in the irrational may spill over into undemocratic practices. There are, as a matter of fact, some unsettling similarities between American New Age interests and interests shared by the Nazis. For example, top Nazi war criminal Rudolf Hess was keen on occultism, mythology, vegetarianism, magic, runes, astrology, the doctrine of correspondences, and herbalism. Nor was Hess exceptional in his interest in "new age" ideas; scholars from Peter Viereck to Goodrick-Clarke have documented the tangled story of the "new age" zeitgeist that informed the Nazi mentality.

Nazi and contemporary American New Age interests overlap in at least three ways 1) fascination with mythology, especially the wish to explore extra-Biblical myth worlds; 2) preoccupation with the body, nowadays called the holistic health movement; and 3) aversion to modernism, scientism, and bourgeois materialism. The commonalities seem real enough. The search for a new myth, the yearning for earthly renovation, the discontent with soul-crushing materialism are widespread signs of desire for spiritual renewal. Are the similarities between Nazi and American New Age ideas cause for alarm?

Dangers no doubt exist, but, in my view, would be greatly exaggerated. I do not believe with the fundamentalists that the New Age is Satan in disguise or with liberal rationalists that it is just "orange crush," devoid of intellectual substance. The American Millennium Myth, as I said in chapter 5, historically goes back to the European Enlightenment and Anglo-Saxon Christian democracy. The psychohistory of the American New Age is grounded in Renaissance-Enlightenment ideals of liberty, equality, fraternity, tolerance, and religious freedom, ideals of individualism and universalism, the pursuit of happiness, and so on. By contrast, the Nazi and Communist Millennium Myth passed through a cultural template stressing race, subservience to the collective (Russian *sobornost*), and less philiac gods (Wotan instead of Christ). The differences seem significant; one version respects people as having certain inalienable rights, the other treats them as cogs in the state machine.

The Millennium Myth expresses itself in two ways. In one, as Norman Cohn has stressed, aspiration is filtered through the disoriented, ignorant, and resentful outcasts of society, justifying violent revolutionary politics; in the other, as I want to stress, the Myth works through the humanistic, life-affirming side of people.

I think it fair to say that in the Renaissance-Enlightenment-American stream of the Myth, the good potential has a better chance of improving the human condition than the murderous Müntzer-Stalin-Hitler stream of influence. I think it important to keep this double focus on the possibilities.

Like the Italian Renaissance, which looked back to the Golden Age of pagan antiquity to restore its waning spirit, the American New Age looks back to perennial Eastern philosophies and shamanic realities to revive its fatigued spiritual imagination. Perhaps the American New Age is just a beginning, the forerunner of an American Renaissance.

Endtime Anomalies

*And it shall come to pass afterward, that I will pour
out my spirit on all flesh, and your sons and your
daughters shall prophesy, your old men shall dream
dreams, your young men shall see visions. And also
upon the servants and upon the handmaids in those
days will I pour out my spirit.*

JOEL 2:28–29

In the Biblical map of the end of history, there are places on the way called "signs" and "wonders." These are part of a wider range of phenomena called "miracles." Three Greek words in the New Testament describe three aspects of miracles: *teras*, "wonder or portent"; *dynamis*, or "power"; and *semeion*, "sign or significance." Taken together, the three shed light on the meaning of miracles. "Miracles" are signs or portents that a new power is about to break into history—a power that promises to transform our lives.

Jesus in the Gospels and John's Book of Revelation refer to false prophets and false miracles; these would be prophets who deceive or miracles without higher meaning. False prophets and false miracles are themselves signs of endtime. Put in secular terms, the riot of claims and counterclaims in matters of metaphysics, controversial reports of unusual phenomena, and paradigm wars are signs of dramatic changes forthcoming in consciousness at large.

According to the Biblical view, unusual phenomena will attend the catastrophic breakup of reality that must precede the end of time and the coming Kingdom of Heaven. Or, in the language of science, signs and wonders are *anomalies* that indicate a new model of reality is in the offing.

It so happens that reports of apparently anomalous events are on the rise. Some of these reports seem to conform to Biblical prophecies. In fact, the anomalous events I shall discuss all seem to be signals of coming changes in the experience of human reality. In what follows, I try neither to explain nor validate current anomaly reports. My concern is with their *semeion*, the significance they may have for our changing consciousness.

I happen to believe that the fictive and factual elements in many if not in most stories of anomalous experience are very hard to disentangle. Their purely objective content is of interest to parapsychologists. But in practical life, fact and fiction fuse, truth and myth blend seamlessly together. It is this domain of creative phantasy, where history and imagination meld, that I look at in this chapter. For whatever the ultimate nature or true explanation of the phenomena, they are changing the way people see reality.

Joel's Outpouring of Spirit Revisited

According to the prophet Joel, the messianic Kingdom will be preceded by an outpouring of spirit: "And it shall come to pass afterward, that I will pour out my spirit on all flesh, and your sons and your daughters shall prophesy, your old men shall dream dreams, your young men shall see visions. And also upon the servants and upon the handmaids in those days will I pour out my spirit" (Joel 2:28-29). The last line is intriguing. The great time of transformation will be marked by a democracy of altered states of consciousness. Young and old, men and women, people from all walks of life will take part in this great outpouring.

Something like a democratic outpouring of spirit seems in fact to be occurring right now in the late nineties. Whether outpourings from channelers or near-death visionaries or UFO contactees or angel seers, Joel's prophecy of a democracy of altered states seems in the process of being fulfilled.

Anomalist John Keel is probably right when he says that "each generation is, from its singular point of view, the last generation." In a way this is inevitable, since each generation must face its own collective death and rebirth. Having said this, it is hard to avoid the feeling that our times *are* unique. For one thing, everything is exaggerated and accelerated by means of technology: the capacity to destroy, the capacity to create. Most of all, the new information technologies are creating a climate of accelerating apocalyptic change. In any case, one is struck by the variety of ways the "spirit" is being poured out. Let us look at some examples.

Channeling and Near-Death Prophecy

In democratic, soul-searching America, Joel's outpouring of the spirit has assumed the form of *channeling*. Estimates vary, but certainly thousands of people in America alone claim to be channeling higher sources of nonphysical intelligence.[1] If we take Joel seriously and think of spiritual outpouring in ordinary people as heralding a transformation of consciousness—the "Day of the Lord" in Joel's language, the "end of an era" in Jung's—then channeling might well seem a symptom of such transformation. I believe, however, that the importance of channeling lies less in the content of the message, but as a sign that the floodgates of the collective unconscious are opening.

Channeling is a modern counterpart to prophecy. A channel, like a prophet or medium, is a vehicle through whom information from a "higher" source of intelligence is said to be transmitted. Among the great mediums of Victorian England and early twentieth-century America, the information was allegedly channeled from discarnate spirits. The Victorian mediums were anxious to confirm the reality of life beyond the grave and to solace the bereaved. Contemporary channeling is closer to Biblical prophecy; the message is said to be from transcendent sources, offering moral directives and metaphysical uplift. Proof of afterlife is usually unstressed. Modern channelers, like ancient prophets, bear the twofold tidings of the world's end and its glorious rebirth.

Images of cosmic cataclysm appear in Chapter 24 of Matthew's Gospel. "The sun will be darkened, and the moon will not give its light, and the stars will fall from the sky, and the powers of the heavens will be shaken." For resolute endtime watchers, current ecological problems such as global warming and ozone depletion are signs of a coming disaster of Biblical dimensions. The Biblical list of portents includes plague, so that some believers, unpleasant to say, have seized upon the AIDS plague as proof of imminent endtime. Earthquakes and other Earth changes are a staple of modern channelers like Edgar Cayce and are taken by many as signs of the coming Millennium.

Contemporary examples of Joel's spiritual outpouring have been studied by transpersonal psychologist Ken Ring. A subset of people **241** who have near-death experiences report having prophetic visions of global significance. The content of these visions shows a pattern that reflects the bipolar Millennium Myth. They foretell cataclysmic wars and geophysical upheavals, to be followed by a "new era of peace and human brotherhood." Ring notes the Christian archetypal underpinning to these visionary episodes and suggests they may be planetary projections of typical near-death experience:

> Whether the earth is shaken by natural catastrophes, or nuclear warfare, or both, earth and the life upon it does survive. More than that, however: A New Age emerges and the devastating changes that have preceded it are understood to have been necessary purgations effecting the transformation of humanity into a new mode of being. By analogy, just as the individual near-death experiencer may have to endure the pain and suffering associated with the trauma of almost dying before positive personal transformation can take place, so the world may need to undergo a "planetary near-death experience" before it can awaken to higher, more spiritual, collective consciousness with universal love at its core.[2]

Every near-death experience (NDE) is a private apocalypse. With Ring's prophetic near-death visionaries, the apocalyptic encompassing of time stretches beyond the personal focus to the world at large. The "trauma of almost dying" is an unavoidable prelude to the "new mode of being." This is pure millennialism.

By focusing on the transpersonal core of near-death encounters, Ring has given us a bird's eye view of the spontaneous eschatological mind—the level of mind in all of us that somehow "sees" the master plan, the telic face of being. What impresses one is the life-affirming optimism; in Ring's prophetic near-death visionaries, we find what William James called the "Yes function," the intoxicated will to affirm life at all costs, even in the midst of death. A power is unfolding before our eyes, a power that likes to wear many disguises; it is, if I am right, the power of the Millennium Myth.

Channeling and visionary NDEs show the same apocalyptic zeitgeist unfolding, the sense that an ending is at hand as well as a new beginning. The fact that so many people seem to be coming up with the same ideas in dissociated states, whether during near-death or trance-channeling, suggests to my mind that a spontaneous reshaping of *collective* consciousness is occurring. The fact that most channelers repeat the same ideas often in the same pseudo-Biblical styles supports this view. It is as if the same message were trying to force its way into the public consciousness; a message that seeks any available outlet and is content to express itself in whatever rough form it can muster. And what is coming through the channels are cries for more life, abundance, yearning for boundlessness. It is Ficino's appetite for the infinite, back to haunt us again, an appetite voiced repeatedly by New Age channelers with their talk of unlimitedness and the coming of godhumanity.

Messengers of Endtime

The word *angel* is from the Greek meaning "messenger" or "bearer of news or tidings." The Greek word for *gospel* (in Saxon, *gode-spell*) is *euangelion*, "good tidings" or "good news." The Christian gospel is thus etymologically related to angels. The good news, the glad tidings that the angels bring are about the coming Kingdom of God—the end of the old and the dawn of a new world. The gospel, in short, is a message of good news; and the good news is that a new reality principle is about to ingress into history—in other words, an apocalypse or *unveiling*. Angels, in Christian theology, are associated with the coming end of time.

We should consider the present revival of interest in angels against this background. The belief in angels is very old; so we need not be surprised at the return of the angel in the late twentieth century. The Catholic cult of the guardian angel was already under way[3] when angel mania broke out in America and began to spread, spilling over from New Agers to the public at large. "Angels in America" is the name of a Broadway trilogy, about AIDS, near-death, and guardian angels. Hundreds of books have been published on all aspects of angels; a new encyclopedia of angels has appeared. Communing-with-angel groups have appeared, along with newsletters, mail order companies, centers, and conventions, all devoted to angel lore. In America, the business of angels is thriving. And, as if to ratify that angels have truly arrived on the American scene, the December 27, 1993, issue of *Time Magazine* ran a cover story called the "New Age of Angels," reporting a survey that sixty-nine percent of Americans believe that angels exist.[4]

"What in heaven is going on?" asks *Time Magazine*. To some it may seem easy to explain the phenomenon. A comment from the editor of a *New Jersey Angel Watch Newsletter*: "The world is in a lot more trouble than it's ever been. People are recognizing their own sense of powerlessness." Stories of encounters with angels vary from genuinely puzzling events[5] to bland coincidences experiencers think proof of angelic intervention.

Like channeled guides and space visitors and Mary Goddess epiphanies, angels seem part of a systemic psychic SOS, a supernormal broadcast for help by a humanity that is teetering on the edge of history. The American collective unconscious has not been cowed by the carpings of rationalism; the popular imagination goes its own way, has its own agenda. No academic schools of thought can stop its course.

Rumors of angels seem like part of the outpouring of spirit that Joel said would signal the "Day of the Lord." The New Testament also bears witness to the link between angels and the Second Coming. Christ is depicted as "sending forth his angels with a trumpet and a great sound, and they will gather his elect from the four winds" (Matt. 24:31). So this may be part of the meaning of angel mania: a ploy to round up the elect, the chosen, the happy ones destined to participate in the coming cosmic breakthrough.

Another job of angels is to awaken the dead for the final reckoning. Thus, according to the First Epistle to the Thessalonians, the Lord will return with angels "and the dead in Christ will rise up first" (1 Thess. 4:16). It is also the job of angels to separate the just from the wicked: "But when the Son of Man will come in his majesty, and all the angels with him, then he will sit upon the thrones of his glory; and before him will be gathered all the nations, and he will separate them one from another" (Matt. 25:31-32).

The New Testament assigns to angels a great task in the mighty drama of the Second Coming. Christian tradition continues in this spirit, for example, in the Second Sibylline Book,[6] which shows the angels breaking the gates of death and raising the dead. The Church fathers share the vision of angels as messengers of endtime. For example, Saint Ephraim, known as the bard of the Second Coming, wrote:

> Then the Lord will appear in the heavens like lightning with unspeakable glory. The Angels and the Archangels will go on

before his glory like flames of fire. . . . Then the tombs will be
opened and in the flash of an eye all the peoples will rise and
behold the holy beauty of the Bridegroom.[7]

In light of the tradition, angels seem forms of the creative energy
needed to force the end of history, raise the dead, face the terrible
beauty of the end of time.

Some accounts of angels can be puzzling. You occasionally find
provocative stories, as in Rosemary Ellen Guiley's *Angels of Mercy*.[8]
These stories of veridical "angelic" assistance, angels who seem to
intervene in the physical world, add to the growing psychic tempest
of the Millennium Myth that is reawakening today after two thousand
years of restless longing, frustration, and renewed expectation.

UFOs and the Millennium

Endtime angels will come "like lightning" and "flames of fire" in the
sky. Such imagery leads one to examine another pattern of endtime
anomalies. Alongside the *fin de siècle* angel revival is the modern UFO
(Unidentified Flying Object) phenomenon.

Are UFOs angels repackaged for people in the space age? Updated
messengers with tidings of the end of history? Such a view is plausible,
I believe. As with the angel revival, much more may be going on with
these exasperatingly complex stories than meets the eye. Millenarian
motifs are subtly and sometimes patently part of the UFO story.
Whatever UFOs are in themselves—and nobody knows for sure—they
ring interesting changes on the Millennium Myth.

The modern UFO era began mid-twentieth century, although UFO
mavens insist that Strange Visitors from Elsewhere have been with
us since the sunrise of history. The Old Testament Book of Ezekiel
is often trotted out to prove that ETs hobnobbed with prophets of
Biblical times. Popular writers like Zecharia Sitchin and Erich von
Daniken are more or less skillful at serving up brain-tickling tales of
ET intervention in human history.

For the past fifty or so years, thousands (perhaps millions) of
people all over the world and from all walks of life have reported
encounters with Unidentified Flying Objects. Pilots and astronauts
have gone public on their sightings, often retracting their statements
or withdrawing in silence after they have done so; radar detection

of alien craft and physiological traces are claimed. Close encounters can reportedly be unhealthy, even fatal. Many say they have talked with occupants of alien craft. The phenomenon becomes even more convoluted with recent reports of alien abduction. David Gotlib, a Canadian physician who edits the *Bulletin for Anomalous Experiences*, has produced a carefully crafted code of ethical behavior for physicians who have to deal with the anomalistically traumatized.[9] I mention this to point out that we are dealing with a powerful phenomenon and that responsible health professionals take it very seriously.

Angels of Deception?

Anyone who looks at the extensive literature is bound to conclude that *something* very puzzling is going on. Even the Condon Report of 1966,[10] which officially disclaimed anything truly anomalous, contains a hard core of unexplained cases. Jacques Vallee[11] (essential reading for the UFO phenomenon) calculates that in the twentieth century, since investigators have begun to collect data, about fourteen million people may have had UFO encounters—far too many, says Vallee, to be visitations from outer space.

Vallee argues for the physical and paranormal reality of the UFO phenomenon. On the other hand, he does not think the evidence points to ETs from outer space. More likely, he contends, UFOs are evidence for an altogether "metalogical" and ultradimensional reality. Vallee's main point is that the X Intelligence that seems quasi-physically to interact with humans is not from outer space but from some unknown dimension of reality. That dimension has a distinct millennial coloring.

In *Messengers of Deception*, Vallee concluded there is a disinformation factor involved in the UFO phenomenon. Now, the Book of Revelation stresses false prophecy, disinformation, as one of the signs of endtime. Fundamentalist preacher George Vandemann,[12] unlike Vallee, has no doubts that the source of this deception is the Devil himself. Vandemann gives examples from John Keel's *Mothman Prophecies* of alien intelligence in our midst that deceives with apparently deadly intent. Folklorist Peter Rojcewicz has called attention to the diabolic component of what are known in UFO research as "Men in Black," uncanny beings said to intimidate UFO sighters and investigators.[13]

The truth is that anyone looking for simple answers to the UFO enigma will be disappointed. UFO phenomena draw the enquirer into a metaphysical fun house full of epistemic trap doors and magic mirrors. Nevertheless, the UFO phenomenon—the nuggets of firm fact, the illusions, the disinformation, even the blatant hoaxes—suggests ideas of apocalyptic renewal. The theme repeatedly emerges: We're heading for a showdown with the Eschaton. Such was the view of an early and distinguished commentator.

Jung, Flying Saucers, Mandalas, and the Changing of the Gods

Early in the UFO era, Carl Jung wrote about the apocalyptic side of UFOs. *Civilization in Transition* (Jung 1950, vol. 10), contains a monograph, "Flying Saucers: A Modern Myth of Things Seen in the Skies." Full of seminal insights, the book is largely about UFO dreams and UFO symbolism in art. Jung was interested in the psychic side of the phenomenon, although he was open to the reality of a physical component: " . . . either psychic projections throw back a radar echo, or else the appearance of real objects affords an opportunity for mythological projections."

Jung makes much of the circular, disclike shape (as well as the luminosity) of the typical flying saucer. Whatever the cause of the sightings may be, he says, they prompt us to project myths of the "gods." The UFO myth is about salvation from gods that come from the sky. Disoriented, we look to the sky for answers to our soul-wrenching questions. "The present world situation is calculated as never before to arouse expectation of a redeeming supernatural event." At the dawn of the Christian era, the redeeming event was the resurrection of Christ; in our time, it is the appearance of flying saucers.

According to Jung, the psychically shattering events of the Second World War have shaped the present world; the Nazi death camps and the radioactive rubble of Hiroshima have made a mockery of Western civilization. This violence done to the collective psyche makes for "changes in the constellation of psychic dominants." We are facing the end of a "Platonic month," moving from the age of Pisces to the age of Aquarius. It will be a transition, said Jung, full of violent transformations.

In the Introduction to his book on flying saucers, Jung became unusually solemn. He felt moved to issue a warning of "coming events which are in accord with the end of the era." This was not the first time he had issued such a warning: in his 1936 essay on Wotan, he spoke of the changing of the gods and the rise of the Nazi movement.

The saucer is a mandala, according to Jung, a circular symbol of the self. People have begun to see symbols of the whole self in the sky—symbols projected "out there"—because they have lost the inner basis of their wholeness. The more psychologically uprooted, the more people project symbols of wholeness on messianic figures. The Christian myth that held the Western world together for the last two thousand years is ailing, and Jung wonders about what rough beast will arise in the interregnum between gods and archetypes.

Seeing mandala-like UFOs in the sky comes from the need "to compensate the split-mindedness of our age." In the chaos of transformation, we "create the image of the divine-human personality, the Primordial Man or Anthropos, . . . an Elijah who calls down fire from heaven, rises up to heaven in a fiery chariot, and is a forerunner of the Messiah. . . ." In an age of space travel, with Christian belief faltering, "modern man" finds it easier to accept a technological miracle—a messiah from outer space. Robert Short's book, *The Gospel From Outer Space*, makes this point clearly.[14]

The Gospel from Outer Space

Another phase in UFO history involves claims of contact with extraterrestrials. Individuals who report such contact are called "contactees." The most famous contactees were prominent during the 1950s, although recently new stars have risen. Whitley Strieber, whose best-selling *Communion* is a story of alien encounter, is a recent example. Strieber is a gifted fiction writer, a master of the macabre imagination, a concerned ecologist, and a liberal of fine stripe. No need to call attention to himself, Strieber nevertheless says he is communing with alien beings he calls "the visitors."

Strieber's *Communion* was made into a movie. And so we should note that Hollywood has done its part in feeding the collective imagination with images of alien contact. Two well-known examples: *Close Encounters of the Third Kind* and *ET*, both smash hits at the box office, were stories about alien contact.

Contacteeism is a form of prophecy, and contactees usually develop a missionary sense after their experiences. The attempt to carry out the mission often disrupts, and may even destroy, a person's life. Like the prophet of old, the latter-day ET contactee is typically at odds with the establishment. Ancient prophet and modern contactee agree that the End is nigh and that a new era is about to dawn.

Dr. Leo Sprinkle, a psychologist from the University of Wyoming, is perhaps the most experienced and sympathetic ear in America for people alleging UFO contact. Dr. Sprinkle is a man with warmth, humor, and a gift for empathy. He has the rare ability to enter the minds of people who have been to the edge of ordinary reality. Says Sprinkle:

> In my opinion, the UFO phenomenon is an important factor in the total experience of a new age: . . . messages suggest that there will be many changes in the condition of the Earth and in the condition of humankind, including an increased emphasis on spiritual development. . . . I believe that we are confronted with a most exciting and challenging task, to understand the physical, biological, psychosocial, and spiritual implications of the ending of a former age and awakening of the "New Age."

Contactees, like ancient prophets, insist that a superhuman, other-worldly power, a superior intelligence and technology oversee the course of human history. These Higher Ones are guiding our history; they plan to intervene, to inaugurate a new aeon of human development. Contactees often have messianic phantasies. In former times, similar types became founders of new religions, were stoned to death, or were burnt at the stake; in our time, they write books and become media stars. Sometimes they lose their jobs, get divorced, and become estranged from peers and community.

During the fifties, many Americans were becoming aware that science had become a threat to planetary survival; the military-industrial complex was busily building world-destroying atomic arsenals. Contactees like George Adamski, George King, and Orfeo Angelucci, psychic antennae of this very real danger, became missionaries committed to saving humanity from nuclear Armageddon.

Consider, for example, the aerospace worker Orfeo Angelucci, whom Jung wrote about in his book on UFOs; Jung thought Angelucci's story showed the tremendous power of the newly emerging "psychic dominants." Here are a few sentences from Angelucci's *The Secret of the Saucers* (1955). The ET intelligence declares to Orfeo:

> It [a devastating Earth change] is permitted as a last hope of waking mankind to the terrible realization of the ghastly price he will pay if he enters the bloody holocaust of Armageddon. . . . But if the horror of the War of the End of an Age shall come, our multitudes are at hand to aid all of those not spiritually arrayed against us.

The tone here is a little less ferocious than John of Patmos and other ancient channelers; the message has become more liberal—extraterrestrial help is available to anyone who does not resist. Orfeo's prophetism began with a classic UFO sighting, developed telepathically and culminating in visions of a pretty Space Sister and a congenial Christ. Thus spoke the Christ-apparition to Orfeo:

> Remember, Orfeo, wherein it was revealed to you not long ago that beings from other worlds now walk upon the Earth. Each is a double [a "walk-in" or angel we entertain "unawares"] of the other and they have of their own free will entered the valley of sorrows that is Earth, to help mankind. . . . Only by their fruits may they be known. This is the beginning of the mysteries of the New Age.

Contactees in the nineties prophesy in the same vein. In 1987, I spoke with a contactee called Ron who worked for Northrop Aerospace. Voices and visions in his head drove Ron from his job. According to Ron, the voices were incessant and interfered with his work, which was related to weapons production. After leaving Northrop, he entered a program for training to become a forest ranger. The gospellers from outer space apparently approved of this ecologically correct profession.

Some people dismiss UFO contactees as insignificant people trying to add luster to their lives. This might have applied to Orfeo. But what about Whitley Strieber, an accomplished man of letters? Nor does it account for Dr. Rauni Leena Luukanen-Kilde, the chief medical officer of Finnish Lapland and also the best-selling author of a book on the afterlife.

A highly intelligent woman, I have met and talked with her on several occasions. Dr. Luukanen-Kilde travels around the world reporting her ongoing telepathic experiences with ETs who are educating her—in preparation of the coming purification of the human race. In a spirit worthy of the ancient prophets, Rauni happily submits to the will of her ETs, who (she says) view us humans as we might view a promising but refractory lower form of life.

But now the ETs are not here as idle sightseers but to carry out an experiment in genetics. As Rauni tells it, the ETs extracted her ova. Extraordinarily intrusive behavior, but Rauni is compliant. It appears that the intruders are here to produce a hybrid race, a new species of humanity, destined, according to the Finnish physician, to replace the current, dysfunctional one. Rauni tells me she is periodically allowed to view and to hold her hybrid offspring.

Dr. Luukanen-Kilde, an imposing woman, says that humans are like "cockroaches" or "puppies" compared to the visitors. Whether we are at all worth saving as a species is a matter of debate for the physician and her extraterrestrial tutors. One story she tells would be terrifying if it were true. The ETs caused the Chernobyl catastrophe, she alleges, punishment meted out to uncooperative Soviets and a warning to other governments. As tutors of the human race, Rauni's ETs are draconian; as we have seen, an attitude of brutality toward the wayward is not untypical of some exponents of the prophetic tradition.

Alien Abductions

The Finnish doctor's story reflects what seems an evolution of the UFO phenomenon. Dr. Luukanen-Kilde is at once a classic 1950s type of contactee, but her story includes the more recent motifs of alien abduction. Since the 1980s, the UFO phenomenon has taken a bizarre turn—if that makes any sense, since the whole phenomenon is quite bizarre. The public imagination—books, media, researchers, CNN— has focused attention on reports of alien abduction. According to these reports, an alien race of bug-eyed, gray-skinned dwarfs is abducting human beings to space ships and using them to create a new species of hybrid humanity. It is quite a staggering claim, yet one you might almost expect to hear in times thick with apocalyptic expectation.

Although other countries report alien abductions, the United States leads in these cosmic rape stories. The Barney and Betty Hill case in 1961, later made into a movie, marks the beginning of the great American end-of-the-century abduction-craze.[15] Once again, events that exacerbate millennial phantasy are rife on the American scene.

According to researcher-historian David Jacobs, thousands, perhaps millions of souls have been abducted by the short "grays," taken aboard extraterrestrial spacecraft, and subjected to medical examination and intrusive reproductive procedures. Budd Hopkins also details the "reproductive focus of the UFO occupants." That focus includes "artificial insemination of female abductees, the removal of fetuses, and the apparent creation of hybrids, offspring showing a mix of human and alien features."[16]

An accomplished American painter turned UFO-researcher, Hopkins has become a human shelter for people who believe they have been kidnapped by aliens. Hopkins is quite zealous in his insistence that aliens are abducting and performing these genetic experiments.[17] Evidence at this point remains circumstantial; there is no medical proof of missing embryos and nothing to support the existence of implants, said to be inserted in abductees and thought to be tagging devices.

Despite the difficulties in accepting abduction stories at face value, one may still believe that these stories contain some kernel of authenticity. John Mack, a Pulitzer prize-winning author and Harvard psychiatrist, has recently made a study of the abduction phenomenon and concluded that the experience is authentic in the sense that it represents a psychiatrically unclassifiable syndrome.

Mack, however, unlike Hopkins, is not convinced that aliens are literally abducting people. He sees a different but no less radical thing occurring; in his view, the UFO phenomenon is part of a mysterious process that is shattering the Western paradigm. He regards this process as painful and wrenching, something comparable to escape from the Platonic cave, a phenomenon pregnant with implications for human evolution. Mack believes that before human beings can transcend their present mode of consciousness, they need to be wrested, violently if need be, from the hypnotic spell of the old Western paradigm. The UFO phenomenon seems to be about doing just that.

Mack has said, "the only war worth fighting today is the paradigm war." The notion of "paradigm wars" is a secular analogue of the final conflict motif in the Millennium Myth. The danger, however, according to Mack, lies in the "reification of metaphor," which happens when dualistic phantasies are literalized and projection of messianic or Antichrist archetypes on individuals or groups occurs.

John Mack spoke to me of the apocalyptic content of the abductee experience. Abductees, most of whom he found were otherwise normal individuals, are filled with "apocalyptic images of destruction of the earth, collapse of the infrastructure, the governmental structure, the desertification of the planet, pollution in the sense of complete destruction of life, geophysical transformation. As they relate these images to me they experience them as truly predictive—this for them is the future, not simply threatening images."

However, in discussing these images after hypnotic sessions, abductees seem more open to the idea that they may be more metaphoric than literal. (John White came to a similar conclusion about the status of poleshift.) Their sense is that the images, put in their minds by the aliens telepathically or through screenlike devices, represent not what must be but what may be. The aliens bring us tidings of possible not necessary worlds. They are true to the prophetic tradition, not necessarily "predictive but possibly as a warning."[18]

Whatever lay behind the UFO mystery, the image content of abduction stories resonates with the Millennium Myth. Alien abduction stories seem to be one way the Millennium Myth is ingressing into contemporary history. To begin with, the very idea of being abducted, swept up by otherworldly beings, is similar to the New Testament prophesy of the Rapture. Here is the classic statement from 1 Thess. 4:16–17:

> For the Lord himself shall descend from heaven with a shout, with the voice of the archangel, and with the trump of God: and the dead in Christ shall rise first. Then we which are alive and remain shall be caught up together with them in the clouds to meet the Lord in the air.

For two thousand years Christians everywhere have been hoping, dreaming, imagining, desiring, praying for, believing in, and thus attempting to elicit the experience of being lifted up out of their difficult lives and away from everything bad and brutal in earthly existence. A deep expectation of being carried off by divinely benevolent beings has colored the collective imagination for thousands of years.

In an age of space travel, one can think of the Rapture in a new way. Many people today believe that they have been raptured away by humanoids, often in alliance with Nordic-type humans; in some cases, there seem to be physical effects, unexplained lesions, gouges, incisions, pains. In this regard, UFO raptures parallel accounts of religious rapture. Teresa of Avila wrote in her autobiography of being abducted by an angel and pierced by a spear in her heart; curiously, her autopsy showed an unexplained spearlike mark on her heart tissue.[19]

The form of the alleged ET ravishers is rich in apocalyptic symbolism. For example, the most popular form of alien abductor—as seen on the cover of Strieber's *Communion*—is clearly childlike or even fetal in its appearance. Students of Jungian psychology might be struck by the symbolism of the childlike ETs. One might, for example, say that the alien stories are about the Divine Child archetype. The Divine Child represents the future, according to Carl Jung,[20] and the human future is increasingly in doubt. In Jung's account of the Child archetype, the child, threatened with destruction, rallies and recovers with divine power. The Child archetype represents indestructible creative power.

The Child archetype—the collective imagination of children—might well be in violent disarray nowadays. One sees the starving faces of children in Somalia and their bruised bodies in Bosnia and the children of intifada hurling rocks at Israeli soldiers and being beaten and shot at. The children's crusade of horror is not only evident in poor or war-torn countries. Kids are killing each other in America in unprecedented numbers, and they are committing suicide at alarming rates. The problem is worldwide. Children, probably never in such great numbers, are going through bad times everywhere. They have to adjust to broken marriages, extended families, economic dislocations. Add to murder, suicide, and abuse, the fact that all over the world today kids are being abducted and sold into sexual slavery.

The turbulence, suffering, deprivation, literal enslavement, and abduction is undoubtedly registering in our consciousness. The horror imposed on children everywhere may, I suggest, be creating living phantasies of alien abduction. Set against a dark apocalyptic landscape of the future, it is possible to think of the alien abductors reported and experienced by so many as unconscious materializations of dissipated psychic energies, the energies perhaps of children murdered, abused, aborted.

These psychic energies might, in ways we do not yet understand, be transformed into quasi-autonomous entities, tulpoidal space-time vagabonds, that randomly or by association are attracted to people in receptive states of mind, perhaps at the edge of sleep or drifting off during highway hypnosis. Dennis Stacy, the skeptical editor of *MUFON* (Mutual UFO Network) *Magazine*,[21] has suggested that alien abductors are the "avenging angels" of American guilt over abortion.

Jung would say that when the child, who symbolizes the future, is endangered, a creative energy is called forth from the depths of nature. The endangered Divine Child is a dangerous force. The idea of an "angry" archetype—chaotic human energies hungry for new forms of expression—ought to give us pause. The abduction stories take us back to the dark side of the Myth. One hears a great deal in these narratives about being used against one's will, being brutalized, terrified, objectified with cold scientific indifference.

Apparently, the aliens treat humans the way humans often treat each other. Perhaps, the "aliens" of abduction stories, who trample human rights, are really ourselves; we might think of them as a living species of nightmare that temporarily materializes and attacks us in acts of revenge. Now, I do not say this is the correct or the complete explanation of alien abduction stories—but something like it seems possible and is consistent with the dynamics of the Millennium Myth. The UFO phenomenon, seen in this light as a disturbance in the Child archetype, is a message about the end of civilization, yet, at the same time, about releasing the energies of the future—for the child is the "potential future."[22]

Crop Circles and the Millennium

One thing to notice about the twentieth century is the appearance of new types of anomaly or, if you are a skeptic, new types of hoax. Far from solving all the mysteries, science seems to keep stumbling upon new ones. So, for example, science has recently discovered that about ninety percent of the matter in the universe is "dark," invisible to human beings; dark matter is known indirectly by its gravitational effects. The fact that cosmologists say we know nothing of ninety percent of the physical universe should be intellectually humbling.

Now, whether hoax or new anomaly, since the 1980s there have been worldwide reports of unaccountable formations appearing in cereal crops and fields. England, within a sixty-mile radius of Stonehenge, is the focal point of these reports. Crop Circle formations became more complicated in the nineties; some claim their shapes follow Mandelbrot sets and are designed in accord with musical intervals. Still, the core image remains the circle, so the mandala or symbol of wholeness is again popping into public consciousness.

Experts say you can distinguish the true from the bogus Circles by the way the grasses are nonharmfully pressed down. I prefer, however, to bracket discussion of their authenticity.[23] *Whatever* the origin of Crop Circles, they stoke, as does the UFO phenomenon, fires of the millennial imagination. Crop Circles have in fact been linked to UFO sightings. One speculation: Crop Circles, appearing among cereal crops, are messages of restoration of Gaia or the Mother Earth Goddess. Now that the notion that Earth is a living organism has been ratified by James Lovelock, the idea of it signaling us through Crop Circles in wheat fields gains a certain appeal. Crop Circle watchers insist that Mother Earth is desperately trying to say something to us.

An American computer-graphics artist, Peter Sorenson publishes *Millennium Magazine*. Sorenson has made several on-site investigations of Crop Circles in England and has described to me his tremendous sense of being in the presence of a transcendent mystery. The lead article by Sorenson in the January 1991 issue of *Millennium Magazine* was called "Crop Circles: Humanity's Wake-Up Call."

Sorenson sees in the Circles signs of eschatological intent. He compares them to the monolith in Arthur C. Clarke's *2001—A Space Odyssey*, that great sci-fi symbol of the monkey mutating into the human. By analogy, Crop Circles signify that once again a critical point in human evolution has evolved. Crop Circles signify that humanity is about to mutate, says Sorenson. "In the face of this presence, business as usual will not be able to go on for long." The End, in short, is near.

An observer of Crop Circles, Paul Von Ward, says, "Upon seeing a fresh formation, one has the impression that the stalks all lay down in response to some command." The suggestion is that a transcendent power over nature is responsible for the Circles. What sort of power? What is behind the pictographs and insectograms and their golden ratios? According to Sorenson, the Circles he photographed display geometric properties that match a sixteenth-century Cabalistic-Rosicrucean diagram of "the Father, the Son and the Holy Ghost." But this, says Sorenson, must be understood in a universal sense, the law of three being a motif in all religious traditions. In other words, the Intelligence behind the Circle Makers is a universal spiritual force. "I submit that anywhere you go among the countless inhabited planets scattered across space, you will find that advanced spiritual understanding recognizes a triune aspect of the Loving Creator Being."

From a logical point of view, there is nothing in this puzzling phenomenon that warrants such an extravagant claim. Sorenson's feelings, however, reflect age-old millennial fervor. Sorenson's zine advocates "a united humanity come the millennium." "It's now or never," says he. "After fifty million years, as we stand just once at the crossroads to Utopia or total ruin, recognizing Love may be the secret to our survival. That seems to be what the Crop Circles are all about."

Let me finish this section with remarks from two of the best-known scientific investigators of Crop Circles. Pat Delgado, for example, is convinced that the phenomenon is a "demonstration of energies and an intelligence beyond the realm of scientific dogma." The Circles, in short, are part of the paradigm war John Mack spoke of—part of a cosmic drama, a cosmic awakening. "The unfolding drama of the crop-formation enigma is a deliberate attempt to expand our awareness."[24]

Delgado's British co-author (also an engineer) Colin Andrews strikes me as a man even more passionately committed to the view that Crop Circles are part of a mounting historic climax of apocalyptic proportions. According to Andrews, the Circles are a sign that "an untouchable distant dimension is becoming nearer as our mental consciousness shifts more quickly than at any time in recorded history."[25]

In a talk I heard Andrews give, he warned darkly of what John of Patmos referred to as "war in heaven." Dark forces, he declared, were massing on the human horizon; a paradigm war, a spiritual war of gravest import is imminent. According to Rosemary Ellen Guiley, a skeptical observer of the Circle phenomenon and the networks it has spawned, Andrews and other Circle enthusiasts strongly believe that a CIA-mediated conspiracy of devilish dimensions is afoot. Once again we meet the conspiracy mentality that pervades the UFO phenomenon, so typical of the Book of Revelation with its talk of false prophets.

Unleashing the Powers of the Future

What can we conclude from this review of the "signs" and "wonders" that, hoaxed or authentic, are reported in such large numbers today?

Carl Jung began his book on flying saucers with an ominous warning about the future. In his essay on Wotan, he also had warnings about the future; Jung saw both the revival of Wotan worship and the flying saucer movement as symptoms of a collective change that would unleash tremendous psychic forces. The ego was going to capsize in a sea of numinosity. Wotan was a magical warrior god, and Jung's Wotan study was an alert to a bloody upheaval, a Nazi-induced mass possession and twilight of the gods. So the question for us is, What might the current spate of anomaly reports signify?

257

Consider the growing reports of visions of the Virgin Mary. Lately, these have been seen, or at any rate reported, with increasing frequency in the United States. Thomas Petrisko, who edits *Our Lady Queen of Peace*, says that reports of apparitions of Mary have so accelerated in the last decade that it is almost impossible to keep up with them.

The Book of Revelation contains a strange vision of a "woman clothed with the sun" (Rev. 12:1), a figure depicted as being at war with a "red Dragon." Conservative Christians have usually thought the red Dragon was the Red Soviet Empire, an Antichrist candidate. But the Soviet Antichrist has collapsed, yet Marian visions are still being reported with growing frequency.

Perhaps we should look in another direction for decoding the Marian mystery. In my view, the sun woman epiphany is archetypal and touches the deepest chords of what Lincoln called our "mystic memory." It is an arresting image of the feminine at war with the dark aspect of the masculine. Are then the current visions of Mary signs of the archetypal rift in the human psyche? Do they perhaps foreshadow in some obscure symbolic way the great paradigm war between Masculine and Feminine—Yahweh and Demeter, Thor and Aphrodite, at war, in a final row, before the end of the old dispensation of history and the dawn of a new?

Nineteenth- and twentieth-century visions of Mary have brought with them times of shattering conflict. A few examples: Catherine Laboure's visions of Mary forecasted the French revolution, foretelling the guillotine for people of the cloth. The 1917 Fatima visions signaled the rise of the Soviet empire, an epoch of dehumanization. The 1968 visions in Zeitun, Egypt, were linked to dissension between Muslims and Coptic Christians, dissension that remains unresolved till today. In 1981, children began seeing visions of Mary in Medjugorje, a mountain village near Bosnia in Herzegovina; the message was peace in a country that since has turned into a hellhole of war. Marian visions seem to anticipate encroaching social tumult.

In the 1990s, Marian visions have begun to occur with increasing frequency in the United States. Thousands of people converge on places of reported epiphany, often trampling on private property, passionate to behold the Mother of God. As in the other examples I gave, the increasingly visible Mother Mary in America may be a signal that forces of change, possibly turbulent change, are afoot.

It is, I admit, a dark reflection, but one that may have a bright side. One wonders if Marian visions in America are somehow a response to the unhappy fate of so many children in our society and in the world at large. One wonders if these persistent images of sacred femininity are signs of an awakening of archetypal psychic forces that have been stifled and distorted for millennia. As the Greek philosopher Heraclitus said long before the birth of Christ: When we stray from the path of cosmic justice, the "Erinyes, ministers of Justice," will find us out. The Erinyes were ferocious feminine chthonic deities also known as "the Furies."

Are these Marian eruptions from the collective imagination a response to the failure of the male-dominated religions of the past two thousand years? Do they in some weirdly mysterious way express unconscious collective forces in revolt against the civilization that produced Hiroshima and the Nazi death camps?

Marian visions, UFOs, and other psychic anomalies may be signs of growing tension in our collective mentality; if Jung is right, they forebode a period where the center will no longer hold, and psychological forces, normally confined to their regular orbits, will be dangerously unleashed. Perhaps psychically anomalous America is moving toward an event that, like the Civil War, may be frighteningly disruptive, but also necessary for a second rebirth of the nation.

Anomalies signify endings and new beginnings. Look around; the evidence is hard to deny. A changing of the gods is upon us. After two thousand years, the cross, undoubtedly still alive and potent, has nevertheless become a question, a burden for many, for others a backdoor to nihilism, as we saw with the messianic-minded Nazis and Communists. Centerless in the interregnum, the cycle starts all over again, and the cross shape-shifts into an ankh, a mandala, a swastika, a serpent, a crystal, a flying saucer—the blue planet in space.

Why are the archetypes exploding? The hypnotic spell of two thousand years of Christianity is lifting. Planet Earth has entered a new phase of its history. Science, the product of human intelligence, has made everything topsy-turvy. In the twentieth century, a species of risible bipeds suddenly acquired titanic power over nature. Human beings now have godlike powers to destroy and to create.

Now, if, as James Lovelock and Lynn Margolis contend, Gaia our Earth Mother is really alive in some sense, she must have a mind, but a mind no doubt far stranger than the human mind. To put the question of our endtime anomalies into yet another perspective, let us say that Gaia is attempting to talk with us. Her mind, lacking a taste for Cartesian clarity, communicates in a language of symbols and archetypes. Perhaps then Gaia is speaking to us in the enigmatic language of Crop Circles and Flying Saucers, angels and Marian visions, Alien Grays and Men in Black, and so on. Perhaps we are being signaled from the depths of nature and collective humanity that we are at a fork in the road of time and history.

Who knows what forces the mind of Gaia might unleash, sensing the attack on life, the ill-treatment of her body and her youngest and most promising human children? Clearly we face an age of spiritual wars. Already we see them on the horizon, shadowy figures ready to kill law-abiding doctors because the voice of conscience whispers to them that abortion is wrong. In Bosnia, Orthodox Christians slaughter Catholics and Muslims, and Catholics and Muslims slaughter each other. In Rwanda, 1994 tribal warfare resulted in the slaughter of hundreds of thousands, and observers speculate that these tribal-spawned carnages presage a return to medieval barbarism (see the cover story in *Time Magazine*, May 16, 1994). The unspeakable stares at us daily on the television screen. No wonder the kids are packed into the video arcades, playing Terminator 2. Are they psyching themselves up for Judgment Day?

Anomalies are symptoms of breakdown, the end of a world view; but they are also signals of the dawn of a new world view. Are the growing reports of anomalies and alien weirdness symptoms that civilization is having a nervous breakdown? Symptoms perhaps of a kind of psychotic breakthrough into the healing depths, a journey through a dark tunnel, at the end of which the light of transformation awaits us?

Technocalypse Now

Then the One sitting on the throne spoke, 'Look, I am making the whole of creation new.'

REV. 21:5

Cyberspace stands to thought as flight stands to crawling. The root of this fascination is the promise of control over the world by the power of the will. In other words, it is the ancient dream of magic that finally nears awakening into some kind of reality.

MARCOS NOVAK
Liquid Archetypes in Cyberspace

n the last chapter, we surveyed the domain of endtime anomalies; in this chapter, we look at the relationship between technology and the Millennium Myth. Technology, too, reflects the pressure of the Millennium Myth to ingress into history. To identify this pressure I have coined the word *technocalypse*, "the convergence of technology and the apocalyptic imagination."

The dimensions of technocalypse have only begun to dawn on us as we approach the end of the twentieth century. Science and technology have begun to utterly transform human existence with such things as the atom bomb, space travel, cryonics, bioengineering, nanotechnology, virtual reality, and so on, developments full of apocalyptic overtones.

The Book of Revelation pictures the complete transformation of nature—"a new heaven and a new earth" (Rev. 21:1). "The world of the past is gone," says the voice speaking to the prophet John; "Look, I am making the whole of creation new." What I want to try to show in this chapter is that technology, taken as a long-range and total pursuit, is being driven to accomplish just such a remaking of the whole of creation. In particular, I believe, the eschatological thrust of technology is toward remaking the human body.

In his Letter to the Romans, Paul wrote of the natural world suffering from a fundamental defectiveness. According to Paul: " . . . the whole creation itself might be freed from its slavery to corruption and brought into the same glorious freedom as the children of God. We are well aware that the whole creation, until this time, has been groaning in labor pains. . . . even we are groaning inside ourselves, waiting with eagerness for our bodies to be set free" (Rom. 8:20–23). The Biblical vision of the total renovation of nature and bodily existence goes back to Isaiah: "For look, I am going to create new heavens and a new earth, and the past will not be remembered" (Isa. 65:17). Gladness, joy, complete harmony with a new nature will be realized in the coming messianic Kingdom. In contemporary language, nature will enter a new epoch of cosmic evolution.

The Technology of the New Heaven and Earth

The belief that a break with nature as we know it is possible is found in many ancient traditions. Mircea Eliade spoke of the human nostalgia for paradise. Besides the Hebrews, the Romans felt it; for example, Virgil's Fourth Eclogue foretold a coming golden age in which the laws of nature and of human society would be radically altered. In chapter 8, I described Plato's vision of the true earth. Henry Corbin has discussed the "celestial earth" of Mazdean and Shi'ite Iranian psycho-visionaries.[1]

Like Plato and Saint John, the Iranian visionaries anticipate a transfigured earth. According to Corbin, active imagination is the faculty for discerning the celestial earth; the image is the locus in our mental life where sense and spirit unite: "And the property of this Image will be precisely that of effecting the transmutation of sensory data, their resolution into the purity of the subtle world, in order to restore them as symbols to be deciphered. . . . Such perception through the Imagination is therefore equivalent to a 'dematerialization.' "[2]

This last point touches on a major theme of technocalypse: the tendency for technology to dematerialize—not just itself—but human existence itself. For example, as may be observed in the tendency of technology toward miniaturization, computers are getting smaller and smaller. This may seem paradoxical, since we associate technology with materialism. But the paradox vanishes once we reflect on what technology actually does, which is to reduce the restraints of material existence on our experience of the world. A phone, for example, annihilates space for the human voice; television, for the human image, and so on—every piece of technology enables us to extend ourselves across time and space. Nature constrains us less and less. Behind technology is the drive to restructure nature, a drive toward a second genesis.

The prophets saw it all in a vision, obscurely. With the rise of the modern world, the vision began to find ways to incarnate bits and pieces of itself. Historian Ernest Tuveson has, in fact, written of the "mechanistic New Jerusalem." Robert Boyle, for instance, saw the "great discoveries" of new science as "pregnant hints" of something wonderful to come, as giving us "grounds of good hope, that God makes haste to finish some great work in a more glorious display. . . ."[3] Boyle spoke of the coming enlargement of human perceptive and intellectual faculties. In "the great renovation of the world" that Boyle envisioned, human beings will carry on exploring nature. Not even death will halt the evolution of consciousness, for "it is likely that all our faculties will, in the future blessed state, be enlarged and heightened." Thus Boyle's idea of scientific and technical progress merges with the eschatological goal of a "future blessed state."[4] The hunger for immortality, for a future new heaven and earth, is here linked to the rise of the new science and technology.

Three Views of the Technology of the New Heaven and Earth

Moving ahead to the present, there are three ways we can meaningfully speak of the technology of a "new heaven and earth."

1) The first deals with the prodigious power over nature that human beings are increasingly acquiring.

2) The second comes under the heading of creating new environments, autonomous worlds. Science and technology have begun to create (or to think about creating) new worlds in the sense of creating new environments; for example, terraforming or shaping a planet like Mars so it can accommodate human space migrants. Terraforming is a literal fulfillment of John and Isaiah's prophecies of new heavens and earths. Biosphere 2, the two-year attempt to create a self-supporting ecosystem, a bio-world unto itself is another recent

example of new-heaven-and-earth making. Another example, which I focus on here, is cyberspace or virtual reality (VR).

3) The third example of technocalypse involves growing efforts at bioengineering; the notion of bioengineering a new type of human being fulfills Robert Boyle's millennial vision of "physico-theology."

Technocalypse carries on the work of the American and European Enlightenment, the progressive side of the Reformation, the humanism of the Renaissance, the hopes of the Iranian psycho-visionaries, and the aspirations of John of Patmos, Plato, and Isaiah. Modern technology, seen in this light, is the latest and most powerful expression of a visionary tradition that stretches back to the origins of human civilization. Modern technology, I am suggesting, is not just the Frankenstein monster it often appears to be, or the mere adjunct to comfort and convenience that Samuel Hopkins lauded, but an instrument unconsciously driven by millenarian visions of the end of history. Now let us look at these three paths to technocalypse in greater detail.

A New Power Over Nature

Machines are secretly driven by eschatological phantasies; the way to see this is by looking at what they do. In general, machines have the effect of lightening the world, of reducing its natural unwieldiness and antagonism to human desire. As noted above, they exhibit a tendency to dematerialize the world. Arno Penzias of Bell Labs who discovered the afterglow from the Big Bang in 1964, says, for example, that we are on the threshold of an "Age of Information Transparency." According to the prophet Daniel (Dan. 12:4): "Many shall run . . . to and fro, and knowledge shall be increased." A revolution in transportation and information is coming, proclaimed apocalyptic Daniel, centuries before Penzias.

So is a revolution of time consciousness coming. Through video, film, and computer projection, technology promises to get us all, like Kurt Vonnegut's Billy Pilgrim, "unstuck in time." Getting unstuck in time, escaping natural time, is a major feature of technocalypse. Technology is accelerating the experience of time and has even created a new type of disease, called by Alvin Toffler "future shock." We are, say the techno-visionaries, heading toward a quantum leap of machine power that is rapidly changing all the rules of the reality game. Quantum physics, say some theorists, may even make time travel possible.

There is no better example of the accelerating expansion of human capacity than what K. Eric Drexler calls the "coming era of nanotechnology." *Engines of Creation*, the title of Drexler's book, takes us on a scientific detour back to the Book of Genesis. Traditionally, creation is the business of gods; in the mechanistic New Jerusalem, it becomes the business of engineers.

Although Drexler's views extrapolate from well-founded areas of science such as organic chemistry, nanotechnology is still a visionary science. Nanotechnology is molecular technology; a nanometer is a billionth of a meter, the size of a molecule. With nanotechnology we embark with Isaac Asimov on a Fantastic Voyage; we accompany the Incredible Shrinking Man in a descent to the world of the vanishingly small.

Since the Stone Age, technology has operated "in bulk," as in stone chipping and wood carving. The artist or builder tackles a bulky object and refines its shape. Nanotechnologists will build from the molecular level up, controlling molecules by controlling the bonding laws of organic chemistry. They will harness the nanomachines that operate living organisms, extract their chemical mechanisms, and put them to work. With nanotechnology, according to Drexler, we will enter an era of millennial abundance, develop ways of producing bionic bodies, and move to the solar system and beyond. American prosperity consciousness finds the supreme ally in nanotechnology.

Among possible technologies, none support the optimism of the Enlightenment Millennium more than nanotechnology. American futurologists generally promote optimism; for example, Naisbitt and Aburdene (in *Megatrends 2000*) and Cetron and Davies (in *American Renaissance*). The latter write, "For the next fifty years the United States will remain the most productive country in the world, the most powerful, the richest, and the most free. By the year 2000, few of us will have reason to doubt it." Esfandiary, self-declared "transhuman" among us, also preaches abundance and optimism. He ends his *Up-Wingers* with the words, "Let us not be afraid of vision and hope. It was the daring of visionaries that brought us this far—from gloomy primordial marshes to where we are today—reaching for the galaxies reaching for immortality." Timothy Leary belongs in the company of these constitutional yea sayers, confident, as he is, that human beings may be on the threshold of learning to "boot up" their own brains. Drexler's optimism beats them all:

> With nanotechnology we'll be able to make almost anything we want in any amount we want, and do it cheaply and cleanly. Poverty, homelessness, and starvation can be banished. Pollution can be eliminated. We can finally open the space frontier. With the help of powerful AI systems, we'll be able to tackle more complex applications of nanotechnology, including molecular surgery to repair human tissue. And that can eliminate aging and disease. People everywhere struggle for greater wealth and better health. With these advances, we can have them—for all of us.[5]

What a statement about human potential! Now note a passage, parallel in spirit, from the early Church father Irenaeus:

> The days will come, in which vines shall grow, each having ten thousand branches, and in each branch ten thousand twigs, and in each twig ten thousand shoots, and in each one of the shoots ten thousand clusters, and on every one of the clusters ten thousands grapes, and every grape when pressed will give five and twenty metretes of wine.[6]

This is a vision of materialistic abundance and, like Drexler's nanotech vision, promises nothing less than a new cosmology of abundance. The difference, of course, is that Irenaeus expects that God will accomplish the miracle, while for Drexler technology is the miracle worker: "The new technology will handle individual atoms and molecules with control and precision; call it *molecular technology*. It will change our world in more ways than we can imagine."[7]

The key to this millenarian miracle of creative power will be the assemblers. "Because assemblers will let us place atoms in almost any reasonable arrangement, they will let us build almost anything that the laws of nature allow to exist." Stewart Brand, who founded the *Whole Earth Review*, talks of the coming age of "designer realities." The encroachment on the turf of deity has begun. Drexler, with the confidence of a Renaissance magus, says, "With assemblers, we will be able to remake our world or destroy it." Assemblers will work with disassemblers. A disassembler is a nanomachine that takes an object apart while recording its structure; once the structural information is down, assemblers will proceed to make perfect copies of the object—cheaply, cleanly, efficiently. The technological Millennium will be a bargain.

Critics say Drexler's ideas are implausible because of the way molecules behave: Drexler thinks of molecules too rigidly and mechanically; his nanomachines will not work because the molecular world is too diffuse; and so on. Such misgivings do not dampen Drexler's confidence and enthusiasm, whose motto is: "If it can be done, it will be done." Nanotechnology will be a "revolution without parallel."

Biosphere 2

The Millennium Myth is driving us to recreate and reembody ourselves—to renew the Earth, to rediscover, and if need be, redesign the Garden of Eden. This is how we can look at Biosphere 2, a much-criticized experimental attempt to create a glass-enclosed, humanmade, energetically open living system—in short, a biosphere. Biosphere 2 was an attempt to build a computerized Noah's ark, a detached, ultimately transportable, living microcosm of Earth.

The biospherians designed a meta-ecosystem in which whatever they breathed, ate, and drank was recycled. And so the circle returns, the mandala of wholeness, the symbol of our divinity, under the guise of a first attempt to prepare whole environments to participate in terraforming or space migration. Biosphere 2 is a good example of secular spinoff from the prophetic imagination of Isaiah and John of Patmos.

Texan tycoon Ed Bass underwrote this two-year southern Arizona experiment in post-Biblical re-genesis. Thirteen biospherians, men and women, were involved, so far the biggest attempt to create a synthetic ecology. The task was formidable, which may have prompted one of the bionauts, Peter Warshall, to remark: "Designing a biome is an opportunity to think like God." That the experiment has apocalyptic overtones is suggested by the fact that there were rumors that the whole setup was a dress rehearsal for post-apocalypse, an evil plan for billionaires to save themselves in the coming breakup of the world order.

About engineering biospheres, Dorian Sagan writes, "We are at the first phase of a planetary metamorphosis, a breaking of the biontic wave."[8] To break the biontic wave means that the future of Earth now lies in the hands of human engineers. Biosphere 2—beyond its technical or protocol achievements—is a landmark in symbolic significance, a punctuation mark in the time wave of Earth history. For, before space travel and space colonization become possible, biosphere engineering will have to be mastered. Biosphere 2, an experiment in space biology, anticipates a challenge that has to be met to engineer a sustainable space habitat. We can not migrate to space alone; we have to take the whole biontic wave, from which we evolved, with us.

Opening the Space Frontier

Drexler paints the future in a chapter called "The World Beyond Earth." The American Space Program bogged down after Project Apollo, which Drexler puts down as a flag-waving ceremony. The Program will be reborn with nanotechnology.

About a century ago, the Russian visionary Konstantin Tsiolkovsky said, "Man will not always stay on Earth; the pursuit of light and space will lead him to penetrate the bounds of the atmosphere, timidly at first, but in the end to conquer the whole of solar space." In 1961, another Russian, Yuri Gagarin, became the first man to travel in space. As usual, vision precedes technology.

According to Drexler, we are about to realize Leonardo's dream of flight in a way that would have amazed Leonardo. We will use the vast sources of solar energy in space, mine the moon and asteroids, fabricate lands as large as Europe and seas as large as the Mediterranean in zero-gravity space. There will be freedom and abundance for all, *literally*, in a new heaven and earth. "Space resources and replicating assemblers," declares Drexler, "will accelerate this historic trend beyond the dreams of economists, launching the human race into a new world."

Timothy Leary, who helped launch America on inner space travel through his promotion of psychedelics in the sixties, has become an advocate for outer space travel. In March 1976, Leary was in San Diego Federal Prison for having had the temerity to reanimate the Socrates archetype in the twentieth century. In prison, Leary wrote a piece called "War and Centralization as Prelude to Space Migration."[9]

It asks about the "goal of evolution." Leary dumps as dead ends the old goals of territorial expansion, technological competition, and cultural homogeneity. The old technology created an "electroid-homo-genized society, almost insectile in its centralization."[10] (*Insectile*, a curious adjective, pops up in John's Book of Revelation and William

Burroughs's Interzone. *Insectile* also figures in Whitley Strieber's description of the Visitors.)

Leary's chiliastic leanings are shown by his optimism: "What gets lost in the pessimism is the fact that our species is riding an enormous evolutionary brain-wave, a gigantic upsurge in information-release which must be designed with some goal in mind."[11] The goal of human evolution, according to Leary, is—S.M.I.²L.E. This stands for Space Migration, Intelligence Increase, and Life Extension. Leary notes that evolution is directed toward progressive mastery of environments, expansion and flight in space, and "away from the pull of gravity." Indeed—away from the pull of the grave. As of old, death and gravity remain apocalyptic foes.

"Most of the religious revelations and cosmologies which have guided humanity in the past have agreed that the goals of life are to be found in 'heaven above.' Surely it is no accident that winged angels, celestial realms, messianic descents and ascensions, are basic themes found in almost all theologies." I agree with Leary's generous evolutionary hermeneutics of religious symbolism and mythical discourse; gods, messiahs, angels, and other agents of supernatural power are here understood as metaphors for human evolutionary potential. Religion, read with polycognitive eyes, anticipates the future of science.

Prophecy, especially where it foretells the coming of the Eschaton, is a portrait of transhuman development. The war between science and religion is needless, Leary implies, the product of minds made superficial by fear. No such wars bothered Galileo, Newton, or Einstein. The war between science and religion is a war between monotheists of the imagination.

As for life extension being a goal of evolution, Leary agrees with Nikolay Fedorov, our death-hating Russian visionary of chapter 6, when he adds, "Death is the only enemy of humanity. The conquest of death should be the basic and central concern of science. Death should be snuffed."[12] Or, as John Donne said, "Death thou shalt die." With Leary the dare flung at death becomes a call for technocalypse. Leary, as a matter of fact, has committed his brain to the millenarian hope of cryogenic immortality. I should say, however, that in Leary's eschato-evolutionary logo, the emphasis is on Intelligence Increase. Leary rightly underscores how ludicrous life extension and space migration would be without intelligence increase. Long-lived, space-hopping folk with retarded minds would make a mockery of any scientific Millennium.

Cyberspace and the New Heaven and Earth

People today are hailing cyberspace—or virtual reality—with the same enthusiasm as nanotechnology. While nanotechnology is a vision of godlike power over physical nature, cyberspace is a vision of a new environment where the human imagination will be free to reinvent and reembody reality. The idea of travels in computerized synthetic realities, like the idea of all-powerful nanomachines, suggests that humans are on the cusp of a new stage of cosmic evolution.

Marshall McLuhan was a prophet of cyberspace when he wrote in 1964, "Today, after more than a century of electric technology, we have extended our central nervous system itself in a global embrace, abolishing both space and time as far as our planet is concerned."[13] Cyberspace extends our nervous systems beyond our individual selves into what McLuhan called the "global village."

Cyberspace was born in the paleolithic caves of Lascaux. When cave dwellers made marks on their cave walls that evoked images of animals, they created the first alternate space for the human imagination to inhabit. They took the first step toward creating the dream machine that is cyberspace. Telling a story is creating a conscious dream; cyberspace is the techno-fiction of conscious dreaming, a technique for producing what novelist William Gibson called a "consensual hallucination."[14]

Humankind cannot bear too much reality, said T. S. Eliot. Cyberspace is the answer to humankind's need to escape the drudgery of life trapped in space-time, a way beyond Freud's reality principle. Let me put it like this: If space is the theater of Realpolitik, cyberspace opens the door to Surrealpolitik.

Egyptian magicians thought they could (or pretended they could) animate images by proper incantations. The Renaissance magi thought humans could control the forces of nature by manipulating icons and verbal formulas; in late twentieth century, we manipulate the icons of Apple Computers or of Microsoft Windows.

America, the birthplace of cyberspace, has led the way in developing phone, phonograph, light bulb, radio, movies, TV, and the computer. Cyberspace is the name for the accelerating convergence of telecommunication technologies. Cyberspace, an inchoate concept, represents a collective lunge toward the Eschaton of information. The Eschaton, on the plane of technology, here signals the appearance of a new environment: the human extension into a new electronic heaven and earth. Invention by invention, advance by advance, this latest surge toward Last Days has been evolving.

The telephone was crucial in making telepresence and interactiveness possible. McLuhan wrote, "with the telephone, there occurs the extension of ear and voice that is a kind of extrasensory perception." Radio provided multiple telepresence but lacked interactiveness. You could turn off Mayor La Guardia while he read the funnies during a newspaper strike, but you could not talk back to him. With today's electronic town halls, we have visual and auditory telepresence, with the ability of millions of participants to interact with each other.

We are watching the beginnings of a new logical space, an instantaneous electronic everywhereness, which we may all access, enter into, and experience. We have, in short, the beginnings of a new kind of community. The virtual community becomes a model for a secular Kingdom of Heaven; as Jesus said there were many mansions in his Father's Kingdom, so there are already many virtual communities, each reflecting their own needs and desires. On the WELL (Whole Earth 'Lectronic Link), for instance, you can log on to virtual communities of interest ranging from comics to cooking, hacking to hypercard, AIDS to angels.

In cyberspace, one leaves the body and immerses oneself in another environment; one enters a world of electronic astral projection. Behind it lay centuries of human aspiration toward transcendence of death and matter. Here we confront a crucial link between ancient eschatology and modern technology. Note what steps were taken this century. The movies made possible the first mass exodus into a partially evolved cyberspace. We experienced partial (mostly visual) telepresence; in a dark theater we had, psychically speaking, our first electronic out-of-body experiences.

The entertainment industry has fueled the search for this aspect of cyberspace, new dimensions of sensory expansion and telepresence. Fred Waller's *Cinerama* did not produce great films, but it was a step on the way of the popular American imagination struggling to liberate itself from space and time. Morton Heilig's *Sensorama* was a machine that took you on simulated motorcycle rides through New York City; **271** you experienced wind in your face and simulated smells of the city that were ejected from the seat upholstery. Although Heilig's enterprise was never a commercial success, the inventor saw *Sensorama* as an educational tool, a way of extending and organizing experience in a world that is increasingly chaotic. Cyberspace, seen in this light, becomes an educational tool for the next millennium.[15]

Another prophet of cyberspace—an electronic version of the new heaven and earth—is Myron Krueger. So far I have made no attempt to define cyberspace (or virtual reality), because the concept remains open-ended. But Krueger's definition is worth quoting at length:

> A virtual reality totally dominates your senses and immerses you in a simulated world created with computer graphics. You interact with this world in a completely natural way using your body. This world can be inhabited by graphic creatures and the images of other people who are in different locations. Since the laws of cause and effect can be composed, any interactive fantasy that can be imagined, can also be experienced.[16]

A virtual reality—Krueger implies the concept is pluralistic—constitutes a new world of graphic creatures, a world we can enter and leave at will, a world where anything we can imagine can be experienced.

With television you are standing outside, peering at a box that contains, and displays, a moving image; in virtual reality you step through the box, pass though the screen, and become immersed in a world, as you become immersed in a dream; you move through a stereoscopic, gravity-altered world. You mount your head display, tighten your data glove—you're there! A surgeon at an operating table, an astronaut jogging on Jupiter, a sugar molecule in the bloodstream.

Krueger's remarks suggest another idea about cyberspace. In cyberspace, we create our own reality. (We encounter the New Age cliché in a post-karmic techno-setting.) We create informational objects— "graphic creatures" as Krueger puts it—and arrange for them to inhabit simulated worlds. We can endow these graphic entities, these budding golems and tulpas, with as much intelligence as we like; then we make up rules or stories and devise ways for interacting with them. Thus, with the machine, we can play god.

Musician-inventor Jaron Lanier is known for designing a tool for cyberspace called the data glove. The data glove orients cybernauts to their virtual worlds. The data glove is a new opposable thumb. With the first opposable thumb, we became *homo faber*; with the data glove, we become *homo imaginalis*. Cyberspace implies the radical extension of our nervous systems into informational spaces whose outreach is as great as the human imagination.

According to enthusiastic exponents, it also implies an extension of our basic freedoms. Thus, Mitchell Kapor, co-founder of the Electronic Frontier Foundation, suggests that the digital highway is heading us toward a Jeffersonian information policy. "In fact," he writes, "life in cyberspace seems to be shaping up exactly like Thomas Jefferson would have wanted: founded on the primacy of individual liberty and a commitment to pluralism, diversity, and community."[17]

Of course, this remains a utopian dream; as things stand, the technology of the New Jerusalem may only deepen the class split between the informationally rich and the deprived. One might reasonably fear the specter of corporate domination, not to mention that the five hundred channels of the new data highway may, like the old media, become five hundred channels for commercial catering to the lowest common denominator.

Satanic Technology: An Interlude

Indeed, not everyone is sanguine about the future of cyberspace. Cyberspace, because of its amazing networking potential, may seem the highway to a Jeffersonian democratic utopia, and Capor is right to press for total freedom at this frontier. However, the Myth we are using as our signpost to the future tells us that the time of transition is a time when we must face the challenge of satanic forces.

The Book of Revelation sees a world enslaved and brutalized by a satanic technology that dominates the mind through manipulation of animated images. The false prophet is the slave of the Beast. By "miracles" the Beast "breathed life into the image, so that the image of the beast was able to speak, and to have anyone who refused to worship the image of the beast put to death" (Rev. 13:15).

In 1987, a brilliant movie appeared that explores the metaphysics of cyberspace and mind control. David Cronenberg's *Videodrome* is a tale of technocalypse. In the movie, videodrome is a video signal that creates a tumor in the brain; according to Professor Brian Oblivion, this "tumor" is actually an organic extension of the brain, an organ

273

for perceiving new realities. Images extrude from TV screens and the boundaries between hallucination and reality dissolve. Max (played by James Woods) puts his head through a TV screen that liquefies, makes virtual love with Deborah Harry, who in turn morphs from a TV image to a 3-D femme fatale. The battle for the mind of America will be fought in the videofield, we are told by Dr. Oblivion. "Television is reality," he proclaims. Television is the human future. Reality is a porno-mystical video with overtones of initiation and self-mutilation.

An air of apocalyptic menace pervades *Videodrome*; we see Deborah Harry ecstatically press a lit cigarette into her breast, in a gesture reminiscent of Russian women of the Skoptsy sect, women who mutilated their breasts to hasten the Second Coming. In a bid for world power via the Cathode Ray Mission, sado-masochistic stimuli trigger the hallucinatory mechanisms for controlling the collective mind. The apocalyptic note is most clearly struck in the culminating theme of Videodrome, the "beginning of the new flesh." True to the Myth, the new flesh of the resurrection presupposes crucifixion.

"To become the new flesh you must kill the old flesh." That is why Videodrome had to emerge out of snuff films, movies about real eroto-sadism that end in death. As in the Book of Revelation, real mass slaughter seems indicated before the Great Breakthrough. The last image of *Videodrome* shows us Max (James Woods) blowing his brains out, dismembering himself, the necessary prelude to his Transfiguration in Cyberspace.

In *Videodrome*, images that come to life threaten to take over the world. In this Hollywood gloss on the Myth, Satan operates a giant hallucination machine, and sadism is deployed to open the neural floodgates, prepare the soul for the epiphany of the "new flesh," and thus for the next dispensation of "mondo weirdo." *Wild Palms*, an ABC mini-series directed by Oliver Stone in 1992, was another foray into the video of technocalypse. And I would include on this short list *Terminator 2* (and the video games it has spawned) as pop apocalypses in which the Antichrist is identified with the Machine. The popular imagination of America is haunted by apocalyptic imagery.

So are certain critical moments in twentieth-century American history. Indeed, some of Saint John's worst nightmares have been realized in the twentieth century. Angry John, exiled on the island of Patmos, saw a time coming when men would call fire down from heaven and rain death on the Earth, a time when people would be destroyed en masse with deadly efficiency.

For a recent example, consider the Stealth bomber, those sleek bird-like agents of mass destruction—Lockheed's legacy to the apocalyptic murder potential of America. The Stealth bomber, undetectable by radar, acquires a sinister supernatural quality. Not one Stealth bomber went down in the Persian Gulf War; the destruction rained on Baghdad was a Patmosian revelation of the dark side of human technology. Meanwhile, the world watched the entire (doctored) scenario on an image device that John of Patmos seems to have prophesied two thousand years ago. Did John see it all, in a glass, darkly?

When Robert Oppenheimer witnessed the first A bomb explode, he quoted Shiva, the Hindu god of destruction: "Now I am become death, the shatterer of worlds." A primeval phantasy of world-destroying power—voiced long ago by the prophets of Israel and the seers of India—became on that day at Alamagordo an all-searing physical reality. The Bomb reified the metaphor of divine destruction. Scenarios of vast decimation, once creatures of the mythic imagination, metastasized in the tissue of human history.

The Book of Revelation is a living museum, a zoological garden of the world's greatest nightmares. They become visible when John gets to work on those terrible seals. After opening the fourth seal, he sees a vision of a "pale horse; and his name that sat on him was Death, and Hell followed with him. And Power was given to them over the fourth part of the Earth, to kill with sword, and with hunger, and with death, and with the beasts of the earth" (Rev. 6:8). As the seals are opened, the bottomless pit yawns, and the fiery abominations below erupt in righteous rage against anyone lacking "the seal of God in their foreheads" (Rev. 9:4).

A new age began with the bombing of Hiroshima, August 6, 1945. On that day the imagination of the End acquired a new meaning, a new power to materialize and stamp itself on the world. The Cold War may be over, but the threat of nuclear apocalypse is not. The arsenals of apocalypse are still in place, and countries like Iraq and North Korea are very intent on joining the Nuclear Club. With political and social instability steadily growing all over the world, the danger of satanic technology remains as real, if nor more real, than ever. For this reason the millennial hope in the renewal of humanity—with the help of technology—assumes more, not less, urgency as we approach 2001.

Bioengineering Superhumanity

The dark side of technology is everywhere, and the potential for destruction, distortion, and domination is undoubtedly vast. But let us return to the positive imagery of the Book of Revelation, the positive vision of the new heaven and earth. At the moment, we are looking at the technical side of that vision. Not only does modern technology give us great powers over nature as well as a virtual environment of the imagination to explore, it also promises to create a new type of human being—a new kind of "flesh," such as imagined by Paul of Tarsus and David Cronenberg.

The idea of superhumanity is found in other and older traditions. In the ancient world, Plutarch wrote concerning the predictions of Tuscan soothsayers:

> One day when the sky was serene and clear there was heard in it the sound of a trumpet, so shrill and mournful that it frightened and astonished the whole city. The Tuscan sages say that it portended a new race of men, and a renovation of the world.

An unidentified sound from a clear and serene sky—a sound like a trumpet. Trumpets also figure in John's Revelation. The trumpet is the signal that vast change is at hand, that an old form of humanity is about to come to an end, and that a new form is about to emerge. This ancient human hope and expectation is reawakening today through science and technology.

Consider, for example, the Promethean, thoroughly heretical idea of bioengineering. Biotechnology suggests that the time of the great quantum leap, the breakthrough to a new cosmic epoch, may really be at hand. Human intelligence is about to gain a significant technical foothold on what used to be God's prerogative: designing, if not creating, life.

The painter Salvador Dali was fascinated by technology and leaped to imaginative conclusions about the future of science. His most famous painting of melted clocks was influenced by Einstein's Theory of Relativity. Dali had high hopes for the potential of bioengineering: "I am convinced that cancer will be curable and that the most amazing transplants will be performed, and cellular rejuvenation will be with us in the near future. To restore someone to life will merely involve an everyday operation. I will wait in my liquid helium without a trace of impatience."[18]

No doubt we are far from the age of bionic superhumanity, but the idea has clearly entered the mainstream (witness the TV series *Bionic Woman*) and is part of the current zeitgeist. Reflected in the recurrent science fiction phantasy of cyborgs (cybernetic organisms), the bionic evolution of a "new humanity" has already begun. In 1990, a bionic show toured twelve cities in the United States with state-of-the-art displays in the field of "replacement medicine."[19] The show featured the latest in prosthetic limbs, organ transplant technology, and other orthopedic aids.

Recently the first lung transplant was performed in Utah. Thanks to a tiny 22-channel cochlear implant inserted in their ears, children deaf from birth may now learn to hear—and speak—words. Antiarrhythmic implants (defibrillation devices) may extend the lives of heart patients. As an example of the "new flesh," plastic skin patches that release nitroglycerine or hormones are now established scientific procedures. By implanting fetal neurons in the patient's brain, medical scientists have made progress in alleviating the symptoms of Parkinson's disease. Penile and breast implants have been less than successful in bringing on the millennium of the perfect body. The injection of silicone gel into the breast may cause scleroderma, a disease in which the body mummifies itself. Truly, an example of technology satanically run amok.

Still, the experimental drive toward perfecting the design of the human body is probably unstoppable. The experiment will continue, and I see no reason to doubt that increasing success is eventual. Technology everywhere is accelerating, and different technologies are converging; everything seems poised for what Whitehead called "creative advance." Given the drive to immortalize ourselves and to perfect our bodies, bioengineering is bound to press forward. Whether Frankensteinian horrors or Plutarch's "new race" of humanity emerges, remains to be seen. Either way, everywhere we see frontiers of human creativity opening up.

The prophets saw a time when nature would lavish its bounty on us—God would step in, make lion and lamb live together in peace, nature forever clement and fruitful. In the old Myth, God makes all this possible; in the new Myth, people do. The FDA does. For example, in March 1990, the Federal Department of Agriculture approved an enzyme, chymosin, that was produced by recombinant DNA techniques. Corporations are therefore the new deities. Calgene, a plant biotechnology firm in Davis, California, has engineered modifications in the biology of corn, a plant normally resistant to change. Thus we have quietly entered the age of designer foods—a significant step, one could say, toward the American Millennium.

But something more radical is in the offing—the age of designer humans. In 1990, the Hastings Center Report discussed genetics and the new "human malleability." It is a phenomenon that opens a huge can of philosophical worms. The options go far beyond gene therapy for current disabilities; they include choosing desirable traits and trying to enhance them by bioengineering. Bioengineering is a late twentieth-century technique for creating Paul's new humanity; in it, we map the human genome—there are 100,000 genes in every human cell—and then proceed, like Renaissance magi, to try to design better human beings.

These are intoxicating prospects. There are bioengineers beginning to speculate on the DNA of love, intelligence, and other sociable traits. No doubt, there will be an outcry against the dangers of creating a mechanistic humanity. Debate, however, is not likely to stop experimentation. The appeal of playing God is too great. Not only can we now imagine engineering an improved version of the human species, but in this time of technocalypse, we can aspire to even greater miracles.

Paul Levinson, in a statement called *The Extinction of Extinction*, claims for science the altogether outrageous potential to reverse the ravages of natural time and resurrect extinct forms of life from fossil death. The idea was suggested in Michael Crichton's *Jurassic Park*. To bring back a dinosaur from the abyss of time is a feat the average person might ascribe to God. In the old Myth, it was God who raised Jesus from the dead; today, Mitsubishi or Calgene promise the resurrection power. As Levinson puts it, "Heaven may well be a huge directory of DNA codes, and coming back from the dead—as far as a species goes—may be as simple as finding the right place in which to insert the code."[20]

Not everyone is thrilled by the prospect of having to deal with designer life forms. Science fiction has canvassed the sinister possibilities. In *Algeny*, Jeremy Rifkin warns of murderous bacteria escaping profit-mad gene-labs, invisible monsters attacking defenseless populations and starting a plague worthy of John's apocalypse. In *Jurassic Park*,

Michael Crichton painted an eco-apocalyptic scene of killer dinosaurs revived from fossilized DNA. Here the phantasy of raising the dead shades off into the primitive fear that the dead are out to wreak havoc on us.

Bioengineering offers hope of rejuvenation and longevity. Revising the script of life and nature—to the point of bringing back extinct species—sounds like something that takes a lot of time. So, not surprisingly, the Myth would have us at least retrieve our allotted lifespan in Eden. Roy Walford, a gerontologist and Biospherian 2, figures that should at least be 120 years. Walford, like his Renaissance predecessor Luigi Cornaro,[21] claims that undereating is the secret of longevity.

At this juncture in the human time wave, human beings seem to be biologically programmed to grow old and die. Entropy is our inescapable predator. But suppose there are knowable mechanisms involved in the design for death? Might it be possible to reset the clock that shuts down the genetics of youth? Redesign our bodies so they begin to age, say, at five hundred?

The lead story in the November 1993 issue of *Health* was called "The Anti-Aging Drug." In 1990, gerontologist Daniel Rudman at the Medical College of Wisconsin in Milwaukee injected a human growth hormone (a chemical produced in the pituitary gland) in a dozen men that produced physiological changes the equivalent of ten to twenty years of aging reversal. Despite mixed results in some who had the injections, one enthusiast saw miraculous potential and started a rejuvenation center in Mexico. "We thoroughly believe we can stop the aging process," he says. Another devotee of the hormone evokes mythology, "This could be what Ponce de Leon was looking for."[22]

In fact, aging seems no different from any other bioengineering problem. Given our millennial yearnings for infinite life, I expect that science will not give up until it understands and learns how to control and even reverse the mechanism of aging. The antiaging project is consistent with Michael Murphy's blueprint for the future of the human body. Murphy saw in his data a supernormal future for the human body. We may be evolving, if Murphy is right, extraordinary bodily powers. Looking at all the data "synoptically," Murphy thinks the human body is poised to enter on a new stage of its cosmic evolution. Similar enthusiasm has been voiced by Drexler: " . . . the ill, the old, and the injured all suffer from misarranged patterns of atoms, whether misarranged by invading viruses, passing time, or swerving cars. Devices able to rearrange atoms will be able to set them right."

Nanotech offers to lend a hand to bioengineering the superhuman. So does Artificial Intelligence (AI). The apocalyptic imagination sees in AI more than just a trick for humiliating humans who think they are good at chess. Vernor Vinge, who writes speculative fiction,[23] speaks of the coming Technological Singularity. Vinge's Singularity is a possible face of the Eschaton. This is an event likely to occur early in the next century (Vinge says between 2005 and 2030), and it will represent the quantum leap of technological progress that has been accelerating exponentially during the twentieth century. "We are on the edge of change comparable to the rise of human life on Earth," proclaims Vinge.

Computers may be about to "awake" to levels of superhuman intelligence and autonomy. This superhuman awakening may occur in computer networks or in other possible ways. The Singularity, when it arrives, will be a "point where our old models must be discarded and a new reality rules." The mark of this AI-induced Singularity will be the "runaway" nature of the phenomenon—a little, I suppose, like Hal of *2001* getting out of control and taking matters into his own hands.

The main idea is that the notion of a quantum leap in machine-mediated intelligence renders concrete and plausible the ancient prophetic dream of a new superhumanity. Cyberspace, the global brain or electronic Mind at Large that we are presently building, and that America under the Clinton administration apparently wants in its fiber optic data highways, may, combined with a possible AI Singularity, be part of the primordial soup out of which a new psycho-physical machine-organism may be evolving. AI is conceivably the key ingredient in our evolving parallel environment, the electro-imaginal networks of cyberspace.

From prosthetics to gene therapy to antiaging technologies, as new information becomes available, and the possible becomes actual, increasing numbers of people will feel the lure of physical immortality—the urge to extend, enrich, and enhance their lives. At first the opportunities for life extension will be available mainly to the rich. But as with all evolving technologies, life-extending technologies will become portable, cheaper, user-friendly. These and new technologies will converge synergistically with the growing drive toward achieving superhumanity. Brain machines, as described in Michael Hutchison's *Megabrain*, or "smart foods" such as hydergine, said to increase access to memory by increasing bloodflow to the brain,[24] will enter the meme pool and attract evolutionary adventurists—people that Timothy Leary calls "futants." And since we mentioned Tim Leary again, let us add psychedelics to the list of futant technologies— those substances that make human brains transparent to informational hyperspace.

Given the Jeffersonian pursuit of happiness and the new cyberspace frontier based on the pursuit of imaginal freedom, I think we can expect, as the pertinent information becomes available to more and more people, increasingly strident affirmations of the expansive rights of life. The Millennium Myth, if it encourages us to predict anything about the future, is that people will continue to suffer from incorrigible divine discontent. As the Enlightenment fought for the rights of humanity, so in the new enlightenment people are likely to fight increasingly for the rights of superhumanity.

Cloning seems natural enough in an age of technocalypse. Cloning will enable us to bank our genetic potential from infancy and draw on our reserves repeatedly, regenerating a wasted kidney here, a wrecked heart there, and with a little luck, extending physical life, both in our own selves and in a potentially infinite family of clones. Cloning, in my opinion, fits perfectly with Mormon Millennialism. Joseph Smith believed that the true Mormon is evolving into a god; but for Smith the way a god proves his godhood is to replicate himself, bring forth, father a kingdom. Mormons become gods by polygamous reproduction. Cloning seems a technology made in heaven for Mormon godmakers.

The Last Garment

The Millennium will have style. People will discover the *last garment*. So prepare for the Eschaton of haberdashery. In the last garment—on the threshold of the End—our clothing will be designed so that our nano-telecommunications gear will be sewn, as it were, seamlessly in our shirts, pants, jocks, and bras. Thus, fashion leader Donna Karan says, "The future of fashion will focus on technology—in fabric and personal electronics."[25] Clothing will merge with telecommunications. The border between skin and garment will vanish; we will become our clothing.

Style in the age of technocalypse will celebrate garments that invest us with the ecstasy of information. Wherever we are—on the job, out for a stroll, flying in a plane—it will be possible to jack into cyberspace—and rove where we will in the electronic Mind at Large. The Brainman in Arthur C. Clarke's *Hammer of God* has images and sounds fed directly into his brain, bypassing the senses, through a helmet made of millions of microprobes. "That way," says Clarke, "virtual reality is theoretically indistinguishable from reality."[26] This would amount to a revolution, Clarke observes, that would change everything.

It would create the potential for connectedness with everything, while freeing us from the physicality of technology. Clarke sees the next step in human evolution as the fusion of machine and human, a cyborgian synthesis leading to emigration from planet Earth and rebirth in the galactic Overmind. In his nonfiction book *How The World Was One*, Clarke says the telecommunications industry should welcome the year 2001 by wiping out all long distance phone charges—a step toward global mental unity and (Clarke suggests) good business.

Arthur C. Clarke's speculations on the integration of communications technology with our future bodies provides an icon for a true techno-Millennium. Robert Boyle in the seventeenth century spoke of future science enhancing our intellectual and perceptive faculties. A cyborgian or electronic information body would fulfill this prophecy. Says Clarke, "I can envisage an era of total couch potatoes, when we have our legs amputated because it wastes energy to keep them functioning." The body itself is insignificant by comparison with the quality of experience. "If you could experience everything, sitting in a chair—'wired' to coin a phrase—why bother with reality?"[27]

Fashion experts and science fiction visionaries here concur that our new clothing—our new bodies—will transcend the old flesh and become increasingly fine-tuned instruments of telecommunication. Our bodies of lovely yet imperfect flesh will turn electronic—then photonic—and thereby become linked to all other bodies and eventually to the whole of existence. So, as the millenarian prophets of old pictured a day when people will put on glorified astral or light bodies, so do today's techno-visionaries, coming from their own prophetic expertise, arrive at a similar view of posthuman hyper-embodiment.

Conclusion

We have entered the age of technocalypse—a time when science and technology have begun to accelerate so rapidly that tremendous ontological shock is about to shatter our old sense of reality; basic assumptions about reality are being overturned, and new possibilities of action and experience are rapidly becoming available.

These poleshifts in our reality-grids and concept-filters seem uncannily like reifications of apocalyptic metaphors and archetypes. Eschatology is ingressing into technology. It seems to be doing so in the following way. The call for apocalypse is a call for the total renewal of nature, a new heaven and new earth, and a new type of human being.

The technological recreation of heaven and earth is taking place on at least three fronts. The first involves the sheer power to dominate nature, for good or for ill—nanotechnological abundance or nuclear perdition. The second extends our capacity for communication, the creation of a virtual heaven we can people with demons or angels of our own invention. The third, through bioengineering, promises to metamorphose the human animal into an etherialized cyborg—analogues of angels, our form in heaven after the resurrection, according to New Testament eschatology.

In the finishing touch that Arthur C. Clarke puts on the idea of virtual reality, we can see very clearly the way the apocalyptic imagination is driving technology. When we put on the last garment, what we wear will be how we communicate; we will wear our world and become our world. Human and machine will merge, and the distinction between reality and virtual reality, technique and myth, body and soul, will vanish.

Prophecy and technology converge, as we mutate into a species of light body. Fulfilling all its historic trends, technology will literally enlighten us, release us from the tyranny of flesh and the constraints of earthly time and space. But will this be the end—or just the beginning? These are the questions we discuss in the last two chapters.

The Future of Death

*Only the feeble resign themselves to final death
and substitute some other desire for the longing for
personal immortality.*

MIGUEL DE UNAMUNO

*Humans are still too death-oriented too guilt-ridden
too submissive and fatalistic to demand immortality.
To even hope for it.*

F. M. ESFANDIARY
Up-Wingers

Technology offers us a bold vision of "wired" freedom. But can this be the last step in our evolution? Is it not possible, as Arthur C. Clarke hinted, that the next step is to get rid of the "wire"? Clarke does just that in *Childhood's End*, where the end of days is depicted as the last people ascending from Earth on a telepathic wave toward the Overmind.

And so one is led to ask: Are there any limits to science and technology? Are there any grounds for hope in salvation from death? According to religious and secular exponents of the Millennium Myth, the answer is yes: there is hope of transcending even this barrier. In chapter after chapter, we have seen this last hope hinted at or blatantly expressed. From Zoroaster to Benjamin Franklin, from Daniel to Joseph Smith, it has been a recurrent motif: one day, somehow, human beings will—as Timothy Leary put it—"snuff" death.

To form a credible picture of how this might be done, we will have to stretch our imaginations to the limit. And we will have to merge a wide array of disciplines. A scientific eschatology of the twenty-first century would be a synergistic blend of several types of tradition, theory, and data. The merger I have in mind remains in the future, for at the moment these areas of interest remain isolated from each other. But, for a full-scale immortalist project, a merger seems essential—religious and scientific, ancient and modern.

There are two traditions, the prophetic and the mystical; the Near Eastern faith in bodily rejuvenation or resurrection, and the Greek philosophical and Far Eastern view that affirms the soul's immortality. The Near East cherishes the hope for a time when the human body is rejuvenated or resurrected; whereas Indian and Tibetan sages and Western philosophers say that the soul is by nature immortal, a fact that we can know by experience here and now.

Now, this traditional contrast is reproduced in modern scientific attempts to make the case for immortality—or at any rate for some form of survival. There are, for example, the modern scientific "immortalists" who carry on the tradition of the Near East and who stress attaining powers, perhaps unlimited, of life extension. Here we find a thread that runs from Gilgamesh through Jesus on through Enlightenment figures like Joseph Priestley and eccentric chiliasts like Nikolay Fedorov, all the way to biotechnology. This thread was alluded to in the last chapter on technocalypse, although we stopped short with Arthur C. Clarke's vision of "wired" transcendence.

Psychical research and transpersonal psychology carry on the tradition of the Greek and Far Eastern faiths. For over a hundred years, a small band of dedicated researchers have been trying to demonstrate, using the methods of science, that some aspect of the human personality survives death. Also, since the 1960s, transpersonal psychologists have been studying peak experiences—mystical, ecstatic, creative, expansive encounters with timeless and nonlocal states of being. Psychical research and transpersonal psychology try to prove there is an eternal component of human personality.

I believe we need to bring all four of these approaches together: Near Eastern resurrectionists and their modern counterparts; the scientific life-extensionists; Greek and Far Eastern eternalists; and modern psychical research and transpersonal psychology.

Approaches to the Abolition of Death: The Tetrad

1) *Resurrection of the Body* Prophetic Tradition: Gilgamesh, Zoroaster, Christ	3) *Immortality of the Soul* Philosophy and Mysticism: Plato, Upanishads, Zen

2) *PK, biotechnology,*
   nanotech
	4) *Psychical research,*
	   transpersonal psychology

Here, of course, I can only outline some connections between these approaches and try to set an agenda for future dialogue. At the moment, there is little dialogue. Barring the few exceptions, science seems uninterested in resurrection or immortality, and religion seems apathetic about building bridges with the scientific prophets of life extension. Neither do the biotechnical immortalists and psychical researchers seem inclined to talk to each other. My call is for them to come together under the banner of the Millennium Myth and to engage in what can only be a dialogue of supreme importance. The Millennium Myth offers to unite humanity in its quest to transcend the curse of death.

Rejuvenation and Resurrection: Prophetic Intimations

The Sumerian Epic of Gilgamesh is the oldest story in the world and concerns the quest for everlasting life. The turning point in the story is when the hero Gilgamesh loses his beloved comrade and alter-ego Enkidu. The shock of his comrade's death awakens Gilgamesh and inspires him to set out on a long journey across the Sea of Dark, past the Scorpion people, through the black depths of a mountain, past Dilmun the earthly paradise, in search of Utnapishtim—the Faraway One.

The Faraway One survived the Flood, as Noah did in another story, for which the capricious Mesopotamian gods granted him the gift of enduring life. When, after his long journey, the hero at last confronts the Faraway One, he is told, "I will reveal to you, Gilgamesh, a hidden matter, and a secret of the gods I will tell." The secret involves a technology of rejuvenation, the basis for a kind of botanical eschatology. "This plant is a plant apart, whereby a man may regain his life's breath. I myself shall eat it."[1]

Gilgamesh, monster slayer and goddess scorner, demanded and obtained from the Faraway One the magic plant. But on his way home to the city of Uruk, he suffered a fatal lapse of attention. To freshen himself from the heat of day, he paused and stepped in a pool of water, whereupon a snake appeared and stole the plant from the absent-minded hero. The snake thus wrested the secret of immortality from Gilgamesh.

In the Old Testament, the snake reappears as the symbol of forbidden wisdom, the tempter and seducer of humankind, the secret bearer of immortality. Said the serpent to Eve about the prohibition against eating of the tree in the center of the garden: "Ye shall surely not die" (Gen. 3:4) On the contrary, says the serpent, "ye shall be as gods, knowing good and evil" (Gen. 3:5). We will come back to the symbolism of the serpent in the last chapter; suffice it to note that these old Near Eastern tales register an approach-avoidance conflict over the idea of immortality and human power.

The idea that humans might be able to change the physics of their mortal bodies, that there exists a food of the gods, and that supernormal rejuvenation is possible was a farseeing one, prophetic of modern immortalism—the techno-pagan belief in the psychophysics of immortality. As the Faraway One said, it is possible to "regain a man's breath."

Of course, the search of Gilgamesh would continue. Others would follow in his trail, in hope that breakthrough beyond death is possible. The Iranian Zoroaster introduced a vision of last things. At the end of time, we enter the world of the resurrected body; we enter what a later Iranian visionary would call the archetypal world of the "Hurqalya."[2] Here, in place of a plant, hope shifts toward the almighty power of Ahura Mazda, forerunner of Biblical monotheism.

It turns out that Zoroaster's vision of the resurrection is surprisingly hedonistic. Thus, in the *Greater Bundahishn* we find this curious image of resurrected sexual function—an image that would delight Isaac Asimov and other antinatalists: "To each man his wife and children will be restored, and they will have intercourse with their wives, even as they do on earth today, but no children will be born to them."[3] This severs the amative from the propagative function of sex, thus making Zoroaster a precursor of mystic sex rebels like John Humphrey Noyes.

Gilgamesh and Zoroaster introduce history to hope in the conquest of death. In the Biblical tradition, the scope of the promise becomes increasingly audacious, for now the entire world of former things shall pass away, as John of Patmos assures us, "and there shall be no more death" (Rev. 21:4).

On this hope Christianity is founded. To the Christian, a general resurrection is possible because Christ was raised from the dead. One divine anomaly guarantees a complete paradigm change, a revolution in the nature of human existence itself. Christ's breakthrough to resurrection makes hope possible for us all. As Paul said, "If our hope in Christ has been for this life only, we are of all people the most pitiable" (1 Cor. 15:19). The resurrection, as told in the Christ story, is the core of Western expectations about the end of history. The Resurrection story climaxes four thousand years of unquiet quest begun by Gilgamesh at the Sumerian dawn of history.

The mythic premise was that death is a mistake—in the Old Testament, the wages of sin, the result of a blunder that could have been avoided. African myth likewise explains the origin of death: the creator sends a message of immortality to humankind, but along the way the message gets garbled.[4] Also, Gilgamesh lost his herb of rejuvenation because of a blunder, a lapse from mindfulness. But—and this is a big point—if we were not meant to die, then death can be abolished. Over and over, hope rises that we can do away with death.

Medieval history periodically witnessed insurrections against the last enemy, outbursts of millenarian discontent based on the hope of abolishing death. The heresy of the Brethren of the Free Spirit shaped a motley international underground that lasted for about five centuries; academics at the University of Paris in the early 1200s promoted a philosophy of total sexual emancipation—which turned out to be the key to the mastery of death.

The heresy of the Brethren claimed quite simply that everything is God and that we are all God! The synod found the Amaurians, who claimed that "all things are One, because whatever is, is God,"[5] guilty of pantheism. But now the worst heresy: "He dared to affirm that, in so far as he was, he could neither be consumed by fire nor tormented by torture, for he said that, insofar as he was, he was God."[6] In short, one snuffed death by believing one was God.

Some mystic rebels thought they were invulnerable to bodily harm, and there were saints in the Middle Ages who apparently did demonstrate immunity to fire and other supernormal bodily marvels.[7] Unusual physical feats are likely to have inspired many people with the hope in immortality. If I witness a saint levitate or show immunity to fire, it becomes easier for me to imagine an extension of such power over death itself. As for immunity to fire, firewalking is a skill that apparently people can learn today. In even bolder displays of contempt for death, ancient Indian wise men, to prove their immortality to Alexander the Great, set themselves on fire in gestures of self-immolating bravado.[8]

Several Chinese texts are based on the idea that through certain meditative techniques it is possible to create one's own spiritual body. Survival, in that case, is not a given but an evolutionary potential.

The *Secret of the Golden Flower* (*T'ai I Chin Hua Tsung Chih*) was first published in the seventeenth century but dates from oral traditions of the T'ang Dynasty (eighth century), and is known as the Religion of the Golden Elixir of Life.[9] The Golden Elixir is the imaginal body of light—the spiritual body. The Chinese offer a manual for constructing the spiritual body. By combining breath control, light imagery, and spiritual discipline, we can prepare for death, retaining a conscious center of personality after death and avoiding dissipation into unconscious shadow-beings. The Taoist search for magical potency in life and death helped inspire the violent millenarian Boxer Rebellion (1900) that was meant to oust all foreigners from China.

Native Americans followed a similar pattern. The Ghost Dance is the most celebrated messianic movement among the North American Indian tribes and had forerunners in the Good Message movement started by the Iroquois Handsome Lake (influenced by Quakers), the Dreamers begun by Smohalla, and the Shakers (not Ann Lee's movement) promoted by John Slocum. These movements arose to expel white civilization, restore the ancient ways, and, after the cataclysm, raise the dead.

In 1886, a Paiute shaman, Wovoka, underwent a visionary experience during an eclipse of the sun while he was ill with a fever. He "went up to heaven," saw God and his ancestors, and was instructed to give the dance to his people. The Ghost Dance, which spread rapidly among the Plains Indians, especially the populous Sioux, was supposed to herald a catastrophe that would wipe out white civilization, restore the buffalo, regenerate Indian culture and, above all, resurrect the Indian dead. If the Indians gave up alcohol, farming, weapons, and technology, the resurrection would occur in the spring of 1891.

289

Wovoka urged his followers to dance for five straight days, then bathe themselves in the river, and go to their homes. This, he said, would bring on the regeneration. In a letter, he wrote:

> Do not tell the white people about this. Jesus is now upon the earth. He appears like a cloud. The dead are all alive again. I do know when they will be here; maybe this fall or in the spring. When the time comes there will be no more sickness and everyone will be young again. When the earth shakes at the coming of the new world do not be afraid; it will not hurt you.[10]

The Sioux had introduced the idea of the "ghost shirt," decorated with images of birds and stars and believed to provide protection against bullets. In 1890, a group of Ghost Dancers resisted arrest by white troops at Wounded Knee Creek, confident in the protective power of their magical ghost shirts. The shirts proved useless against the two-pound shells of Hotchkill guns, and about three hundred men, women, and children were massacred.[11]

The core hope that drove the Plains Ghost Dancers was that the Indian dead would rise and unite with the living upon a regenerated earth and dwell forever in paradisal harmony with nature. Confidence in the existence of a power to rejuvenate and even transform the human body took possession of thousands of Native Americans. The Ghost Dancers were deluded about their magical shirts. But not all traditions are deluded in their belief in the supernormal. There is real empirical data to suggest that powers over certain routine "laws" of nature do in fact exist.

Supernormal Physical Powers and the Future of Death

The belief in a spiritual power of rejuvenation is part of an old prophetic tradition—Gilgamesh, Zoroaster, Daniel, Jesus, Paul. An impressive roster. These and other traditions contain intriguing stories of saints and adepts with supernormal physical capacities. Are these stories true—or sheer fabrications? If there is truth to them, they would support the prophetic vision of abolishing death.

Phenomena associated with Catholic mysticism and Tibetan yoga—as well as other traditions—suggest that human beings do possess extraordinary physical capacities. The question is: What bearing do such paranormal capacities have on the future of death? The examples I am about to give suggest that latent powers of the human body may exist, capable of rejuvenating, even transforming the physical structure of the body. They hint of something that might be strong enough to reconstitute nature in a way that it becomes possible to overcome death itself.

Phenomena of Catholic saints and mystics are a case in point. The Jesuit scholar Herbert Thurston has written about some of the strangest of these in his classic *The Physical Phenomena of Mysticism* (1952). Several types of prodigy that Thurston reviews involve the dead bodies of saintly people. Phenomena such as bodily incorruption, absence of cadaveric rigidity, blood prodigies, and the odor of sanctity may seem to have little directly to do with heroic sanctity or high spirituality; they were, apparently, anomalous by-products of lives lived in pursuit of the holy. No one has a clue to why Saint John of the Cross's body has remained incorrupt for centuries. But these bizarre effects—especially the retardation of physical decay—raise interesting questions.

What was it, one would like to know, about the lives of so many saints and yogis that interfered with the normal mechanisms of bodily decay after death and kept their bodies intact, often warm, moist, flexible, occasionally bleeding, and frequently emitting not the odor of decay but pleasant fragrances? What was it about their lives that kept their demised bodies in such a condition for months, years, decades, and, in some cases, centuries?[12]

Might we here be observing effects of what John Humphrey Noyes called the "resurrection power"? There may be some important clues here for death abolitionists. So far as I know there has never been a serious scientific investigation—beyond attestation of the phenomena themselves[13]—of any of these strange corporeal artifacts of heroic sanctity. It would make a nice project for an energetic scientific eschatologist.

Let us suppose there is a transcendent vital factor—a metadeath factor. Such a factor seems in evidence in other prodigies observed among the Catholic saints and raises similar questions about latent rejuvenation powers that may be at large. Take, for example, *inedia* or *near-inedia*, the ability to live without eating, or on really minute amounts of food, as was observed in the recent case of Padre Pio.[14]

Catholic hagiography contains creditable accounts of saints enjoying full vital functions, yet abstaining nearly or completely from food for long periods of time, sometimes decades.[15] Saint Catherine of Genoa, who led an active life, is a well-documented case.[16] On the other hand, some modern inediacs were invalids who lived on the fringes of religious pathology. Dominica Lazzari and Louise Lateau, for example, were very queer hyperaesthesiacs; Dominica would contort in pain at the smell of toast, then faint away. The slightest contact with food would drive these ladies into convulsions. (Today we talk about eating disorders.)

Bodily incorruption and inedia suggest the presence of an anomalous degree of vital energy operative in some exceptional human beings. The existence of such a hypervital energy indirectly supports the prophetic myth of the mastery of death. The Catholic saints have produced other phenomena that testify to a hypervital energy; for example, they abound in anomalous manifestations of bodily heat. Tibetan lamas are noted for practicing *tummo* yoga, a technique for producing sacred heat.

The ardors of the mystic heart cause the entire physiology to burn, if the depositions and observations of eyewitness accounts are correct. For example—one of my favorites for high strangeness—the body of eighty-six-year-old Maria Villani had an autopsy performed on it, nine hours after her death. Onlookers were dumbfounded at the sight of "the smoke (*fumo*) and heat which exhaled from the heart," described as a "veritable furnace of divine love." The surgeon found the heart too hot to proceed with the autopsy; he was obliged to remove his hand from it because it burned him (*scottandosi*).[17]

Similar reports of what Catholic mystics call *incendium amoris*— "the fire of love"—occur in Hindu Tantrism and kundalini yoga. Gopi Krishna, a twentieth-century yogi and apocalyptic prophet, gives a vivid account of his incandescent meeting with *incendium amoris*. Gopi Krishna related his fiery experience to *kundalini*, "the serpent power," which he deemed the energy of evolution and immortality.[18]

The experience of hypervitality, the excessive heat, the ability to live without eating—all suggest the reality of a latent metadeath factor. What this factor may have to do with levitation, the ability to defy gravity, and with immunity to fire—also well-attested phenomena— are further questions that beg for answers. Finally, there is the phenomenon of luminosity, described so well by Patricia Treece in her book *The Sanctified Body*.[19] The bodies of many saints have repeatedly been observed to radiate strange forms of mystic luminosity.

The Millennium Myth promises that human beings will one day transcend death. The unusual phenomena I have mentioned here provide hints of possible empirical stepping stones to fulfilling this part of the visionary Myth.

Documented reports of *spontaneous* supernormal healing also have bearing on the future of death. The alleged healings of Jesus, as recounted in the New Testament, may be construed as evidence for the resurrection power.[20] Indeed, the resurrection of Jesus may be seen as the ultimate symbol of psychophysical healing power. All spontaneous healing phenomena, as observed in the lives of saints, shamans, and avatars, and as are reported at famous healing shrines like Lourdes belong to the rejuvenation-resurrection paradigm. Likewise, all types of *experimental* evidence indicative of supernormal healing power belong in this paradigm.[21] The experiments of Bernard Grad, for example, in which healing and other biological processes were affected by the "laying on of hands" through an energy or life force belong in this perspective. Experimental prayer in a modern hospital setting also seems to have proven itself effective.[22]

The idea of a sanctified or resurrection body is related to what Deepak Chopra calls "the body of bliss." *Bliss*, according to Chopra, is the subtle emanation of the divine intelligence of the universe; it is the essence of our bodily life and both emanates from and transcends DNA.[23] Dr. Chopra's concept of a body of bliss lends itself to millenarian immortalism. The body of bliss—its potential for hypervitality and radiant joy—also takes us back to Joseph Campbell and Thomas Jefferson with their declarations of the right to pursue our bliss and happiness.

To pursue the body of bliss will demand a daring synthesis of disciplines. Large areas of research need to be integrated, viewed synoptically. For example, A. P. Elkin, anthropologist from the University of Australia, describes what he calls "aboriginal men of high degree,"[24] people capable of extraordinary powers. In Elkin's account, the Australian medicine man, after a ritual of "death and rising," acquires abilities such as the *strong eye*, "clairvoyant inspection of diseased bodies"; the power of disappearance, which may be part of the skill of creating illusions; *fast traveling*, which merges with teleportation and bilocation; walking on fire; use of a *magic cord* by means of which the *clever man* is able to project fire; visiting the sky to make rain; and tracking down a wanted killer.

Elkin notes the similarity between the reported abilities of aboriginal medicine men and Tibetan yogis. In both, supernatural power is shown by people who somehow penetrate the barrier of death. Aboriginal medicine men and Tibetan yogis do rituals at graveyards in order to evoke the spirits of the dead and, with them, metadeath powers. As for the methods of Australian people of high degree and Patanjali's siddha yogis, in both, preparation involves "concentration."

Another psychic phenomenon that may be related to human death-transcending potential is the poltergeist: cases of poltergeists demonstrate a powerful psychokinetic power at large that seems to erupt from time to time in the lives of troubled adolescents. Consider a spectacular example: In 1967, a German girl, Annemarie S., was responsible for a series of inexplicable incidents in the law office where she worked in the Bavarian town of Rosenheim; in her presence, bulbs exploded, neon lights repeatedly went out, sharp bangs were heard, fuses were blown without cause, copying machines broke down, telephones rang inexplicably, and so on. Technicians, police, and physicists from the Max Planck Institute of Plasmaphysics in Munich were called in to explain what was going on; they concluded that "the phenomena defy explanation with the means available to theoretical physics."[25] The "new force" that the physicist William Crookes described in the setting of physical mediumship may be related to the force evinced in poltergeist cases.

About poltergeists and the Millennium Myth, I will say this: If a) poltergeists involve phenomena that defy explanation by theoretical physics, and b) if they are produced by human beings, then we should consider the possibility that poltergeists involve a force related to the potential to abolish death.

The poltergeist suggests the reality of a phantastic human potential totally out of control. Instead of ignoring it, we need to put it into a framework that gives it meaning—as I am suggesting, the millennial hope of transcending death. William Roll,[26] a leading investigator of poltergeists and a maverick theoretician, has suggested that we teach the poltergeist person to take command of his or her poltergeist power and try to learn to convert its random destructiveness into deliberate creativeness. The English psychic Matthew Manning seems a case in point. Manning began his psychic career as a poltergeist victim—his own psychic power on the rampage against himself—but apparently acquired control over the disturbing force. Now he puts his demons to work for him, instead of the other way round, and uses his psychic powers for healing purposes.

In the context of this story, we should include the data of physical mediumship. The materialization powers of famous mediums like Eusapia Palladino, D. D. Home, Rudi Schneider, and Sai Baba, for which there is much provocative testimony,[27] belong among evidence that may have bearing on the future of death. The British physicist Sir William Crookes and the Nobel prize-winning physiologist Charles Richet made observations and performed experiments with mediums that convinced them of the reality of supernormal physical forces. Crookes, for example, concluded that his experiments established "the existence of a new force, connected in some unknown manner with the human organization."[28] Richet admitted he found it "painful" to admit the reality of materialization and maintained that his observations provided "entirely new and unforeseen" data.[29] For accounts of the materializations of the contemporary Sai Baba, there are several useful reports.[30] Sai Baba is reported to materialize food, jewelry, and sacred ash.

Assume that there is something to phenomena such as materialization. Again, we ask: If a power at large can materialize physical objects apparently from nowhere, what may be its relationship to the metadeath factor? None of these effects directly attest to a rejuvenation or resurrection power, but, taken together, they provide grounds to speculate that they may be part of a system of reality that does, or one day may, lead to the abolition of death. But let us shift our focus to another type of data.

Rejuvenation and Resurrection: Scientific Immortalism

If myth, prophecy, hagiography, anthropology, and parapsychology all testify to the existence of a latent death-transcending power, it ought to come as no surprise that confidence in such a potential should reappear in secular-minded moderns. That confidence is alive among contemporary "immortalists" who pursue the hope of Gilgamesh through the agency of technology.

Indeed, the mythical idea that death is a mistake and can therefore be eliminated has reappeared today in a secular setting. The impulse to transcend death has worked its way into modern science. So, for example, latter-day immortalists and life extensionists claim that aging—and by implication death—is not a biological necessity; they believe it possible to dismantle the genetics of aging and ultimately death itself. They think it possible to tinker with the mechanics of time itself, thus to hasten the coming of the "end" of ordinary time.

The dream of rejuvenation—the dream that drove Gilgamesh to search for Utnapishtim's plant of immortality—is reawakening today among American techno-pagans. Take the Flame Foundation in Scottsdale, Arizona. Run by a trio of unconventional lovers, two men and a woman, they declare, "Death is not real for us."[31] According to the Flame, life everlasting is realizable through science, and the secret consists of "cellular awakening," rejuvenation through deep erotic intimacy.

The alliance of Eros and immortality is as old as Plato, and, as I said above, medieval mystic rebels promoted a philosophy of erotic anarchy and self-deification. American social revolutionaries like the Shakers, Seventh-day Adventists, Mormons, and Oneidans also believed that physical immortality depended on the right use of erotic energy, despite differing greatly in their view of how to deploy this energy.

A Flame enthusiast remarked about his *ménage à trois*: "I've never had the kind of intimacy I feel with John and Ann. And I'm never leaving them." The intimate bond they cultivate awakens their cells and will increase their longevity, they say. "It is not normal to die. It's not natural," declares a member, repeating the teaching of the Book of Genesis. But science, not the Second Coming, will save people from death: "Scientists are finding clues in DNA that show there are ways to switch off the dying and switch on our regenerative capacities." (Note the core metaphor of our Myth—regeneration.) According to a spokesman for the Flame, the new erotic immortalists represent the new edge in human evolution; those who ignore the call will suffer extinction. The yearning of Gilgamesh for a technology of regeneration is alive and well in America.

Let us backtrack a little to the utopian sixties to pick up this particular thread of millenarian aspiration. For a brilliant American statement of the immortalist project, look at Robert Ettinger's *The Prospect of Immortality* (1964). Ettinger's outlook is that of an updated eighteenth-century *philosophe*; with the nonconformist Joseph Priestley, he shares the optimistic enthusiasm of contemporaries like Tim Leary and Esfandiary. Because it denies the creative imperative of DNA, Leary believes it defeatist to worry about the population explosion;

we should accept the challenge of our growing numbers, prepare for space migration, do everything in our power to increase the collective intelligence, and apply ourselves to the technology of life extension.

Leary shows a fine Buddhist indifference to the mere fact of his personal survival, but, in the spirit of the Vikings—as he told me once—feels driven to explore a new land, and has committed himself to what Ettinger calls the "freezer program."[32] Leary totes a card with instructions to have his head hastened to the nearest icebox, in the event of his death. Committed to the prospect of cryonic immortality, the project includes digitizing his personal history.

This is how it works, according to Ettinger and Leary. First, it is possible to suspend an inanimate body or brain by freezing. All, or nearly all, bodily decay and decomposition may be stopped. According to Ettinger, who believes in the unlimited powers of science, one day it should be possible to revive, restore to youth and even greatly improve dead, frozen bodies—or, in Leary's case, dead, frozen brains. It is simply a matter of staying frozen long enough until the Golden Age of science dawns. The point of storing extensive digitized memories is to fill the gaps likely to result from a century or so of being encrypted in liquid helium.

Meanwhile, expect an era of "unlimited wealth," one that is similar to K. Eric Drexler's vision of nano-assembled abundance. Ettinger on cryonics:

> One may picture the Golden Age society in which every citizen owns a tremendous, intelligent machine which will scoop up earth, or air, or water and spew forth whatever is desired in any required amounts—whether caviar, gold bricks, hernia operations, psychiatric advice, impressionist paintings, space ships, or pastel mink toilet rolls.

Ettinger sees no conflict between his vision of cryonic immortality and the true humanistic intent of the higher religions. In the chapter "Freezers and Religion," he states that "the freezer program represents for us now a bridge to an anticipated Golden Age, when we shall be reanimated to become supermen with indefinite lifespans." Superhumanity will result from the growth of knowledge, in effect, of living hundreds or even thousands of years and thus being able to apply the latest technology to perfecting the resuscitated freezee. "With an extended lifespan, the soul has a chance to grow nearer to perfection."

The millenarian heresy of perfectionism thus reasserts itself under the guise of science.

Like that prescientific eschatologist, Paul of Tarsus, Ettinger foresees the coming of a new humanity. He envisions more than the mere extension of years. People will be totally different, Ettinger thinks. "Mental qualities, including both intellectual power and personality or character, will be profoundly altered." Genetic science will enable us to mold our children into superhumans, a new species. Far from seeing this as being at odds with the Book of Revelation, Ettinger thinks it conceivable "that the freezer era—if it develops into an age of brotherly love and a living Golden Rule, as I believe it will—may be accepted by some as the embodiment of the Millennium."

Not long after Ettinger's manifesto on the coming freezing era appeared, Michael Harrington published *The Immortalist*, a book that Gore Vidal said may be the most important of our age. Harrington's thought rivals in force the antideath philosophizings of the Russian Nikolay Fedorov.

As Fedorov thought death an affront that science had to deal with, so does Harrington see immortalism as essential to complement humanity's graduation from mythic adolescence. According to Harrington, humanity is going berserk because the old myths have been demolished. As Nietzsche based his vision of the superman on the premise that God is dead, Harrington bases his vision of the abolition of death on the same premise. God is dead, contends Harrington, therefore humans must immortalize themselves. Esfandiary put it poignantly: "It is outrageous that such a beautiful phenomenon as life should be encased in such a fragile thing as the body."[33]

In Drexler's vision, nanotechnology holds the answer to outrageous death, thinking it possible to build "cell repair machines" that can halt the entropy of aging:

> Aging is fundamentally no different from any other physical disorder; it is no magical effect of calendar dates on a mysterious life-force. Brittle bones, wrinkled skin, low enzyme activities, slow wound healing, poor memory, and the rest all result from damaged molecular machinery, chemical imbalances, and misarranged structures. By restoring all the cells and tissues of the body to a youthful structure, repair machines will restore youthful health.[34]

In every century, humankind should abolish at least one bad thing. In the nineteenth century, it was slavery; in the twentieth, it was patriarchy and cancerous smoke in the workplace; in the centuries to come, if Diderot and Ettinger and Vidal and Harrington and Drexler are right, death will be abolished. From Gilgamesh's magic plant to K. Eric Drexler's cell-repair nanotech machines, the Myth hammers away at the hope of abolishing death.

The Sociology of Human Finitude

Harrington—along with Ernest Becker and Norman O. Brown— argue that we *must* beat death because our entire civilization is distorted by the denial of death. The fact that we are both conscious and finite beings makes for much trouble. The question is: What happens to people when they lose touch with their instinctive, mythical hope of immortality?

First of all, they develop a lust for surrogate immortality; people are driven to woo that fickle temptress, fame; they strive, at all costs, to become noticed, recognized, admired, adored—according to Hegel, this is the spur that keeps history galloping forever onward.

Gilgamesh was the one who set the pattern for countless strong-willed, unhappy, death-defiers: slay the monster, build the wall of Uruk, found a city. Our last image of Gilgamesh, home from his failed immortality quest, is of a man chipping away on stone tablets, telling the story of his life, carving an epitaph for himself; in short, trying for substitute immortality.

By denying death, said Ernest Becker, we force ourselves into false heroics.[35] We are driven to achieve and perform and prove our worth, power, significance, hoping thereby to salve the hopeless impotence we feel in the face of death. Harrington remarked about "showing off in front of the computer of excellence."[36] Yet all to no avail. For, from the immortalist perspective, the pursuit of excellence is just another boondoggle, a way of dodging our true metaphysical dilemma, a balm for hurt mortal minds.

Having to face death short on vision has political effects. Not everybody is as well endowed as Gilgamesh to bargain with fate with a shot at surrogate immortality. For most people the more likely fate is service and submission to others. Hitler and Stalin seduced people into mindless immersion in mass movements; hypnotized by messianic symbols, the masses enjoy a transient illusion of godlike power, a way of forgetting one's powerlessness before death.

One effect of being mythless before death may be the most damaging; depression of one's capacity to live. For the fear of death is at the root of the fear of life; because of it we tend to retreat from all but the most routine ways of encountering the world. Think of it like this: If death is the enemy of enemies, every rendezvous with life becomes laden with risk, a challenge that threatens to wreck our hard-earned defenses against the last anxiety. To take any risk, to break our habits, to shake up the status quo, these might upset one's fragile sense of security. Even to feel strongly about anything might become a danger; to love exposes one to rejection and loneliness—which are like shadows of death. The fear of death makes us all agoraphobes— neurotic about the open spaces of existence.

The first step toward renewal, say the immortalists, is to affirm the desire for infinite life. It ill serves us to deny what Unamuno called the "hunger for immortality." We have to admit what Ficino called the "divine appetite" for abundant and eternal life. We have to quit repressing our longing for the sublime, quit feeling cowed in the face of destiny. Saint Augustine said yes to immortality; the Eastern sages celebrate consciousness as eternal bliss. Even Nietzsche who announced the death of God professed immortality in the form of eternal recurrence. And Jung said, to heal the soul we need to come to grips with death, and heal the imagination of death.

Platonic and Far Eastern Testimony of Eternal Consciousness

Beside Near Eastern prophecy, there is another tradition that affirms a happy future of death. Instead of resurrection of the body, this tradition affirms the immortality of the soul. Clearly, there is a difference: One anticipates the renewal of the body at the end of historical time; the other maintains the intrinsic indestructibility of the soul. Perhaps in the end these traditions converge—we will consider that possibility later.

Parmenides, Plato, Plotinus, Meister Eckhardt, the Upanishads, Taoism, the Chinese, Japanese, and Tibetan meditative (or Zen) traditions, and so on, despite many variations on the theme, assert that at the core of the human personality is a reality identical with an eternal, a transcendent ground of being. Whatever name one attaches to this eternal reality—Soul, Self, Purusha, Atman, Brahman, God, Goddess, Divinity—the assumption is that it is possible to experience it here and now and thus know, immediately, nonanalytically, and noninferentially, one's transcendent nature. This experience, in principle open to us all, is described paradoxically by saying that our minds are inherently enlightened—indeed, as the Zen masters put it, that earth is heaven. We have only to clear away all the rubbish that obstructs our intrinsic immaculate perception.

A few examples from sacred text: In the Katha Upanishad, Nachiketa dialogues with Yama, the god of death. He is anxious about death. Yama replies that the Atman, our true Self, is deathless: "The knowing Self is not born; It does not die. It has not sprung from anything; nothing has sprung from It. Birthless, eternal, everlasting and ancient, It is not killed when the body is killed." The moment one "realizes" this, one is "freed from the jaws of death."[37]

The Chinese and Tibetan teachers relentlessly underscore the futility of the wrong kind of effort toward "achieving" or "attaining" enlightenment. There is nothing to "do" to achieve enlightenment; in fact, craving it, and in particular, craving immortality becomes an obstacle. Thus, Huang Po, a ninth-century Chinese Buddhist, said, "But to awaken suddenly to the fact that your own Mind is the Buddha, that there is nothing to be attained or a single action to be performed—that is the Supreme Way."[38] The contrast with the rejuvenation-resurrection paradigm needs to be underscored here; for the prophetic tradition, as opposed to the mystical, the answer to death is yet to come. The New Jerusalem must descend. For the mystical, we already have the "answer" to death; it lies within us—our own eternal nature.

In the Tibetan Book of the Great Liberation, we hear of the "self-originated Clear Light." Again, it is a question of gnosis, of becoming aware of the Clear Light (which we intrinsically are): "Without meditating, without going astray, look into the True State, wherein self-cognition, self-knowledge, self-illumination shine resplendently." All that we "need" is in the here of here, the now of now. "Nothing more is there to be sought; nor is there need to seek anything" except the "beginningless, vacuous, unconfused Clear Wisdom of self-cognition."[39]

One point of contact between the Tibetan doctrine and modern near-death research: according to the Tibetan Book of the Dead, we encounter the "self-originated Clear Light" at the moment of death. Interestingly, an encounter with Transcendent Light is typically reported by people having near-death experiences. It is not quite clear what to make of this coincidence. One might at least say the following: According to Tibetan doctrine, the Clear Light is not something external that visits us at the moment of death; it is our own inner reality; we *are* the Clear Light, always, in life, before life, after life.

If so, there is a profound practical lesson: we do not have to wait till near or after death to discover that we are "immortal." It is open to us here and now to uncover that we are; the experience of eternal life is permanently just below the surface of ordinary consciousness. As the German mystic Jacob Boehme said, "If a person could stop thinking and willing for an hour, he would see God." This approach to survival was suggested by the parapsychologist William Roll, who maintained that the way to study survival is to study expanded states of consciousness in living people. These expanded states associated with after death he called *theta* states (after the first letter of the Greek word for death, *thanatos*.) Are there any empirical grounds to support the claim of our inherently immortal nature?

Empirical Intimations of Immortality

The answer seems to be yes. For, just as the tradition of bodily regeneration has spawned its empirical offspring, so has the tradition of psychic or atmanic immortality; at the moment, there are two scientific disciplines that study the eternal, the timeless, the nonlocal factor in human experience. One is transpersonal psychology; the other is parapsychology.

Modern transpersonal psychology studies states of consciousness that transcend ordinary time, space, and personality.[40] Transpersonal experiences—of bliss, ecstasy, rapture, mystical transport, cosmic consciousness, near-death epiphany, esthetic contemplation, shamanic voyage, and so on—represent excursions into transcendent, in a sense, "afterdeath" states of consciousness. They do this while the experiencer is embodied. Transpersonal experiences seem like reconnoiterings of last things; they constitute a kind of avant-garde in practical eschatology. What we can say with confidence is that the mystics, poets, prophets, and ordinary folk who report having these experiences come away *convinced* of their immortality.

"I know I am deathless," announces Walt Whitman, adding:

The smallest sprout shows there is really no death,
And if ever there was it led forward life . . .
All goes onward and outward, nothing collapses,
And to die is different from what anyone supposed, and
    luckier.

Richard Bucke, the author of *Cosmic Consciousness* (1901) and an early investigator of what Abraham Maslow, Charles Tart, Stan Grof, and others in the 1960s and 1970s came to call transpersonal psychology, had this to say about individuals who have these experiences: "Each soul will feel and know itself to be immortal, will feel and know that the entire universe with all its good and with all its beauty is for it and belongs to it forever."

Bucke, who wrote his classic study at the dawn of the twentieth century, was filled with millenarian enthusiasm. Compiling his study of people transformed by cosmic consciousness, he wrote that the "immediate future of our race" is "indescribably hopeful." The reasons for this hope lay in what he imagined was an imminent economic and social revolution and a "psychical revolution" of cosmic consciousness. Everything, he dreamed, was about to converge to "create a new heaven and earth. Old things will be done away with and all will become new."

Not quite a hundred years have passed since Bucke wrote this, and indescribable hope has turned into indescribable misgivings for the immediate future of our race. Nevertheless, Bucke's idea that the key to a millennial future lay in a "psychical revolution"—in what he called the "evolution of cosmic consciousness"—is still a motivating force of transpersonal psychology. Of continued relevance, in light of our discussion of the sociology of death, is the belief that certain states of consciousness reduce or eliminate the normal fear of death. This, as suggested above, may very well be a key variable in the transformation of human society. A society in which the common person was on familiar terms with transpersonal states of consciousness would indeed be a transformed society. I believe this so-called "fifth force" in psychology, because of its transformative potential, deserves far more attention than it has received so far.

The same might be said for another area of neglected scientific research that has an even more direct bearing on the future of death—

parapsychology. Modern parapsychology, like transpersonal psychology, also testifies to the reality of a nonlocal, nontemporal factor in human experience; as such, it merits an important place in the present outline of scientific eschatology.

Extrasensory perception (ESP) itself is an indication of a nonlocal, nontemporal factor.[41] ESP includes telepathy, clairvoyance, and retro- and precognition. In telepathy, one mind communicates with another mind, directly, independently of the known senses; in clairvoyance, minds apparently interact with physical reality independently of the known senses; and in retro- and precognition, minds transcend the present and range directly over the past and the future. In short, all three forms of ESP add credence to the idea of an unlimited, immortal soul or Buddha mind. They are like flares that shoot up against the dark sky of opaque materialism, empirical pointers to where we may be going, or rather, where we essentially are. In themselves often trivial, occurrences of extrasensory perception may be thought of as mini-flashes of the apocalypse, little signals from eternal life.

More directly related to scientific eschatology are the types of survival evidence collected by psychical researchers. For reasons I will not go into here, most educated people today seem strangely turned off by this particular type of information, by anything that seriously suggests the possibility of postmortem survival. This disdain may say more about a hard-to-exorcise fear of death than about the unworthiness of the evidence.[42] I believe the evidence is worth taking seriously and belongs in the armory of data that bolsters the Millennium Myth's hope for immortality.

Several types of data suggest postmortem survival; I am talking about more or less well-documented accounts of out-of-body experiences, apparitions of the dead, hauntings, reincarnation memories, cases of possession, near-death and deathbed experiences. One recent attempt to critically review the evidence for life after death is by the philosopher Robert Almeder.[43] Almeder concludes that the case for personal survival is on a par with the case for the existence of dinosaurs. Here I can hardly do justice to Almeder's careful analysis of the data, but I will mention two types of argument he uses.

Philosophers distinguish between "knowing that" something is the case and "knowing how" to do something. In one case reviewed by Almeder, the medium, Mrs. Willett, was able to display philosophical skills she did not possess but that were characteristic of the deceased communicators allegedly speaking through her. The argument is that Mrs. Willett could not have displayed these skills—"knowing how"—unless she actually was acting as a medium for discarnate minds who had *acquired* them during *their* lifetimes. A similar type of argument is made in cases where a medium displays *responsive xenoglossy*, which is "the ability to converse in a language (she) never learned." The argument is that one could never display responsive xenoglossy unless an external, discarnate personality who *had* learned the language were speaking through the medium.

Almeder also discusses evidence for veridical out-of-body experiences, for example, as reported in the near-death situation. In some cases a person who is clinically dead can demonstrate that he or she was observing actual events occurring at a location at a distance from their clinically dead bodies. Almeder reviews experiments in out-of-body projection with the late psychic Alex Tannous, conducted at the American Society for Psychical Research by Kārlis Osis and Donna McCormick, that seemed to show that a real localizable entity can leave the body and correctly observe the external world. If a localizable entity can leave the body while one is living, or clinically dead, the idea that it may continue to exist after death becomes more credible.

The near-death experience is in some ways especially interesting because it provides tantalizing hints of what the experience of eternal life might be like. Let me mention three examples of how.

First, there are reports of panoramic memories, the sense of seeing the whole of one's existence before one, in a kind of apocalyptic summing up, a state described by the Roman philosopher Boethius as *totum simul*, a sense of total simultaneity and full possession of life.

Second, there is an overwhelming luminosity, a feature that pervades the landscape of prophetic visionary experience. In Raymond Moody's book, *Reflections on Life After Life*, the author reports that many of his subjects saw, in addition to mysterious beings of light, "cities of light." (The New Jerusalem of John of Patmos, the Celestial City of the Iranian mystical prophets, the *Citta Felice* of Tommaso Campanella.)

Third, there are feelings of transcendental love. This love, this peace that passes understanding, is perhaps the supremely defining feature of the heavenly destiny that awaits us, at least according to makers of the Millennium Myth who belong in the camp of Zoroaster, Jesus, Paul, Jefferson, Solovyov, and Whitman. Looked at in this way, the near-death experience, while it provides weak evidence for life after death, does seem to contain a kind of preview, in its transient epiphany of love, light, and simultaneity, of the great visionary world that the prophets say will unfold for us at the end of time.

Psychedelic Eschatology

Near-death epiphanies are a little like psychedelic visions; both are expansions of ordinary consciousness. Both suggest that we are immersed in a Platonic matrix of timeless being, although ordinary consciousness, veiled with its fixations, blocks awareness of the fact. Psychedelic, like transpersonal and supernormal, states of consciousness, offer glimpses of nonlocal, atemporal modes of being—and as such, previews of the death state. The psychedelic shaman, like the mystic and the near-death experiencer, is a reconnoiterer of possible postmortem states of being. Some comments on psychedelic eschatology therefore seem to the point.

Ever since the modern psychedelic movement emerged, with Aldous Huxley's *The Doors of Perception* and *Heaven and Hell*, there is a growing sense that psychoactive plants are doorways to extraordinary states of consciousness. Huxley's title *The Doors of Perception*, a book about mescal intoxication, is from William Blake: "If the doors of perception were cleansed every thing would appear to man as it is, infinite." The idea that we can learn to crash the gates of time and enter the infinite worlds of heaven and hell via mescal inebriation was explored again in Huxley's *Heaven and Hell*.

Gordon Wasson, banker-mycologist-explorer, in his book *Soma: The Mushroom of Immortality*, argues that certain plants have played a lively role in opening up human mental vision to the prospects of immortality. Soma was ingested by the Indian *rishis* who saw the timeless nature of consciousness. Irwin Rhode made a similar case for the experiential discovery of immortality among the Greeks in the cult of Dionysos. As Rhode explains it, the bacchants, inebriated by a combination of potent Greek wines mixed with hashish, danced until they became *ek-static*, literally, "outside themselves." In this out-of-body state, celebrants experienced themselves as godlike, in effect, immortal.[44]

Wasson has also suggested that the Eleusinian Mysteries were used to induce vivid experiences of nonlocality and immortality.[45] The

Eleusinian Mysteries lasted two thousand years, were the spiritual mainstay of generations of Greeks, and inspired great poets and philosophers like Sophocles and Plato. This ancient psychedelic cult induced an experience of immortality in the form of goddess consciousness, the rite invoking visions of the Kore—the divine maid, anima, nymph.

Recently, the American writer Jean Houston has been busy reviving and modernizing the Eleusinian Mysteries; she has done pioneer psychedelic research and performed experiments with an out-of-body launching device she called the "witch's cradle." A world-traveler, empathetically exploring indigenous cultures on the brink of extinction, she has been shoring up images of the human adventure, as if she would enrich our panoramic memory for an encroaching planetary near-death experience. Jean Houston is an American psychonaut in the court of Teilhard de Chardin's noosphere.

Psychedelic eschatology has been around since the dawn of civilized life. I mentioned the plant that Gilgamesh let slip through his fingers, the one that Utnapishtim promised would rejuvenate the user. According to Charles Muses, a tradition of psychedelic eschatology existed among the early Egyptians. Speaking of ancient Egyptian ethnobotany, Muses writes, "Ingestion of the sacred material was designed not merely to give 'a high' but to trigger and impel the *metamorphic process* leading to a theurgic transformation of human nature . . . , in which the previously merely mortal is to be, using Meister Eckhart's graphic word, *vergottet*, 'begodded'."[46] According to Muses, this ethnobotanical begodding of humanity is the basis of the *Egyptian Book of the Dead*.

In Leary's view, the brain is a "reality-tunnel" machine; our neuro-circuits determine what reality-tunnels our brains enable us to navigate. Most of us most of the time navigate a tiny band on the spectrum of the possible. Psychedelics interfere with the routine operation of our neuro-circuits and hence open our reality-tunnels. Leary, with Richard Alpert (now Ram Dass) and Ralph Metzner made the connection between death and psychedelics in their book *Psychedelic Experience* (1964), which used the *Tibetan Book of the Dead* as a basis for guiding psychedelic sessions. The last word in practical epistemology, psychedelics become tools for researching afterdeath states of consciousness.

The question is whether the entire planet, as the Millennium Myth envisions, is to be drawn into a world of imagination eschatologically **307** detached from the ailing body of old Gaia. Leary speaks of an imperative to leave the planet, Arthur C. Clarke of a telepathic journey to the Overmind. Space travel and telepathic travel seem natural allies to psychedelic travel, technologies for experiments in endtime.

Psychedelics provide tools for a scientific eschatology. Unfortunately, the mental climate of the country is hostile to the use of psychedelics. The reason, in part, has to do with drug-related problems that are the antithesis of the expansive potentials of psychedelic substances.[47]

It is against the confusion between mere drugs and the psychedelic poetics of consciousness, a confusion that insults the right to pursue happiness in whatever way befits the choice of Jeffersonian free spirits, that Terence McKenna has emerged in the 1990s as bard of the psychedelic Millennium. According to McKenna's incantatory mythos, history is hurtling us toward a singularity in which the human spirit will be launched into a new dimension, into what William Butler Yeats called "Magic" or Henry Corbin the "Mundus Imaginalis." According to McKenna, we ought not to resist the impetus of this unraveling time-spirit; in fact, he recommends "heroic dosages" of psychedelic mushrooms as a way of escalating the eschatologic drumbeat. Psychedelics unveil the present, actualize potential, render explicit, open clearings, allow epiphanies, make the unconscious conscious. The psychedelic imagination is the road to the end of history.

The entire thrust of our planetary culture, according to McKenna, is toward compression, complexification, etherization. Says McKenna, "Possibly the world is experiencing a compression of technological novelty that is going to lead to developments that are very much like what we would imagine time travel to be."[48] The new technology of simulated or virtual reality may be seen in this light as weaning human consciousness from its dependence on linear time. These new technologies may, for all we know, be exciting the psychic functions and thus disengaging consciousness from the restraints not only of time but of space.

McKenna, with Jung and the Mayan calendar, attaches chiliastic import to the year 2010; at that point in time, he thinks, this chaos of compressed information—accelerated by psychedelics and simulation technologies—is going to send us into a metaphysical tailspin and bounce us through the "white hole of time"[49] and out—but into what?

We are not told precisely what the Eschaton will be like—to get too specific on the rebirthings of time is bound to be an exercise in futility. All that McKenna is sure of—the Logos, he says, has been chatting with him—it's going to be one helluva party! So we come full circle with Zoroaster, who, like Terence McKenna, sees the end of history as a gigantic party—a party to which the entire human family, including the dead, will be invited.

The UFO Link in the Chiliastic Chain

I discussed some aspects of the UFO enigma in chapter 9, mainly with respect to their symbolic significance for the Millennium Myth. UFOs are also important in forming a new picture of the future of death. The UFO phenomenon—after you eliminate the hoaxes and the cases with normal explanations—involves a residuum of fact that shatters our routine ontology, forcing us to admit we are in the presence of unknown realities.[50]

Most careful students of UFO phenomena have been driven to conclude that there is some real, objective, invasive core to these reports. The mistake is to assume that they necessarily imply machines from outer space. The evidence does not warrant that conclusion. For one thing, there are too many encounters, landings, abductions, and the whole phenomenon, though quasi-physical, is too visionary in character. Something more interesting and more revolutionary seems to be involved than visitors from another planet. I agree with Jacques Vallee when he concludes in one of his books: " . . . the UFOs seem to represent an alien force that anticipates our own scientific development by decades, mocks our efforts to identify its nature and its long-term intentions."[51]

With regard to the future of death, there are features of these phenomena that connect with eschatology. UFO-related entities disobey the laws of physics; they pass through solid walls, materialize, and dematerialize, showing many of the earmarks of ghostly or other paranormal phenomena. Now, whatever the correct explanation of UFOs, they seem part of an alternate system of reality whose temporal dimension differs from ordinary reality's. One effect widely reported is "missing-time." Travis Walton, whose story was (inadequately) told in a movie, *Fire in the Sky*, missed an entire week. Walton, who passed lie detector tests, experienced an end of ordinary time and apparently vanished from the face of the Earth.[52] This type of datum is important for a new death paradigm. All anomalies of time are important, because the question is whether human personality is stuck inside or capable, like Kurt Vonnegut's Billy Pilgrim, of getting "unstuck" in time.

UFO phenomena bear on the future of death in another way. Whether or not human beings have a future beyond their bodily death seems linked to the question of other worlds. As far as transcending death, there is the question of locale. If, for example, some aspect of our personalities escapes bodily death, it will have to go or be somewhere, exist in some otherworldly or ultradimension of reality.

The UFO phenomenon may relate to the ultraphysical dimension of postmortem life. UFOs seem not only otherworldly but ultradimensional, as Vallee argues in his book *Dimensions*. UFOs, in short, may be aspects of last things; cross-sections of a nonlocal, nontemporal world; anticipations of, accelerations toward, the end of time. We must put them in our eschatology data bank. Let us turn now to another question.

The Obsolescence of Aging

It has often been noted that it is just when people start to get old and their bodies begin to go that their souls begin to ripen; by the time they begin to master the art of living, they are slipping into life's late afternoon. There is point to the quip that youth is wasted on the young. The question is: Is getting old becoming obsolete?

Aging may have made sense in the early stages of human evolution: to succeed as a species, the population had to expand; slowly ripening individuals would have been a luxury from the standpoint of the survival of the whole species. In the early stages of evolution, survival as a whole was more important than highly evolved individuals. In the early days of human life on earth, quantity was more important than quality.

But this arrangement no longer makes much sense. First, the obvious reason: Quantity of population is no longer a problem—or rather, it is, but in a different way. Today the problem is that quantity is excessive; there are too many people, and exploding population is a positive menace. At this stage of history, what we need for survival is not randomly proliferating numbers but conscious refinement of values—not quantity but quality of life.

People need more time to assimilate the enormous amounts of information rapidly becoming available; information is outstripping our capacity for understanding. And people need more time to explore their enormously expanded environments. In the age of cosmic exploration, long-lived people will be a necessity. Moreover, if Einstein is right, aging *will* slow up as we learn to travel at speeds approaching that of light.

But before we get into star trekking, immortality—extended life-spans—is a necessity here and now on earth. It may seem a paradox, but we need temporal abundance to reduce population growth. People reproduce because they crave symbolic immortality. But an immortal individual would not need to reproduce to carry on his or her name; each of us could carry our own names on, as the decades and the centuries unrolled. Immortal people would always be evolving. The fullness of time, and the absence of the old life-denying psychology, would make it easier for us to live as friends to each other and friends to our home planet.

Instead of being neurotic consumers of the goods of the Earth, we might learn to become galactic citizens. Given that biostasis technology will most likely be mastered, it will be possible to take periodic vacations from conscious existence; one might, for instance, decide to skip half a millennium. What an interesting experience it would be to go to sleep on New Year's Eve 2001, and wake up five hundred years hence!

Modification of the aging process might conceivably involve more than just slowing or stopping the aging mechanisms; it might involve *reversing* them. Once that is accomplished, we could select from a variety of age styles. Some might enjoy being adolescents for a long time; others might prefer ripe middle age as the best temporal persona; others might be content with the more tranquil life styles of wise old men and women, making themselves available as consultants for people with more ambitious, driven, and mobile temperaments.

Type A diseases would vanish because there would be no rush to achieve or compete; the declined population—an inner and practical necessity among immortals—would alter the complexion and the quality of life on earth. There would be an end to the harmful psychic mechanisms of death-denial, neurotic flight from the body, and robotic servitude to causes. Life extension would entail the end of history as we know it and the dawn of a new epoch.

Death and the Informational Singularity

The Millennium Myth contains a vision of the end of death as we understand it. My contention is that there is a fourfold division of data that bears on this vision. First, a division between the prophetic and the mystical traditions: The prophetic tradition (Gilgamesh to Jesus) tells of the rejuvenation and resurrection of the body; the mystical tradition tells of the immortality of the soul.

The data tetrad also divides between ancient-intuitive and modern-scientific. To support the prophetic are such modern technologies as cryonics, bioengineering, nanotechnology, gene therapy, and so on; to support the mystical tradition are transpersonal psychology, parapsychology, psychedelic research, and possibly ufology. In short, contemporary studies provide enough data to suggest that death is a more malleable concept than scientific materialism would have us believe.

Moreover, it is now clear that as we come to the end of the twentieth century, the spiritually stupefying philosophies of Marxism, Freudianism, behaviorism, and some versions of Darwinism have proven inadequate to the complexities of human experience. There are good reasons for entertaining the notion of scientific eschatology; the coming informational singularity is very likely to throw the idea of death into new perspectives.

The intellectual landscape of the next century is likely to be more, not less, open to new ideas concerning human transcendence. Instead of a universe of changeless being, we face a multiverse of becomings— a place where the old idea of eternal law has broken down into one of succeeding epochs and novel ingressions. In the simple solid unchanging mechanistic universe of a Hobbes or Helvetius, it was hard to imagine escaping the ravages of time. Before evolutionary cosmology, time was the enemy; after it, time acquires a creative dimension.

The new cosmology with its quantum packets of possibility, its subtle energies and many dimensions and ceaseless novelties, its sharp beginnings (the Big Bang), its punctuated evolutionary leaps, and its overall marvelous chaotic creativeness seems to me a place where human immortality might turn out to be—or to become—possible. My general feeling is that posthumous or vastly extended life is no more improbable a fact than life emerging from nonlife—or there being a universe rather than there not being one. The climate of thought created by the new science ought to alert us to all manner of marvels, not strangle our sense of the possible.

The new physics and its metaphors of breakthrough, the appearance of virtual environments as liberators of the imagination, post-Darwinian evolutionary theory, biotechnology, nanotechnology, kundalini yoga, psychedelics, transpersonal psychology, ufology, parapsychology, AI, electronic communications, and countless other informational novelties—once the combined perspectives of these approaches begin to cross-pollinate, there is good reason to anticipate sea changes in the paradigm of death.

Lastly, consider the emergence of the Anthropic Principle. In 1974, the physicist Brandon Carter introduced what he called the "Anthropic Principle," which attempts to account for the many remarkable life-facilitating coincidences of nature. This principle, which has several formulations—weak, strong, participatory, and final—reintroduces the old argument from design for a cosmic intelligence. Another way of putting it, it brings back teleology, purpose, and final causation to our understanding of the universe.

John Casti's version of the Anthropic Principle is perhaps the most radical: "Once life is created, it will endure forever, become infinitely knowledgeable, and ultimately mold the universe to its will."[53] As Michael Corey observes about this "final" version of the Anthropic Principle, it asserts that "intelligent life will eventually grow to the point of becoming godlike."[54] As such I take the Anthropic Principle as an intellectual expression of the Millennium Myth; its vision of a godlike capacity to "mold the universe to its will" is compatible with the prophetic vision of the abolition of death.

In the final version of the Anthropic Principle, the whole of human potential is destined to be realized. A full and complementary development of human potential would be reflected in the complementary nature of the human psyche—psychokinesis *and* extrasensory perception. Psychokinesis, I suggest, corresponds to the prophetic tradition, the drive to transform the body. Extrasensory perception corresponds to the mystical tradition, the drive to unfold the whole of consciousness.

This is what the Logos whispers in my ear: At the end of time, the split will be overcome; PK and ESP, prophet and mystic, body and soul, action and contemplation, earth and heaven, time and eternity—all will converge in an act of cosmic copulation.

After the End of Death, What Then?

The Millennium Myth promises immortality; it also promises a transformation in human relationships—liberation from ages of flawed love. If we think about it a moment, love is more basic than death; it is not enough to extend—even to eternalize—life. I therefore place the theme of love at the end of this book about the End. I conclude with speculations on the future of love, the heart of the Millennium Myth. *L'amore*—the stuff Dante thought made the stars go round! Technology, space migration, infinite intelligence, even immortality, what good are they without love? Without heart to guide them, they are worse than useless—they are downright dangerous. So let us look at one last great image in the gallery of the Millennium Myth.

Love and Sex in the Millennium

*Of one thing I am certain. The sexual force is the
nearest thing to magic—to the supernatural—that
human beings ever experience. It deserves perpetual
and close study. No study is so profitable to the
philosopher. In the sex force, he can watch the purpose
of the universe in action.*

COLIN WILSON
Sex Diary of a Metaphysician

In the great day that is to come, not only will nature be transformed
and the sorrows of death banished, but human relations—the true
powers of love and sex—will be freed from the ancient curse against
Adam, Eve, and the Serpent. At the core of the Millennium Myth we
find a dream about a new world where love, sex, and all life-affirming
instincts are fully free, fully realized.

Nowadays, in the accelerating nineties, there are good reasons to
reexamine our thinking on love and sex. High divorce rates, the
breakdown of the family, AIDS that forces a sinister coupling of sex
and death, feminism, the challenge of gay and lesbian life styles, the
battle of the sexes that seems to be getting uglier—all these, and much
more, add to the confusion and the challenge.

Then there is the growing violence that mars life everywhere—
no need to run through the usual litany of horrors. But if there is
an answer to violence, it must have something to do with love; for
surely, where there is love, violence cannot be. Our modern physicians
of culture—Freud, Marcuse, Norman O. Brown, and many others—
have spoken of the battle that Eros is fighting against Thanatos, yet
somehow the dark forces continue to have an unusually tight grip on
the world at large. So we need to review our resources and consider
the public habits of mind, the institutions that shape the evolution of
our amative and peaceful potential.

Love, one might (perhaps foolishly) protest, is the only antidote to the forces of barbarism everywhere on the march. The truth is that after the "triumph" of the West, there is little sign of growing love in the "new world order." That triumph has in fact led to a worldwide explosion of human discontent. Nor do the old high creeds inspire much confidence. After thousands of years of Western idealism and religiosity, governments still swear by Machiavelli, not the Sermon on the Mount; and the people idolize Rambo, not Rimbaud—Schwarzenegger, not Schweitzer. So, rethinking our ideas on love and sex might be the best thing we can do to prepare for the next millennium.

Binding and Unbinding the Dragon of Life

Love and sex are central to the Millennium Myth; in fact, the core image of the Myth is symbolically related to love and sex. The key passage is one we have cited before from the Book of Revelation: "And I saw an angel come down from heaven, having the key of the bottomless pit and a great chain in his hand. And he laid hold on the dragon, that old serpent, which is the Devil, and Satan, and bound him a thousand years" (Rev. 20:1–2). (A similar idea is evoked by Isaiah for whom Yahweh's "unyielding sword" will punish "Leviathan the coiling serpent" and "kill the dragon" [Isa. 27:1].)

Thus, the Millennium represents that time or condition of being in which the dragon, the old serpent, identified with the Devil and Satan, is bound and locked in a bottomless abyss. Is this image a clue to what went wrong with love in the Western tradition?

One has only to contemplate this old serpent a little, and something seems not quite right. First of all, the symbolism of snakes, serpents, and dragons is very rich. In China, for instance, the dragon was revered as King Lung Wang or god, had a pearl of great price in his throat, and lived in underwater palaces; the Chinese dragon was a symbol of life's abundance. In Greece, the serpent was the emblem (as in China) of healing in the cult of Asclepius; the caduceus, symbol of the healing profession, is a wand twined with two serpents, surmounted by two birds. Here the serpent forms an image of life in balance with itself. At Epidaurus, the God of Health was represented by a living serpent. In India, the serpent power of kundalini is a feature of Tantric yoga—a symbol of sexual energy and transcendence.

Serpents, dragons, and marine monsters appear in Mesopotamian creation myths, where they do symbolize evil and deception. In the Near East the primordial marine monster Tiamat was the foil of the creator Marduk; Marduk slays the marine monster Tiamat but creates the world from her corpse. So even here evil contains the future of good, and destruction is a prelude to creation. The truth is, in the wider tradition, the serpent is an ambiguous and morally plastic symbol. "The serpent almost everywhere," writes Mircea Eliade, symbolizes "what is latent, preformal, undifferentiated."[1]

If then, as in Greek, Indian, and Chinese cultures, we take the dragon as a symbol of "latent" life, the image of the Millennium, as it appears in the Book of Revelation, ties the goal of history to a ruthless repression of the life instincts—a demonizing of life itself. Demonizing the serpent already occurs in the Book of Genesis, where it appears as a messenger of deception, leading to the expulsion of Adam and Eve from the garden of Eden. The equation "dragon-serpent=satanic deceiver" reaches a climax in the passage cited from the Book of Revelation. Christian civilization, to the degree it is informed by that Book, may therefore be said to be based upon antagonism to the life instincts.

The Book of Revelation represents a departure from a wider and more open-ended dragon tradition. It makes the dragon, a many-valued symbol of life force, into a thing of pure evil—as John says, into the *Devil*. John, blistering with righteous indignation, wants to hurl it into the shade, place it under lock and key, bind, control, and repress its writhing rebellious life; John invests the dragon with supernatural negativity. The dragon is satanic, the adversarial father of lies and deception. Where the Eastern sage was content to call the dragon of life *maya*—the magical, often misleading, iridescence of our own minds—John of Patmos saw in the dragon's firepower a will to deception, an absolute enemy to all human interests.

Antipathy toward the "dragon" has pervaded Western culture. Western science has been very successful in controlling the dragon of nature, by putting nature, as Francis Bacon once said, to the rack; or, as Martin Heidegger put it, Western metaphysics, ruled by a Nietzschean will to power, has turned nature into a gigantic factory. This enterprise of subduing satanic nature advanced when science, capitalism, and the Protestant Reformation converged. The tremendous will to power over nature, the Baconian will to put nature to the rack and make her do our will, carries out the project of dragon repression envisioned in John's Millennium Myth.

But halt. At this point in our history we need to court a new attitude toward the "old serpent"—John's metaphor for nature. In an age of ecology and depth psychology, paranoid, repressive, and exploitative attitudes toward nature are no longer defensible. Now that we have gained such power over nature and have come to know the dangers of that power, it is time to deconstruct the New Testament image of the dragon as enemy. It is, I want to argue in this chapter, in our interest to nurture images of the dragon *unbound*.

War Against the Dragon of Natural Life

Duke anthropologist Weston La Barre's *They Shall Take Up Serpents* is a study of the psychology of snake-handling cults in rural southern America. The basis for the cult is a passage in the Bible about signs of endtime: "And these signs shall follow them that believe: In my name shall they cast out devils; they shall speak with new tongues; they shall take up serpents; and if they drink any deadly thing, it shall not hurt them; they shall lay hands on the sick, and they shall recover" (Mark 16:17–18).

Most American snake-handlers were poor and uneducated; the cult was a way of attesting to a faith-power over nature as embodied in poisonous snakes. In handling the snake one handles the forces of life and death. The prophet Isaiah envisioned messianic times when children would play with snakes, immune to their danger. "The infant will play over the den of the adder; the baby will put his hand in the viper's lair" (Isa. 11:8). When the Kentucky snake-handler holds a dangerous rattlesnake in his hands or lets one coil itself around his neck, he defies death and nature and for a moment tastes the power of gods. As the serpent in the garden of Eden said, "Ye shall be as gods" (Gen. 3:5).

La Barre, unsurprisingly, sees symbolic identity between snake and phallus. Indeed, snake cults and snake myths abound, and they all pay homage to phallic power. Richard Payne Knight's learned book *A Discourse on the Worship of Priapus* (first published in 1786) shows how deeply rooted in Western culture was the teaming up of religious passion and the "generative power" of the snake-phallus. Western worship of Priapus is paralleled by the Eastern cult of serpent power.

The phallic mythos runs deep in the ancient and medieval mind. Knight observed:

> In an age, therefore, when no prejudices of artificial decency existed, what more just and natural image could they find, by which to express their idea of the beneficent power of the great Creator, than that organ which endowed them with the power of procreation, and made them partakers, not only of the felicity of the Deity, but of his great characteristic attribute, that of multiplying his own image, communicating his blessings, and extending them to generations yet unborn.[2]

So, in declaring war against the dragon-snake—the symbolic equivalent of bringing about the Millennium—John declared war against the phallic-generative forces of nature.

This ascetic war against sexuality can be grossly literal or subtly abstract. For example, millenarian antiphallicism took place with particular literal-minded ferocity among the castrants, groups like the Old Believing Russian Skoptsy who, taking the metaphor of a poet to literal extremes, "made themselves eunuchs for the sake of the kingdom of heaven" (Matt. 19:12).[3]

On the other hand, we can say that the Western world's preference for the Promethean work ethic over the Orphic play principle,[4] its puritanical discomfort with Renaissance *voluptas*, and its slavish subjection to a punishing superego (in Freudian lingo), represents a more subtle form of self-emasculation, a more socially distilled animosity against the old dragon of life. The idea of the Millennium, as it reflects a will to power over the life force itself—symbolized in the image of binding the dragon—indicates a dangerous turning point in the history of Western consciousness.

Nevertheless, a secret tension remained, an underground rapport with the wisdom of the dragon, a recurrent millenarian impulse to unbind the serpentine power and release the renovating energies of sex and love into a society that had built itself up for centuries on the habit of self-repression. From time to time this underground serpentine wisdom—it is part of the secret history of the Millennium Myth—reasserts itself and sets about to overthrow the established order and usher in an age of unrepressed love.

Contrary to John of Patmos, *liberating* the "dragon" has for many radical utopians been the basis of their vision of the Millennium. From

Jesus to John Humphrey Noyes, from Zoroaster to Norman O. Brown, they have dreamed of living on earth in the fullness of life and love. Let us therefore look at examples of the attempt to unbind the dragon and institute the liberation of love.

The Pursuit of the Millennium as the Liberation of Love

For traditional Christianity, sex belongs to monogamous marriage and the business of reproduction. Consider what the angelic doctor of the Catholic church, Thomas Aquinas, had to say about "inordinate emission": "The inordinate emission of semen is incompatible with the natural good; namely, the preservation of the species. Hence, after the sin of homicide whereby a human nature already in existence is destroyed, this type of sin appears to take next place, for by it the generation of human nature is precluded."[5]

In other words, the purpose of sex is to make babies and to waste semen is to commit murder. Birth control and abortion thus become a type of murder, and masturbation, a moral cousin to murder. Needless to say, the latter is a problem for young people just getting acquainted with the *ophos archaios* ("old serpent"). Nor has the Church's position changed much since the days of Saint Thomas. In 1993, Pope John Paul published *Veritatis Splendor* (The Splendor of Truth), where he pronounced premarital sex, masturbation, homosexuality, and artificial insemination "intrinsically evil."

The millennial underground takes a different view. The radical makers of the Myth picture a day when sexuality—the whole gamut of human loves—is completely emancipated from traditional constraints. In what follows, I want to look at six different ways that millenarians and mystic rebels have pursued love and its radical possibilities. Is there any commonality among the six? I think there is. Each is a way of unbinding the dragon; each aims, directly or indirectly, to release and then to integrate the serpent power and thus renew and transform society. The six ways involve:
- The art of inhibition
- A revolt against conventional marriage
- The millennial uses of "polymorphous perversity"
- Eroticizing work
- Art and the erotic sense of reality
- A revolution of cybersex

I start with a way that is traditional and end with one that is futuristic.

The Art of Inhibition

The first way involves developing a common human faculty, the will—the curious capacity we have for voluntary delay and inhibition of our bodily impulses. (Inhibition is not the same as repression: repression, in our book, is the enemy; inhibition, an ally.)

In the art of living and loving, all is not constant release, dilation, expansion. The yoga of love that Plato taught in the *Symposium* and the *Phaedrus*, although it has its eye on blissful expansion into the great "ocean of erotic beauty," begins with inhibition—the ability to play meditatively with and channel the erotic impulse. Platonic inhibition of Eros differs sharply from John's compulsion to hurl the serpentine power into the abyss. Platonic love is far gentler in its approach to Eros, which it respects as a daimonic power that connects human and divine reality.

Platonic love begins with erotic attraction to particular bodies but disallows complete physical gratification (the "Platonic" thing about Platonic love). The goal is to sublimate the erotic impulse until the candidate for enlightenment learns to enter the "ocean" of erotic beauty. Plato's sublimated Eros overflows into all social activities, creating an erotic Millennium akin to Joachim's community of ecstatic monks.

Eastern traditions also value inhibition as a tool in the art of spiritual transformation. Patanjali, for example, defines yoga as the effort to inhibit the spontaneities of our basic mindstuff. Tantric yoga also begins with the common-sense idea of self-control; but, by carrying it to extremes, Tantrism uses self-control to shatter the illusions of what Freud called the "reality principle"—that is, the mental bulwark of ordinary civilization. Tantric yoga confronts John's unruly dragon but instead of consigning it to the bottomless pit, recognizes that the dragon, or serpent, is inside ourselves. The "devil" that John projects "out there" is really within our own bodies. One neither represses nor renounces the dragon; one inhibits its refractory movements for the sake of a final satisfying embrace.

The idea of inhibition for the sake of union comes out in the Zen Oxherding Pictures, a brilliant product of Rinzai Zen Buddhism. There are different versions of the Oxherding Pictures, images (with poetry and commentary) of an ox and an oxherder, symbolic of nature and spirit, force and will. The ox, I take it, is functionally equivalent to the serpent; the goat and the bull also symbolize the generative powers of nature. The Oxherding Pictures tell the story of the way to a Zen Millennium.

Following Kakuan's version, the gist is this: At first the ox (or dragon) is unruly, then it is gently prodded into a relationship with the oxherder. In the fifth picture we read, "When the ox is properly tended to, he will grow pure and docile; without a chain, nothing binding, he will by himself follow the oxherd."[6] No need to bind the ox—the dragon. In the eighth picture, ox and oxherder vanish. "All is empty—the whip, the rope, the man and the ox." The duality of good and evil is overcome; conflict converts to harmony. The last picture is called "Entering the City with Bliss-Bestowing Hands." In the Zen Millennium, after union with the ox-dragon, one returns to the throng of life—"he touches, and lo! the dead trees are in full bloom." Opposition dissolves into unity, alienation into friendship, force into persuasion, discipline into love, death into life. In the Zen tradition, the ox-dragon is seen as both outside and inside, other and lover, real and unreal.

Once we compare the Zen Oxherding Pictures—not to mention Platonic love and Tantric yoga—with the Book of Revelation, the latter, from the standpoint of psychological finesse, comes off as crudely inferior. John's vision leaves us forever at odds with nature, with life, with the other; instead of peace it preaches apocalyptic war; instead of tranquillity, repression; instead of love—an elusive word in the Book of Revelation—curse and condemnation. Thus, at the very end of the Book of Revelation, we read: "If any man shall add unto these things [the words describing John's revelations], God shall add unto him the plagues" (Rev. 22:18).

Platonic love, Tantrism, Zen, and the Christian Book of Revelation all affirm the importance of engaging the serpentine life force in a strategy of delay and inhibition. The difference in the actual deployment of this strategy becomes evident once we compare the Book of Revelation and the Oxherding Pictures: in the former, delay and inhibition turn into ruthless repression; in the latter, they are steps toward playful integration and sublime transcendence.

Nevertheless, the tension created by Saint John's apocalyptic legacy has left in its wake a secret subtext that has kindled some of the boldest social theories and experiments in Western history. The repressed dragon keeps returning and wants to undo thousands of years of paranoid aggression against life. One way it has done this is by instigating a revolt against conventional marriage.

The Revolt Against Conventional Marriage

Freud, who knew a few things about the human psyche, once wrote a pessimistic piece about marriage called " 'Civilized' Sexual Morality and Modern Nervous Disease."[7] The marriages that Freud observed were a sorry compromise, a sacrifice of vital instinct to the Moloch of civilized life. Most marriages, according to the Viennese physician, were "doomed" to "spiritual disillusionment and bodily deprivation." The naturally effervescent love instincts end up bottled and deflated in the flask of unholy matrimony. Freud, denounced by feminists, once said, "Women, when they are subjected to the disillusionments of marriage, fall ill of severe neuroses that permanently darken their lives."

Whereas men, in most "civilized" marriages, are driven to "violently suppress" their emotions, which consumes their energy and enervates them. The choking up of the life force results in the impotent, resentful "little man" that Wilhelm Reich wrote about so tellingly.[8] Asks Freud: Is civilization worth all the sacrifice?

History is full of examples of people who have said "no" to civilization, rejecting marriage and by implication the established society. Jesus himself said there would be no marriage in the Kingdom of Heaven and that when history finally wound up, people would live like "angels," somehow emancipated from common fallen sexuality. The remark has been the basis of many a strange social experiment. Throughout the Christian era, millenarians of all stripes have jumped into radical social experiments, in pursuit of postmatrimonial "angelic" perfection. The visionary word was out: In the coming world—in the new age—institutions of repressive worldliness such as marriage will be finished. Any society that merits the name of heavenly will be a society free from repressive marriage.

Medieval visionaries such as Joachim of Fiore and Amaury of Bene saw most worldly—Freud would say "civilized"—institutions as destined to come to an end, and in their place, a postcivilization of free lovers. Joachim and his followers, like the American Shakers, pictured this "free love" as a communal life of seraphic monasticism. In the words of Father Joseph Meacham, a Shaker theologian: "The time is come for you to give up yourselves and your all to God, to possess as though you possessed not."[9] The Shakers' dance was their outlet to erotic ecstasy. Amaury's Brethren of Free Spirit were more like John Humphrey Noyes and the American Spiritualists and pursued a more emancipated erotic Millennium. The dance shades off into the orgy, with innumerable possibilities of experimentation in between.

Twelfth-century Europe seemed to have grown weary of marriage. Not only did the revolutionary Joachites and the anarchic Brethren of Free Spirit unleash their heretical ideas into the stream of Western history, but something was ignited the same century in southern France that started two new trends in the arena of love and sexuality: the birth of romantic love and the liberation of women. Both trends were inimical to conventional marriage.

The art of courtly or chivalrous love began in Provence. It was essentially adulterous love. Thus, Andreas Capellanus says in the *Art of Courtly Love*, "I am greatly surprised that you wish to misapply the term 'love' to that marital affection that husband and wife are expected to feel for each other after marriage, since everybody knows that love can have no place between husband and wife."[10] The rebellion began with the poetry of the troubadours, war-loving aristocratic French knights who took to writing exquisite poetry to the women of *other* knights.

Adulterous love was love for the sake of love itself. The conscious pursuit of Eros aimed for a transcendent experience, and as such it declared itself free from the conventions of marriage and as well from the duty to breed. The pursuit of love for love's sake had implications for overturning established society. For one thing, it opened a way to soften the savage mores of the warrior caste, making room for gentler habits of mind and heart. This became possible through poetry, the fine art of articulating the movements of the passionate heart.

The troubadour sublimation of savagery into poetry was an index of a wider change of consciousness taking place; Denis de Rougement writes of the "psychical revolution of the twelfth century."[11] The nub of this lay in a new attitude toward women that encouraged civility. Flirting with your peer's lady had to be done with extreme caution; meanwhile, caution, applied to passion, gave rise to *cortezia*, or "courtesy." Courtesy, like poetry, became another formal device for sublimating the warlike instincts. (It would be nice if today's gun-toting savages could learn from the old French troubadours and take to writing sonnets to beautiful ladies, instead of blowing each other's brains out.) For the troubadours, courtesy and poetry became strategies for awakening and artfully playing with the serpent power—the power that Saint John wanted to bind up and banish from the playing fields of history.

The art of courtly love was undertaken in an atmosphere of extreme danger; recall, for instance, the unfortunate Abelard and his lover Eloise. In the most celebrated love story of the Middle Ages, Abelard, philosophy professor and troubadour, suffered the indignity of mutilation because of his romance with Eloise, one of his gifted students. The risk of death and mutilation romanticized illicit love, as Capellanus implies, and even jealousy was recognized as useful for intensifying romantic love.

Although its methods may appear extreme, courtly love was an experiment in psychological wholeness; the *animus* (male principle) tried to temper its animosity by uniting with the *anima* (female principle). In the great epics of the world, women were never subjects of rhapsodic romantic relationships; the great relationships were between men. In the Sumerian epic, it was Gilgamesh and Enkidu; in the Iliad, Patroklos and Achilles; in the *Aeneid*, Dido plays second fiddle to Aenias's love affair with Empire. Women stay in the background; for the most part, as chattels—of utilitarian, never ideal, worth. As Pietro Aretino remarked during the Italian Renaissance, women had three options in life: they could be wives, nuns, or whores.[12]

In the twelfth century they became *fair ladies*. The poets of Southern France created a literature that helped men begin to see the Goddess in women, idealizing, eroticizing the image—as Dante does in *The New Life*—of the female anima. Here is what Dante wrote: "Nine times already since my birth the heaven of light had circled back to almost the same point, when there appeared before my eyes the now glorious lady of my mind, who was called Beatrice."[13] It is a lady of Dante's "mind," and the key to her "glory" is her distance; she thrives as a power in Dante's erotic *mundus imaginalis*.

The Dantean elevation of the Shakti image is a rebirth in Western consciousness of Plato's erotic imagination; but there is a break with the Greek, Arab, and Persian tradition, for the new focus is heterosexual, no longer homosexual. This shift toward a richer heterosexual imagination in the cult of chivalrous love was linked to another twelfth-century phenomenon, the cult of Mary. In the Middle Ages, France exalted and venerated the imagination of the Goddess under the cult of Mary. It may be surprising to some, but in the Middle Ages the figure of Mary is anything but pious and conformist in her inclinations.

What drives her is the need for passionate devotion. She embodies the divine pleasure principle and bears a secret (but neglected) potential for overthrowing male-dominated modes of consciousness.[14]

There were other indications of this insurgence. In the twelfth century, for example, the rules in the game of chess changed: instead of four kings, the new game featured one king and one queen[15]; moreover, the king is neither mobile nor very powerful. A precious drone, the single king's reason for being is to be protected; treated as a mere token of honor, he does nothing to earn his keep. The queen, on the other hand, bounds freely, powerfully, and dangerously across the board. Does the game of chess, whose rules were changed in the twelfth century by subversive troubadours, conceal a prophecy? Does it herald a new epoch, the feminine principle restored from centuries of Patmosian repression?

It was the century that Joachim of Fiore prophesied that the third *status*—the new age—would witness the Holy Spirit incarnate in a feminine body.[16] Prous Boneta, a millenarian forerunner of today's return of the Goddess movement, said she held the key to the bottomless abyss and claimed she had power over the *ophos archaios*. For eight centuries now the return of the Goddess has been underway, anticipated by medieval monks and troubadours. What I want to stress here is that the psychic revolution that de Rougement refers to—the new exploration of the feminine, the cultivation of erotic consciousness, and the synthesis of barbarism and poetry—thrived in an atmosphere of hostility to conventional marriage.

In those days, hostility to conventional life took the form of underground wars and cabals against the Catholic church. Manicheans, Bogomils, and Cathars shared the American Shakers' dislike of "slavish subjection" to sexuality, which encouraged revolt against marriage and economic slavery. The Brethren of the Free Spirit, the radical Franciscans, and the Waldenses, in a spirit akin to Joseph Smith and John Humphrey Noyes, were passionate about the prospect of paradise here and now, in embodied life. The Adamites, in particular, sought to restore paradise through revolutionary nudism and antinomian orgies; medieval streakers with a mystic vengeance, they liked to foregather in caverns in perfect nakedness. They proscribed marriage and advocated community of women and promiscuous sex.

The heretics attacked the Church as the bastion of bestial patriarchy; the established Church, they complained, inverted the very name of

God—AMOR (love) into ROMA (Rome)—an unpardonable aberration. For the mystic rebels of the time the potential for "higher consciousness" implied the need to subvert established institutions. And the main institution that had to go was marriage.

Let us move ahead to more recent times. The eighteenth-century philosophers also mounted an attack against marriage. Consider, for example, the Marquis de Sade's opinions on marriage. Marriage, as one may have guessed, was a constraint upon his gods—Nature and Freedom. And so, to all women he proclaimed: "O charming sex, you will be free: as do men, you will enjoy all the pleasures of which Nature makes a duty. Must the diviner half of humankind be laden with irons by the other? Ah, break those irons; Nature wills it."

The romantic god of nature decrees the "right of enjoyment" to all men and women. Happiness, to the millenarian mind, must be collective. In de Sade's view, all men have a right to enjoy all women— not to own but to use "temporarily"—like somebody who drinks freely from a fountain but makes no claim of ownership. So it is natural for men to take their pleasure in women—even, if need be, by force. The personal ego has no say here. De Sade's sadism is a kind of ultrahuman mysticism, a "dark Eros,"[17] an eschatology of unbridled lust: "Love, satisfying two persons only, the beloved and the loving, cannot serve the happiness of others, and it is for the sake of the happiness of everyone, and not for an egotistical and privileged happiness, that women have been given to us." "Never," says de Sade, like a good eighteenth-century *philosophe*, "may there be granted to one sex the legitimate right to lay monopolizing hands upon the other."

De Sade sees the marital contract as more burdensome to women than to men, because women are "endowed with considerably more violent penchants for carnal pleasure than men." Consequently, they require freedom from monogamy. In de Sade's republic, there are special houses for women, so that from a tender age a girl will

> be able to indulge in everything to which her constitution prompts her, she will be received respectfully, copiously satisfied, and, returned once again into society, she will be able to tell of the pleasures she tasted quite as publicly as today she speaks of a ball or promenade.

The last point about publicity is crucial; it means the end of repression, the end of shame consciousness, the end of the Augustinian equation: female genitals=*pudenda* (the Latin word means "shame" and "female genitals"). Disregarding the absurd denial of a woman's right to say "no," de Sade is, after his own fashion, a type of feminist.

For those who find the Marquis's rough-sex philosophy distasteful, a gentler but no less spirited anticipation of the end of repressive marriage may be found in Tom Paine, a man, like the Marquis, who spent a good deal of his time behind bars or in flight from the law. The writing of Paine I have in mind is called "Reflections on Unhappy Marriages." Paine concludes this ironical essay with advice received from an "American savage." The "savage" thinks Christian marriage neither a good nor a wise thing. Conventional, merely legally constituted, marriage he deems a form of imprisonment.

Because neither can escape the bond, by way of revenge each prisoner of marriage can only "double each other's misery." Paine therefore calls for the liberation of love. Says his "savage" persona, "Whereas in ours, which have no other ceremony than mutual affection, and last no longer than they bestow mutual pleasures, we make it our business to oblige the heart we are afraid to lose; and being at liberty to separate, seldom or never feel the inclination."[18]

The noble-savage persona evoked by Paine was a common device with the French *philosophes*. Here Paine uses it to dissolve "unhappy marriage" into the natural affection and pleasure of Eden's savage enlightenment. The tone differs from de Sade's, yet both men share a vision of the end of oppressive marital law and evoke the god of "Nature" to ratify the call to liberation.

In the nineteenth century, we find that American social visionaries were also hostile to marriage, although their arguments were shaped by Bible Communism as much as by eighteenth-century philosophy, and the practical applications of their antiwedlock sentiments were less overtly libertine than de Sade's. In chapter 6, for example, I discussed the saying of Jesus about the end of marriage in the Kingdom of Heaven. The Mormons, the Shakers, and the Oneidan Perfectionists—all millenarian movements—placed different interpretations on that saying, leading to different revolutionary sex practices: polygamy, celibacy, and complex marriage, respectively. I will not repeat that material here, but hostility to conventional marriage was also evident among Swedenborgians, Owenites, and Spiritualists.

Take the latter. The doctrine of free love may not be linked in the contemporary mind with Spiritualism, but the tie was strong during the heyday of the movement. How it relates to the words of Jesus on the end of marriage is worth noting; this is how C. M. Overton put it in the free love journal *The Social Revolutionary*:

> But will any intelligent Spiritualist deny that the concurrent testimony of the spheres proves that their inhabitants are controlled in their love relations not by arbitrary outside authority but by the law of attraction, affinity or Free Love? Is it not a conceded fact that the angels do not have to be hauled up before a magistrate to legalize their marriages? How supremely ridiculous the idea that the men and women of Paradise live together on the cat and dog principle because it wouldn't be respectable to separate?

Angels in paradise are not tied down by marriage, so why should Spiritualists, who model themselves after the angels? Robert Owen, the Welsh-born reformer and millennialist, came to Spiritualism late in life. Founder of New Harmony in Indiana, and like many progressive Americans of his day, he was critical of conventional marriage, condemning it with private property as a product of irrational religion and as an awful oppressor of humankind. Owen wrote of the "evils of indissoluble marriages." His son Robert Dale Owen, also a Spiritualist, published in *Moral Physiology* in 1830, a pioneer tract on birth control in the United States. I should also mention here the many American followers of Fourier, who believed their social program would lead to "higher degrees of amorous freedom." (Back to Fourier below.)

The social reformer Josiah Warren invented the phrase "Individual Sovereignty." An ideal dear to the Enlightenment, it goes back to Aristotle's *autarkia*, or "autonomy," the condition for true human happiness. We are not made to be slaves—not even the slaves of God. To put it another way: If God is within, then nobody (and no human institution) has the right to dictate to people the manner of their pursuit of love and happiness.

In the best of all possible worlds, individual sovereignty combines with the law of attraction to guide human relations. Like Tom Paine, American free lovers thought it ridiculous "to stay together and scratch and pull hair from a sense of duty." In the society of the Millennium,

329

relations will transcend duty without being irresponsible, since relations compelled solely by force of duty might well be a recipe for hell.

In the Spiritualist Millennium, as Esfandiary today recommends, instead of families there will be "mobilia," loose and changing erotic and philiac relationships. In the new dispensation, relationships will break up fairly readily—as they do in America today—but this need not be an unhappy custom. Yes, Overton agrees, the liberation of love is bound to mobilize, and sometimes to destroy, relationships.

But what of it? Contemporary Americans may think such a philosophy of amorous instability distressing. But not, however, our optimistic Free Love millenarians; on the contrary, in their view it is good that false relations be purged by the fire of emotional honesty from time to time. That, according to Spiritualist belief, is the way it works in the much happier realms of the afterworld: "The fact that they break up false relations there and form new ones is as well established and is just as much a part of the Spiritual or Harmonic Philosophy as the doctrine of Endless Progression."[19] It is not a bad thing for relationships to break up, because without a little periodic chaos, our soul's birthright to "endless progression" would be impeded. To hazard a comparison, as Roger Lewin shows in his book about life at the edge of chaos, the greatest evolutionary moments occur after mass extinctions.[20] Something comparable, according to free-love millenarians, applies to human relationships.

Does any of this throw light on the high divorce rate in America? If half the marriages in America end in divorce (extinction), then on Overton's Spiritualist principles, it would seem that half the marriages in America are "false." In other words, they violate individual sovereignty and the law of attraction. High divorce rates may be seen as birthpangs of still undefined forms of love relationship, destined, perhaps, to fully emerge in the coming Millennium. At the least, they seem proof that half the population is unconsciously at war with the institution of marriage-as-it-is, evidence for long-standing discontent more boldly advertised by millenarians.

The Millennium Myth points beyond what Paine called "false relations," and not merely the false relations in marriage but those that infect the whole of human society. A more enlightened form of love will one day transform not just family life but religion, education, government—and, above all, work. But before looking at love and work, I want to consider a Freudian idea employed by some recent utopian thinkers on the theme of Eros and civilization. What I have in mind is that lurid-sounding notion of *polymorphous perversity*. Let us see if it sheds any light on our subject.

The Millennial Uses of "Polymorphous Perversity"

Jesus once said that we have to become like children before we can enter the Kingdom of God. The idea can be given a Freudian twist. According to Freud, children have a nonspecialized capacity to enjoy erotically the whole of bodily existence. Instead of the intensely localized genital sexuality of adults, reality itself is erotically tinged for a child. Freud used the somewhat misleading expression *polymorphous perversity* to describe this situation.

Polymorphous erotic potential seems a better way of putting it. Some radical Freudians talked about the "erotic sense of reality." (See below, the section on art.) In the child, the capacity for pleasure is not fixated upon a few erogenous zones, as it is with mature adults; it permeates the whole of its embodied existence. Every sensory encounter affords a chance of playful enjoyment and gratification. As we mature, (according to the Freudian model) our childlike genius for delight in sense-life gradually shrinks, and a more narrowly focused, more anxious need for pleasure becomes organized around, and dominated by, the genital functions. Willy-nilly, we are forced to renounce our polymorphous potential for bodily love and enjoyment. Growing up leads to an impoverished capacity for erotic sense-enjoyment. To recapture that potential—to become like children again—is for Jesus and Freud the royal road to the Millennium.

Nevertheless, the potential for the erotic sense of reality remains. The mystic sex rebels believed in reawakening that potential. As we saw in the section above, a potent tactic for reversing the civilized regimentation and specialized parceling of our love potential is to stand up against monogamous sex and the common zeal for propagation.

The "perversity" of the sex mystics consists in their refusal either to bind or to be bound by the serpent power. Or, to put in a way that Schopenhauer might have liked, perversity lies in the refusal to let the species use the individual as a mere tool for its own perpetuation. The love rebels want to harness the impersonal serpent power for personal enjoyment; they want progress, not just replication—individuality, not just collective immortality. Above all, they want freedom, not the economic and psychological slavery that, for the mass of humankind, results from bondage to the procreative instincts. Gautama Buddha, realist that he was, put it like this: "Another child, another fetter." Recreation, not procreation, is the motto of sex millenarians.

The principle of polymorphous "perverse" eroticism was present in germ in Plato's philosophy of love. In the *Symposium*, Socrates distinguished "pandemic" love from the superior love of the educated pederast (needless to say, this ideal relationship between boys and older men is tough to appreciate these days). Plato thinks of sexual love as a symptom of human fragmentation, a stimulus for achieving wholeness.

The comic Aristophanes, present at the Symposium, invoked the androgyne to explain the dynamics of love. We love because we remember and long for something we once had but lost. Once we were androgynously complete, before Zeus in cowardly fear of our independence—"polymorphous perversity" if you like—saw fit to cut us down to size by slicing us in two, thus dooming us to a fate of forever searching for our lost halves—or, as people say today, our soul mates.

Herbert Marcuse used the notion of polymorphous perversity in *Eros and Civilization*. According to Marcuse, we should cherish our polymorphous sexuality for at least two reasons. First, it prevents us from adapting easily to the nuclear family, which Marcuse thought the social cement of repressive capitalism. Marcuse's theory of the perversions was no friend to traditional "family values"; the "perversions" undermine the cohesive fabric of repressive civilization. Second, polymorphous sexuality fosters the play principle; people in touch with their bodies resist being used as mere tools in the soulless world of economics. The Marcusan critique implied a changing of the gods, new culture heros; instead of Prometheus, hero of the work ethic, Marcuse would have us venerate Orpheus the musician, the one who tames the savage forces of nature with the charms of music.

The garishly provocative phrase *polymorphous perversity* is theoretically important; for instance, it relates to the idea of androgyny. The great mystics often cast their speculations on future love in images of the androgyne (or hermaphrodite.) Androgyny—as I wish to use this term—denotes the psychic plenitude of masculine and feminine traits in individual people. Most men have underdeveloped feminine psychic glands; ditto, in reverse, for women. The quest for the Millennium is a quest for wholeness of being—a Blakean marriage of heaven and hell. Balzac's *Seraphita* and Hesse's *Narcissus and Goldmund* describe the mysterious power of the androgynous personality. A moment ago, I mentioned Aristophanes's androgyne, the idea that love always conceals a secret longing for a half-remembered wholeness.

Throughout history the psychic underground has been drawn to images of men-women. Thomas's Gnostic Gospel, for example, tells us (without using the word) that androgyny is the secret to entering the Kingdom of Heaven. "When the male becomes female and the female becomes male, when the inner becomes outer and the outer inner, when the end becomes the beginning and the beginning becomes the end." The clairvoyant poet Arthur Rimbaud in his *Season in Hell* abjures what he calls "those lying loves" and wistfully evokes an image of liberated love in "one body." Whitman is perhaps the greatest visionary of androgynous love:

> I sing the body electric,
> The armies of those I love engirth me and I engirth them.
>
> *   *   *
>
> I am the poet of the women the same as the man.

Whitman's omnierotic sentiments are plain enough. An aficionado of Walt Whitman, the Englishman Edward Carpenter, published in 1908 a book called the *Intermediate Sex*. Carpenter was interested in "transitional types of men and women" he called Uranians, or people given to "homogenic attachment." Uranians, according to Carpenter's studies, were less driven by purely carnal motives; in their attractions, they were more esthetic, personal, and spiritual. In "gradations of Soul-material," Uranians enjoy a less specialized degree of feminine and masculine traits. They are more psychically balanced than normal people; intellect, for example, is anchored in feeling and intuition. Uranians, in other words, are more androgynous than normals.

Carpenter, drawing on some fascinating clinical and biographical data, makes a spirited case for the hypothesis that Uranians represent the evolutionary future of humankind. "We do not know," he observes about sex, "what possible evolutions are to come, or what new forms, of permanent place or value, are being already slowly differentiated from the surrounding mass of humanity." Carpenter concluded that "at the present time certain new types of humankind may be emerging, which will have an important part to play in the societies of the future—even though for the moment their appearance is attended by a good deal of confusion and misapprehension."[21]

According to Carpenter, Uranians are less sensual than ordinary people; their vice is sentimentality; their temperament, philanthropic; and, like the immortalists we met in the last chapter, they seem in touch with a mysterious source of youthfulness and vitality. Add to this their psychic and esthetic leanings; they are likely, says this English disciple of Whitman, to be the "teachers of future society."

For an up-to-date discussion of the evolutionary potential of androgyny, the reader might turn to the American Jungian, June Singer. Singer, in a way that supports Marcuse, points out that androgyny or psychic wholeness subverts the tyrannical one-sidedness of monotheism and patriarchy.[22] Now, a form of psychic wholeness in which patriarchal oppression comes to an end, leads us, as we found in our discussion of Joachim, to the heart of the Millennium Myth. Androgyny means the end of patriarchal dominance and one-sidedness; carried to revolutionary extremes, it would mean the end of Western civilization. If men stopped behaving exclusively like typical men, and if women stopped behaving like typical women, the world would never be the same again.

The issue for the future therefore transcends the issue of gay and lesbian sex. I say this without meaning to underrate the importance of gay and lesbian rights or without disparaging the sufferings of these minorities. But sex, as N. O. Brown reminds us in *Love's Body*, means "sections." The idea is to get beyond the "sections" and hang-ups of sex, hetero or homo, and move beyond mono- or bisexuality toward omnisexuality, omnieroticism. In the omnierotic universe of the Millennium, there will be room for the gamut of erotic possibilities—from Henry Miller's pagan enjoyment of sex on impulse to the passionate celibacy of Shakers.

But what about the question of "perversion"? Are no limits to be placed on the omnierotic people of the future? I will answer with the help of the Russian eschatologist we met a while back, Vladimir Solovyov. In *The Meaning of Love*,[23] Solovyov tackles the question of sexual perversion. Perversion, according to the Russian thinker, consists in any failure to love the whole person; fixation on a part, neglect of the whole, is the essence of perversion. Thus, a heterosexual male or female who relates to the opposite sex partially, abstractly, selfishly—who fixates on the other's bodily parts or on some other limited part of the whole person—would, according to Solovyov's criterion, be "perverted." Whereas, it would follow, a same-sex relationship in which partners loved each other unselfishly would not at all be "perverted." In other words, the only "perverted" love is selfish love. In this sense, we are all more or less perverted, and not till the Millennium will love be freed from the stigma of "perversion."

Work In the Amorous New Age

To imagine with conviction a world graced by unperverted love, we have to deal with the question of work. Work came up in the last section; the more "polymorphous perverse" we are, the less inclined we are to abuse our bodies, to allow them to be used as mere tools. The antidote to degrading work is play; in the world of play, we open ourselves to the serpentine power and surrender to what Deepak Chopra calls the "bliss body." Work, at the end of time, will become a vehicle for bliss, for play. Play is the life style in Eden.

The fall from Eden was a fall into the world of work—the toiling pain the Greeks called *ponos*. "In the sweat of thy face shalt thou eat bread," Adam is told (Gen. 3:19). "Therefore the Lord God sent him forth from the garden of Eden, to till the ground whence he was taken" (Gen. 3:23). After the fall, we have to work for a living. The Genesis myth portrays our essential misery, our "fallenness" as the theologians say, as being subject to the tyranny of economic necessity.

Karl Marx, that modern secular prophet, brings Genesis up to date with his critique of "alienated" labor. In a world of alienated labor, the ability to love, for most of us, is woefully restricted. It is hard to live a loving life in a society ruled by dehumanized labor. Love is inconsistent with inequality; hence the importance of our work world. Richard Heinberg, philosopher of primal humanity and author of *Memories and Dreams of Paradise*, believes that equality (by which he means the mutual recognition of basic human worth) is the only soil where love can grow.[24]

Capitalism may support economic freedom and individualism, but as a system ruled by the bottom line it is forced to treat people as means to an end, as more or less useful and expendable commodities. In Marxist lingo, people become a "means to production"; capitalism

335

is an economic system that disposes the majority of workers to emotions of envy, resentment, and discontent. None of these fertilize the possibilities of love.

The Millennium Myth makers want a world where work ceases to be dehumanizing. The German tongue illustrates the intimate relation between work and reality; what we work at (*wirken*) is what is real (*wirklich*). Reality (*Wirklichkeit*) is how we work; our job is our metaphysics. To change our work relations is therefore to change our reality. The radical implications of this were explored by American thinkers who came into prominence in the 1960s. Norman O. Brown and Herbert Marcuse shared a millenarian insistence on reversing the fall and overcoming alienated labor. Brown did it by seeking to unbind the dragon of the logos; Marcuse, by exposing the arbitrariness of repressive civilization. In *Eros and Civilization*, Marcuse argued for the overthrow of the Promethean work ethic, invoking Orpheus and the play principle, a new mythical hero for a new postcivilization. "I loaf and invite my soul," chanted an orphic Whitman in *Song of Myself*. "I loaf and observe a spear of summer grass."

Brown, Marcuse, Whitman—all in their own way makers of the Myth—saw in our amative potential the power to transform work, and hence everyday life, into play. Just as androgyny would call for the end of the old civilization, so does the idea that our work should be our play have similar subversive implications. However, before Marcuse and Brown—and influencing them both—was the Frenchman Charles Fourier (1772–1837). To make the point about work in the amorous new age, I will focus on his ideas.

Fourier was a strange, extravagant, prophetic thinker. An armchair revolutionary and self-taught clerk, he was financially wrecked by the French Revolution. Embittered by this, he plotted a detailed critique and overthrow of civilization. Fourier produced a huge following in the United States during the early 1840s and, through his influence on Marcuse and Brown, planted seeds of intellectual discontent again in the 1960s. Marx despised Fourier as utopian and unscientific. Fourier's appeal differs from Marx's, touching, I think, more on the life-affirming instincts and less on the resentment that Marx exploited so successfully.

What was the secret to Fourier's huge appeal in nineteenth-century America? In my opinion, it lay in his sweeping millenarian phantasies about freeing the serpent power whose repression has been the bane of Western civilization for two millennia. Here is how Frank Manuel sums it up: "Unrepressed sexuality, pervading relationships of love and labor, would regenerate the human race, now decaying in fraud, deprivation, and odious, unremitting toil."[25]

Fourier saw the possibility of regeneration in the future of the senses. Neither the lofty ministrations of spirit nor the archetypal imaginings of soul will save humankind, but rather the complete liberation of sense life. Not even a refinement of the visual or auditory senses will accomplish this miracle of social transformation; rather, it will be the exquisite cultivation of taste and, in particular, the enjoyment of the fruits—not even the grains—of the Earth. Fourier wanted to literally build the garden of Eden; Marx and other puritanical communists regarded Fourier's pleasure-loving utopia as if it were a brothel.

But Fourier saw himself as a new Newton, a discoverer of the spiritual counterpart to the law of gravity; in the human world, he claimed, attraction is the analogue to gravity. By applying the law of attraction, he thought it possible to transform human society; unlike Marx, he rejected force as a means to implement social revolution. (No dictatorship of the gourmand.) Revolution meant allowing the "attractive" forces of our divinely orchestrated sensual natures to govern our lives and to guide the manner in which we associate in work and love. The master key was *attraction passionelle*—"passional attraction" was the principle of the rebirth of global civilization. Fourier urged his followers to organize in groups, governed only by the law of passional attraction.

To accomplish this, Fourier recommended a special social unit he called a "phalanx," a term ironically borrowed from military usage. The idea was to combine work and fun, business and Eros—America heard the call; in the fall of 1843, Fourierism broke out everywhere. Phalanxes sprang up like wild mushrooms all over God's country. The vision of Eden restored caught fire. Americans came forth by the thousands, "rampant," as Noyes observed, "against existing civilization."[26] There was the Pennsylvania Phalanx, the Marlboro Association, the Trumbill Phalanx, the Prairie Home Community, the Ohio Phalanx, the Wisconsin Phalanx, the North American Phalanx—dozens of phalanxes scattered all over the country. Men and women banded and bonded together for the high purpose of reinventing civilization.

The old civilization was rotting with discontent. Fourier would liberate everybody, men and women, kids and the elderly, from boredom and drudgery. He catalogued the passions and devised schemes for gratifying them; he discerned a passion for cabals, intrigues, and a "butterfly" passion for novelty, and arranged for their satisfaction in his phalanxes. But an obstacle had to be overcome. The mentality of the West was built on resistance to passion, resistance to the wisdom of the serpent, and repressive morality stood in the way of Fourier's fruitarian Millennium.

"Morality," said Fourier, was "a mortal enemy of passional attraction." The morality Fourier inveighed against was the morality of the "savage, patriarchal, barbarous and civilized forms of society." His diagnosis of the disease came to this: The cause of the misery of the world is labor without love. For Fourier, as for Marx, wage-based industrial civilization was a system of forced labor, a system in which love and human values are compelled to give way to the profit motive.

The cause of our social ills, our essential lovelessness, according to Charles Fourier, lies in "industrial parceling or incoherent labor which is the antipodes of God's designs." "Incoherent labor" is labor that has nothing to do with anybody's real needs or anybody's real humanity. After considering all his data, Fourier concluded that God's design for the human race is to evolve beyond industrial, capitalist civilization.

So the world as we know it must come to an end. The only hope, according to Fourier, is to rise from present civilization to a new tree-centered existence. In a tree-centered postcivilization, work will marry the pleasure principle. Fourier wants to take us back to the tree in the garden of Eden; he wants to undo the curse of ordinary work. Fourier is clear on the purpose of work. The true purpose of work is to afford all people a continual banquet of constantly varying, constantly interesting and delightful experiences. The salvation of humankind is to lift the ban against repression and gratify the *papillon* within, the butterfly principle of novelty.

In the social universe, there are but two choices: force or attraction. One is the distempered product of civilized humanity; the other is the birthright of God and Nature. Fourier and his American disciples rejected civilized humanity: "Voluptuousness is the sole arm which God can employ to master us and lead us to carry out his designs; he rules the universe by Attraction and not by Force; therefore the enjoyments of his creatures are the most important object of the calculations of God."[27]

Fourier's phantastic vision excited the American psyche in the nineteenth century, drawing on the country's deep reservoir of millenarian feeling. In 1843, the year Fourierism took off in America, a hundred national conventions were held on antislavery. A good part of the Northeast was fired up by Millerite expectations of the imminent descent of the New Jerusalem. The spirit of discontent with existing civilization ran high; there was a burning confidence that transformation was not only possible but part of America's manifest destiny. The *New York Herald Tribune* served as Fourier's messianic trumpet and produced a huge amount of propaganda for the cause. Read, for example, the words of a Fourier enthusiast, Parke Godwin, who spoke at a national Convention of Fourier Associationists in New York City, April 4, 1844:

> To the free and Christian people of the United States, then, we commend the principle of Association. . . . The peculiar history of this nation convinces us that it has been prepared by Providence for the working out of glorious issues. Its position, its people, its free institutions, all prepare it for the manifestation of a true social order. Its wealth of territory, its distance from older and corrupter nations, and above all the general intelligence of its people, alike contribute to fit it for that noble union of freemen which we call association. That peculiar constitution of government, which, for the first time in the world's career, was established by our Fathers; that signal fact of our national motto, *E Pluribus Unum*, many individuals united in one whole.[28]

This knits Fourierism into the fabric of the Founding Fathers—the founding visionaries of the nation. The pursuit of happiness becomes the pursuit of association, of passional attraction. America is the place destined to witness to the full this postcivilization power. There were, in the eyes of many, plenty of signs of it rising. In 1844, Whitman was roaming the streets of New York City humming the first tunes of the body electric, while John Humphrey Noyes was gathering disciples in Putney, Vermont, preparing his followers to embrace each other in the healing raptures of complex marriage.

Some people thought Fourier was a madman; I conclude this section with a quote from him illustrating what kind of a madman, namely, messianic. Fortunately, he was more like Nijinsky than Hitler, in the manner of his madness:

> I alone shall have confounded twenty centuries of political imbecility [says our impecunious bachelor clerk], and it is to me alone that present and future generations will owe the initiative of their boundless happiness. Before me, mankind lost several thousand years by fighting madly against Nature; I am the first who has bowed before her, by studying attraction, the organ of her decrees; she has deigned to smile upon the only mortal who has offered incense at her shrine; she has delivered up all her treasures to me. Possessor of the book of Fate, I come to dissipate political and moral darkness, and, upon the ruins of uncertain sciences, I erect the theory of universal harmony.[29]

Art and the Erotic Sense of Reality

In *Eros and Civilization*, Marcuse discredits Prometheus, god of the old workaholic dispensation, substituting a new culture hero, Orpheus. Orpheus embodies a new reality principle—promising a world of song, peace, and pleasure. Orpheus is the prophet of an esthetic Millennium, and art becomes a revolutionary path. Art, however, as a way of cultivating the erotic sense of reality must take us beyond the artwork as cultural fetish and capitalist commodity—beyond the museum as a mausoleum of the "masterpiece." Art, in the Marcusan perspective, is erotic metaphysics in action, a sacred revival of the senses, an awakening of the visionary imagination.

In an article called "Art as a Form of Reality," Marcuse discusses the future of art. Art for Marcuse has a distinctly prophetic function: its job is to indict established civilization and prepare the way for a new erotic-orphic civilization. Art becomes an instrument of prophetic negation, a surrealistic technique for dissolving the dominant cultural ego.

Art—understood by Marcuse as a socially critical activity—gives us images of alternate "form[s] of reality." This, however, means not "the beautification of the given, but the construction of an entirely different and opposed reality." Art, in short, is not a decorative but a truly creative enterprise. Because its job is to construct an entirely different and opposed reality, art is necessarily a revolutionary, a futuristic pursuit. Art is not to help us adapt to the existing world (the beautification of the given) but to create other worlds—a "beauty and truth antagonistic to those of reality."

Art thus becomes eschatology; a pursuit that seeks its own end, its own self-transcendence. Art is a form of reality whose aim is to overcome itself. The end of art will come when for the first time people "see with the eyes of Corot, of Cezanne, of Monet because the perception of these artists has helped to form this reality."[30] Robert Hughes remarks in a related vein about van Gogh: "Art influences nature, and van Gogh's sense of an immanent power behind the natural world was so intense that, once one has seen his Saint-Remy paintings, one has no choice but to see the real places in terms of them."[31] Art assumes a visionary vocation, acquires a prophetic identity as transformer of people's perceptual existence. The work of art is not an end in itself but a sign of the transformation of consciousness, the recreation of reality. Several modern artists stand out for their attempt to bring art to an End—to make art a handmaid to eschatology. Consider a few examples.

Modern art is a project sworn to repudiation of the past, a wiping clean of the Lockean *tabula rasa*. Marcel Duchamp's Mona Lisa with a moustache is the supreme gesture of hyper-esthetic iconoclasm, a way of dispelling the spell of the past, escaping the tyranny of authority, recapturing the innocence of perception. The "masterpiece" becomes a master that the slave must revolt against; the masterpiece becomes the enemy, the violator of innocent perception that must be overthrown.

Marcel Duchamp made a conscious decision to abdicate the gross physicality, the fussy interventionism of traditional art. He despised what he called the "retinal" aspect of art. Art, he said, is an act of the will; to illustrate, he submitted a porcelain urinal to the New York Independents in 1917, signing it with the pseudonym "Mutt." Art is not an object but a position we take toward objects. We saw this hatred of objects and objectivity in the Russians Berdyaev and Kandinsky; the object is a kind of Antichrist to be dissolved in the fire of artistic apocalypse.

By about 1917, Duchamp had given up painting, wishing to create an art strictly for "the mind." For a while he toyed with creating objects that were projections of four dimensions. "I thought, by simple intellectual projection, the fourth dimension could project an object

341

of three dimensions." The painting that made his reputation, *Nude Descending a Staircase*, was an attempt to capture such a projection, which reduced the simple solidity of the object to a cascading display of fluctuating planes of shimmering light.

Every move in his career—and Duchamp made it a religion not to repeat himself—was for the sake of "freedom" or "amusement." "I have had an obsession about not using the same things," he said once in an interview. "One has to be on guard because, despite oneself, one can become invaded by things of the past."[32] Whether in art, philosophy, or prophecy, this obsession with obliterating the past is a recurrent millennial motif. Duchamp was a prophet of the end of art. Art belonged to the dispensation of work, hence Duchamp's notion of "the readymade"—the porcelain urinal, for example, which he titled "Fountain." Instead of painting, he played games, especially chess; his contribution to millenarian eroticism, a fondness for playing chess with nude women, a gesture that combined Shaker detachment from sexuality with the medieval Adamite's scorn of clothing as sign of expulsion from Eden.

Jackson Pollock, like several American avant-gardists, turned to exotic sources of inspiration as a means to overcome the European tradition. Pollock, who came from Wyoming, was influenced by Navaho sandpainters. Like the Navaho, he tried to enter into the image of his painting. He did this by breaking with the European tradition of the easel; Pollock's art—again like the Navaho's—was an art of the earth. "On the floor I am more at ease," he wrote. "I feel nearer, more a part of the painting, since this way I can walk around it, work from the four sides and literally be 'in' the painting. This is akin to the Indian sandpainters of the West."[33] Pollock entered into his painting but was unable, like the Navaho sandpainters, to let the artwork vanish back into its source.

Pollock took another step toward the end of art; he identified his painting with the act of creating it, defining a new movement in modern art called "action painting." Art thus becomes a ritual for the constant recreation of the world and ends by overflowing its traditional boundaries, in Pollock's case by giving up the stationary easel and reentering the archaic space of Native dance and prayer.

The apocalyptic tendency to wipe out boundaries, to merge art and everyday life, dream and reality, is typically American. Pollack is a rerun of Paine's American Revolution—a meta-political event—a meta-art event. American modernism continues in the spirit of Kandinsky and Malevich, Marinetti and Russolo, the impulse toward crashing the gates of heaven by making all-out efforts to break, Marilyn Ferguson-style, from the European past—perhaps from the whole of the human past. Pollock took painting off the easel; he wanted to take it out of the museum and the art gallery where it became a commodity. (He failed in this; American capitalism has a genius for coopting everything, even the apocalypse.) He tried to bring art back to nature and to the vast spaces of the far West—to the free action or gesture of the shaman or vision hunter. He died in a car crash—a futurist death.

John Cage was another American prophet of the end of art. Cage, mycologist and student of Zen, sought to eliminate the difference between music and noise. The distinction between music and noise is as fundamental as the distinction between the self and the not-self. Cage wanted all these boundaries dissolved. For John Cage all noise is music. Like Duchamp, for Cage art is an act of the will—or rather, a willingness to abdicate the will; music is the way you listen to whatever is sounding. The supreme art demands total detachment from the esthetic ego. Random noises recorded at Times Square, New York, become "music" in the same way that Duchamp's urinal becomes a sculpture called "Fountain"; after the end of art, everything becomes art.

By destroying the concept of harmony and the notion of music as such, Cage opened the entire field of experience to art, beauty, and esthetics. Cage, like Pollock, sought through his experiments in randomly produced music to free the listener from the ego, from all conscious expectations of what music is. Cage—like Pollock and Duchamp—went beyond conscious intention toward unconscious spontaneity. Cage, Pollock, Duchamp, by dissolving—deconstructing is the vogue word today—the boundaries between art and nonart, were opening a clearing for an erotic sense of reality, a paradisal restoration of the innocence of the senses. Just as all sounds acquire a musical value—in the freedom of the millennial mind—all encounters with reality become occasions for love.

Ad Reinhardt was another American artist, also interested in Zen, whose paintings were meant to alter the state of consciousness of the viewer. Reinhardt's notorious black paintings were icons of the end of art. Critic Barbara Rose comments, "In order to bring their barely **343** distinguishable pattern into focus and to discriminate their minutely varying hues, it is absolutely necessary to shut out the din and roar, the visual and aural shocks and cacophony of our mundane world of sensory overload."[34] The painting disappears, all that remains is a poised, superdiscriminating eye. In a sentence bursting with paradox, Reinhardt wrote in 1959, "My painting represents the victory of the forces of darkness and peace over the forces of light and evil."

Surrealism was another attempt to shatter mundane perception and descend into creative darkness. Surrealism was an attempt to overthrow the hegemony of the Cartesian linear ego and in its place to exalt "the omnipotence of the dream" and "the disinterested play of thought."[35] Surrealism, with its techniques of "pure psychic automatism" was a latter-day reversion to prophetic possession, a systematic pursuit of a super or "sur" reality. Here is how André Breton defined surreality: "I believe in the future resolution of two states (in appearance so contradictory) dream and reality, into a sort of absolute reality: Surréalité." The unconscious made conscious; the hidden uncovered; in a word, apocalypse.

"And there was no more sea," said Saint John. The sea is sucked up into the light of the surrealist imagination. Surrealism sought to expand the experience of reality, transmute the sea of the unconscious into a new earth. The aim behind liberating the mental automatisms was the apotheosis of chance, a way of creating an erotic sense of reality, which, for example, permitted the surrealist hero Lautreamont to imagine himself copulating with a shark. Every metaphor becomes an act of love; *metaphor*—literally, "a transfer"—a copulation of strange meanings. "The poetic embrace," wrote Breton, "like the carnal while it endures, forbids all lapse into the miseries of the world."[36]

Making the Millennium will require a psychic revolution of the type Denis de Rougement said occurred in twelfth-century Provence. To imagine a new day for the human heart means we have to imagine new methods of seeing the ordinary, new ways of experiencing concrete relationships from moment to moment in daily life. That is the apocalyptic task of the arts.

In the poetics of the Millennium, there emerges a new type of Antichrist. It is Vico's *malizia di riflessione*, "the malice of the reflective mind"; the self-obsessed, carping-captious mind that destroys the *sensus communus*, "the common sense" and shared sensibility that makes life civil and lovely. Vico's "deep solitude of spirit" is what finally destroys a culture in its dying days; the people become litigious and meticulous, narcissistic and cruel. In the end, the fatigued culture "goes mad and wastes its substance." In Vico's eschatology, there is a redeemer—the return of the language of the gods. N. O. Brown calls it "sovereign imagination"—the orphic pacifier of savage souls, the weaver and binder of peoples. Art is the redeemer—the poetic Christ in alliance with the angels of primary thinking—the one who overthrows the autocrats of malicious reason.

Politics and morality give way to art—art understood as the making, the poetry, the nurturing metaphors of the Millennium. In this view that I am inviting you to contemplate, each of us becomes a maker—a *poetes*, or "poet"—of the Millennium. The Millennium is now a work of art, a collective project of the whole human family, in the sense that Walt Whitman said the United States was a great poem. *Verum factum ipsum*, Vico's dictum—truth is poetry. There is no Millennium but the one we call into being poetically. There is no messiah but sovereign imagination. And there is no religion, as William Blake said, but art.

Does this sound crazy, utopian, unrealistic? It is supposed to. The great prophets were crazy; they were seized by powers beyond their control. Crazy is what we need to be in a world dying of rationalism, egoism, scientism. But we are lucky to have Plato to help us remember the distinction between types of madness; there is, for instance, the madness of people who go berserk and shoot everybody in sight—the antipodes of love. There is another kind of madness that we do need, the type of madness Plato calls "god-given."

In Plato's *Phaedrus*, a dialogue about love and language, Socrates makes a remarkable statement. He says that people's greatest blessings arise "through madness" (*dia manias*). And there are four types of god-sent madness—healing, prophetic, artistic, erotic—each conferring a blessing. *Mania* implies ecstasy—being out of one's body— and *ekphron*, being out of one's mind. Art, like love, is a creature of inspiration, an overflow from the wisdom of the unconscious. The makers of modern art—Cage, Duchamp, Breton, Pollock, Reinhardt, and all the rest—each, in their own way, hewed a path to Plato's erotic mania.

There are also traditional channels to experience these sacred energies. We talked (in the chapter on the Russians) about the Orthodox art of the icon, how painted sacred images were used as tools for facilitating grace. Giuseppe Tucci describes the Tibeto-Indian art of the mandala. Tucci calls the mandala a "psychic cosmogram."[37] Mandalas are maps, psychic highways for traveling transcendent planes. Mandalas, often aesthetically fine, are psychic tools for transcending ordinary consciousness.

So are Native sandpaintings, as made by the Navaho, the Papago, the Zuni, the Hopi. A book by David Villasenor, *Tapestries in Sand*, shows how sandpainting is a shamanic healing ritual. The shaman prepares by fasting, self-purification, and eating peyote. Then the paintings are performed; laying down the "paint" is a dance, a shamanic song in color. Each sandpainting is a visual prayer. Images are created by dropping sand, flower pollen, cornmeal, roots, and barks in patterns of snake or star or thunderbird. At rite's end, the painting is destroyed; the materials return to chaos and to nature. The artwork disappears, a traceless gesture of contact with the Great Spirit; Mother Earth sighs with relief—one less piece of clutter to deal with.

Native American sandpainting has apocalyptic overtones. The art object disappears into nature. Art enhances—while it vanishes—into experience. John Dewey's notion of *art as experience*[38] comes to mind. For Dewey, experience, at its human best, is suffused with the esthetic. For Dewey art, as known in the Western world, was at an end. A singularity in art history occurs in the twentieth century: art breaks away from its gallery-and-museum mediated existence and becomes a mode of reality, in the happenings of the sixties and the lalapaloozas of the nineties, a celebration of love's body—a road, an inlet to the American Millennium.

One could talk a great deal more about this struggle to transform art into reality. We might profit, for instance, from a meditative reading of Oscar Wilde's brilliant dialogue *The Decay of Lying*, in which the author laments the loss to society of the fine faculty of imaginative lying. Let me end instead by recalling the Shakers—a people who called themselves "the United Society of Believers in Christ's Second Coming"—a group of spiritual originals led by a poor and oppressed woman, Ann Lee, who arrived in New York on the eve of the American Revolution. It was a group that still boasts of a few faithful followers, heirs to a great American millenarian tradition.

The experience of the Shakers nicely illustrates the relationship between love, art, and the Millennium. First of all, the Shakers excelled in the art of inhibition and tried to live like androgynous angels, single, celibate, communally. The Shakers based their entire philosophy of life, love, and art on the premise that existing civilization was a corrupt and dying animal, and that a new world was emerging. To speed the onset of this world they radically inhibited their sexuality; nevertheless, they learned how to dance with their "dragons." The Shaker dance was an artistic ritual in which they sought to elevate themselves in a spiritual embrace—with each other and with God. It was a daunting spectacle for outsiders.

Observed Hannah Chauncey in 1780, "I saw a Shaker woman who was under great operations of the power of God. She shook and trembled mightily, and was carried here and there, and shook till her hair was thrown everyway. I felt struck. I was afraid it was the way of God, and that I would have to embrace it or never find salvation."[39] The Shaker dance was an ecstatic love-embrace with the divine. In the heyday of the movement, the dances were Dionysian revels; according to Valentine Rathbun, celebrants ran about in the woods in the dead of night, hooting and tooting like owls; "some of them have stripped naked in the woods, and thought they were angels and invisible."[40]

The Shakers surrendered to ecstatic love through dance; they were also masters of the practical and inventive arts. Their lived motto was "Hands to work; hearts to God." The simplicity and perfection of Shaker chairs, furniture, and homes are legendary. An aphorism of Mother Ann's affords a glimpse into the mentality that inspired the Shakers to produce their exquisite handicrafts: "Labor to make the way of God your own. Let it be your inheritance, your treasure, your occupation, your daily calling." It was an attitude that brought hand and heart together to make the art of living suitable, if need be, to visiting angels.

The spirit of the Millennium Myth ran high in those dawn days of the nation. So impressive were the Shakers that Thomas Jefferson wrote enthusiastically of them in 1808: "If their principles are maintained and sustained by a practical life, it is destined eventually to overthrow all other religions."[41] The Shakers were a brilliant example of a community who developed a highly evolved erotic sense of reality, evident in their dance and handicrafts. Love, art, and the Millennium came together in an original way among them; in a modified form, I can imagine the Shaker spirit appealing to spiritually adventurous people sick of today's civilization. But now let us finish with a speculative horse of a very different color.

Cybersex and the Millennium

Cybersex is a recent addition to our vocabulary; it links two themes of the Millennium Myth, love and technology. Cybersex is another case of technocalypse and involves the idea of making love with, to, or through a computer. Coupling love and technology is bound to strike some people as pathetic or downright depraved. John Dvorak, writing for *PC Computing*, thinks machine-mediated sex is the reserve of gynophobic hackers. Says he with genial detachment, "The VR sex concept is also subscribed to by screwballs and insatiable sex fiends who look forward to it as another cheap thrill."[42]

I want to look at cybersex from another perspective. Cybersex may well be something whose time has come, a step toward the American Millennium. Cybersex promises to launch us into a world of pure erotic imagination. As I write, of course, the incredibly sensitive technology required for serious, wired love is a long way off. Of course, breakthroughs in technology occur nowadays faster than most people expect, so instead of wondering when this might happen, let us try to imagine how it might happen; let us, in short, discuss the concept of cybersex as it relates to the millennial phantasies of humankind. Oddly enough, the concept of an electronic extension of sexual experience converges with the old idea of a light, or resurrection, body. Shocking as such a prospect may appear, cybersex offers a technology for entry into a paradise of expanded eroticism.

The first component is telepresence. Telepresence implies being present to each other across space and time. Television, for example, involves visual telepresence; the telephone, auditory telepresence. The latter is crucial for any cybersex that wishes to be more than onanistic; the telephone takes us out of ourselves and allows us to interact with others. The videophone is a further step along the way, combining the interactiveness of visual and auditory telepresence.

But the crucial extension is tactile interactive telepresence. (I omit discussion of the olfactory and the gustatory for the moment, but true cybersex will not be satisfied without them.) Love is about feeling, and the physical prototype of feeling is touch, the most intimate of the senses. If the Italian engineer Danilo de Rossi keeps working on his "smart skin,"[43] it will one day be possible to touch, stroke, fondle, and caress each other with the help of our Apple or PC hardware;

across space-time, we will enter a world of wired intimacy. It will all be available online in the LoveNet of the future.

Virtual reality (VR) will make possible a complete immersion in synthetic space. We will not only see, hear, and touch each other but be immersed in a complete, synthetic world of the erotic imagination. VR adds yet another dimension to the future of dalliance—in cybersex our personae will be as multiple as imagination permits or as desire decrees. Since cyberspace exists in its own dimension, all customary rules of identity, morality, and legality will vanish in the hum of your hard disk. Bodies that sexually meet in cyberspace will be electronic, or perhaps, photonic; they will occupy their own space, exist in a parallel imaginal universe. They will be bodies that represent us to our partners; as in the world of art, they will be *expressive* bodies, whose sole and whole reason for being will be erotic. They will have no other purpose and be bound by no other obligations than to serve as vehicles for cybersex.

It follows that the phenomenal features of our cyberbodies may be completely revised. Again, on the reasonable assumption that technology will eventually find a way, we will have it in our power to select from a repertoire of cyberbodies to represent ourselves in any number of possible amative adventures and relationships. The menu of possibilities makes precybersex look positively dowdy by comparison. We could, for example, customize our cyberbodies according to archetype, celebrity, historic personage, idealized versions of ourselves, and for those who wish to indulge, the monstrous, and the nonhuman. (Zeus, you might recall, ravished Leda in the form of a swan, which might make an attractive cyberscene for the classically minded.) Choice of gender will also be optional; so will concealing or revealing our real-world ID. For the highly motivated, it will be possible to develop a rich repertoire of encryption cybererotic personae.

Cybersex may well become a millenarian craze in America, for the appeals are many. Those who, like John Humphrey Noyes, distinguish the amative and social from the propagative function of sex will welcome it; cybersex would free the amative and social function, while the risk of unwanted pregnancy would be eliminated. In fact, anybody concerned with overpopulation is bound to look forward to the coming of cybersex with more than a bit of enthusiasm. I can imagine massive campaigns to introduce cybersex (at the moment a utopian idea) in the underdeveloped areas of the world where exploding population is a menace. Even if a modest percentage of the population converted from real to surreal cybersex, the benefits would be significant. Cybersex technology, in a millennial society, would promote cybersexual education; the values promoted could be planet enhancing, soul enhancing, and life enhancing.

An obvious reason people will find cybersex appealing is the fear of sexually contagious diseases. Cybersex is the last word in safe sex. Without fear of contracting AIDS or other ills, it will be possible to abandon ourselves to the infinite world of the amative. All restraints will fall away, and the old, the infirm, the ugly, the shy, the underendowed, and the morbidly frightened will, assuming they can muster a quantum of imaginal energy, be able to join in a Dionysian revel or hurl themselves into a Wagnerian *Walpurgisnacht*—and all this, assuming Barlow and Kapor's Electronic Freedom Foundation does its job, for a pittance—or I should say, for a pixel.

The mental health of the nation would also improve; for we could explore the impulses and phantasies we repress in our world of civilized discontent. What a boon to humankind, to be able to virtually act out what might in reality destroy our lives. We could pursue these imaginal journeys incognito or wallow in rank exhibitionism—and after a fling in the parallel universe, return to the serenity of our chosen family life style. Conventional life might become very exciting, or at any rate, comfortably tolerable, once we knew that an infinitely expanded virtual life was available online.

Cybersex will allow us to experience varying degrees of intimacy and self-disclosure; and there will always be the chance of our cyberventures leading to relationships in real space and time. Virtual relationships may serve as practice for real relationships. (The day may come when real space-time relationships seem quaint.) In any case, the utopian aspiration of living an unrepressed life, of living our polymorphous potentialities gains an ally in cybersex.

Is cybersex the unconscious goal of telecommunications? The techno-analogue to the celestial city of the Millennium dream? The apex of endeavor that began with the paleolithic cave paintings of Lascaux and the Rubenesque goddess figurines? Perhaps the end of civilized unrest will come when we build a virtual Noah's Ark, a New Jerusalem of the imagination, a place where we can strip (or don playfully) our masks and meet in the fullness and openness of being.

History, in that case, would be the tortuous spiral leading from the Venus of Willendorf to the chiliastic climax of the LoveNet.

The Threshold of the Infinite

Love and sex in the next millennium? I considered six elements based on the prophetic phantasies of past and present—a short inventory of love at the frontiers of the possible. The first candidate dealt with the will. The will was central to the humanistic Renaissance. In a humanistic Millennium, passive faith yields to active will.

There is a reason why even in the midst of love's raptures, the will, somewhere in the quiet depths of our being, must at all times be on call: the will is essential to an important type of love I have yet to mention specifically, at least not by its Greek name, *agape*. Agape is spiritual, universal love. Unlike Eros, agape proceeds not from the need to take but from the will to give; and unlike philia or friendship, it is impartial and unconditional. There are times when "attraction" fails, but love is still mandated; then the will must act against inclination. Because agape is based neither on need nor self-interest, it is the form of love that most clearly seems to mirror the "divine" aspect of human potential. Agape, in a sense, is the freest form of love; nevertheless, I believe it is incomplete without some tincture of Eros and philia. Spiritual love bereft of the earthy warmth of Eros and of the sociableness of philia would, in the long run, prove insufficient, even a danger.

If a Renaissance restoration of will is the first inner step to utopian love, the first institution that must be radically revised is marriage. According to our consultants—Jesus and Plato, the Marquis de Sade, and John Humphrey Noyes—there is something deeply flawed about the traditional mating habits of human beings. In the Golden Age dreamed of by the prophets, our amative potential will no longer be restricted to the selfish interests of family or the bio-compulsions of propagation but will overflow the boundaries of all narrow and confining relationships.

Love will fill our lives when we are full—complete human beings ourselves. The Myth says there is a source of completeness within; after all, we are made in the image and likeness of God. Like the angels, we are, at our divine core, beyond sex—that is, containing all the qualities of both sexes. In Plato's *Symposium*, in the gnostic Gospel according to Thomas—in a long underground tradition—androgyny is the guiding metaphor for this state of being, this place inside ourselves that transcends the one-sidedness of sectarian sex. Our androgynous, polymorphous plenitude is the psychic basis of spiritual freedom and generosity, without which we remain forever disposed to be takers rather than givers.

As we kindle the spark of this many-sided soulfulness within, it becomes easier to negotiate the world of institutions. The Millennium Myth, from the beginning, has called for the end of our conventional institutions, particularly such bastions of the status quo as marriage. All the prophets agree, marriage is a roadblock to the Millennium. Work is the second institution in need of radical revision. Work must cease to be a soulless activity, divorced from pleasure, creativity, dignity, and real human needs, as it has been for the majority of people since civilization began. Too long has humankind been forced to live under the yoke of economic necessity and the spur of savage competition.

Since the first cities were built in the ancient Near East, human beings have been forced to eke out a hard-scrabble existence that leaves neither time nor energy to spend on cultivating a loving or a lovely existence. With the Promethean "mastery" of nature in essence complete, there ought to be sufficient goods for all of us to pursue the happiness that love, liberated, promises. The obstacle is the manner in which the goods we extract on loan from nature are used, shared, and distributed.

This, of course, boils down to the pathologies of politics. Why self-defeating selfishness instead of cooperation and common decency? Why the ruling class instead of unclassifiable originality? The answer, as I gather it from thinkers who range from Friedrich Schiller to Ernest Becker, is as simple as it is profound: for reasons both deep and devious, we are ignorant of the art of enjoying the present. We cannot see a world in a grain of sand, as William Blake did, or a heaven in a wildflower. Because of this blindness to the presence of the present, this inability to "hold infinity" in the palm of our hands, we are forever in quest of the Great Something Else—whether material goods, or power to awe and dominate the other, or kudos and credits for afterworlds to come. The remedy is art. To open our senses to the gifts of the present is the millenarian task of the arts—the true religions of the soul and the enemies of empire and tyranny.

The last issue addressed was techno-futuristic. We are, as Marshall McLuhan said, wired together in a quasi-telepathically linked global village. This affords imaginative seekers of enhanced life an enormous field for exploration. And yet, cyberspace, like every other technology invented by our species, is a Janus-faced wonder. We may use it for ill or for good, create a network for Antichrist or a vestibule to the new heaven and earth.

Marsilio Ficino was right: the appetite for experience, for reality, for love, is all-sided and unlimited. This appetite to transcend humanity—*trashumanar*, as Dante put it—cannot be reduced to words or explained by concepts. But it drives us on, nevertheless, as it drives the Millennium Myth. Arthur C. Clarke enriched the Myth with his view of the next step in the evolution of cyberspace: the machine will etherialize itself by merging with our bodies. Then, but for the physical trappings and underpinnings of technology, we will attain a godlike ability to explore infinity.

But could this be the last step? Not if Hegel, prophet of the American Millennium was right; the last stage of history will be a journey toward freedom. Nor if Joachim was right, who saw the end of history as freedom from fear and all oppressive institutions. Anyone who cherished this ideal of the End would never be content with a wired paradise. If anything, the Millennium Myth shows we are not likely to be content with anything. No matter how far we travel, the eyes of imagination will see another bend in the road of time; whatever satisfaction the heart discovers will whet desire for something new. The odyssey is eternal; the End is always beginning.

Conclusion:
The Meaning of the
Millennium Myth

Are all nations communing?
Is there going to be but one heart to the globe?

WALT WHITMAN
Years of the Modern

So, the story of the Millennium Myth is far from finished. It is still a telling force in our lives. Where is it leading us? Is it going to bring us together or rip us apart? After six thousand years of history, we are prompted to ask with Walt Whitman, Is there any hope of people "communing" or of the globe discovering its "one heart"?

I believe that the Millennium Myth touches the globe's "one heart," touches our common aspiration for all that is good and life enhancing. I am convinced that streaming through the history of the Myth is a living force that secretly connects all traditions, all peoples, all souls. Thus, in touching this force, we touch the soul of humanity.

In tracing the highlights and byways of the Myth, I found that the American dream is steeped in ancient prophecy. The American dream goes back a long way, through its land and great-spirited Native peoples; through the democratic Reformation, the optimistic Enlightenment, the creative Renaissance, the mystic Middle Ages; through the master millenarian Jesus, the inspired Jewish prophets, the generous Iranian Zarathustra, the dauntless Sumerian Gilgamesh, and back, I believe, to those Neanderthal proto-people who buried their dead in sleeping postures, thus obscurely expressing the hope that one day they would awaken from death to new life.

The Millennium Myth is a report on the human psyche's passion for regeneration, its desire to shatter the chains of death and, in Dante's phrase, to "imparadise" our minds with love. Modern science and technology give this passion a new lease on life. Suddenly, we find ourselves in an evolving universe in which novelty and breakthrough are the rule, a universe in which time is a creative genius, the universe itself a place for producing miracles.

We seem to be rushing dreamlike toward fulfilling, in reality-twisting ways, the phantasies of the Millennium. Indeed, when we look about and survey the big picture, we see signs of all manner of futuristic forces of transformation. Winding restlessly through the centuries from the Book of Daniel to the Renaissance, from the Enlightenment to the present, has been the idea that knowledge would one day enable our species to recreate nature and, above all, to regenerate human reality.

Glancing backwards in time, one reels at the distances covered, the dizzying velocity of change. A thousand years ago, people lived on Earth in total ignorance of the possibility of H bombs, VCRs, cryonics, chaos and complexity theory, bioengineering, virtual reality, nanotechnology, ten-dimensional space, and a good deal more that lay shrouded in the shadows of the future.

But now consider this. Since knowledge is increasing exponentially, we can expect that in the *next* thousand years new quantum leaps of progress lie in store for us. Will they make those of the last look lame by comparison? Will they carry us closer to realizing the dream of a new resurrection, of a new Teilhardian genesis in which the energies of love are at last harnessed in the creation of a new world?

The Myth is a map of our possible futures, a storehouse of chronic dreams forever seeking to embody themselves. It is as if we are standing at a door that is slightly ajar, a bright light streaming in—a door that leads to a landscape of marvels, perhaps (say the wilder visionaries), even a passageway into a new dimension. Those who have peeked through this door say we should brace ourselves for what is coming. We may even beat the last enemy, they say. John Humphrey Noyes said that death can be abolished, but only through love and what he called the "resurrection power." The postmodern techno-pagans of the Flame Foundation also thought life extension possible through deepening intimacy. So one of the great meanings of the Myth is, perhaps, that love itself is the answer to death, Eros the sole power to charm Thanatos.

And yet, there is also a dark side to a Myth that, as we have seen, can cast dangerous spells on zealous believers. So we have our homework cut out for us. We have to learn to see through our divine fictions, nurture the vision, avoid the danger.

One danger is that, in the pursuit of our bliss, we dehumanize each other. To see how this works, study the Book of Revelation. In that fateful scripture, contactee John of Patmos imagines pure, alien evil in the form of an old serpent. Comparison with other mythic takes on the serpent is instructive. The Chinese Zen tradition, the Greek Asklepian tradition, the Tantric kundalini tradition, all see the serpent as a primal generative force, the priapic sap that flows through the tree of creation. In Mesopotamia, China, India, Greece, Africa, and the New World, the serpent is a figure of tantalizing ambiguity, sometimes sinister and bewitching, but more often a pointer to the creative, the evolutionary forces of nature.

The Book of Revelation, at odds with this great symbol of vitality, equates the serpent with Satan (the adversary) and with the Devil (the deceiver), and it does so in no uncertain terms. This may make for fine drama but sets a time bomb for eschatology. According to the logic of the image, the Millennium—in other words, the goal of Western history—will only come about by burying the serpent in the "bottomless pit," by binding and placing under lock and key the great life force.

In a way, the Book of Revelation is one of the world's most dangerous documents, for John's image of evil, and its seductive theatrics, lends itself to creating climates of suspicion and rancor toward, well, *other* people—toward anybody we happen to imagine is our enemy. Something, in fact, seems to have been lost in this book, a falling off from what D. H. Lawrence once called the "aristocratic spirit of love" of Jesus; something else has reared its head, a more vindictive spirit that revels in visions of sheer triumphalism. What turns Saint John on are images, not of love, but of victory and power. A Christ unknown to Paul or to the Gospels says these chilling words: "And he that overcomes, and keeps my works unto the end, to him will I give power over the nations. And he shall rule them with a rod of iron; as the vessels of a potter shall they be broken to shivers" (Rev. 2:26–27).

What leaps out here is an unvarnished Nietzschean will to power. Vengeance, not forgiveness, is the mental climate of the Book of Revelation, and Saint John's mentality—I hesitate to say it—has more in common with Adolf Hitler than with Jesus. One looks in vain for words of mercy or compassion in this text, the last canonical word of Christianity. The Book of Revelation might very well appeal to people who want to simplify their map of the moral universe. A yea or a nay—so easy. Unfortunately, John's phantasy lends itself to some pretty nasty habits of heart and mind, as we found in the discussion of Communist Russia and Nazi Germany. The disturbing fact is that the same barbarous mentality is alive and well today, in the new tribal warfare, in the plague of "ethnic cleansing," and in the growing pestilence of "hate crimes."

The habit of dualizing and demonizing the other pervades our mental life. An aspirin for ontological panic, it helps focus existential rage on simple, clear targets. But, need I utter the obvious? The real world is an infinitely fluid, nuanced, and fine-textured place. To understand the problem, we have to note something about language itself—or rather, about the way we use language—its unwitting proneness to filter (and lacerate) experience with crude abstractions. No wonder the mystics urge us to lay off the psycho-babble; no wonder we need poets to shatter the clichés of consciousness.

Let's face it; Saint John's image of the Millennium, which splits the universe in moral halves, is seriously flawed. It is the product of a primitive mind, and however beautiful it may be in a gothic way, is a thick-headed oversimplification. Once you apply it to real events and real life, it blinds perception and ends by ratifying the use of violence. John's map to the Millennium is worse than misleading; its attitude of loveless intolerance, its brutal aspiration for power and judgment, poison the creative power of the Myth.

Recall again the key verses: "And I saw an angel come down from heaven, having the key of the bottomless pit and a great chain in his hand. And he laid hold on the dragon, that old serpent, which is the Devil, and Satan, and bound him a thousand years" (Rev. 20:1–2). Let us, as we said, suppose that the serpent symbolizes our creative power. In that case, our mythic legacy puts us at odds with the best part of ourselves.

Writer Arthur Koestler[1] and neuroscientist Paul MacLean have much to say about human neurosis, in which they see "a paranoid streak" busily at work. This paranoid streak is based on a kind of schizoid fracture in our poorly evolved neural apparatus. The reptilian brain is off on its own, incommunicado with the neocortex—our "new" thinking cap. In short, ideas and emotions are out of synch; conscious and unconscious are strangers to each other. The neocortical ego strikes a pose, keeps a stiff upper lip, and will not talk with the reptilian id—that monster John called the *ophos archaios*, the old serpent, which, for all future paranoiacs, he dubbed His Satanic Majesty.

The devil is also called a dragon. The dragon is a fabulous beast, a serpent with wings. As such, it suggests the marriage of earth and heaven. The dragon symbolizes the Tao, the harmony of yin and yang, the dance of Shiva and Shakti, the coincidence of opposites. The dragon, thus seen in a more congenial, Eastern light, turns into a symbol of synthesis, of dialogue between the new and the old brain. As such I take the dragon to be a fine image of the future of human evolution. John's error, then, is worse than we thought. Not only did he create the perfect myth for compulsive dualizers and demonizers, but he hobbled, by indulging in dragon baiting, any hope of improvement. Obviously, if the dragon symbolizes our evolutionary future, we need to embrace it, not ban it from consciousness. In short, the Book of Revelation, by divorcing us from the wisdom of the dragon, becomes a stumbling block to our spiritual evolution.

What to do about it? A place to begin is to work through the images of the Millennium, to meditate upon and enter into their living spirit, to make contact with and thus possess their power instead of letting their power possess us. But to manage this, we need to learn to talk with the old dragon-serpent within. A gesture of politeness will do for starters. The key is conversation—learning the language of the dragon. I call this kind of conversation soulmaking; it involves bringing to life, and somehow creatively embracing, the demons of our personal and mythical past.

So Saint John got it all wrong. The lesson we have to learn is not to repress, alienate, or imprison but to irrepress, make friends with, and liberate the old dragon. This, I reckon, is the way to free ourselves from what Jung called the Shadow—all the dark, slithery stuff inside us that makes us cringe with embarrassment and that we try to reject and want to disown.

Instead of trying to overpower the dragon-serpent, let there be a dance; instead of rape, rapture. The Hindu serpent signifies kundalini, the Shakti or Goddess energy. Bedeviled John not only tried to crush irrepressible phallic magic but—foolish man—dared to scorn the Goddess. Where has the Goddess been all these millennia? Is it not time to recant, to undo this malediction against the fullness of life? Instead then of binding, let us unbind the Shakti-serpent, for unbinding is the prelude to the dance, and the dance is all there is.

And let neurology help us revise the Revelator's image of evil. Let there be dialogue between the neocortex and the reptilian brain. The possibilities are infinite. Every moment of our lives, every time we find ourselves eye to eye with the other, opportunity for divine dialogue knocks. If John of Patmos had known some neurology, he might have avoided his blunder, and history might have been a different story, sung to a sweeter tune. John forgot that each of us *is* a serpent, a coiled kundalini-charged spinal cord, a ripple of life force, and, yes, attached to a brain, that marvel of marvels, that problem of problems. The brain is a brilliant upstart with a tendency to forget the snake that bore it. So, in working through these millennial images, let us drop the pose of neocortical superiority and assume some reptilian humility. And instead of pitching him into the bottomless pit—a gesture incompatible with polite dialogue—why not a little sympathy for the devil? Even Jesus said, "Be ye wise as serpents," thus honoring the wisdom of the serpent.

Like Gilgamesh, we have been on a long journey, and the question now is, What conclusion shall we write on our stone tablets?

First of all, I would say, we are riding a time wave toward the Eschaton. Utter amazement may lie just around the corner. The signs of the times say that something very strange is indeed afoot, that this time it is for real, that we really are about to take a quantum leap in our very mode of existence on Earth. Joachim said it eight hundred years ago: the New People are coming. Like it or not, we are swept up in waves of transformation, and we are poised (let us hope) for a new Renaissance, a new Enlightenment.

If we take our cue from the Millennium Myth, the war between the real and the ideal promises to come to an end, and we can expect the New Jerusalem to descend from heaven and wrap her gorgeous arms around the Earth in a great nuptial embrace. If the Myth be our guide, people will pursue that perfect embrace in the decades and centuries to come—the eternal quest to heal the breach between body and soul, sex and spirit, male and female, time and eternity, and science and religion.

The Myth is carrying us toward a fabulous future. The voice of timeless urges, it tells us it is okay to dream of heaven, it is okay to expect miracles. It signals us to detonate the divine spark within; it kicks us toward creativity, shouts to us that the universe is a theater where nothing is impossible. The Millennium Myth says we are made in the image and likeness of Something Divine, hence are destined to snuff death and grow into love's light-body.

If the drive toward metamorphosis is as powerful as the millennial data indicate, there can be no stopping our pursuit of happiness through the effort to evolve our minds and bodies. It is futile to deny Pico's "ambition" for omnipotentiality. Our true future lies in the hands of artists, scientists, shamans, poets, lovers, dreamers, mystics, all the people who want to unlock the treasure trove of our godlike potential—the people at the fringes, dreaming impossible dreams; the space colonizers; psychedelic eschatologists; mapmakers of inner worlds; explorers of hyperspace and cyberspace; brain machinists; smart-food farmers; Platonic-Tantric dragon masters; wiccan whole-brainers; the entire motley tribe of reality hackers; indeed, everyone and anyone who wants to push beyond present dysfunctional humanity toward becoming New People in a new universe.

In the end, the meaning of the Millennium Myth depends on us, on the ways we put flesh and color on the vision and make it come true in our lives. Moreover, the meaning of the Myth is evolving, just as we are evolving. What is clear is that this immense project of the soul to shake the foundations and reach for the stars refuses, in spite of all setbacks, to go gently into the night. All the data of human experience lies before us; we can use it to build a highway to heaven—or to hell.

Notes

Introduction

1. Clifford Linedecker, *Massacre at Waco, Texas* (New York: Saint Martin's Press, 1992), xv.

2. See the discussion of Tom Paine in chapter 6.

3. Paul's First Letter to the Corinthians helps us understand the extent that extreme psychic phenomena were rampant in the early Christian communities. Paul sounds a moderating note, suggesting that the most important gift of the spirit is love.

4. Eusebius, *History of the Church* (London: Dorset Press, 1984), vol. 16.

5. Harry C. Schnur, *Mystic Rebels* (New York: Beechhurst Press, 1949).

6. Schnur, *Mystic Rebels*, 218–19.

7. Melford Spiro, *Buddhism and Society* (New York: Harper & Row, 1970).

8. Chapter 10 examines the notion of *technocalypse*.

9. See Hal Lindsey, *The Late Great Planet Earth* (New York: Bantam, 1973). A runaway bestseller that feeds the phantastic imagination of endtime.

10. Grace Halsell, *Prophecy and Politics* (Chicago: Lawrence Hill Books, 1986). See section, "The Saved Will Be Raptured," 36–39.

11. Robert I. Friedman, "Revenge," *Village Voice*, 20 November 1990.

12. Bernard McGinn, *Visions of the End: Apocalyptic Traditions in the Middle Ages* (New York: Columbia University Press, 1979), 10.

Chapter One ◆ *Origins of the Great Vision*

1. Carl G. Jung, *Aion* (Princeton: Princeton University Press, 1968), 264.

2. James M. Robinson, ed., "The Gospel of Thomas," in *The Nag Hammadi Library* (San Francisco: Harper & Row, 1978), 117–31.

3. In chapter 12.

4. See Friedrich Nietzsche, *Beyond Good and Evil* (New York: Modern

Library, 1927) and Max Scheler, *Ressentiment* (New York: Schocken Books, 1972).

5. Wallace Budge, *Egyptian Magic* (Secaucus, N.J.: Citadel Press, 1978).

6. R. H. Charles, *Eschatology* (New York: Schocken Books, 1963), 403.

7. Halsell, *Prophecy and Politics*, 39.

8. For a good anthology, see S. Scott Rogo, *Mind Beyond the Body* (New York: Penguin Books, 1978). For a detailed discussion of Paul's conversion experience and its psychic component, see Michael Grosso, *Frontiers of the Soul* (Wheaton, Ill.: Quest Books, 1992). See especially the chapter on Saint Paul and the near-death experience.

9. See the discussions in chapters 10 and 11.

10. Weston La Barre, *They Shall Take Up Serpents: Psychology of a Southern Snake-Handling Cult* (New York: Schocken Books, 1969).

11. Berthold Schwarz, "Ordeal by Serpents, Fire, and Strychnine," *Psychic-Nexus* (New York: Van Nostrand, 1980), 3–24.

12. James Mooney, *The Ghost-Dance Religion* (Chicago: University of Chicago Press, 1965).

13. The term used for apocalyptic writings with mythical authors, a device for remaining anonymous.

14. Duncan Greenlees, *The Gospel of Zarathustra* (Wheaton, Ill.: Theosophical Publishing House, 1978), 147. My discussion of the Zoroastrian apocalypse relies heavily on this book.

15. Greenlees, *Zarathustra*, 141.

16. Greenlees, *Zarathustra*, lxxxix.

17. T. S. Eliot, "Four Quartets," *The Complete Poems and Plays* (New York: Harcourt, Brace & Co., 1968), 145.

18. Mircea Eliade, *Cosmos and History: The Myth of the Eternal Return* (New York: Harper Torchbooks, 1959). See especially chapter 2, "The Regeneration of Time." Also Alexander Heidel, *The Babylonian Genesis* (Chicago: University of Chicago Press, 1951).

Chapter Two ◆ *Joachim of Fiore: Prophet of the New Age*

1. Augustine, *The City of God*, ed. David Knowles (New York: Penguin Books, 1980). See Book XX, chapters 7–9, 906–18.

2. Bernard McGinn, ed., *Apocalyptic Spirituality* (New York: Paulist Press, 1979), 85.

3. Norman Cohn, *Pursuit of the Millennium* (New York: Oxford University Press, 1961), 108.

4. McGinn, *Apocalyptic Spirituality*, 99.

5. McGinn, *Apocalyptic Spirituality*, 99.

6. Carl Löwith, *Meaning in History* (Chicago: University of Chicago Press, 1958). See 145–59 and Appendix 1, "Modern Joachism."

7. McGinn, *Apocalyptic Spirituality*, 105.

8. McGinn, *Apocalyptic Spirituality*, 101.

9. Leonardo Boff, *Saint Francis: A Model for Human Liberation* (New York: Crossroad, 1984), 155.

10. G. G. Coulton, *From Saint Francis to Dante* (London: David Nutt, 1906), 55.

11. Jacopone da Todi, *Le Laude* (Firenze: Libreria Editrice Fiorentina, 1955), 200.

12. Leo Sherley-Price, *St. Francis of Assisi: His Life and Writings as Recorded by his Contemporaries* (London: Mowbray, 1969), 28.

13. Max Weber, *The Protestant Ethic and the Spirit of Capitalism* (New York: Charles Scribner's Sons, 1958).

14. Cohn, *Pursuit of the Millennium*. See especially chapter 3, "The Messianism of the Disoriented Poor."

15. See Richard Kieckhefer, *Repression of Heresy in Medieval Germany* (Philadelphia: University of Pennsylvania Press, 1979). See especially chapter 3, "The War Against Beghards and Beguines."

16. Marjorie Reeves, *The Influence of Prophecy in the Later Middle Ages* (Oxford: Clarendon Press, 1969), 248.

17. Kieckhefer, *Repression of Heresy*, 22.

18. Vincent Bugliosi, *Helter Skelter* (New York: Bantam, 1974), 292.

19. Herbert Marcuse, *Eros and Civilization* (Chicago: University of Chicago Press, 1958). See chapter 12 for a further discussion of Eros and the Millennium.

20. Löwith, *Meaning in History*. See Appendix 1, "Modern Transfigurations of Joachism."

21. See R. Hinton Thomas, *The Classical Ideal in German Literature* (Cambridge: Bowes and Bowes, 1939), 35.

Chapter Three ♦ The Renaissance: World Renovation Through Arts and Sciences

1. Jacob Burckhardt, *The Civilization of the Renaissance in Italy* (New York: Harper Torchbooks, 1958), vol.1, 15.

2. Burckhardt, *Civilization*, 303.

3. See James Hillman's important *Revisioning Psychology* (New York: Harper & Row, 1975). See also Thomas Moore, *The Planets Within: The Astrological Psychology of Marsilio Ficino* (Great Barrington, Mass.: Lindisfarne Press, 1990).

4. Reeves, *Influence of Prophecy*, 429.

5. Reeves, *Influence of Prophecy*, 429.

6. Reeves, *Influence of Prophecy*, 439.

7. A. Chastel, quoted in Reeves, *Influence of Prophecy*, 430.

8. For a discussion of this, see Eugenio Garin, *Italian Humanism* (Oxford: Basil Blackwell, 1965), 90.

9. Friedrich Schleiermacher, *On Religion* (New York: Harper Torchbooks, 1958).

10. Charles Trinkaus, *In Our Image and Likeness: Humanity and Divinity in Italian Humanist Thought* (Chicago: University of Chicago Press, 1970).

11. Bruno Snell, *The Discovery of the Mind* (New York: Harper Torchbooks, 1960).

12. This and the remaining quotes in this section are from Trinkaus, *In Our Image*, vol. 2.

13. This and the following quotations are from Ficino's *Theologica Platonica*. They are taken from chapter 9 in Trinkaus (*In Our Image*, vol. 2), to whom I am indebted for guidance and for making available materials which were difficult to come by.

14. "Five Questions Concerning the Mind," in *The Renaissance Philosophy of Man*, eds. Ernst Cassirer, Paul Oscar Kristeller, and John Herman Randall (Chicago: University of Chicago Press, 1948), 211.

15. Cassirer et al., *Renaissance Philosophy*, 210.

16. Pico della Mirandola, *Oration on the Dignity of Man* (New York: Bobbs-Merrill, 1940).

17. Mirandola, *Oration*, 20.

18. Frances Yates, *Giordano Bruno and the Hermetic Tradition* (New York: Vintage Books, 1964), 156.

19. G. S. Kirk and J. E. Raven, *The Presocratic Philosophers* (Cambridge: Harvard University Press, 1957), 229.

20. I owe this excellent word to my old classics professor Moses Hadas.

21. Eliade, *Cosmos and History*, 9.

22. Frank Manuel and Fritzie Manuel, *Utopian Thought in the Western World* (Cambridge: Harvard University Press, 1979), 154.

23. Manuel and Manuel, *Utopian Thought*, 158.

24. Frances Yates, *The Art of Memory* (Chicago: University of Chicago Press, 1966). See chapter 6.

25. Yates, *Art of Memory*, 132.

26. Manuel and Manuel, *Utopian Thought*, 160.

27. Lorenzo Valla, *On Pleasure* (New York: Abaris Books, 1977), 37.

28. John Addington Symonds, *Renaissance in Italy: The Revival of Learning* (New York: Henry Holt, 1908), 521.

29. Girolamo Savonarola, "The Compendium of Revelations," in *Apocalyptic Spirituality*, ed. McGinn, 238.

30. Niccolò Machiavelli, *The Prince & Selected Discourses* (New York: Bantam, 1966), 106.

31. McGinn, *Apocalyptic Spirituality*, 279.

32. McGinn, *Apocalyptic Spirituality*, 267.

33. In Pasquale Villari, *Life and Times of Savonarola* (London: T. Fisher Unwin, 1939), vol. 2, 388.

34. McGinn, *Apocalyptic Spirituality*, 197.

35. Paolo Rossi, *Philosophy, Technology and the Arts in the Modern Era* (New York: Harper Torchbooks, 1970), 101–2.

Chapter Four ◆ *The Enlightenment: Progess and the Millennium*

1. Mircea Eliade, *The Two and the One* (New York: Harper Torchbooks, 1962). See especially the chapter, "Experiences of the Mystic Light," 19–77.

2. Carl L. Becker, *The Heavenly City of the Eighteenth-Century Philosophers* (New Haven: Yale University Press, 1948), 43.

3. Condorcet, "Sketch for a Historical Picture of the Progress of the Human Mind," in *French Philosophers: From Descartes to Sartre*, ed. Leonard Marsak (New York: Meridian Books, 1970), 265–82.

4. Benjamin Franklin, *The Autobiography and Other Writings* (New York: Penguin Books, 1986), 255.

5. Becker, *Heavenly City*, 145.

6. Marsak, *French Philosophers*, 267.

7. Manuel and Manuel, *Utopian Thought*, 497.

8. Manuel and Manuel, *Utopian Thought*, 507.

9. Denis Diderot, *Oeuvres* (1876), vol. XVIII, 100–101.

10. Immanuel Kant, *Groundwork of the Metaphysics of Morals* (New York: Harper Torchbooks, 1956), 85.

11. Garry Wills, *Inventing America* (New York: Doubleday, 1978), 254.

12. Francis Birrell, ed., *Denis Diderot: Dialogues* (New York: Capricorn Books, 1969), 117–18.

13. Sidney Hook, ed., *The Essential Thomas Paine* (New York: Free America Press, 1968), viii.

14. Christopher Dawson, *The Gods of Revolution* (New York: Minerva Press, 1975), 45.

15. Thomas Paine, *Rights of Man*, vol. 7 of *Collected Works* (New Rochelle, N.Y.: Thomas Paine National Historical Association, 1925).

16. John A. Garratry and Peter Gay, eds., *The Columbia History of the World* (New York: Harper & Row, 1972), 771.

17. A key notion in Vico's work, similar to Jung's collective unconscious.

18. Quoted in Löwith, *Meaning and History*.

Chapter Five ◆ *Yankee New Jerusalem*

1. John Noble Wilford, *The Mysterious History of Columbus* (New York: Alfred A. Knopf, 1991), 216.

2. See Pauline Moffitt Watts, "Prophecy and Discovery: On the Spiritual Origins of Christopher Columbus's 'Enterprise of the Indies,'" in *American Historical Review* 90 (February 1985); and Delno C. West, *Joachim of Fiore in Christian Thought: Essays on the Influence of the Calabrian Prophet* (New York: Princeton University Press, 1975).

3. Quoted from a personal communication in Wilford, *Mysterious History*, 225.

4. James H. Moorhead, *American Apocalypse* (New Haven: Yale University Press, 1978), x.

5. William Bradford, *Of Plymouth Plantation: 1620–1647* (New York: Alfred A. Knopf, 1963), 3–10.

6. Bradford, *Plymouth Plantation*, 58.

7. Bradford, *Plymouth Plantation*, 62.

8. In Thomas Wertenbaker, *The First Americans* (New York: Macmillan, 1927), 94.

9. Wertenbaker, *First Americans*, 94.

10. Cotton Mather, *Magnalia*, I., 266.

11. Philip Gura, *A Glimpse of Sion's Glory* (Middletown, Conn.: Wesleyan University Press, 1984), 91.

12. Gura, *Glimpse*, 53.

13. Gura, *Glimpse*, 80.

14. For a discussion of this see Richard Hofstader, *Anti-Intellectualism in American Life* (New York: Alfred A. Knopf, 1974). See especially chapters 3 and 4.

15. Robert Leckie, *George Washington's War* (New York: Harper Collins, 1992), 250.

16. Thomas Paine, "A Serious Note," vol. 2 of *The Life and Works of Thomas Paine* (New Rochelle, N.Y.: Thomas Paine National Historical Association, 1925), 2.

17. Christopher Collier and James Lincoln Collier, *Decision in Philadelphia: The Constitutional Convention of 1787* (New York: Random House, 1986), 38.

18. Leckie, *Washington's War*, 128.

19. *Works of John Adams* (Boston, 1865), 3:447.

20. Ernest Lee Tuveson, *Redeemer Nation* (Chicago: University of Chicago Press, 1968), 22.

21. Joseph Priestley, "Notes on All the Books of Scripture," in *Theological and Miscellaneous Works* (London, 1806–32), vol 14, 443.

22. Priestley, *Works*, vol. 14, 476.

23. Robert Hieronimos, *America's Secret Destiny: Spiritual Vision and the Founding of a Nation* (Rochester, Vt.: Destiny Books, 1989).

24. Moorhead, *American Apocalypse*, 86.

25. Wills, *Inventing America*, xviii.

26. William L. Gaylord, "The Soldier God's Minister" (Discourse delivered in the Congregational Church, Fitzwilliam, N. H., 5 October 1862, on the Occasion of the Departure of a Company of Volunteers for the Seat of War), 19.

27. Winthrop S. Hudson, *Religion in America* (New York: Charles Scribner's Sons, 1983), 183.

28. See also Matt. 22:15–22; and Mark 12:18–27.

29. Charles Nordhoff, *The Communistic Societies of the United States* (New York: Schocken Books, 1875/1970), 133.

30. Lawrence Foster, *Religion and Sexuality: The Shakers, the Mormons, and the Oneida Community* (Chicago: University of Illinois Press, 1984), 32.

31. Foster, *Religion and Sexuality*, 34.

32. By mid-nineteenth century the Shaker dance had become more staid and controlled, although during times of stress they reverted to the ecstatic mode.

33. Foster, *Religion and Sexuality*, 34.

34. Foster, *Religion and Sexuality*, 30.

35. The letter is reprinted in George Wallingford Noyes, ed., *John Humphrey Noyes: The Putney Community* (Oneida, N. Y.: by the author, 1931), 1–10.

36. Report of the Oneida Association, "Bible Argument," 24.

37. Bhagwan Shree Rajneesh, *Tantra Spirituality and Sex* (New York: Rainbow Bridge, 1976).

38. Foster, *Religion and Sexuality*, 91.

39. Jacques Vallee, *Passport to Magonia* (Chicago: Henry Regnery Company, 1969).

40. For an early detailed critique see William Alexander Linn, *The Story of the Mormons* (New York: Russell & Russell, 1901/1963).

41. Quoted in Tuveson, *Redeemer Nation*.

42. John Humphrey Noyes, *Strange Cults and Utopias in Nineteenth Century America* (New York: Dover, 1966). Formerly titled *History of American Socialisms*.

43. See, for example, John White, *The Meeting of Science and Spirit* (New York: Paragon House, 1990).

Chapter Six ◆ *The Proletarian Paradise*

1. Nicolas Berdyaev, *The Russian Revolution* (Ann Arbor: University of Michigan Press, 1961), 5.

2. Berdyaev, *Russian Revolution*, 7.

3. Leonid Ouspensky, *The Meaning of Icons* (Basle: Otto Walter, 1969), 27.

4. Ouspensky, *Icons*, 50.

5. Ouspensky, *Icons*, 212.

6. See article on Skoptsy in *Man, Myth and Magic*, ed. Richard Cavendish (New York: Marshall Cavendish, 1970), vol. 19, 2594.

7. Benedetto Croce, *History: Its Theory and Practice* (New York: Russell & Russell, 1960), 207.

8. Berdyaev, *Russian Revolution*, 8.

9. George Woodcock, *Anarchism: A History of Libertarian Ideas and Movements* (New York: Meridian Books, 1967), 13.

10. Woodcock, *Anarchism*, 151.

11. Woodcock, *Anarchism*, 153.

12. Woodcock, *Anarchism*, 155.

13. Woodcock, *Anarchism*, 155.

14. Isaiah Berlin, *Russian Thinkers* (London: Penguin Books, 1978), 103.

15. Ronald Hingly, *Nihilists* (New York: Delacorte Press, 1967), 57.

16. Woodcock, *Anarchism*, 173.

17. Berlin, *Russian Thinkers*, 217.

18. Hingly, *Nihilists*, 38.

19. N. O. Lossky, *History of Russian Philosophy* (London: George Allen & Unwin, 1952), 78.

20. Nicholay Fedorov, "The Question of Brotherhood," in *Death as a Speculative Theme in Religious, Scientific, and Social Thought*, ed. Robert Kastenbaum (New York; Arno Press, 1977), 17.

21. Kastenbaum, *Death as a Speculative Theme*, 20.

22. Lossky, *Russian Philosophy*, 79.

23. John Weir Perry, *The Far Side of Madness* (Englewood Cliffs, N.J.: Prentice Hall, 1974), 66.

24. Vladimir Mayakovsky, *Poems* (Moscow: Progress Publishers, 1972). See the Preface by Victor Pertsov, 11.

25. Mayakovsky, *Poems*, 14.

26. As quoted in Frank Whitford, *Kandinsky* (London: Paul Hamlyn, 1967), 17.

27. Whitford, *Kandinsky*, 33.

28. Kasimir Malevich, *Essays on Art* (Copenhagen: Borgen, 1968), vol. 1, 19.

29. Fyodor Dostoevsky, *The Brothers Karamazov* (New York: Modern Library, 1950), 298.

30. Vladimir Solovyov, *War, Progress and the End of History* (New York: Lindisfarne Press, 1990).

31. Nicolas Berdyaev, *The Beginning and the End* (New York: Harper Torchbooks, 1957), 231.

32. Gary Hart, *Russia Shakes the World* (New York: Harper Collins, 1991), x, Foreword.

Chapter Seven ♦ *The Messianic Third Reich*

1. Nicholas Goodrick-Clarke, *The Occult Roots of Nazism* (Wellingborough: Aquarian Press, 1985), ix.

2. See Peter Viereck, *Meta-Politics: The Roots of the Nazi Mind* (New York: Capricorn Books, 1941/1965).

3. Carl Jung, *Civilization in Transition* (New York: Bollingen Foundation), 185.

4. Löwith, *Meaning in History*.

5. Cohn, *Pursuit of the Millennium*, 239.

6. See Ernst Bloch, *Man On His Own* (New York: Herder and Herder, 1966).

7. See Georg W. Hegel, *Introduction to the Philosophy of History* (New York: Dover, 1956).

8. Hegel, *Philosophy of History*, 30.

9. Otto Strasser, *Hitler and I* (Boston: Houghton Mifflin, 1940), 66.

10. William L. Shirer, *Berlin Diary: The Journal of a Foreign Correspondent (1934–1941)* (New York: 1941), 16–18.

11. Walter Langer, *The Mind of Adolf Hitler: The Secret Wartime Report* (New York: New American Library, 1943/1972), 64.

12. Langer, *Mind of Adolf Hitler*.

13. Albert Speer, *Inside the Third Reich* (New York: Macmillan, 1970), 32.

14. Speer, *Third Reich*, 32.

15. John Toland, *Adolph Hitler* (New York: Ballantine, 1976), 194.

16. Toland, *Hitler*, 302.

17. James M. Rhodes, *The Hitler Movement: A Modern Millenarian Revolution* (Stanford, Calif.: Hoover Institution Press, 1980), 22.

18. Rhodes, *Hitler Movement*, 24.

19. See Donald M. McKale, *Hitler: The Survival Myth* (New York: Stein & Day, 1981).

20. Quoted in Joscelyn Godwin, *Arktos: The Polar Myth in Science, Symbolism, and Nazi Survival* (Grand Rapids, Mich.: Phanes Press, 1993), 71.

21. Adolf Hitler, *Mein Kampf* (New York: Houghton Mifflin, 1971).

22. "Is Wagner a man at all?" asked Nietzsche in *The Case Against Wagner*, 11; "Is he not rather a disease?"

23. Viereck, *Meta-Politics*, 229.

24. Viereck, *Meta-Politics,* 229.

25. Viereck, *Meta-Politics*, 232.

26. Viereck, *Meta-Politics*, 238.

27. Michael Barkun, *Disaster and the Millennium* (New Haven: Yale University Press, 1974).

28. These quotes appear in Robert G. Waite, *The Psychopathic God: Adolf Hitler* (New York: Basic Books, 1977), 418.

29. See the *Reader's Digest Illustrated History of World War II*, ed. Michael Wright (London: Berkeley Square House, 1989), 190.
30. Pierre Grimal, ed., *Larousse World Mythology* (Secaucus, N.J.: Chartwell Books, 1965), 399.
31. See Goodrick-Clarke, *Occult Roots*, 34.
32. Viereck, *Meta-Politics*, 292.

Part Two ◆ *Futuristic*

1. Hegel, *Philosophy of History*, 85.
2. See G. W. Hegel, *The Phenomenology of Mind* (New York: Macmillan, 1931).
3. John Dewey, *Art as Experience* (New York: Capricorn Books, 1958).
4. Richard Bucke, *Cosmic Consciousness* (New York: Dutton, 1969).

Chapter Eight ◆ *New Age America*

1. Terence McKenna, *The Archaic Revival* (San Francisco: Harper, 1991).
2. See Michael Parenti, *Land of Idols* (New York: Saint Martin's Press, 1994).
3. J. Gordon Melton, *New Age Encyclopedia* (New York: Gale Research, 1990).
4. Harold Bloom, *The American Religion: The Emergence of the Post-Christian Nation* (New York: Simon & Schuster, 1992). See the chapter, "The New Age: California Orphism."
5. Michael Kelly, "Hillary Rodham Clinton and the Politics of Virtue," *New York Times*, 23 May 1993.
6. See Grosso, *Frontiers*. Especially the chapter, "The Psychic Origins of Christianity."
7. G. W. Noyes, *John Humphrey Noyes*, 119.
8. One has to go back to the sixties to the writings of Herbert Marcuse and N. O. Brown for radically consistent philosophies of healing. James Hillman today is another voice that would awaken us from the slumbers of socially uncritical philosophies of healing. See also the author's "The Power of Imagination: Toward a Philosophy of Healing," in *Cultivating Consciousness: Enhancing Human Potential, Wellness, and Healing*, ed. Ramakrishna Rao (New York: Praeger, 1991), 165–79.
9. The phrase itself is from Michael Lerner, editor of *Tikkun*, a Jewish New Age periodical whose name (*tikkun*) means something like rebirth.

10. See Ronald Numbers, *Prophetess of Health* (New York: Harper & Row, 1976).

11. Bloom, *American Religion*.

12. Michael Murphy, *The Future of the Body* (Los Angeles: J. P. Tarcher, 1992).

13. See Henry Corbin, *Spiritual Body and Celestial Earth* (Westport, N.J.: Princeton University Press, 1977).

14. Corbin, *Spiritual Body*, 205.

15. Edwin Burtt, *The Metaphysical Foundations of Modern Science* (New York: Doubleday, 1954).

16. Joseph Campbell, *Myths to Live By* (New York: Bantam, 1972).

17. Interview with Michael Toms, New Dimensions Radio.

18. David Bohm, *Wholeness and the Implicate Order* (New York: Ark Paperbacks, 1983).

19. Michael Talbot, *The Holographic Universe* (New York: Harper Collins, 1991).

20. Fred Alan Wolf, *Taking the Quantum Leap* (San Francisco: Harper & Row, 1981).

21. Donald Phillip Verene, *Vico's Science of Imagination* (Ithaca: Cornell University Press, 1981).

22. John White, *Pole Shift* (Garden City, N.Y.: Doubleday, 1980).

23. White, *Science and Spirit*.

24. White, *Science and Spirit*, 45.

25. Kenneth Ring, *The Omega Project: Near-Death Experiences, UFO Encounters, and Mind at Large* (New York: William Morrow, 1992).

Chapter Nine ♦ *Endtime Anomalies*

1. Jon Klimo says "hundreds of thousands." See his *Channeling* (Los Angeles: J. P. Tarcher, 1987), 3.

2. Ken Ring, *Heading Toward Omega* (New York: William Morrow, 1984), 203.

3. See chapter "The Cult of the Guardian Angel," in Grosso, *Frontiers*, 119–29.

4. Around the same time, Newsweek also ran an article on angels.

5. See Rosemary Ellen Guiley, *Angels of Mercy* (New York: Pocket Books, 1994).

6. Jean Danielou, *The Angels and Their Mission* (Westminster, Md.:

Newman Press, 1957), 108. See especially chapter 10, "The Angels and the Second Coming."

7. Danielou, *Angels and Their Mission*, 108.

8. Guiley, *Angels of Mercy*.

9. David Gotlib, "Ethics Code For Abduction Experience and Treatment," *JUFOS*, in press 1994.

10. For a critical discussion, see J. Allen Hynek, *The UFO Experience: A Scientific Enquiry* (Chicago: Henry Regnery, 1972), chapter 12.

11. Jacques Vallee, *Confrontations* (New York: Ballantine, 1990); Vallee, *Revelations* (New York: Ballantine, 1991).

12. George E. Vandeman, *The Telltale Connection* (Boise, Idaho: Pacific Press, 1984).

13. For a penetrating account, see Peter Rojcewicz, "The Folklore of the Men in Black: A Challenge to the Prevailing Paradigm," *Re-Vision* 11.4 (1989): 5–16.

14. Robert Short, *The Gospel from Outer Space* (New York: Harper & Row, 1983).

15. John G. Fuller, *The Interrupted Journey* (New York: Berkley Edition, 1966).

16. Budd Hopkins, "Invisibility and the UFO Abduction Phenomenon," *MUFON*, 1993.

17. Budd Hopkins, *Intruders* (New York: Random House, 1987).

18. These remarks are taken from an interview I conducted with John Mack on October 9, 1993.

19. D. Scott Rogo, *Miracles* (New York: Dial Press, 1982).

20. Carl Jung and Carl Kerenyi, *Essays on a Science of Mythology* (New York: Harper Torchbooks, 1963). See especially Jung, "The Psychology of the Child Archetype," 79–100.

21. The 1993 *Proceedings* was dedicated to him; ironically, most MUFON members are not entirely sympathetic to Stacy's nonliteral minded approach to the UFO phenomenon.

22. Jung and Kerenyi, *Essays*, 83.

23. Investigative reporter Rosemary Ellen Guiley, who has done on-site investigations of the circles asserts that most of the elaborate circles are hoaxes but that there may be a residual core of simple, unexplained cases.

24. Pat Delgado and Colin Andrews, *Crop Circles: The Latest Evidence* (London: Bloomsbury, 1990), 80.

25. Delgado and Andrews, *Crop Circles*, 9.

Chapter Ten ♦ *Technocalypse Now*

1. Corbin, *Spiritual Body*.

2. Corbin, *Spiritual Body*, 10.

3. Ernest Lee Tuveson, *Millennium and Utopia* (New York: Harper & Row, 1964), 10.

4. Tuveson, *Millennium and Utopia*, 104.

5. K. Eric Drexler, *Engines of Creation: The Coming Era of Nanotechnology* (New York: Doubleday, 1986).

6. Quoted in Tuveson, *Millennium and Utopia*, 11.

7. Drexler, *Engines of Creation*, 4.

8. *Whole Earth Review* 92 (Summer 1967): 2.

9. Timothy Leary, *Neuropolitique* (Scottsdale, Ariz.: New Falcon Press, 1991).

10. Leary, *Neuropolitique*, 141.

11. Leary, *Neuropolitique*, 142.

12. Leary, *Neuropolitique*, 147.

13. Marshall McLuhan, *Understanding Media* (New York: Signet, 1964), 19.

14. See William Gibson's novel *Neuromancer* (New York: Ace Books, 1984).

15. For an excellent account, see Howard Rheingold's *Virtual Reality* (New York: Simon & Schuster, 1991).

16. See *Cutting Edge Video*, 2a Red Plum Circle, Monterey Park, CA 91754.

17. "Where is the Digital Highway Really Going? The Case for a Jeffersonian Policy," *Wired* (July 1992).

18. Robert Descharnes, *Salvador Dali* (Berlin: Taschen, 1992), 188.

19. Mary Ann Seamon, "Hands on Bionic Show Tour," *Medical World News* (26 February 1990).

20. *Wired* (September 1993): 92.

21. Luigi Cornaro, *The Art of Long Life* (Milwaukee: Butler, 1903).

22. Rick Weiss, "A Shot at Youth," *Health* (December 1993).

23. See his "Across Real Time," *Whole Earth Review* (Winter 1993).

24. See Ward Dean and John Morgenthaler, *Smart Drugs and Nutrients* (Santa Cruz: B & J Publications, 1990).

25. *Time Magazine* (Special Issue, Fall 1992): 66.

26. *Wired* (July/August 1993): 96.

27. *Wired* (July/August 1993): 96.

Chapter Eleven ◆ *The Future of Death*

1. See Gordon Wasson, *Soma: Divine Mushroom of Immortality* (New York: Harcourt Brace Jovanovich, n.d.) for a possible interpretation as to the psychedelic nature of this plant.

2. Corbin, *Spiritual Body*.

3. Mircea Eliade, *Death, Afterlife, and Eschatology* (New York: Harper & Row, 1967), 78.

4. La Barre, *They Shall Take Up Serpents*. Especially the chapter, "Snake Cults in Africa," 53–64.

5. Cohn, *Pursuit of the Millennium*, 154.

6. Cohn, *Pursuit of the Millennium*, 154.

7. See, for the best accounts, Herbert Thurston, *Physical Phenomena of Mysticism* (London: Burns Oates, 1952).

8. Carl Kerenyi, *Eleusis* (New York: Pantheon, 1967).

9. Richard Wilhelm and C. G. Jung, *The Secret of the Golden Flower* (New York: Harcourt, Brace & World, 1962).

10. Eliade, *Death, Afterlife, and Eschatology*, 88.

11. Dee Brown, *Bury My Heart at Wounded Knee* (New York: Bantam, 1971).

12. Filippo Caraffa and Antonio Massone, *Santa Cecilia: Martire Romana* (Roma: Centro di Spiritualita Liturgica, 1982).

13. Joan Carroll Cruz, *The Incorruptibles* (Rockford, Ill.: Tan Books, 1977).

14. Grosso, *Frontiers*, 165–67.

15. Patricia Treece, *The Sanctified Body* (New York: Doubleday, 1987).

16. Baron Friedrich von Hugel, *The Mystical Element of Religion as Studied in Saint Catherine Genoa and her Friends* (London: J. M. Dent, 1973).

17. Thurston, *Physical Phenomena*, 220.

18. B. K. Karanjia, *Kundalini Yoga* (New York: Kundalini Research Foundation, 1977).

19. Treece, *The Sanctified Body*, 64–82.

20. Morton Kelsey, *Healing and Christianity* (New York: Harper & Row, 1973).

21. See, for example, Stanley Krippner, *Spiritual Dimensions of Healing* (New York: Irvington Publishers, 1992).

22. Randolph C. Byrd, "Positive therapeutic effects of intercessory prayer in a coronary care unit population," *Southern Medical Journal* (July 1988): 826–29.

23. Deepak Chopra, *Quantum Healing* (New York: Bantam, 1989). See chapter, "Body of Bliss."

24. A. P. Elkin, *Aboriginal Men of High Degree* (New York: Saint Martin's Press, 1977).

25. See Hans Bender, "Modern Poltergeist Research," in *New Directions in Parapsychology*, ed. John Beloff (Metuchen, N.J.: Scarecrow Press, 1975), 122–43.

26. William Roll, *The Poltergeist* (New York: Signet, 1973).

27. Stephen Braude, *The Limits of Influence: Psychokinesis and the Philosophy of Science* (New York: Routledge & Kegan, 1986).

28. R. G. Medhurst, *Crookes and the Spirit World* (New York: Taplinger, 1972), 65.

29. See Charles Richet, *Traite de Metapsychique* (Paris: Felix Alacan, 1922). Especially chapter 3, "Des ectoplasmies" (Materializations); for a critical account of physical phenomena of mediumship, see also Hereward Carrington, *The Physical Phenomena of Spiritualism* (New York: American University Publishing, 1920), and Braude, *Limits of Influence*.

30. Erlendur Haraldsson, *Modern Miracles* (New York: Fawcett Columbia, 1987); Grosso, *Frontiers*, chapter 11.

31. See the article by Michael D'Antonio, "New Edge," *Bazaar Magazine* (June 1993).

32. Personal communication.

33. F. M. Esfandiary, *Up-Wingers* (New York: John Day Company, 1973), 129.

34. Drexler, *Engines of Creation*, 115.

35. Ernest Becker, *The Denial of Death* (New York: Free Press, 1973).

36. Alan Harrington, *The Immortalist* (Millbrae, Calif.: Celestial Arts, 1969).

37. Nikhilananda, *The Upanishads* (New York: Harper, 1962), 75–76.

38. John Blofield, trans., *The Zen Teaching of Huang Po* (New York: Grove Press, 1959), 40.

39. W. Y. Evans-Wentz, ed., *The Tibetan Book of the Great Liberation* (New York: Oxford University Press, 1954), 224.

40. For an excellent overview of transpersonal psychology, see Frances Vaughan, *The Inward Arc* (Boston: New Science Library, 1985).

41. For the best single study of ESP, see John Palmer, "Extrasensory perception: research findings," in *Advances in Parapsychological Research* (New York: Plenum Press, 1978), 59–241.

Notes

42. See the chapter, "Fear of Life After Death," in Grosso, *Frontiers*.

43. Robert Almeder, *Death and Personal Survival: The Evidence for Life After Death* (Lanham, Md.: Rowman and Littlefield, 1992).

44. See Irwin Rhode, *Psyche*, 2 vols. (New York: Harper Torchbooks, 1966).

45. G. Gordon Wasson, Carl Ruck, and Albert Hofmann, *Road to Eleusis* (New York: Harcourt Brace Jovanovich, 1978).

46. Christian Ratsch, ed., *Gateway to Inner Space* (New York: Avery Publications, 1989), 148.

47. See Peter T. Furst, ed., *Flesh of the Gods: The Ritual Use of Hallucinogens* (New York: Praeger, 1972).

48. See McKenna, *Archaic Revival*.

49. The title of an excellent book by Peter Russell.

50. See Vallee's speculations on this in *Dimensions*.

51. Vallee, *Confrontations*, 206.

52. See Travis Walton's account in his *The Walton Experience* (New York: Berkley Medallion, 1978).

53. John L. Casti, *Paradigms Lost* (New York: William Morrow, 1989), 482.

54. Michael Anthony Corey, *God and the New Cosmology* (Lanham, Md.: Rowman and Littlefield, 1993), 4.

Chapter Twelve ♦ *Love and Sex in the Millennium*

1. Eliade, *Cosmos and History*, 69.

2. Richard Payne Knight, *On the Worship of Priapus* (Secaucus, N.J.: University Books, 1974), 17.

3. Benjamin Walker, *Sex and the Supernatural* (Baltimore: Ottenheimer, 1970).

4. Marcuse, *Eros and Civilization*.

5. Thomas Aquinas, *On the Truth of the Catholic Faith*, Book Three, *Providence* (New York: Doubleday, 1956).

6. D. T. Suzuki, *Manual of Zen Buddhism* (New York: Grove Press, 1960), 131.

7. Sigmund Freud, *Sexuality and the Psychology of Life* (New York: Collier Books, 1963), 20–40.

8. Wilhelm Reich, *Listen, Little Man!* (New York: Noonday Press, 1948).

9. Amy Stechler Burns and Ken Burns, *The Shakers* (New York: Portland House, 1987), 37.

10. Andreas Capellanus, *The Art of Courtly Love* (New York: Frederick Ungar, 1957), 17.

11. Denis de Rougement, *Love in the Western World* (New York: Fawcett, 1940), 115.

12. See the hilarious *Dialogues*, trans. Raymond Rosenthal (New York: Stein & Day, 1971).

13. Mark Musa, *Dante's Vita Nuova* (Bloomington, Ind.: Indiana University Press, 1973), 3.

14. See "The Marian Morphogenesis," in Grosso, *Frontiers*.

15. See de Rougement, *Love in the Western World*.

16. See chapter 2 (on Joachim).

17. See Thomas Moore, *Dark Eros: The Imagination of Eros* (Dallas: Spring Publications, 1990).

18. Paine, *Collected Works*, vol. 2, 77.

19. John Humphrey Noyes, *The Putney Community* (New York: Oneida, 1931), 189.

20. Roger Lewin, *Complexity: Life At The Edge of Chaos* (New York: Macmillan, 1992).

21. Edward Carpenter, *The Intermediate Sex* (London: George Allen & Unwin, 1908), 11.

22. June Singer, *Androgyny: Toward a New Theory of Sexuality* (New York: Anchor Books, 1977). See chapter 7.

23. Vladimir Solovyov, *The Meaning of Love* (New York: International University Press, 1947).

24. Personal communication.

25. Charles Fourier, *Design for Utopia* (New York: Schocken Books, 1971), 5.

26. J. H. Noyes, *Strange Cults*, 161.

27. Fourier, *Design for Utopia*, 61.

28. Fourier, *Design for Utopia*, 220.

29. Fourier, *Design for Utopia*, 14.

30. Herbert Marcuse, "Art as a Form of Reality," in *On The Future of Art*, ed. Edward Fry (New York: Viking Press, 1970), 123–34.

31. Robert Hughes, *The Shock of the New* (New York: Alfred A. Knopf, 1991), 271.

32. Pierre Cabanne, *Dialogues with Marcel Duchamp* (New York: Viking Press, 1967), 38.

Notes

33. Alberto Busignani, *Pollock* (New York: Hamlyn, 1970), 22.

34. Barbara Rose, *Ad Reinhardt* (New York: Marlborough, 1968), 18.

35. Herschel B. Chipp, *Theories of Modern Art* (Berkeley: University of California Press, 1969), 412.

36. Anna Balakian, *Surrealism* (New York: Macmillan, 1970), 33.

37. Giuseppe Tucci, *The Theory and Practice of the Mandala* (London: Rider, 1961).

38. Dewey, *Art as Experience*.

39. Burns and Burns, *Shakers*, 36.

40. Burns and Burns, *Shakers*, 28.

41. Burns and Burns, *Shakers*, 15.

42. *PC Computing* (12 September 1993).

43. Rheingold, *Virtual Reality*, 347.

Conclusion

1. Arthur Koestler, *The Ghost in the Machine* (New York: Macmillan, 1967).

Index